The Cooking Gene

THE
COOKING
GENE

*A Journey Through
African American Culinary History
in the Old South*

MICHAEL W. TWITTY

Amistad
An Imprint of HarperCollins *Publishers*

HarperCollins books may be purchased for educational, business, or sales promotional use. For information, please email the Special Markets Department at SPsales@harpercollins.com.

FIRST EDITION

Designed by Suet Yee Chong

Grateful acknowledgment to Stephen Crotts for permission to include his drawings throughout this book.

Library of Congress Cataloging-in-Publication Data

Names: Twitty, Michael, 1977- author.
Title: The cooking gene : a journey through African-American culinary history in the Old South / Michael W. Twitty.
Description: First edition. | New York, NY : HarperCollins Publishers, 2017.
Identifiers: LCCN 2017003374 (print) | LCCN 2017004857 (ebook) (print) | LCCN 2017004857 (ebook) | ISBN 9780062379290 (hardcover : alk. paper) | ISBN 9780062379276 (pbk. : alk. paper) | ISBN 9780062379283 (ebook)
Subjects: LCSH: African American cooking—History. | Cooking, American—Southern style—History. | African Americans—Food—Southern States—History.
Classification: LCC E185.89.F66 T95 2017 (print) | LCC E185.89.F66 (ebook) | DDC 641.59/296073—dc23
LC record available at https://lccn.loc.gov/2017003374

21 LSC 10

FUNTUMFUNEFU
There are two crocodiles who share the same stomach
   and yet they fight over food.
Symbolizes unity in diversity and unity of purposes and
   reconciling different approaches.

—THE ADINKRA WISDOM OF THE AKAN ELDERS

——

I dedicate this book to my board of directors, My Ancestors, with-out whom none of this would be possible, but more specifically

With respect to my Mama

With respect to my Daddy

For Meredith, for Fallan, for Gideon, for Kennedi, for Grace and Jack, for Malcolm, for Ben—souls in and out of the Newest South

CONTENTS

—

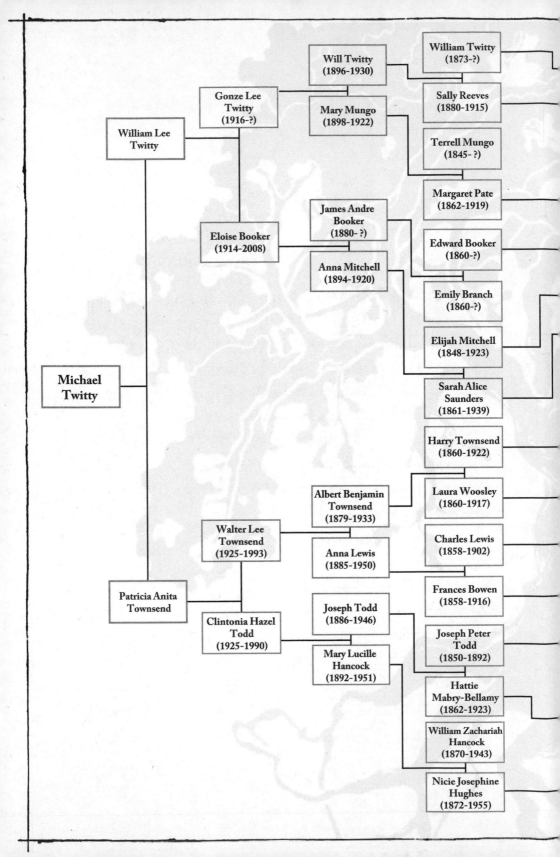

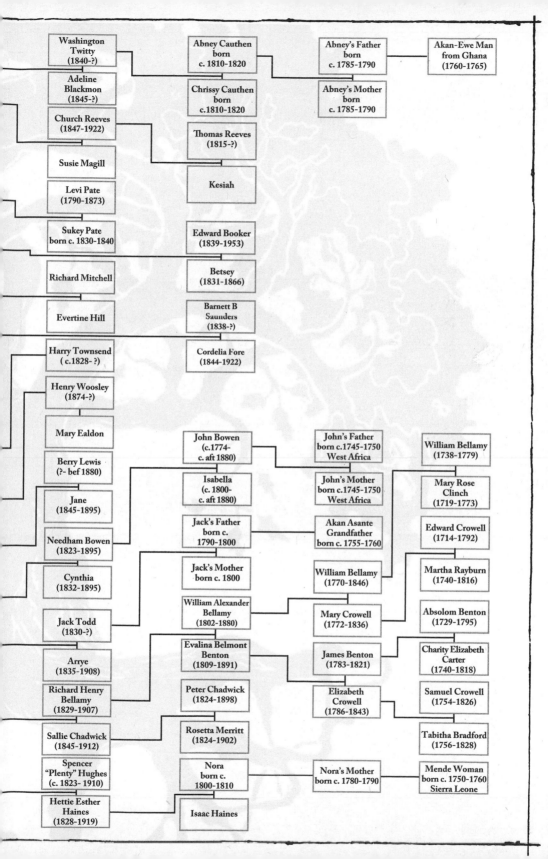

—

THE OLD SOUTH

Negroes in the North are right when they refer to the South as the Old Country. A Negro born in the North who finds himself in the South is in a position similar to that of the son of the Italian emigrant who finds himself in Italy, near the village where his father first saw the light of day. Both are in countries they have never seen, but which they cannot fail to recognize. The landscape has always been familiar. . . . Everywhere he turns, the revenant finds himself reflected. He sees himself as he was before he was born. . . . He sees his ancestors, who, in everything they do and are, proclaim his inescapable identity. And the Northern Negro in the South sees, whatever he or anyone else may wish to believe, that his ancestors are both white and black.

—JAMES BALDWIN, "NOBODY KNOWS MY
NAME: A LETTER FROM THE SOUTH"

The Old South is a place where people use food to tell themselves who they are, to tell others who they are, and to tell stories about where they've been. The Old South is a place of groaning tables across the tracks from want. It's a place where arguments over how barbecue is prepared or chicken is served or whether sugar is used to sweeten cornbread can function as culinary shibboleths. It is a place in the mind where we dare not talk about which came first, the African cook or the European mistress, the Native American woman or the white woodsman. We just know that somehow the table aches from the weight of so much . . . that we prop it up with our knees and excuses to keep it from falling.

The Old South is where people are far more likely to be related to one another than not. It is where everybody has a Cherokee, a Creek, a Chickasaw, a Seminole, or a Choctaw lurking in their maternal bloodlines but nobody knows where the broad noses or big asses come from. It is a place where dark gums and curly hair get chalked up to lost Turks and meandering mystics but Nigeria and Gambia are long forgotten, unlike everything else that is perpetually and unremittingly remembered. Proud bloodlines of Normandy and Westphalia and County Armagh and Kent endure here and, like it or not, it is often in the bodies that bear no resemblance to those in whom those genes first arrived, bodies like mine.

The Old South is a forgotten Little Africa but nobody speaks of it that way. Everything black folks gave to the aristocracy and plain folks became spun gold in the hands of others—from banjos to barbecue to Elvis to rice and cotton know-how. Everything we black Southerners kept for ourselves, often the unwanted dregs and markers of resistance, felt like markers of backwardness, scratches of the uncivilized, idolatry, and the state of being lost. And yet I loved that Old South, and loved it fiercely in all her funkiness and dread. To be honest, I never hated white people for their strange relationship to us, their colored kith and kin, but I grew up with the suspicion that they had no clue just how much of us there was in their family trees and stories and bloodlines and on their groaning tables. Maybe if they did, we would know less enmity toward one another.

The Old South is where I had to return.

The Old South is my name for the former slaveholding states and the history and culture they collectively birthed from the days of contact through civil rights. My Old South doesn't end when white people start recovering from the Civil War and move to Southern cities and start working in mills and factories. My Old South ends when black people are formally and forcefully brought out of the nineteenth century—in the middle of the twentieth. Maryland, Virginia, West Virginia, North and South Carolina, Georgia, Florida, Alabama, Tennessee, Kentucky, Missouri, Arkansas, Mississippi, Louisiana, Texas, and Oklahoma: pretty much the census South. Heads may shake over this list, but my geography is determined by the fact that the South is multiregional. Landscapes, politics, subcultures, climates, ecosystems, and crops separate Blue Ridge from bayou country, Chesapeake from the Ozarks, the Black Belt from the Low Country, the delta from bluegrass country, and middle Tennessee.

Old South culture is also not bound by growing up in the former Confederacy. "Where are you from in the South?" privileges settlements and cities, not to mention the white-folks version of what "Southern" means. The former Confederacy is not the totality of the South or Southern culture, and the Deep South is younger than the seaboard and Upper South. The prominent cities of the New South, while markers of the Sunbelt, are not really where the vernacular culture of the South came to be. It was in the wide swaths of densely populated rural country, often not far from rivers, where the elements came together.

In 2011, I remembered that I had started to forget where I came from. I became aware of my own apathy and amnesia. I had a responsibility to study the generations before me and use that to move forward. So I worked with my then partner to craft a crowdfunding campaign called the "Southern Discomfort Tour." My goal was for us to travel the South looking for sites of cultural and culinary memory while researching my family history and seeing the food culture of the region as it stood in the early twenty-first century.

There are giant peaches on top of towers, and statues of boll weevils and giant mammies, and country stores that sell pig parts aplenty and have coolers that can keep a deer carcass or a mess of largemouth bass cold for three days. Nothing can prepare you for the sea of green cane or rice or tobacco or the way cotton looks when it's young and bushy and putting out mallowlike blossoms. The road signs are clear—three crosses on a hill, "Get Right with God," signs for cans of field peas and succotash, buffet-style halls and "meat and threes" off the highway, and nondescript adult entertainment centers. Old plantations lend their name to actual historical sites on the brown landmark signs as well as to apartment complexes and resorts, and battlefields are everywhere. In some town centers, the auction blocks are remembered. From the town I live in in Maryland, to Oxford, Mississippi, the Confederate soldier stands guard near the old courthouse, and people will point out to you where the hanging tree stood—or stands.

There is a lot of beautiful and a lot of ugly mashed together. Pecan trees are my favorite thing and they stand guard over my grandfather's home in South Carolina. Nothing matches light filtering through Spanish moss in the latest part of the day. The elders talked about how beautiful this place was, and if you are lucky, you will learn why they left it and what that first taste of Northern cold was like and the realization some things were no better no matter where you lived. In the words of my maternal grandmother, "The day I learned up North wasn't streets paved with gold and that white people there could be just as bad was the way I learned that sometimes the grass is greener because there's more shit to deal with." But she missed the crepe myrtles, and my grandfather missed the taste of ripe cane nabbed from a neighbor's yard; I had come to see it all for myself.

It's a misnomer. "The Old South."
The South has never been still, or merely aged. It is not stagnant and it is not as set in its ways or physical boundaries as much as some would like to pretend. Perhaps there is nothing old about the South except its airs. Mississippi, Alabama, Georgia, Arkansas, old? The first two were barely middle-age, Georgia was just starting to think about being emeritus, and Arkansas was in puberty when the "War between the States" (because *real* Southerners don't say the "Civil War") broke out. The New South waits for us, but it's less place than lingering idea. And the postmodern South? Who cares, nothing is made there. In our minds, nothing is like the Old South, home of the original American rebel.

The Old South was introduced to me in movies and magazines as the bizarre place we black Americans owed our identity. Untanned, ageless white ladies in pastel crinolines . . . Carolina blue, pale jessamine yellow, dogwood blossom pink, mint julep green . . . bedazzled with stars and bars and frills aplenty. Parasols and fat black crones called "mammies" and crusting, crooning, near-senile ex-bucks fondly called "Uncle." Everybody and everything was satisfactual, and in their right place. White men and white columns and bow ties on white suits, the kind you'd never dream of getting chicken gravy or whip blood on. Blemishless and benign, a patriarchy overlooking a peaceable racial hierarchy ordained by a Creator with a permanent beef with Cain and Ham, and then Joshua butted in:

"Now therefore ye are cursed, and there shall none of you be freed from being bondmen, and hewers of wood and drawers of water for the house of my God." (9:23)

"Hewers of wood and drawers of water." The *Oprah Winfrey Show*, 1987. Oprah goes to Forsyth County, Georgia, where no black person had "been allowed to live" in seventy-five years. She had been on the air five months. Confederate battle flags were on display; a people unreconstructed came out in force to show America's future richest black person where she stood. What seemed like the entire town showed up to justify their whiteopia.

No racial description whatsoever appears in the Scripture for Cain or Canaan, son of Ham, and the verse from the book of Joshua has nothing to do with anyone living in America, and yet a man had his Bible open, ready in 1987 to justify a permanent and seemingly ancient division that did not exist in the British mind before the late sixteenth to mid-seventeenth centuries. My Alabama-born-and-raised grandmother, a refugee of "Bombingham," is folding clothes; under her breath is a constant stream of "God damn *them*." Her breath slowed to a seethe and her eyes became fixed into what seemed like a cut from which she would never return. I was ten and I was barely taught in school that in my own area—the Washington metroplex—slavery and racism had defined the economy, politics, and social order. Seeing this made me dread my own country and, presumably, my own ancestral homeland— the Old South.

"The lazy, laughing South / With blood on its mouth / . . . And I, who am black, would love her," wrote Langston Hughes, a refugee of Joplin, Missouri, the poet laureate of black America. The poems I was bid to remember frequently referenced a place that was caught up in a weird braid of nostalgia, lament, romance, horror, and fear. Forsyth County, Georgia, is no longer the same place it was nearly thirty years ago, and black people have long since moved in. And yet across the region, flashpoints continue, the shootings, the draggings, the overreach of police authority, the obstruction of the vote, inequalities and inequities and silent and sturdy boundaries between white and black. For some, "we" are the South, but "they" are Dixie, and yet we and they all know the old hanging trees and the strange fruit they once bore.

I dare to believe all Southerners are a family. We are not merely Native, European, and African. We are Middle Eastern and South Asian and East Asian and Latin American, now. We are a dysfunctional family, but we are a family. We are unwitting inheritors of a story with many sins that bears the fruit of the possibility of ten times the redemption. One way is through reconnection with the culinary culture of the enslaved, our common ancestors, and restoring their names on the roots of the Southern tree and the table those roots support.

The Old South is where I cook. The Old South is a place where food tells me where I am. The Old South is a place where food tells me who I am. The Old South is where food tells me where we have been. The Old South is where the story of our food might just tell America where it's going.

The Old South / With soul food in its mouth / and I, who am African American, must know her.

The Cooking Gene

1

NO MORE WHISTLING WALK FOR ME

MORNING PRAYER

Five a.m.

The sun isn't quite up.

When I cook on a plantation, before I do anything else, I put on the representative clothes. I prefer the long rough trousers to breeches; either way, I'll still feel the heat. Next come the long wool stockings, or more frequently cotton tights. Then the long shirt I barely wash that's full of little tears and rips, the waistcoat, the kerchief. They call this a costume but it is my transformative historical drag; my makeup is a dusting of pot rust, red clay, and the ghost smells of meals past.

"Now we are slaves in the land of Egypt." I tie the kerchief around my neck.

The smell of the burning wood becomes the smell of your clothes and your body. It gets down to the root of your hair follicles. Your sweat marries with the smokiness until every bacon lover in the world—from human to canine to feline—can't resist you for at least thirty-six hours after cooking, three showers later. The hair on your arms singe off, and wisps of burned hair and the iron-laced smell of fresh blood drawn from cuts or meat, herbs, spices, onion, and earthy pungent roots mix to make for the most confusingly fragrant skin. The ringing in your ears always sounds like a beat on the door-frame, the tuning of the banjo, a misplucked fiddle.

I don't know what kind of wood I'll use or even if the dampness will make much of a difference, but the first task is always to get kindling and wood—thirty to forty pieces—and once you have it, get the fire started quickly and clearly so that the flames dance in the air like Pentecost. Resinous and juicy, the softwoods—the lightwood—start the show when I wrap them in a little cotton. I like burning a little raw cotton with the pine and her needles—it feels like poetic justice, my own little taste of revenge. I know that's silly, but I am captive to blood memory visions of the cotton bales burning and the soldiers marching on and jubilee coming. Nothing ever really escapes memory, and even the things we forget often are condemned to it.

The hardwoods are like friends, and each one has a different conversation with your food—the smell, the burn, the coals, the heat, the smoke—the hot intensity of white oak; the savor of hickory; the mellowness of pecan, the red oak, ash, apple, and maples. Sometimes you have to split the big logs up so that you can stack them like a chimney. When that happens, the day begins with the brooding energy of iron and all of its accompanying West African spirits—Ogun, Ta Yao, Ndomayiri. I sing the song quoted by Fannie Berry, a formerly enslaved informant, to the WPA interviewers in the 1930s: "A cold and frosty morning / the niggers is feeling good / take ya' ax upon ya' shoulder and talk to the wood . . . talk [chop] . . . talk [chop] . . . talk [chop] to the wood . . . talk . . . talk . . . talk to the wood. Talk! Oh yeah! I'm talking, talking to the wood . . . Talk come talk to me, talk to me wood!" Like the recipes I work with, it starts off as a formula from the past, and ends—naturally—with my ad libs, improvisation and tradition chasing each other like fish rippling through a pool.

"N-word" and all, the song gives me an undefinable phantom pleasure. I'm giving energy to the wood I'm cooking with and starting the day the way my ancestors started their own—singing despite the drudgery. Before I started cooking this way, I didn't know that you *had* to sing, and that it wasn't a pastime. Every tool you touch becomes a scepter, and the way you start and finish the task opens and closes the doors of time. Visitors to the South before the Civil War spoke of enslaved men talking to their farming tools and axes and finishing the work with a part yodel, part cry—part prayer. Fannie Berry had her own moment of satisfaction in the southern Virginia Piedmont, hearing the axes fall and the voices rise through the oak-hickory forest and pines until the sun came up with our song. The songs are where the cooking begins—because it must.

You have to know a lot of songs to cook the way our ancestors cooked. The songs are like clocks with spells. Some enslaved cooks timed the cooking by the stanzas of the hymns and spirituals, or little folk songs that began across the Atlantic and melted into plantation Creole, melting Africa with Europe until beginnings and endings were muddied. My favorite is the ambiguous anthem of resistance and removal, "Many Thousands Gone." "No more peck of corn for me, no more, no more / No more peck of corn for me, many thousands gone. / No more auction block for me, no more, no more / No more auction block for me, many thousands gone."

When I started going to plantations, you would often hear tour guides (sometimes dressed like Southern belles in hoopskirts, or as fifty-year-old Confederate soldiers sausaged into uniforms) and docents talk—actually they joke—about the "whistling walk," a path, often covered, leading from the outdoor kitchen to the Big House, the plantation house. Supposedly this was the space where "the slaves" had to whistle as they brought the food in, to prove they were not eating. It was actually just an old architectural covenvention, though, that prevented rain and bird droppings from getting into the food, but the old white men chuckle, the white ladies guffaw, and I feel my inner Nat Turner raging. They must giggle and grin because they think it's quaint and tender as light biscuits to revisit in mind the Old South, where the pilfering nature of the tricky Negro was an accepted consequence of benign paternalism. In all of my days, I have been asked to prove everything I have ever said, but I have never heard a single one of these docents challenged for using racist folk history as fact. One day, improvisation chased tradition, and I started to sing a new song as I worked: No more whistling walk for me / No more, no more / No more whistling walk for me / Many thousands gone.

BURNING IT DOWN

The fire is easy if you know how to use a match or have banked coals. Screw flint and steel. I stack them up in a crisscross tower, gather dead-red pine needles and cones, raw cotton, and paper with a little bacon grease at the base, and set them alight, and the wood begins to crackle and flame. Anyone can turn on a stove, but this is a far more satisfying feeling. Out comes the fire-fan made from the gorgeous iridescent feathers plucked from the unwilling ass of a turkey, the kind of tool my father inherited from his great-grandfather, born enslaved in Appomattox County, Virginia, not that far from Fannie Berry herself. Start a fire, then keep it stoked; fan your fire and make it blaze, then tame it.

The plantations of the American South and other spaces associated with slavery have often been unwelcoming and dishonest spaces
for African American visitors. The whistling walk was just one way
of telling black visitors that their experience was superfluous and
negligible. Still is. The American plantation wasn't the quaint village
community you saw depicted in your history textbook. It was a labor
camp system for exiled prisoners of war and victims of kidnapping.
In this light, it is no wonder many African Americans do not flock
to but altogether avoid the plantation and urban sites where enslaved
people—our ancestors—lived, worked, and died.

The body count alone marks the plantation as a sacred place,
and yet that's not what hallows the grounds to most. Traditionally,
the plantation is a place where architecture and windows and wall-
paper are lauded but the bodies who put them up are not. It is still
marketed as the crux of the Old South, a place of manners, gentility,
custom, and tradition; the South's cultural apogee. It is where much
of Southern culture was born, and that includes much of Southern
food, and it is the place where, by and large, black America was
born—and that's precisely why I use the plantation as a place of
reclamation.

Soul food (or "African American heritage cooking") and its umbrella cuisine, Southern food, are the most remarked and most maligned of any regional or indigenous ethnic tradition in the United
States. They are also big business and key to the aforementioned
cultural tourism. Southern and soul foods are seen as unhealthy,
self-destructive, and misguided, even as modern Southern chefs
try to recast and reinvent the canon, emphasizing fresh ingredients,
balance, and seasonality. And yet the arguments are not just about
how much lard is too much. The connection between and heritage
of both Southern and soul cuisines is hotly debated and arouses old
racial stereotypes, prejudices, and cultural attitudes and intercultural
misunderstandings. It's an easy metaphor for the "two" Souths—

one black, one white—intertwined and complicated. That storm of history—from Africa to America, slavery to freedom, Middle Passage to this, our now—is not trivia. It is in every cell of our bodies.

Today's American food culture is a contested landscape in search of values, new direction, and its own indigenous sense of rightness and self-worth. It's a culture looking toward ecology, the regional flow of seasons, and opportunities for new ways to invigorate and color the American palate. Our new foodies are concerned with health, sustainability, environmental integrity, social justice, and the push-pull between global and local economies. Our food world is a charged scene of culinary inquiry continually in search of ancestors, historical precedent, and novel ways to explore tradition while surging forward. The chefs and culinarians of twenty-first-century America have become hungry for an origin story all our own.

The lofty goal of participation in the praise fest for rediscovering and sustaining America's food roots seems trivial at best when going to your source is traumatic. The early and antebellum South is not where most African Americans want to let their minds and feet visit. It's a painful place, and the modern South is just beginning to engage the relationship between the racial divide, class divisions, and cultural fissures that have tainted the journey to contemporary Southern cuisine. It's an entangled and deeply personal mess that has been four centuries in the making. This book is about finding and honoring the soul of my people's food by looking deep within my past and my family's story.

There is no chef without a homeland. To be a chef today is to center yourself in the traditions of your roots and use them to define your art and speak to any human being about who you are; your plate is your flag. Many of our most pungent memories are carried through food, just as connections to our ancestors are reaffirmed by cooking the dishes handed down to us. For some chefs, this bond is as easy as pointing to a Tuscan village or a Korean neighborhood, while others adopt the foods of culinary kinfolk outside their own background and use them to express their personal identity. Many take for granted their fast and easy connections to a food narrative that grounds them in a tradition, gives them a broad palette to explore, and affords them a genuine taste of eudaemonia, all of which is the holistic feeling of flourishing in life; and of course it is often blissfully apolitical.

I am at least the eighth, and in some cases the ninth, tenth, or twelfth generation of my family to be born in America. I say "America" because the term "United States" conveys politics but not dreams. There is no "United States dream," but apparently there is an "American dream," so I call out America with all due respect to all lands involved in the legacy of Amerigo Vespucci, as if his name above all others was perfect for naming places or dreams. If nothing else, it forces me to confront what "American" means and how I became one other than by nascence. I am an American by the consequence of the long path of slavery, migration, and the search to satisfy hungers—for sustenance, money, sexual gratification, racialized egos. Hunger pushed humanity across Africa and then out of Africa into the world, and ever since, humanity has found ways to push other humans to satisfy their hungers—until they drop.

There is being American and then there is being Southern, and when you move across its face, the South feels endless. For all its familiar tropes, there are multiple Souths, not just one, just as there are multiple ways of being Southern. The differences in the landscape are subtle, and like going from lover to lover, things seem to meld until names are meaningless. Another battlefield, another burial ground. Soulscapes and foodsteps and mysteries and myths. Then, before you know it, the stories begin to pile up like particles of clay and loam and sand until you can't breathe. We Southerners are now as Vietnamese and Mexican and transgender as we were once Muskogean, Anglo-Celtic, Gallic, and fundamentalist. Add the exile of fifty-plus nations of Africa, and this is my heritage, and for some reason, I wrestle with it endlessly—how could I not; I have nothing else. I am African American, and for the majority of us, this is the genesis we freely share with the New South as we did with the Old.

The travels to discover my heritage revealed to me that the South might not be a place so much as it is a series of moments, which in proper composition communicate an indelible history that people cling to as horseshoes do to old barns. In cooking, the style of Southern food is more verb than adjective; it is the exercise of specific histories, not just the result. In food it becomes less a matter of location than of process, and it becomes difficult to separate the nature of the process from the heritage by which one acquired it. Southern cuisine is a series of geographic and gastronomic mutations made long ago by people whose fade into the earth provides half of the justification for why their descendants keep the process going at all. Our ancestry is not an afterthought; it is both our raison d'être and our mise en place, it is action and reaction.

FIGHTING OFF AMNESIA

APPRENTICES WANTED. One or two colored or black Girls will be taken as Apprentices, for a certain term of years, to the PAS-TRY BUSINESS, by a free colored woman, who is a complete Pastry Cook. Proper care will be taken of those placed with her. Apply at the fruit store, No. 81 East Bay.
　　　　　—*CHARLESTON COURIER* (DECEMBER 2, 1830)

Therese Nelson, a dear friend and chef, and I are talking in her Harlem apartment. It's crowded with cookbooks stacked to the ceiling. Therese is a passionate creative and learner, and we share a love of black culinary history. She runs a site and Facebook page that celebrate just that. For Therese, and many chefs of color, the classroom was not the place where they learned about themselves and the culinary past of the African American people. "Culinary schools, just like regular school growing up, don't really teach you your history. You never heard about James Hemings or Hercules or Malinda Russell or Abby Fisher or anybody like that in any of your classes. Or Africa, or that the Caribbean or Brazil have anything to do with Africa, let alone the United States. Here I am trying to be an authentic American chef, which necessitates exploring my African heritage, and we didn't get that in culinary school, and a lot of students still don't."

James Hemings. Currently championed by our fellow friends Chef Ashbell McElveen and culinary historian and sommelier Tonya Hopkins through the newly founded James Hemings Foundation, James Hemings is the household name that should have been that never was. "When I was growing up, I remember all these books talking about what Jefferson did for the American table, and he did make contributions, but he outsourced a lot of his learning to the people who worked on his plantations as his cooks. James Hemings, Edith Fossett, Fanny Hern; they have French training, but then there are these African and Native American ingredients and flavors, and all of it—England, West Africa, and indigenous food—is getting mixed up in their hands. And the thing is, it's not just them. It's generations of black cooks like Solomon Northup's wife—she's illiterate but she's conversant in haute cuisine. A lot of fine restaurants have a pedigree of having black chefs, cooks, whatever you want to call them, powering their kitchens. Delmonico's, Gage and Tollner, North and South, we were there," says Tonya.

Indeed we were. James Hemings (1765–1801) was a "bright mulatto" from Albemarle County, Virginia, who died at his own hand in Baltimore at the age of thirty-six. He is the brother of Sally Hemings, who will go down in history as the mother of Jefferson's African American children. From the same region that would later produce the indomitable Edna Lewis, the author of *The Taste of Country Cooking*, known as "the South's Julia Child," James Hemings saw the birth of the United States and was, without much exaggeration, its most accomplished and educated chef. Accompanying his slaveholder to Paris when he is nineteen, James is officially free the minute he hits French soil during Jefferson's ambassadorship. However, his whole world is atop the mountain known as Monticello, including his mother and siblings. The mountain was a complicated place. His late young mistress was his half sister, Martha; long before Paris, blood and culture lines had already been crossed.

James, "at great cost" to Jefferson, is tutored in French and goes to work in some of the best kitchens Paris and Versailles have to offer. He suffers through being yelled at in a language he gradually gains fluency in and acquires skills that are being snuffed out as America is handed the complete reins of racial chattel slavery—he is multilingual, he is traveled, he can read, and he can write. Jefferson gives him a salary and extra money. He looks every bit the part of a talented chef. He is a cook worthy not only of a plantation kitchen, but of French royalty itself. Many of the foods that Jefferson is credited with introducing to the American diet are in fact learned and translated under James's hand. They worked in concert with each other to develop the kitchen that Jefferson wanted, the reward upon training his brother Peter being James's emancipation. On February 5, 1796, a black man received his freedom and became an American professional chef.

"James's story and Edna Lewis's story and everybody in between 1776 and 1976—these early black cookbook authors and famous chefs and enslaved chefs and free men and women of color who owned taverns and catered in Philadelphia and Washington—those are our ancestors," Therese says. "We need to know where we come from." Therese's own roots are in Newark, New Jersey. She is the second generation born up North to a family with roots in Latta,

South Carolina. "We went down for reunions every summer. My grandmother talked about not being able to go to school until the tobacco harvest was over, but I never really heard them talk much about segregation, and just about nothing from slavery time. Put all of that together from not learning my history at school, and only knowing a little bit from home, and I felt fraudulent because I didn't know my roots, I didn't know where to start." She looks at me intently. "We need a blueprint as individuals and as a people. We live in a puzzle where the pieces don't even fit together. We need a path so we can put it all together again."

My Southern credentials once came from rattling off "home places" in my presentations as if I had been to all of them, seen the counties and creeks and courthouses. Some I had, some I had not. Phenix City and Seale, Alabama; Prospect, Virginia; Lancaster, South Carolina; Halifax County, North Carolina; Athens, Georgia; Tennessee; Mississippi; New Orleans . . . the list kept getting longer and longer as I added up all the spots and stops that led to me—crumbling kitchens, rotting auction blocks, graveyards iced in asphalt. With each deterioration, I was becoming someone fading from who I was and where I came from, just in time for the rest of the world to catch amnesia with me. I began to have the urge to see the places, imagine the ancestors whose lives I could barely know otherwise, and taste the food.

My entire cooking life has been about memory. It's my most indispensable ingredient, so wherever I find it, I hoard it. I tell stories about people using food, I swap memories with people and create out of that conversation mnemonic feasts with this fallible, subjective mental evidence. Sometimes they are people long gone, whose immortality is expressed in the pulp of trees also long gone and in our electronic ether. Other times they are people who converse with me as I cook as the enslaved once cooked, testifying to people and places that only come alive again when they are remembered.

In memory there is resurrection, and thus the end goal of my cooking is just that—resurrection.

Before I officially began the journey to dig deeper into my food and family roots and routes, I was racking up an internal encyclopedia about other people and how food affected their lives as proxy for the stories in my own bloodline and body. This made for really uncomfortable armor. It never really fit me right. These were other people's tales and paths—not my own. I began to wonder if I ever really would be able to locate myself in the human experience. What good is it to learn the flow of human history and to speak of the dead if their stories don't speak to you? What of food history and facts and figures and flashpoints? What good is your own position as a culinary historian if you can't find yourself in the narrative of your food's story, if you don't know who you are?

6:30 A.M., READYING THE POTS

No matter where I am the next work involves the pots. Most of my cooking spans from 1730 to 1880, the generations of my family from when I estimate the greatest number arrived from Africa, to the end of Reconstruction, and fortunately for me, open-hearth cookery in that time doesn't change much. Clunky Dutch ovens (an old legend says if you treat it wrong it will use its legs to run away) and rusty lids, leggy spider skillets, and tin kitchens that look like incomplete George Foreman rotisseries, and lots and lots of wooden spoons and ladles that give me the feeling of being a sorcerer. You have to have imagination to cook this way—first, to put yourself outside of your own time; second, to believe that what you are actually doing is a form of magic. My favorite tool to hate is the waffle iron with its exacting timing and choreographed dance of greasing, heating, pouring in batter, counting seconds, flipping it, counting again, then removing it gently as not to mar a single inch of cake.

If the pots and utensils are not clean, I scrub the pots free of any rust, bug carcasses, or mouse scat. In goes a little boiling water, out goes the water; they dry near the fire; and then comes the grease inside and out until all of the pot is covered. It boils on the pot until it creates a filmy screen blocking the possibility of rust. Dutch ovens, skillets, saucepans, gridirons, stewpans, spit racks, griddles, spatulas, and meat forks—all of this eighteenth- and nineteenth-century Westernness, a far cry from the simpler ensemble of Africa's pot on three stones—must be seasoned lest the food taste of metal and dust, giving off an unsavory essence reminiscent of old blood.

The West and central African cooks—my grandmothers—had a much simpler plan. They set a pot on three stones; earthen pottery made by women in the days before anyone knew what a white person was, versus the cast-iron pots from England for which one of my ancestors may well have been traded. This wasn't just practical; it was their symbol of the universe. Just as the planet seemed to hover in the hands of the Creator, the pot was propped up, and earth, stone, fire, air, and water joined together to bring sustenance. The little hearth—located under heaven or a thatch structure or building used during the rainy season—was itself a ritual space, an altar, a face of spirits, usually a female entity representing motherhood and nurture, the pot itself a kind of womb. To be certain, many of us cooked this way in the slave quarters in our swept yards and at the edges of the fields.

"What's the best thing you ever cooked?" I asked my mother.

"A little black boy named Michael; I cooked him long and slow," she replied.

The metaphor outlasted the women who stirred pots like that, living on in the hearts of our mothers—the notion that cooking and eating were chasing each other. Eating and ingesting—plays on modest terminology for sexual intimacy and conception, followed by more cooking—the preparation and crucible of the womb where the next generation is made. Blood memory? In the genes? Where did we get all this from, this complicated blend of Africa, America, and the West, these Atlantic bodies and selves?

I know there is no such thing as a "racial" "cooking gene." Let's get that straight. I am not one to indulge in too much biological essentialism; that can be very, very, very tricky as a black, gay, Jewish guy. "Don't talk about dry bones around an old woman," the Igbo of Nigeria say. However, I wonder if blood memory, which I do believe in, contains some clause for the ability not to burn water. For generations, when black cooks were enslaved they were called "born cooks," our ability to slay in the kitchen considered a genetic ability rather than a combination of circumstance, nurture, and personal choice and ability. Only now that cooking with a story becomes a jackpot and an ideational diamond mine does this particular branding of people of color become conspicuously quiet, and there is something unmistakably peculiar about that.

And yet there is another part to all this genetic stuff. If you're African American, the urge to know your parts and origins is intense. It has become in the past few years nothing short of a national passion. At first, in the shadow of Alex Haley's *Roots*, it was a quest to embrace family histories that were largely quiet to obfuscate the grief of being oppressed. Then it was the dream of getting back to Africa and repairing the links destroyed or corrupted by slavery. Now there is a full-on movement in genetic genealogy, and black people are leading the vanguard. Four hundred years after 1619, the fire to understand where we come from and to retrieve the valuable parts of our heritage has not gone out.

What does it mean if the person staring back at me from my reflection in an iron pot full of water identifies as a cook, as black, and descendant of the enslaved? Who is this staring back at me? If I could identify where my ancestors came from given genealogy, genetics, and guesses, then I could pinpoint my food heritage and chart a journey across the globe. I could identify the parts of Africa where the men and women who produced me came from, and look at the traditions from Europe and America they came into contact with as genes mixed—by choice and by force.

I've never been satisfied with the generic narrative. It profits me nothing to be a culinary orphan of the West sans pedigree. We Africans in the Americas have not just been adopters, we are border crossers and culture benders. We have always been at play with what was presented to us. The Atlantic world has been an incredible experiment in how an enslaved population could get away with enslaving the palates of the people who enslaved them. From Boston to Bahia, the black cook—enslaved or free—was second to none. To go beyond assumptions; to interrogate our pain; to see the faces of my ancestors, to cook with them, to know them intimately the only way I can know them after decades of memory loss—those are my paths.

8:00 A.M., INGREDIENTS AND MISE EN PLACE

The old cookbooks or "receipt" (recipe) books so lauded in the world of early American and proto-Southern food get a vote but not a veto with me. I am not the white plantation owner's wife reading the recipes aloud after her reverse journey down the whistling walk. I am the enslaved hearing the recipe, or already knowing it and just humoring Big Missy. There are many things in those books that are not African in conception, spirit, delivery, or form. On the other hand, there are many things that are African or Afro-Creole—okra soup, barbecue, red rice or tomato pilau, pepper pot, fried chicken, peanut soup, and the like. The European dishes full of Native American ingredients were changed by black hands, and in reverse you can see how the West and central African dishes with African and

Eurasian and Native ingredients were toned down for European American palates. In these books you can feel the culinary birth pangs of America. North and South, the black cook was the midwife of something new.

So they are all there—Mary Randolph, Annabella Hill, Elizabeth Lea, Lettice Bryan, Hannah Glasse; Carolina, Virginia, and Kentucky housewives; Creole gastronomic manuals, copies of pages from receipt and commonplace books written in fading ink from long-gone plantations, old British classics, and cookbooks that look back on the nostalgia of having the power to own a black cook. In the middle—the few books we have by black folks born into slavery who were cooks—Abby Fisher, Malinda Russell, Rufus Estes, Tunis Campbell. Most are not fat at all. Some are fully annotated with instructions on how to be a good servant and how to set a table, how to serve, how to dispense with the dishes and transition from one part of the evening to the next.

In our own time we have the voices of Edna Lewis, Austin Leslie, Sallie Ann Robinson, Mildred "Mama Dip" Council, Sylvia Woods, Leah Chase, and many others. The white women of the far past, writing and reading in days when it was illegal for much of their enslaved chattel to do the same, held in check by the voices of emancipated cooks and women whose grandparents cooked using the same methods they had seen their grandparents, the last generation born and raised in slavery, do. The last part comes from the formerly enslaved themselves, including emancipatory narratives written or communicated by men and women who had successfully escaped, or the 3,500-plus recorded oral histories of men and women born in slavery who were liberated in 1865 and were interviewed during the Depression as part of the oral history efforts of the Works Progress Administration. An incalculable wealth of knowledge about food and slavery was rescued with this single effort.

It inspired me to harvest the memories and seeds and recipes that travel within my family, and anyone else I could find. Nothing lacks importance; no detail is to be left behind. Our stories and our parents' and grandparents' stories—and even beyond to their parents' and great-grandparents' stories—are precious in a world where the narrative of who we are and were usually lasts no more than three generations. I have spent just as much time with the living as with the dead, collecting their stories and comparing and contrasting them in hopes of a consensus.

I had to commit to doing. To be able to say that I cook in the tradition of the Old South, to the cooking of kitchens high and low, is to affirm that I didn't just read about it distilled on a page. There is no armchair in this work. In cooking, your informed imagination fills in the blanks. The dead and the living cook with me, and things once forgotten come to life. George Washington Carver once said, "If you love something enough it will give up its secrets to you."

STILL LIFE

I have always admired the work of the Dutch masters—kitchen tables and marketplace stalls spilling over with food often in veiled references to a uniquely Protestant spirituality and sense of mortal urgency. Crisscrossed fish tails and sausages on high; and on the ground, rotten fruit, once vain and gorgeous, lying in a putrid state. As much as I love the attempt to cram cardoons and skirret into a painting with religious meaning, it's the larded quails and bubbling pots that catch my eye. These same motifs transferred well to plantation scenes where enslaved men and women are surrounded by the groaning table and wisps of smoke.

The still-life paintings are the way in to many of the foods of the past. A gargantuan ear of Maryland gourdseed corn, a ruddy sweet potato, a horn-shaped okra, and watermelons that burst with juice— all pour out of early American paintings apprehending the early

African American influence. Then there are the people—sometimes our ancestors are shadows, and other times they are front and center. I am the man in the waistcoat and trousers, the billowy shirt surrounded by complicated and ugly produce and foul smells and spices that cut through rain on red clay. I am the new still life—a black man standing on the brick floor feeling the flames lick and the smoke choke, surrounded by the plantation larder.

I have put myself in a world of edible antiques. The food that we have received is not the same as that which our ancestors knew. I once had no clue what an heirloom vegetable was, or a heritage fruit or breed, and I didn't know that the foraging that I loved to do per my grandparents' instructions had the cute little moniker "wildcrafting." My first "historic" foodways demo used anything and everything that gets buried in a landfill or takes thousands of years to disintegrate. I was going for expediency, not accuracy; I had children to teach. I was quickly warned away from this.

Get the pots and the spoons and something to put the food in and eat it from and eat it with. Next came the food. I would have to learn to maneuver the cooking utensils of old and learn how to keep time as I cooked. I lost arm hair and eyebrows, a little blood here and there; I was scalded and branded, burned and seared. These are the marks of my tribe.

I had to learn an entirely new language of measurements—gills (1/2 cup), teacups (3/4 of a cup), drams, jiggers, wineglasses, and pecks. A peck was two gallons of dry cornmeal, or about the amount of food a full hand working on a plantation received per day. This was a world of bushels and hogsheads and barrels and casks. A world full of people unlearned but trained to note on sight distance or volume.

The pots are extremely heavy when filled with water. One event involved cooking at a kitchen until darkness settled, with one modern light and a few candles. I struggled to get the massive pot, filled with water, to the fire. Then I tripped over something near the fire, sending a bit of the water spilling into it. The large group of visitors for the plantation Christmas event, almost completely white, thought this was rather funny. Nobody asked me if I was all right, and most shook their heads in amusement. I have never been so angry at one of these events. I wanted to tell them that if a slaveholder saw fit, an enslaved person in a house could be sold, beaten, or in a few extremely rare but gruesome cases, like an incident in Martinique, cooked alive in an oven for an imperfect cake.

Some people were certainly amused by my path at first. Some thought I'd never make it—but I was just enthusiastic, not daft. One woman challenged me at an early appearance atop Monticello as to whether the fish peppers I was seeding were *annum* or *chinense*. It was a trick question—most peppers are *annum*. Instead of pretending to know, I looked it up. She was not amused, as if my ignorance, which was quickly self-corrected, was an affirmative action dagger with which she had been stabbed. In resistance, I went home and, in the example of Malcolm X in jail, began writing down every single possible animal and plant species used by enslaved people as food, and began to memorize their scientific names. *Sus scrofa, Gallus domesticus, Diospyros virginiana, Brassica oleracea var. acephala, Citrullus vulgaris* . . . music to my newbie ears.

I've gotten used to being challenged on every fact or word that comes out of my mouth. I am not white, and white men and women make up the majority of credentialed experts in this field. I am often the only person of color on a panel, or one of a handful of people of color at conferences on historical foodways and horticultural practices. I am used to being seen as a smack-talking blowhard who thinks he knows but knows nothing—those seeds were planted in those early presentations—but thanks to the miracle of the Internet, I reached out to the lions of the field.

Because of the work of a varied cast of characters ranging from plant and horticulture enthusiasts like heirloom vegetable gurus

William Woys Weaver and Benjamin Watson, and heritage fruit expert Tom Burford, to historical landscape scholars like Peter Wood of Monticello and Wesley Greene of Colonial Williamsburg, I was able to enter a world that until very recently was off the radar of most American eaters. This work is complicated by the searching and plumbing of David Shields and Glenn Roberts and others who have sought to bring old field crops to life and reinvigorate their place in the Southern diet. None of them are black; that is not to say they must be black, but as far as passion and love of the knowledge will take them, not one of these figures can look at their family tree and imagine in their mind's eye an enslaved person munching on Green Glaze collards or Sea Island red field peas or Carolina Gold rice middlins (broken rice reserved for the enslaved).

It's this particular argument about the importance of being able to have that connection that has often gotten me into trouble. It's not that I want them to be African American. I just think there is a measure of gravitas in black people looking at the same food culture and not only learning important general information but being able to see themselves. This is greater than the intrinsic value of knowing where our food comes from and rescuing endangered foods. That *Lost Ark*-meets-Noah's-ark mentality is intellectually thrilling and highly motivational, but it pales in comparison to the task of providing economic opportunity, cultural and spiritual reconnection, improved health and quality of life, and creative and cultural capital to the people who not only used to grow that food for themselves and others, but have historically been suppressed from benefiting from their ancestral legacy.

So much was lost—names, faces, ages, ethnic identities—that African Americans must do what no other ethnic group writ large must do: take a completely shattered vessel and piece it together, knowing that some pieces will never be recovered. This is not quite as harrowing or hopeless as it might sound. I liken it to the Japanese art of *kintsugi*, repairing broken vessels using gold. The scars of the object are not concealed, but highlighted and embraced, thus giving them their own dignity and power. The brokenness and its subsequent repair are a recognized part of the story of the journey of the vessel, not to be obscured, and change, transition, and transformation are seen as important as honoring the original structure and its traditional meaning and beauty.

The food is in many cases all we have, all we can go to in order to feel our way into our past. For others, we are an interesting note on the pages of a very different conversation. For African Americans and our allies, food is the gateway into larger conversations about individual and group survival. Ron Finley, an African American food activist from South Central LA, speaks of "drive-thrus killing more black people than drive-bys." Vacant lots in Detroit and Milwaukee, Atlanta, Athens, and Baltimore are being turned into urban agriculture spaces in neighborhoods where fresh produce and jobs are scarce. While other communities might seem only passively interested in their histories, genes, and genealogies—the African American people struggle between nihilism, passing interest, activism, and obsession—and more often than not these are found not only within the same social circles or households, but within the minds and hearts of black individuals when they look at their relationship to their past.

This reconnection meant I had to take myself back to botany and anatomy classes—one student, one teacher: me. I studied parts of plants and bones so that I could accurately describe in the jargoniest of jargon every single species-specific part from petiole to scapula, from tibia to sepal. Okra was no longer just okra; it became a member of the mallow family domesticated in the ancient Sahel, while it was still verdant and predictably rich, crowned in Linnean-speak *Abelmoschus esculentus*—a mucilaginous vegetable, actually a fruit whose mucopolysaccharides help okra act as a lubricant for the body to expunge that which it no longer needs.

Beyond the language of science came a litany of old-time names for the same parts of the plants and animals I began to work with—chines and trotters and jowls; potherbs and sprouts. Then came knowing the signs to plant, both in the heavens and in nature—waxing moons, waning moons; oak leaves as big as baby squirrels' ears; nights cold enough to gauge the rightness of the hog butchering, or a frost so killing it turned persimmons into sugarplums. Winter is possum time, late autumn is raccoon time, late summer and early autumn are squirrel time, spring is rabbit time. You must know a nice catfish from a muddy one, and count on the guinea hens to be too lean.

Each vegetable has its own timing; each smell and sound is part of your internal timer. I have gone from burning things by following the books' instructions to being able to tell from a feeling in my stomach when the rolls were perfect or the fried chicken was done, crispy and beautiful on the outside and clear juices in the middle. There is a relationship you develop with your food that is built on practice and experience, but also on the feeling that you bring to your pots. They know you because pots have souls—at least that's what I'm told. Pots are to African and African Diaspora mythology what bottles are to genies in the Middle East. They are like shells for hermit crabs—the pots contain wisdom and the dead—and if you don't treat them right you might just watch one run off down the road.

Magical realism aside, there is a magic in being able to take the hot coals and shovel them above and below and cook something and break the expectations of the people you cook for. Equally powerful is imagining that twelve-course meals were once made using only fire, iron, copper, wood, flint, clay, and pewter. Cooks built their reputation on this ancient, common way. Men and women who had ancestors who only used a pot on three stones were now in command of a Western cuisine with African influences, flourishes, and aesthetics. I can't stir a single pot without remembering or acknowledging that—this is where our power was.

MARCHING AS TO WAR

I bring all of this into the historical kitchen with me: politics and race, sexuality and spirituality, memory, brokenness, repair, reclamation and reconciliation, and anger. I bring in moments from my own childhood and wince sometimes at the feelings of mourning and pain I get from them. Moments of shame and failure, moments of incredible love and affection. Before these were my grandmother's hands. I was trained to use my hands to measure as accurately as possible dry ingredients; to this day I can give you any teaspoon or tablespoon or cup measurement you want by just holding my hands a certain way.

My mother gave me three lifetimes of scoldings and sayings that still swirl around me every time I cook: "Integrity in the kitchen!" (Always wash your hands, keep things clean, clean as you go.) "RTFM—Read the F—— Manual." (Don't ignore the instructions or order of the recipe—it's there for a reason. Learn the formula first and then you can experiment, not the other way around.) "Save the best for company." (Give yourself the half-burned, off-looking stuff—always give the best to your guests.)

It was the way I held my hands when I stirred things in a bowl—I remember the pain of having my hand yanked into position and held in the exact bend it took to properly incorporate moisture into a dry mix. It was my father asking me to describe the perfect color of barbecued meat, and when I replied "a pecan-colored brown," my father smiled with satisfaction (a rare look if you know my father) and said, "I like that color, son." It was being kicked out of the kitchen innumerable times for not complying with the exact instructions of the presiding adult. It was sitting at my grandmother's kitchen table waiting to be her official taster and unofficial sous.

It is not enough to know the past of the people you interpret. You must know your own past. I'm in the clothes that call to mind what the enslaved wore, making food like the enslaved made for themselves and their slaveholders. I am in plantation kitchens that are haunted to the rafters in places that few African Americans dare to tread. I watch ghosts walk by, and among them is me. I am seeing myself at seven, at thirteen, twenty-one, thirty, now. I am stirring the pot wondering, How exactly did I get *here*?

Kitchen Pepper

Goes in everything in place of just pepper.

1 tsp coarsely ground black pepper	1 tsp ground Ceylon cinnamon
1 tsp ground white pepper	1 tsp ground nutmeg
1 tsp red pepper flakes	1 tsp ground allspice
1 tsp ground mace	1 tsp ground ginger

Mix together, store in a cool place.

Fish Pepper Sauce

15 to 20 fish peppers	4 cups apple cider vinegar
Kosher salt	or rum

Take fish peppers, and cut off the tops and tips of the pods. A few peppers, say 5 or so, should be hopped to a pulp in a food processor. Add a pinch or two of salt. Take this pulp and place at the bottom of a jar. The rest of the peppers can be sliced down the middle, exposing the seeds, or left whole. Place them on top of the pulpy mixture and cover in the bottle with apple cider vinegar or rum. Shake well and let steep 2 to 3 weeks before using.

2

—

HATING MY SOUL

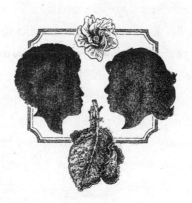

Before I tell you all about my glorious and proud culinary heritage, I have to confess two things about me as a little kid:

I hated soul food and I didn't really like being black. My mother never failed to remind me about my frequent and bloodcurdling toddler tantrums against my own people, although when she told it, it was something akin to Dave Chappelle's blind, black KKK leader, Clayton Bigsby. I cried during every minute of *Song of the South*, *The Wiz*, and *Roots: The Next Generations*, yelling at the top of my lungs, "I don't wanna watch those ugly [black] people!"

For the former, my mother had to "ease on down the road" and remove me from the theater. For the latter, she blessed God for the newfangled invention of the remote control.

Black cuisine was no different. Although my first nonmilk food was the venerable cornbread mashed in potlikker—the juice from cooking Southern-style greens—my palate and nose were soon tainted by fast food, and I had no need for most of the African American heritage cooking that surrounded me. My mother liked to remind revolutionary, Afrocentric, teenage me of these eternally embarrassing moments because she liked to say, "I want you to know no matter how far you go, you need to know how far you've come."

Blame it on Bo Derek and her Columbused cornrows in *10*. Blame it on John Travolta and his black moves in an Italian American body, and Farrah and *Dynasty* and *Dallas* and *The Colbys* and Richie Rich comic books. Blame it on a world that taught me early on and repeatedly that the only people who actually mattered were pretty white people getting laid and living large, and their cute children living without want. All self-hatred is nonsense, and it's a sickness only your soul food can cure.

The kitchen was my crib. The first kitchen I remember was at my grandparents' house on Kennedy Street in Northeast Washington, DC. After a brief stint of living on her own, my mother moved us in with my maternal grandparents and three of her younger brothers. My father lived in another part of Northeast and his mother, Eloise Booker, my Virginia-born grandmother, lived in the Brookland neighborhood in a little house she bought after years of being a domestic, surrounded by a garden planted full of spearmint she grew just for iced tea. My maternal grandparents, Walter (Granddaddy) and Hazel (who I called Grammy) Townsend, had first migrated from Birmingham, Alabama, to Cleveland, and then later Cincinnati after World War II to work on the railroads and in the factories of the Midwest. My grandfather, a former Pullman porter, attended college and studied for a time at Cornell, learning about negotiation—a skill he took to the railroads and railway unions of Africa, from Liberia to Ethiopia, from Tanzania to Mozambique. After a brief return to Cincinnati after living in England and Kenya, my grandparents relocated to Washington, DC. After living in a haunted house on Oakwood Terrace that was tormented by the spirit of a murdered girl and a malicious phantom that danced on the walls at night, they settled in my very unhaunted favorite childhood home.

I was blissfully unaware of all the debts that had been paid and all the intrigues that had occurred to give me a relatively happy childhood. I was born and raised in the census South, beneath the Mason-Dixon Line, in the shadow of slavery, but just beyond the reach of Dixie with border-state taste buds. By design I was not born in the former Confederacy or in the Rust Belt. If I had, I might not be in a position to write this. My grandparents left a dying Midwest for a Washington where federal work and other opportunities were giving people aiming to be in the black middle class a new start. My paternal grandparents, Gonze Lee Twitty and Eloise Booker, had come to DC long before. Grandmother Eloise left Prince Edward County, Virginia, for Philadelphia, then for DC, where she worked as a nurse and a domestic. My grandfather began his new life as a waiter alongside my grandmother, then sold cars. Within a decade they divorced, and he returned to South Carolina to farm and harvest lumber, living on his own land. He was the immigrant who went back home with money from "off."

By the late 1970s, my "people" were a family scattered across the United States and around the world. We had lived in Germany, England, Kenya, Tanzania, Jamaica, and across Latin America. We had fought in Vietnam. The generation before broadcast themselves up and down the East Coast—New York, Philadelphia, Baltimore, Washington; and across the Midwest—Detroit, Akron, Cleveland, Cincinnati, Milwaukee, and Chicago. Within a decade of the civil rights movement some of us were already moving back down South. We met and married into other black families from the South, Africa, the Caribbean, and Latin America, and some of us went west to California; we were, in short, an atypical but typical black American family, each of us occupying a small part of a diaspora created in part by the need to get away from the past.

My mother carried in her body the genes of the South, but not its magnetic pull. Her parents never took her to Alabama, and she and her siblings never went as a family or on their own. She spent summers in Cleveland, Chicago, or Detroit, where Aunt Mu had a Cadillac and taught her to love roller coasters and her Sunday dinner roast chicken with butter and herbs under the skin. During my Mom's childhood, *Jet* magazine circulated with the image of a murdered Emmett Till that gave her nightmares and caused her to never want to go to the Deep South. Daddy, ten years older, went as far as Virginia and South Carolina, and lived a country life each summer and for a full year in Lancaster, where he went to a one-room schoolhouse with eight grades; "At least in DC, school was segregated, but you didn't have eight grades in one room."

When she arrived in Washington, my mother was appalled by just how Southern DC was. There was greater separation there than she had experienced even on the shores of Dixie in Cincinnati. When they arrived, Peoples Drug Store sold Confederate flags proclaiming, "The South Shall Rise Again." There were still places you just didn't go, and people you still didn't talk to. Within a year of their arrival, Reverend Martin Luther King Jr. was assassinated in Memphis, and like 109 other cities, Washington, DC, knew civil unrest and riots. My family's aspirations for job opportunity and a new start were already in doubt. By the time I was born in 1977, on the windy first day of spring in the year of Alex Haley's comet, order had been restored and we were living in Chocolate City.

BABY FOOD

My best pal was a Saint Bernard named Brandy. It took me a millennium to figure out that he was named so because of the custom of attaching a small keg of brandy to the necks of these rescue dogs. He was protective of me, and he shared our home with a Persian cat named Benny. After one knock-down, drag-out fight they became fast friends in our happy home. Our house always smelled of spices, bubbling piquant sauces, and frying. Pepper steak, beef Stroganoff, a Sri Lankan "curry" surrounded by relishes and fixings, marinara sauce, and puff pastry from desserts to samosas—this was my earliest culinary life, salivating with our pets. There were fried apple pies, apple butter, pot roast, hickory-perfumed turkeys resting from my grandfather's smoker, piles of mustard and turnip greens in the sink, black-eyed peas staring back at me under a pool of clear water soaking for New Year's Day, sweet potatoes lusty with nutmeg, and me, Brandy, and Benny waiting for someone—usually my grandmother—to give us something. That's the earliest memory I have of the kitchen. I was a peace-loving boy, except when it came to my grandmother's potato and yeast rolls.

My grandmother would make hot potato bread and yeast rolls for our neighbors present and past, and they would come by the house to get the finished product, all of them filing in in their various occupational uniforms, like a sketch from *Sesame Street*. There are pictures of me in a soldier's helmet my father gave me, and with a toy gun; I forgot my tour of duty guarding the kitchen as my grandmother baked—which was very butch of me, in sharp contrast to my Fisher-Price toy record set, which I had already reimagined as Blondie and Donna Summer albums. Daddy sought to counteract this and my (homosexual-making) play stove that I adored by giving me a helmet, guns, and play ammo. Speaking of homosexual, the kitchen is also the place I once cut myself badly with a knife trying to discover what my toy G.I. Joe and He-Man looked like "under there"—so I guess his tactics to thwart the gay almost worked. What a fucking disappointment and waste of blood.

My grandmother would make the bread, and the whole house would smell of the prediction that I was on the verge of slathering peach, blackberry, or apple jelly on a hot, buttered piece of bread. Being a greedy and jealous kid, I thought all the bread was for me, no matter how many times we had been through the ritual of her giving it away. Her bread was one of six things I ate without a fight. Candied yams (despite Grammy's heavy hand with nutmeg, and never with marshmallows, among our kin), barbecue (which I pronounced "bubble cool"), fried chicken, buttermilk biscuits, and red rice—which the old folks called "Spanish rice" or "mulatto rice," but was really just the American descendant of Jollof rice.

When people came over, they got a good laugh from me crying my eyes out and begging for bread, and nothing calmed me down until I had my own slice with butter melting on it, jellies making abstract art on my plate as foretold by the prophecy of the scent. I was a sensitive little soldier. In the little Kodak picture, I'm sitting under all these doodads and tools and utensils hanging from nails on a sea-foam-green wall. The wall color was ugly, but I didn't care; at the time, everything in my little world seemed magical and scary and potent.

MOTHER'S LAND

I was convinced that pictures of Africans on our dining room wall watched me. Tiger lily—that was the color of the wall. In that room, the remnants of Africa—a drum covered in zebra skin, wooden figurines from the markets of Nairobi, and paintings of Ethiopian saints and East African tribesmen—looked down at me with white, piercing, damning eyes. None of the pictures smiled. There was an Afar man from the dry hell of the Danakil and its salt flats. There was a Kikuyu woman who looked like "Johnson's Mother," a woman both feared and revered in family lore. Joining them was a Masai mother and a Masai warrior, her baby hanging on her back with a very unmaternal stare at the artist, and a man who wore the mane of a lion, defiantly proud of the ultimate kill.

My mother's adolescent experience in Africa with her sisters was something right out of *The Poisonwood Bible*. They didn't know Africa beyond *Tarzan* and movies about voodoo and cannibals. In some ways East Africa did not disappoint, with its repetitive meals of stiff corn mush and constant flow of unidentifiable bush meat swarming with flies that might make cannibalism seem forgivable. Yet there were also new treats like *kachumbali*, a spicy vegetable relish, pumpkin stews, Swahili duck, samosas and chapatis from Indian migrant workers, and a smaller but familiar variety of a plant they knew back home, *sukuma wiki*, collard greens.

They enrolled in Kenya High School; I still have my mother's report cards as life returned to something resembling normalcy. Grammy went back to cooking on a woodstove, and one day as she was cooking skulked into the house "Johnson's Mother," her very traditional Kikuyu neighbor and parent to their hired helper, a young man named, well, Johnson, and a source of great terror and humor. She introduced herself by swinging a panga (machete) in the air, eventually wedging it into the wooden kitchen table on her first visit in protest of the "Englaisah!" (British), sending my mother and her sisters screaming from doing their homework to hiding in the closet. Once my grandmother decided not to cut her, they spent many afternoons patiently working out venting sessions about the meanness of white folks. She wore a Kikuyu tunic, her ears were pulled and pierced, and she introduced herself to my newborn youngest uncle by spitting in his mouth to give him a blessing on his health. She had few teeth with which to smile, and when our family returned to America, never to see Kenya again, Johnson's Mother sent up the death wail, deeply aggrieved.

Johnson took my mother and her sisters to see sunrises at Mount

Kenya. I spent hours looking through old photos of Johnson's Mother—who looked no different than the women in the paintings in the dining room. There were black-and-white pictures of the flower market in Nairobi, the orphaned dik-dik they briefly kept as a pet, the green mamba Johnson killed in the backyard, and proud Masai boys tending cattle, standing on one leg like storks. My mother had her first boyfriend in Kenya—a beautiful boy from the Seychelles named Simon. Had he come to study in the United States, this might well have been a different book. My mother left Africa in love rather than in fear, and came armed with Swahili just in time for black power and Kwanzaa. Every night she would count me down to sleep—*tatu, mbili, moja, sifuri,* and then a kiss.

ALBUMS

Hugh Masekela and Miriam Makeba joined Lena Horne and Kraftwerk and Afrika Bambaataa and Devo on the record player below the African paintings. Depending on who cooked in the kitchen, the tenor of the music changed. I heard gut-bucket blues and classical music and I could identify Isaac Hayes (*Hot Buttered Soul*), Carole King (*Tapestry*), and Al Green (*I'm Still in Love with You*) from album covers. Come on the right day and you could hear Billy Joel and Chic. Then there was the rainbow-colored cover with a white man (Steve Curry) with a fro. From this album came the forbidden song that almost everybody, except my grandfather, seemed to get great pleasure poking fun of:

> I'm a colored spade
> A nigger / a black nigger / a jungle bunny / jigaboo coon /
>   pickaninny mau mau / Uncle Tom / Aunt Jemima / Little
>   Black Sambo . . .

And then comes the menu:

> And if you ask him to dinner you're going to feed him
> Watermelon
> Hominy grits
> An' shortnin' bread
> Alligator ribs
> Some pig tails
> Some black-eyed peas
> Some chitlins
> Some collard greens
> And if you don't watch out
> This boogie man will get you
> Booooooooo!

How exactly did the rainbow-colored white man on the album cover know (except our ribs were pork, not alligator) what they served in my house? I didn't like eating watermelon, and to this day I confess I will not eat it in front of white people—probably because I saw Petey Greene devouring watermelon on his Channel 20 television show. Hominy grits were that really bad un-oatmeal in drag that I saw people put butter and black pepper and salt on. I never saw shortening bread or heard it talked about except for some stupid song about "Mammy's" (Who the hell is "Mammy?") little baby loving it. Pigs' tails and pigs' feet could be found at my other grandmother's house, especially the latter, and they were horrifying. Only superstition made me swallow three black-eyed peas and a spoonful or two of collard greens on New Year's Day, and then came chitlins. . . .

Both of my grandmothers made chitlins (excuse me, "chitterlings") although I never actually saw either one of them eat any.

Grandmother Eloise would make them for Daddy on holidays and New Year's, to lots of grins and laughter, and my chagrin. Grammy would make my grandfather and my uncle chitlins, which she detested, and so did the rest of us, and my mother would use those occasions to take me to the zoo with all its funk and elephant house–ness. Apes throwing vomit, and a whiff of maned wolf in the breeze, smelled better than our house when chitlins were made. Those were the days of hot dogs from a cart with sweet relish; red, white, and blue Popsicles; and astronaut ice cream in all its freeze-dried perfection. I did anything and everything to avoid the smell and savor of "slave" food.

And I didn't really understand why people ate that shit. Literally, I didn't get it—nobody explained to me the cuisine of want until much later. I still will never eat chitlins and I was perplexed, as I learned to read, why the word on the plastic tub was "chitterlings" but everybody said "chitlins"—another reason simply not to trust this food.

Another black medieval torture was okra. In our next kitchen, I remember my grandmother forcing me to eat okra. And all I knew is that it was pinkish on the inside for some reason and snotty and viscous, and looked as if it was going to come alive at any point and have me for dinner. My mother encouraged me to have one bite, but I knew one bite would translate into four bites, so I refused as if I were being sent off to the gulag. Finally, I put a piece in my mouth and marched upstairs to bed, but not before I spat it out in the toilet. Heritage, my ass.

I was horrified by hot sauce. I didn't like the way the bottle smelled, and it was streaked in the inside, really turning me off. Buttermilk, the same thing, streaking the glass. More than one person has joked to me that all gross black food should be consumed on an African American equivalent of both Passover and Yom Kippur, where we atone for our sins and remember our history by being forced to partake in an obligatory feast of chitlins, okra, black-eyed peas, hog maws, pigs' feet, funky greens, pork rinds, and ashcake (flavorless cornbread baked in the ashes of the fire) to get it out of our systems once a year. Like a seder plate, we could have a slave plate and watch one another's faces turn awry as we choked down our oppression and washed it away with a glass of, you guessed it, Kool-Aid, four cups to symbolize our liberation from bondage, four cups of sugar per cup to make up for the horrific meal and all the shame and guilt with which it was flavored.

I remember all these soul food horror stories and shudder. They came from a cultural disconnect based on an interruption in the generations. It wasn't regional, because there were black people who ate the same exact food no matter where they lived, but it was a grandmother who left behind certain foods, and a mother who did the same. Add a grandson who lived in a world that was being taken over by Pizza Hut and McDonald's and Kentucky Fried Chicken, and convenience foods splattered with additives, flavorings, artificial colors, and tons of seduction, and this could have been the end of my soul.

REDEMPTION

Food was supposed to be perfect, almost mathematical. I remember being obsessed with the image of a sandwich when we were being taught phonics. It was so perfect and balanced and colorful that I had the idea in my head that food was supposed to be ideal and not rough; tidy and not confusing. Our food was anything but tidy and not confusing. Those pots with bones sticking out looked to me like bubbling graveyards. Most confusing was why anybody wanted bones in their food or wanted to eat hog intestines or a slimy vegetable like okra that came from the Black Lagoon and, worst of all, bottles that evoked mirrors in horror movies streaked with blood.

It's not surprising that my culinary adventure began with ramen and hot dogs. Today, I eat neither, but I do make my own hot sauce, grow and eat okra, and keep the bones in the pot. But not until Judgment Day on G-d's command will I ever eat a chitterling or do the infamous chitlin strut, as the Carolinians do.

Around six or seven, I began to learn how to cook, mostly out of boredom as the only kid in a house full of adults. The conversion began. My first task was to be the official taster when Grammy prepared meals, and I learned bite by bite the proprietary taste of our favorite dishes. This was followed by the rolling of dough and cutting biscuits out with a floured mason jar. The complex ritual of washing, scrubbing, rolling, and cutting greens followed, and pretty soon I was peeling sweet potatoes and snapping beans, learning how to buy the best peaches, and judging boxes of berries. Canned vegetables were emergency rations, not something anyone used for any good reason; the ways of the Lord are many, but they did not include canned yams, black-eyed peas, collard greens, or string beans.

I slowly learned that the best food was homemade, fresh, and from scratch. As cheap and efficient as Kool-Aid—the source of many racialized jokes—was, we did not rely on it. Grammy's lemonade was special. The juice was mixed with sugar cubes to make lemon simple syrup, we added a pinch of soda or salt, the water was chilled with the lemon shells giving off their oils, and then finally the two were combined, and we would stir and sing:

> *Ice cold lemonade,*
> *stirred with a spade,*
> *made in the shade,*
> *cools your teeth and*
> *parts yo' hair,*
> *makes yo' feel good, everywhere!*

This was called the "slave song" in our family. It was Daddy Ellis's song, my grandfather's stepfather's tune. I've since learned it was
a pretty common folk song, but it was through this song, making
Grammy's special lemonade, that I was introduced to the word that
would change my life and my perspective on being an American. For
all the times I sang that song making lemonade, I didn't know what
a "slave" was, until one day I asked. I don't really remember what the
answer was, but I know that immediately my mind went to a place
dim and murky, bizarre and quiet. Three centuries were explained
to me with books full of pictures opened wide, and my hands felt
around in the darkness of my imagination for the women and men
who felt completely beyond my reach.

THE TWO MAMAS

My mother and grandmother represented to me the last two generations and their strivings. They unified over the cleaning, sorting,
and cooking of collard greens, although my mother began to insert
smoked turkey after Grammy's passing. This was the ritual that tied
them to the women of the past. Many things were discussed over
greens, but I don't remember much banter. My eyes honed in on the
hands, the sounds, what was scrapped and what made it into the pot.
My grandmother, marked with something of an exotic ancestral look
with her memories of John de Conqueror root in her daddy's pocket
and trips to the Holiness church for entertainment purposes and fatback and crowders talking to her daughter, my mother, seasoned in
black pride and black power, a cheek permanently memory-stained
with the kiss of James Brown after a concert, a feminist, classical
music enthusiast, with both of them insomniac puzzle junkies—
and if a weak memory serves me correctly, that's probably what they
chatted about most.

My grandmother would fight bacon grease on summer mornings,

and she would fry green tomatoes in that grease, poking at the cast-iron skillet like she was a fencer and using her housecoat as a shield as the grease popped and threatened to light her hair. Summer mornings were the smell of bacon and grapefruit. The smell of fried green tomatoes and scallions—which were a relish for everything. And the smell of my grandmother's greased, slightly singed reddish brown hair. (She came from mixed stock and was called "Dirty Red" because of her natural hair color, although a family legend says that it actually came from wearing a red dress at her wedding, but to my knowledge all pictures have been destroyed as to not bear witness to this allegation.) I still have the Madam C. J. Walker–invented hot comb that my grandmother bought in the 1930s and my mother used for a lifetime after her. I swear to you that I still keep it in the kitchen. Although I have no long hair to straighten, I bring it out every now and then and smell it and immediately I'm brought back to my childhood—presumably in the same way that one hears the ocean in a seashell. You really don't experience the same sensations—you just imagine you do, and that's enough.

At the end of her life, my grandmother, a lifelong smoker as her daughter would also be, left the world after a mounting second heart attack, her last meal a pot of great northern beans and a chunk of ham boiling on the stove and a cast-iron skillet of cornbread. I remember holding her when the paramedics came and looking at her arthritic hands in which she cut tomatoes, and the blue veins running through her thin, yellow skin. I dared peek inside her journal after she was dead because I wanted her to linger in my life as long as possible. The first thing that struck me was how many grocery lists and meals were listed painstakingly (something my mother also did), and the most jarring entry was one of the meals that I helped prepare. It was collards, candied yams, barbecued spareribs, iced tea, and cornbread muffins, and she said, "And Michael helped, and it, thank God, it was a good Southern meal."

My grandmother loved everyone. She had a great universal love and patience for all people, and collected friends of every background throughout her life. However she never really "had good blood" for the white Southerners who persecuted her and her family. It was something akin to the feeling I've gotten from Shoah survivors who wouldn't think of even getting in a Volkswagen. It was a strange push-pull. It wasn't that her bias was against white Southerners; she was the biggest *Waltons* fan ever (it reminded her of the world she grew up in). She could not simply forget the fears and indignities visited on her and her kin, and the mean and cruel people who did them. My grandmother nevertheless owned being Southern on her own terms, and like so many black grandmothers from beneath the Mason-Dixon line saw it as her personal responsibility to produce in me a true "Southern gentleman."

If my grandmother was tradition, my mother was innovation, and she was less forgiving of my nonsense. I had to learn all of the culinary terms in volume one of the *Better Homes and Gardens Encyclopedia of Cooking*, with its checkerboard, wipeable tablecloth cover. I read and reread them until I could answer anything my mother asked as she strung along culinary terms from "flambé" to "vichyssoise." My grandmother did a certain repertoire without fail, but my mother took things to the next level and pushed us and me further. My mother was pomegranate molasses, hoisin sauce, brioche, and samosa—tastes far beyond the Cotton Kingdom.

My mother's world was the Great Migration. She was the first generation to go to school with white children or to know education beyond the one-room schoolhouse. Even my father, raised in segregated Washington, DC, and South Carolina, never went to school with white kids, and he remembers the one-room schoolhouse. She was a striver. She read and spoke German with near fluency, was good at languages, and would often give me instructions in other languages without translation. Her childhood took her around the world and across the cities of the then thriving Rust Belt, but most of all my mother never identified with nor cared for the South.

The kitchen was where I ate my first Jewish food, thanks to my mom. Challah, golden, sweet challah, cut into pieces for toast with blackberry jam. The first person I made challah with was my mother and she was the best challah braider I have ever known. In Cincinnati, the Jewish baker was your only option on a Sunday, and that's where she picked it up. As soon as my aunt Sheila ("Cookie") got in from Cincinnati, the first thing to do was make fresh coffee and pop open the boxes of pastries and bread from their favorite bakeries back home.

Our kitchen was my mother's office. Using an old Danish cookie tin to hold her Wilton decorating tools and dyes, she made extraordinary cakes—which I loved helping her make, being a color spectrum queen of the first order—and occasionally sold them. It was where I was fired multiple times for disobedience and dishonesty from the job of helping her cook, and where I was hugged and kissed for being a good kid. It was there I heard about the porcupine Johnson caught in the backyard in Nairobi and killed to take home to eat, and the hippo steak my father bought at the "International" Safeway that she marinated for three days before it was edible. Incidentally, the Safeway was also where you could acquire squirrel and kangaroo meat in a can. The kitchen was where Mama and I danced and made spritz and vanilla crisps every Christmas, and made our own colored sugars. Sink after sink of collard greens were cleaned, cut, and boiled, and my mother was assured I was inheriting something meant to be passed down.

Our kitchen was also the place I came out to my mother at the age of sixteen. The kitchen table, to us, was a place of worry, argument, and resolution, and I had no idea where else we should have the conversation. The ironic part about all of this is that the kitchen was where I heard most of my first show tunes—and they were not mine. My uncle and mother would cook and play everything from *La Cage aux Folles* to *Dreamgirls*. There was a lot of gay culture in our kitchen—right down to figure skating—but I didn't know it. But when I came out I came out to RuPaul rocking "Supermodel" . . . and my mother thought I had lost my mind.

In the kitchen, my mother did the look of sarcasm mixed with sympathy, turned to my aunt Sheila and said, "So tell your aunt your big announcement . . ." She looked down and rolled her eyes while I blurted out, "I'm gay."

She looked at my aunt as if she was going to tell me just how crazy I was and pursed her lips. My aunt's response was, "Oh really, well, that's not really surprising at all. Congratulations."

Jaw drop.

I just felt being gay was nothing, so I treated it as such, even though I came up during the time of Afrocentrism, when authors like Shaharazad Ali said black men were being ruined by confusing their roles. Books like hers alleged that cooking made black men gay and that black gay men could cook better than women and that they would swish around—and that was something that really impacted how I viewed myself in the kitchen. I knew I was different, but I didn't connect cooking to the idea of being gay. I had so many men who cooked in my family that the idea of cooking as gay was not part of my world. I hated that stereotype; I didn't see myself as a woman or even like a woman, and didn't think cooking particularly belonged to women or men. In fact, I was very confused because I envisioned myself based on my father and my grandfather, and I didn't see myself as passive. I was confused because I wanted to be "the man," yet I didn't really engage in a lot of masculine pastimes. I didn't like most sports, beyond looking at the men who played them, especially baseball. I had books and I felt like my engagement with them and my knowledge was my masculinity.

Our kitchen was where I learned to hide myself. I asked my

mother for permission to go to speak at a program in the city to talk about gay youth issues. She said no. She stirred the pot of chili once, twice, then withdrew the spoon and slammed it down on the stove, the stain looking like a sign a druid priest might read as something died. "Why do you always have to be the fucking oddball of the family? *Why?* You lost your best friend."

The truth was, I wasn't the oddball of the family. We all were. We were a family set apart in many ways, from our travels to our education to our resistance to feeling as if we had to belong. I didn't catch on to this truth until after the damage of what my mother said was already done. It took me many years to mature into the realization that what she said was not personal, it was a lashing out against our collective abnormal nature as the Todd-Townsend kin. I went upstairs and sulked but couldn't cry. I loved my mother and always would, but the kitchen no longer felt safe if I couldn't use it to tell the truth.

MISE EN PLACE

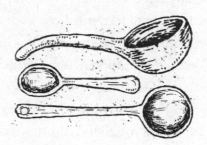

GEOG(R)APHY

My daddy was the first to make me taste Virginia. Actually, he shoved it into my mouth before I could say no. It was not the Virginia of soft, hot, pale gold spoonbread, or corn pone brown as coppery oak leaves on the rim, or even the state meat—salty, cloying, peanutty country ham, the kind that makes your tongue feel as if it should be sweating, and which every Virginian must by consequence of birth have between two pieces of biscuit. The August sun powered the yellowing of the edges of the tobacco leaves, signaling priming time, and the air was hot, but the copperheads lurking in brush piles compelled us to wear long pants and long sleeves. The air was tasty with the delectable stench of burning trash.

"Hah! Smells good, don't it?"

"Is that barbecue?" I got food horny.

"Naw, son, they call that garbage. . . ."

Daddy hauled his heavy, worn-handled, long shovel past the scrub trees—sweetgum, pine, red cedar—to the ancient oaks and hickories, looking for my first real taste of Virginia. Every now and then, a breeze would make the Queen Anne's lace dance along the roadside, knocking into the cherry dock he called "coffee" as a kid and the green pokeberries they called "peas." He dug into the soil of an exposed hillside looking for a perfect, unblemished nugget of Prince Edward County red clay. I had no idea my father, who I felt was mostly sane, was about to feed me dirt.

Prince Edward County is at the heart of Virginia's dying south-central "fire-cure" belt on the Appomattox River, and it smells like heavy mint and pine needles when the sun hits the broad tobacco leaves in late summer. The county's main claim to fame was that it was front and center during the civil rights movement for the crime of closing public schools for nearly a decade, rather than integrating, in a move called "massive resistance." Even though it had a sizable free black population during antebellum times, and later a significant number of independent black landowners and farmers like those in my family, Jim Crow was strong here—strong enough to deny a generation basic learning in the name of white supremacy. By the time massive resistance was enacted, my grandmother Eloise Booker had already migrated to Washington, DC, where she would marry my grandfather Gonze Lee Twitty, a migrant from South Carolina, have two children, and become a cook and domestic for several white families. My father, my teacher, was their firstborn.

You will hear many stories, myths, and rumors about Southerners eating dirt. There's some truth in it. Iron-deficient peasants across the world, most notably, in this case, Africa, have often popped bits of earth like we do vitamins today. After a couple of whacks to get to the perfect, pure piece of ultisol soil, my father said, "Try that!" Mouth open and tongue set to spit, I had earth in my mouth for the first time—well, on purpose, at least.

"Tastes like chocolate, don't it?" My father's laugh was a joyful chirp—the kind he only let out when he was truly tickled beyond taking a next breath.

He was sort of right. There was something chocolatey-coffee-tea-like beneath the mineral saltiness and chalkiness. It wasn't unpleasant, but it was my last encounter with eating red clay.

I was not just of Virginia—Virginia was in me.

When I was seventeen, I saw Prince Edward County for the first time as I accompanied my father to drop my grandmother off for the August church homecoming. Homecoming was traditionally a season where black migrants to the cities and the North returned to catch up with family and friends. It was also the time when children like my father, who were sent South for the summer, usually got to return home to the cities from whence they came. Held during the laying-by period when the crops needed little tending, the week of church and visiting relatives lasted from Saturday to Saturday and usually ended with the migrants returning home with extra bags of gifted produce and homemade syrup and bits and pieces of the country tied in sacks and bags and captured in jars. It was in this world, some seventy years ago, still populated by V-notch log cabins and clapboard houses, that my father obtained a merit badge in growing tobacco, a rudimentary sex education thanks to Ida and Henry (the workhorses and my great-grandfather's main mode of transportation), and his first encounter with a man who had been born enslaved—my great-great-great-grandfather—the patriarch Edward Booker, the First.

Edward Booker was not the first centenarian in the family tree. His likely ancestor, a man named Wonder Booker, so named because he was born when his mother should have had menopause and not because of his extreme longevity, was apparently born in 1690 and died in 1810, serving his later years in the vegetable garden of one of the many Booker plantations. Nearly everyone in that line lived to be in their nineties or even hundreds. Our family photograph of Edward details his life span—1839 to 1953. Born a hundred years before my father, he died when Daddy was thirteen.

The same creek in which my father pointed out to me bullfrogs and crawfish, and deep pools where the quick, silvery turns of bream and minnows made the water sparkle, was the place where "Old Edward" splashed his back with water on a similarly hot day, at which point my father saw long scars across his back. In the twenty-five or so years he spent in bondage, my great-great-great-granddaddy had not managed to avoid the lash. My father helped the old man walk back home, holding tightly to the hands of a man born before my people were considered citizens—or human. Every time I remember the story it never fails to amaze me that I have never been more than one person's touch away from the world of American slavery. Chicken hutch in the background, crooked glasses, overalls, Jesus fan, and boots caked in Virginia clay, pipe tucked away ready with homegrown, dark, fire-cured 'bacca . . . I look at the photograph of Edward the First, and own a part of my past that stares into my soul.

THE PUNKAH

The homecoming-revival and celebratory dinners of the Virginia countryside my father was introduced to on his trips home with my grandmother were sumptuous affairs. My grandmother, born in 1912, said these country feasts were made up of the ever-present Virginia country ham from hogs raised on chestnuts, acorns, hickory nuts, and peanuts; chicken that was fried or fricasseed; wild turkey; corn pone; spoonbread; hot biscuits; and whatever greens were in season: from poke, dandelion, and lamb's-quarters in the spring to turnip and collards in the fall. Springtime and summer meant fried or roasted fish would be on the menu—from shad to bream to catfish—or fried rabbit, stewed okra and tomatoes, fresh field peas studded with salt pork, and huge peach cobblers with heavy, sweet crusts seasoned with cinnamon and brandy (which good Baptists only used for cooking). Fall and winter brought venison, apple cobbler and fried apples, dense spicy persimmon bread, and possum roasted suckling pig–style with a variety of white-meat sweet potatoes nefariously called "nigger chokers" by the white humorists of old.

My great-great-grandfather Elijah Mitchell was born enslaved in Appomattox County, Virginia, around 1844 to a man named Richard and an enslaved domestic servant, possibly the cook, named Evertine Hill. He was known in family oral history as a "house slave," and he was a domestic servant after the "Surrender." Every evening during his childhood, he, like his hero, Booker T. Washington, another African Virginian, he "pulled the punkah." Letitia Burwell, who wrote of her Virginia plantation memories, reminisced:

> It was natural to ask for a drink of water when the water was right at hand, and to have things brought which you easily have gotten yourself. . . . A young lady would ask black Nancy or Dolly to fan her, whereupon Nancy or Dolly would laugh good-naturedly, produce a large palm-leaf, and fall to fanning her young mistress vigorously, after which she would be rewarded.

"Punkah" was the name for the palm leaf, feathers, paper fan or, in the case of wealthier families, an actual elaborately carved wooden device that was pulled by cord to keep off flies and keep the guests cool. Its exotic name came from Hindi and migrated to the South on trading ships along with other hints of the British-Indian colonial presence, like recipes for curried catfish, "country captain," mulligatawny soup, and pickling bell peppers in the manner of mangoes for chutney. Its name was rooted in another word for "wing," and indeed many enslaved children simply used a bunch of peacock feathers tied together for the purpose. Punkahs, once reserved for Indian nobility and still used to honor the sacred text of the Sikh faith during temple worship, became devices to reinforce white supremacy during slavery.

Black children were sometimes placed in a swing above the table where the movement kept the fan going. One enslaved man even bragged about falling asleep thanks to the rocking motion of the device. For most it was drudgery, but it also afforded those who did the job the opportunity to learn about the wider world and to hear and master the speech patterns of the "white folks" (important skills if you wanted to escape). They listened in and spread the word among the enslaved community—news of war, possible sales, financial troubles, debts—details that could prove invaluable to keeping families together and be of use to other enslaved people to manipulate their slaveholders and alter their decisions. Young Elijah wasn't just the human A/C; he was a critical and important lookout.

At the homecoming suppers, my father took up Elijah's chore of fanning the adults sitting down to eat dinner on the grounds, using a bamboo pole covered in strips of newspaper to keep flies off the food. You guessed it, he hated it too, but he also learned about the ways of the world at his task. This was the Virginia my father knew nearly sixty years before on his visits from Washington, DC. Vestiges of slavery like this remained alive and well in "Old Virginny," where the main house on Uncle Johnny's farm was still called the "Big House," and the landscape was one of emerald-green "pretty fields of tobacco," as my grandmother called them, weathered tobacco barns of chestnut and locust with patinas of moss, apple, peach, and pear orchards, smokehouses and "necessaries" that had not yet fallen to the ground. Sixty years later, I walked with my father through graveyards and tobacco fields learning these stories; collecting chinaberries, persimmons, and sweetgum balls in canning jars and freezer bags; drinking water from a well with a tin dipper; and starting to write down everything I could, not realizing my homecoming had started long before.

HELLO BEAUTIFUL

My first encounter with living history was the result of several well-timed commercials on the part of Colonial Williamsburg in the 1980s. Daddy begrudgingly took me three hours south to the world's largest living history museum, rolling his eyes and dreading every single thing I would possibly want—I was one of those kids, the opposite of Buddha the Enlightened One, a hotpot of desire. What I remembered most was the haunted way the sun glowed through the water and live oaks, and the sound of the cannons being fired. I got creeped out by walking over tombs at the Bruton Parish Church. And I fell in love with historical cooking.

We went to the Governor's Palace—which you had to pay extra to see—another cause for fatherly frown. We made our way past the tall catalpa trees of the palace green, and I had never seen anything grander. The hearth—charcoal fired behind an iron grate—looked like hell itself but I was in heaven, and then entered a pheasant, a hot little green, red, and autumn brown number, and all I could think was "Hello beautiful!" My father wanted to visit the magazine—where guns were stored, and cannons and military maneuvers—and all I wanted to do was stay in that kitchen and cook. The two hours we spent there were proof my father was more indulgent than he looked.

Out of the deal, I got a coloring book, a feather quill pen—the kind you need actual ink to use, which I tried to make from various burned things—and a tricorn hat. If this wasn't enough—and I chose my battles wisely—my father bought me a book titled *Colonial Virginia: A Picture Book to Remember Her By*. I wanted the book full of plantation centerfolds for one reason and one reason only. The tall, handsome black man making candles was enough. I liked the way he was dressed, I liked how proud he looked, and I wanted to do what he was doing. His name (not noted in the book) was Mr. Robert Watson, and as fate would have it, he would later become one of my most important teachers in historical interpretation.

The consequence of that visit was trouble turned into trouble turned into surrender. First test—make water boil using rocks. I put a bunch of pebbles in a spent grill, using the white-hot coals to heat them, and then I put them in a broken pot to see if the water would boil. Within seconds of hearing the bubbles made from contact, I noticed a familiar, hovering shadow.

"Michael, what in the hell are you doing?"

This might as well have been my name from seven to seventeen. My father had named me "Michael," "William," and "Twitty." My mother had little say, since she was knocked out from her caesarian. So, I always imagined that, if she had her druthers, she might make matters easier and just go ahead and legally change my name to "Michael, what in the hell are you doing?"

As he stood over my shoulder, I explained myself and promptly was made to dump my boiled-water experiment. This happened quite a bit until I was caught trying to make old cornucopia Indian corn into hominy, and my exasperated mother finally said the magic words:

"You have baking soda all over your face. The stove is on. Clean up my kitchen after you finish and whatever you do, don't kill yourself. Or at least make sure the kitchen is clean first."

That corn was terrible, but I was satisfied that I had won a major battle in the mother-son wars. I made my first slavery-inspired meal at fourteen. There was coush-coush—a Louisiana corn mush with cane syrup, fried salt pork, and a pecan-broth-based soup I couldn't eat because of a nut allergy, and couldn't get my mother to eat because she had sense. I learned to love making mistakes, and trying as much as I learned to love making the foods of the past that much more. I wasn't famous for leaving a clean kitchen, cleaning as I cooked, or being particularly responsible, but I loved my mother more because she gave me a chance.

DADDY'S JAR

When I was six Daddy took me to discover the South's past in an empty jar. Somewhere on I-85, just after entering North Carolina on our way to the family homestead in Lancaster, South Carolina, my bladder was full. My expectation was that Daddy would take me to the nearest gas station and walk in with me to make sure nobody snatched me up—this was of course the time of Adam Walsh. Nope. Daddy handed me an empty glass jar, stopped on the side of the road just off 85, and told me to go into the field and pee in that jar.

Fun game? I went into that field, peed, emptied it out, peed, emptied it out, then peed, and brought a full jar of steaming piss back to my father's Jeep.

He laughed. "What are you going to do with that, son?" I replied, "Daddy, didn't you want me to give a sample to the doctor?" (This I understood.)

"No, son, pour that out now. Back when I was your age, your grandfather took me to South Carolina for the first time, and we couldn't use the bathroom at the gas station because we were colored."

"Like crayons or markers? Did someone draw on you?"

Daddy laughed with a sweet chuckle, the kind that told me he loved me.

"Naw son, white people were white and black people were 'colored,' and just like you had to go pee in the jar, your grandfather made me do the same thing."

"Why did they care where you went to the bathroom?"

"It wasn't just the toilet, son; it was the water fountain, the bus, the train. You couldn't go anywhere white people could go and do the same things they did. Not even eat or sit on the same bench. When your grandmother and I would go up to Philadelphia and New York, the minute the train got to the Maryland border, we had to get back to where we were supposed to sit. That's segregation."

I liked big words, but I knew I didn't like this one.

"What if you didn't want to do that?"

"They arrested you, son. Or they beat you up, or killed you."

I sat there in the car on the way to the next stop, contemplating this weird little universe my father grew up in. I wasn't sure I was going to like this "South" place. We stopped at a popular fried chicken restaurant, and the chicken was golden, greasy, sweet, and plump. It was the first time I ever had the glorious convention of a "refill," but the place was filled with flies and the air conditioner was broken and there were a lot of people sweating in unison like teamwork. Four cups of sweet tea, and I was worried my daddy was going to send me out into a field again to pee, but he didn't.

"So they give you all you want to drink, and lots of chicken and stuff, but there's flies everywhere and it's really hot all the time?"

Daddy nodded affirmatively, head to the side with a smirk.

"That must be what they call Sou-thern hos-pi-tal-i-ty."

Daddy laughed damn near to Lancaster on that.

The first meal I ever saw in South Carolina was a nightmare waiting to happen. It was a pile of hoppin' john on a plate, and it was exotic and awful. It was field peas, rice, and various animal parts and bones. I cried and screwed up my face and demanded chicken noodle soup until a caravan was made to Piggly Wiggly. I love "the Pig" now, but my Lord, at six, I thought, Who in the hell decided to name a store Piggly Wiggly? The grinning piglet didn't seem promising, but we exited with bags of ramen and Campbell's chicken soup and that—along with one plate of fried chicken and biscuits—was what I ate on my first trip to the Deep South.

What my mind cannot remember, Kodak and Polaroid did. I picked yellow-meated watermelons with my grandfather—his favorite—and met my ever-overall-wearing grand-uncle Tillman, named after his maternal uncle, who looked like he was brought right from Africa. My father got a kick showing off how "smart" I was.

"Son, tell them who is from South Carolina."

"Melba Moore and Jesse Jackson—he's from Greenville."

"And what's the capital of South Carolina?"

"Columbia."

"Where are you?"

"I'm in Lancaster County, home of the Twittys!"

My cousins thought I was hilarious—and very city. Every morning began with me pronouncing, grinning from ear to ear, "It's a sunny day!" I was very theatrical and quiet as it's kept—as future gay of America as they come, as I was all about drama and putting on a show. Cotton was long ago phased out of Lancaster, but I still gave the performance of a lifetime on showing my cousins—born and raised in the country—how to pick it.

"You see, you gotta jump down, spin around, and pick a bale of cotton." I even had a dance. Thanks, Mom and your Harry Belafonte records. . . . I actually thought this was a thing. Agile and skinny for the last time in my life, I jumped down low, spun around like Michael Jackson, and mimicked picking a bale of cotton—totally unaware that a bale weighed more than the queerness I had just introduced into the swept yard in front of the pecan tree. I really thought that there were whole armies of black cotton pickers in the past who did a dance, sang a song, and made cotton fields tremble in their wake—and that *this* was the only way to pick cotton.

I saw a Brahma bull—from afar. I saw guinea fowl for the first time and, much to my excitement, turkeys—my then spirit animal!

There are pictures of me with turkey, rooster, goose, and guinea feathers, smiling as if I had found jewels. I dared my father to show me how to milk a cow and we went to my grandfather's neighbors to do so. Much to my genuine heartbreak, my father's instructions on just how to hold my thumb and finger to trigger milk from the teat got me about a tablespoon of milk. I'm really surprised that trying to get to second base with the cow didn't get my little ass kicked by a well-directed hoof, but she had pity on me for being the most inexperienced milkman in dairydom.

HEART OF DIXIE

My maternal uncle Stephen Townsend became the genealogist of the family ever since the day the *Roots* bug bit him in 1976; he took me to Alabama for our second family reunion. We flew to Atlanta and took a bus all the way to Columbus, Georgia. I was thirteen and unbelievably excited to see the "homeland." My grandmother was still alive, and though she did not come with us I carried her stories—stories of her father, born and raised here in the Deep South's most famous and infamous region, the "Black Belt." Named partly for the smile-swath of black prairie stretching into central Mississippi, the Black Belt came to mean the cotton-growing counties across the lower middle of Alabama that at one point were majority black and a powerhouse of slavery, agricultural production, and white supremacy. This is where the trees hung heavy with "strange fruit."

I remember crossing the Chattahoochee on foot across a bridge. The water was clear, and you could see to the bottom like the river was glass. Twenty-twenty vision at full tilt, which I have no more. I saw a huge catfish and a snapping turtle and something bass- or troutlike below. To me, a Pisces, a nature and aquarium lover, and all-around fish fetishist, seeing them was the ultimate sign of the presence of life, a good sign of things to come.

We went to the little library so my uncle could do research, and I set to looking up things about the South while my uncle conducted his work. An hour later, he came back agitated. There in the middle of the book was a white man I had never seen before . . . my presumed great-great-great-grandfather, Richard Henry Bellamy. Having looked at everything I could to pass the time, I remembered that the sword in the case at the front of the library was labeled "the sword of Captain Richard Henry Bellamy, C.S.A."

"What's CSA stand for?"

"Confederate States of America."

My uncle was matter-of-fact. I took a second to ponder. Ms. White Librarian lady studied us until she came over to the case of Civil War—excuse me, "War between the States"—memorabilia, and asked—you guessed it, in the slowest way—"Can I help you?" We weren't buying anything; we were looking, at artifacts. One of them happened to be a part of our story, and she presumed that it didn't.

I just looked at the white librarian lady and was equally matter-of-fact. "That sword was my great-great-great-granddaddy's." She wasn't responsive to that. My uncle forgot himself and inquired after our ability to look at it closer. She flatly said, "I don't think we can do that." A little more research and an armful of photocopies and we left the little library. All eyes were on us, and not in a nice way. I had never felt all the eyes in a room on me like that before.

We made our way to the church on the family reunion bus, passing kudzu-covered poles and fields of pampas grass. I kept the lookout for a cotton field, but no such luck. It was hot and all, but there wasn't any Spanish moss. I wanted some serious Southern stereotypes, so I was sorely disappointed. None of the things in the books seemed to be here. We finally got to St. Peter AME church. I began to meet them one by one—ancestor after ancestor on my maternal grandmother's father's side. When we got to Hattie, my great-great-grandmother, the presumed daughter of Captain Richard Henry Bellamy, born 1862, the sandy soil had given away. There was a crack in the grave and you could peer into the dark finality of death.

This was the reality, Southern country graveyards, especially those held by black folks, often undermanaged and unkempt. It wasn't because we lacked love—we lacked resources. As the dead's living died, and memory began to recede, the ones who honored specific relatives and their graves disappeared. I knew this woman was a part of me, and there was nothing I could do but feel a weak and immature sadness. Fortunately, my uncle kept up with the politics of the church and the graveyard, and fighting development interests ensured many years later that the site would be given historically protected status. Otherwise—like many other black Southern cemeteries—it would just be a bunch of paved-over bodies, and the further erasure of slavery.

My great-great-great-grandparents, Peter and Rose Chadwick, gave land to start that church and graveyard. The Todds, Bellamys, Mabrys, and Chadwicks—black families brought on foot, by wagon, and by railcar from Virginia, North and South Carolina, and Georgia—were all buried up together, the result of plantation marriages and remarriage under Emancipation, sharecropping, farming, and a life lived in cotton and toil. In Alabama, the seaboard South—the Tidewater, the Low Country, the Piedmont—met the Black Belt. And there they were, planted in the same soil from which sweet potatoes, rice, sugarcane, peanuts, and collards sustained them.

When I got back home I told my grandmother everything, detail by detail, and she savored it. I had been to the old country. "I used to love the crepe myrtles and camellias. You don't see those anywhere like Alabama." She didn't cry, she didn't look wistful; she turned her head and changed the subject. Once she left Alabama, she never went back to Alabama. The heart of Dixie was her Poland.

The year after next we traveled as a family to northern Alabama, to Madison and Jackson Counties, where my maternal grandfather's family came together. These families—enslaved to the Townsends and Woosleys and others—had come overland from Virginia and North Carolina and south from Tennessee. I saw the beautiful hills and bushes full of berries, but still no cotton. The hallmark of the trip was seeing an old, very Norman Rockwell–looking black man, reddish brown skin, long beard, straw hat, overalls, and pipe, sitting on the porch of his shack—which of course was across the tracks with his dog.

Whatever archive or courthouse we visited in Huntsville left one impression on me above all others. There was a huge mural tracing Alabama history. It started with the Native Americans—the Cherokees in the Northeast, the Creeks across the East, the Choctaws in the Southwest, and the Chickasaws in the Northwest. It then moved on to planter after judge after governor after businessman, as if that's all Alabama history was—a series of successful white men who came after the removal of noble, civilized, but still-in-the-way savages. There was not one black man or woman on that mural. For all of our suffering and sacrifice, turmoil and toil, it was like we never even existed, or—better yet—built Alabama.

But we had. I was the evidence we had. My great-great-great-grandfather Harry Townsend had been separated from his kin in North Carolina to Alabama to labor on one of the state's largest cotton plantations, and become the unwitting patriarch of a new line of an American family. His son's wife's family, the Woosleys, had come from Virginia to Tennessee to Alabama. That's a lot of bleeding feet and tears from lost family and memories fading of Africa, the Middle Passage, first steps on American soil, becoming a new people, enduring unbelievable mental anguish and, then, only to see two or three generations dissolved to satisfy greed. This loss was incalculable despite all of the victories and recoveries that followed slavery even to the present day. It made us, in many ways, an incomplete and ever-searching people without a clear understanding of how we got here and how that journey shaped who we are.

LOUISIANA

I didn't make it to Louisiana until I embarked on the Southern Discomfort Tour. The crossing of Lake Pontchartrain was a ritual moment for me, after a lifetime of dreaming of the Big Easy. In New Orleans, even post-Katrina, it was clear; there was no mistaking it—Africa was always on parade. The ever-present onions, garlic, peppers, tomatoes, and hot sauce laced the air. First stop—Café Du Monde for beignets across the street from Jackson Square and the Cabildo. You can find it by following the trail left by the powdered sugar massacre.

On one side of the street I'm eating two plates' worth of beignets, hot with chicory coffee, and my face looks like a still from the last scenes of *Scarface*. Then I hear some women talking and I close my eyes; they are West African, and from what I can tell they are speaking the tonal drum music of Yoruba—a language I studied at Howard University. They are tourists too, but they are wedged at this moment between the Mississippi on one side, and the slave auction block on the other inside the museum. I close my eyes, feel the humidity and moisture, and listen to a few kids strike up percussion to get tips from the tourists.

And it's too much. I can't relax myself into this re-memory. The women's tonal words mix with Southern twangs and Louisiana's unique Franco-African way with English and the bucket drums. It's a whole new jazz and though I thought I was prepared, I wasn't—my mind was re-creating a place that was too dangerous for me to enter.

We walked to Congo Square, the place where enslaved people

danced as they did in Yoruba country, Dahomey, Kongo, and Senegal. They sang as they danced and called out to their gods. For a brief window of time in the late-eighteenth to mid-nineteenth centuries, the bamboula beat was passed down from generation to generation, as well as songs for the orisha and vodu from the ancestral spirits and spiritual forces of the Lower Guinea coast all the way to Bo Diddley and Mardi Gras. It wasn't enough to call on the spirits on those Sundays when the dances took place. They had to be fed.

Traditional African religions have a complex understanding of food in the service of faith. Food is often a necessary vehicle between one's ancestors or the spiritual forces that guide their destiny. Each one has its favorite foods. Sometimes these were plain and unremarkable, and other times they were heavily intricate dishes prepared as if the deities were gourmands on high. Even as each "nation" sang out to the universe with drumbeats to match their memories, somebody was stirring a pot of food—coush-coush, deep-fried balls of black-eyed peas or rice, roasted spicy turkeys, jambalaya, and gumbo. All of this energy was not far from St. Louis Cathedral—Catholic saints' days, African gods, French technique and provincial flourishes, Spanish forms, deep frying, bubbling stocks and sauces, chopping, scraping, fish, produce, heat, celebration.

There was nobody there but us and a few homeless folks looking for rest. Yet the minute I got there the vibration of the energy hit me. In a place where there was so much motion, I was perfectly still. Africa was here, morphing, struggling to survive, and she did—by wearing new masks. I have been to many places in my country, but this was the first one in which I can genuinely say I felt I had a mystical experience. I know this because like other seekers before me, I was suspended there in Congo Square between self-awareness and losing my mind.

New Orleans and its surrounding Gulf ports were the colonial entry point for nearly twenty-five thousand enslaved Africans, some being sent north into Mississippi and Missouri. Later it became the antebellum South's largest slave market. That auction block sitting in the museum was real. Every street was like the Toni Morrison quote from *Beloved*, "packed to the rafters with some dead Negroes' grief." Hurricanes, yellow fever, malaria, bodies worked to death, heat exhaustion . . .

The cemetery in which Madame Marie Laveau and her daughter lie in rest is itself a shrine. Now it's closed off to passersby—you have to be part of a funeral or a tour group to walk in. New Orleans's famous "Voodoo Queen" (although she was more than that) and her daughter bear too many legends, memories, and stories to be repeated here. This I know—at their graves were coins, conch and cowrie shells, cigars, bottles of liquor and cups of gumbo, sacred beads, cane syrup and pepper seeds. The walls of their tombs are pockmarked with X marks, signs that devotees have come to repay their respects and make requests of Marie and her daughter, her heir as religious leader.

I was warned by a woman in the marketplace not to make an X mark. "You don't know who you signing a contract with, so mind that X." I don't know if she was a "Voodoo Queen," but she was a devout Catholic who was equally a devotee of vodun—by all accounts a keeper of our heritage and an excellent cook. New Orleans's deep relationship with the French Caribbean saw a flood of migrants from Haiti during and following the Haitian Revolution, and from that moment on it became vodun's American Jerusalem, a place of African spiritual resistance. You can still leave Louisiana with beignet mix, a jazz CD, a can of cane syrup, hot sauce, and a voodoo doll, and nobody will look askance. I did what I knew—I went Jewish and left a pebble and a little note for blessings on whatever was to come.

When you are poor, television and movies and other popular culture allow you to simulate travel in ways few other things can, except for food. My favorite show growing up was the short-lived CBS situation comedy *Frank's Place*, starring Tim Reid, a show about a man who inherits his family's institutional New Orleans restaurant. It was partly based on the goings-on at Chez Helene, the once hopping soul/Creole digs where pre-celebrity chef Austin Leslie with his afrolicious muttonchops and penchant for fried turkeys made his name; and a little Dooky Chase, where the beautiful Leah Chase still reigns. Chefs battled it out over secret recipes and I learned a whole new vocabulary—étouffée, grillades, bananas Foster, daube glacé.

To be sure we had been availed of white Louisiana culinary talent and culture, but until I was a tween, I didn't know how black this part of the world actually was. The show opened with Louis Armstrong singing about Creole stews, and "Do you know what it means, to miss New Orleans?" My heart said, "Yes, I've never been there, but that's where I left my heart." Over the next few years, my Creole play-cousins would bring Steen's cane syrup and frozen crawfish tails and beignet mix and hot sauce back with them as gifts, and of course my first taste of chicory coffee. The waxy covers of New Orleans pralines were my first taste of marketed racism, with their pitch-black mammies with bloodred lips.

In my head I was going to go to this glorious outdoor food market in the French Quarter where Native American women still sold bunches of sassafras leaves for filé powder. I would second line in every parade or funeral and unfurl my umbrella and open the gates to the other world and shake my ass to some street drums. Charleston is where African America never forgot her language; New Orleans is where it never forgot its rhythm or the African gods. Between the two, the recipes never died, they syncretized and survived, and all I ever wanted to do was see for myself our resilience and cook alongside the masters of the Creole tradition.

In 2005, Hurricane Katrina came to visit. It was not the goddess of the wind, but the goddess of the river who ended up taking her toll on New Orleans. I watched in horror as my people died and spent weeks crying over people stranded and left to die. A part of me wondered if I had waited too long to see my Oz. Thousands upon thousands of people were displaced. As much as I worried about never seeing black New Orleans, these incredible people still remained to welcome me, including Chef Leah Chase.

Leah Chase is the chef and owner of Dooky Chase, started by her parents-in-law in the 1940s. It was not just a restaurant; it was a center of the civil rights movement and a place of refuge. Along with nearby Willie Mae's Scotch House, where you can obtain some of the South's best fried chicken always made to order, the Treme institution survived Katrina through cooperation across racial lines, rebuilding after nearly losing everything. After beignets, my first real Creole meal had to be there. Mrs. Chase heard about what I was doing from the waiter, and we were brought back into the kitchen after our meal.

A Leah Chase meal of red beans and rice and chicken gumbo is the real thing. She doesn't need my advertisement but I'll give it anyway. The heart of southern Louisiana cuisine, Creole or Cajun, is the roux, the thickening mother sauce brought from France three centuries ago. It can come in as many colors as the people you see on the streets of New Orleans. Each presents the main ingredients in a different way and these become the dishes we crave; they are laced with the holy trinity of bell peppers, onions, and tomatoes (some say green onions, some say garlic) that is as Senegalese as they come, or Dahoman or Kongolese. Her gumbo is like everybody else's gumbo in one respect: it is as unique as a fingerprint and is a text, but don't tell her that.

"Now look, Mr. Culinary Historian! You can do all that, I'm just a cook! I don't have time for all that, but I'm glad you do. I'm very pleased; you keep doing it, young man. I told my grandson, 'Now look, you think you're special because you've been to Paris and studied at the Cordon Bleu, just wait until you get home and Grandma teaches you some Cordon Noir!'" Anybody who has met Leah Chase can tell you acres about her generosity of time and spirit. She is a polymath who has soaked up every bit of the city's artistic fervor and has a steel-trap mind of stories of everyone famous she's ever served, from Ray Charles to President Obama. We excused ourselves but not before Jacob, Johnathan, and I each got grilled a little and pinched, hugged, and kissed. Her final command: "If you're going to take my picture, you better make me look like Halle Berry!" Sometime later I visited New Orleans and was informed by her granddaughter that Mrs. Leah would be waiting for me in her kitchen. While she directed her army of family and friends from a wheelchair, she was ten cups of chicory coffee ahead of me, knowing my recent sins before I could report them. "Twitty, where you been? I've been waiting for you, and you know what somebody told me, you tried to make gumbo filé without the filé! Come on, maaaan!" She winked and shook her head disapprovingly. "Now give me my hug!" The pebbles had worked; I was in.

4

MISHPOCHEH

To know who you are you often have to be able to see outside yourself. To look beyond the bubble you were born in doesn't come easy to all of us. In the world of my childhood, I constantly left my bubble for the sanctuary of other cultures. My family, on both sides, were tough gatekeepers. There was our way and there was the way other people did things. Nobody ever said outright anything disrespectful or dismissive of another culture or food tradition, but the snorts and garumpfs, side-eyes and rolled eyes told all. My mother was always worrying I was confusing myself, becoming something I was not.

In the Washington suburbs I grew up in, we didn't have a word for diversity yet, but whatever diversity is we were it. You had to be able to go over to a friend's house and communicate in worlds and words outside your own. Many people still had the grandparents who were from the old country. Some didn't speak English, and others had parents who were born at the end of the nineteenth century and who remembered all the culture and history and songs and lore and foods that their grandparents gave to them. Those people gave me my first education in terms of international food.

There was no Internet to look up what a food or an ingredient was, or to diagnose its provenance. You were simply told—in another language—to sit down, shut up, and eat what's offered to you, and don't be rude and refuse it. That's how I met Indian-Caribbean roti, Korean squid chips, Greek *tzatziki*, Italian cannoli and zeppoli, tabbouleh, falafel, rugelach, *pupusas*, empanadas, *bhel puri*, dim sum, and an entirely new vocabulary outside of collards, cowpeas, yams, and rice. I listened to the way people talked about their food, the poetry and power of what it meant to them, and I absorbed it as if it were my own. I read cookbooks and watched cooking shows and connected the dots.

To be honest, I was just mirroring the values of *Sesame Street*, *The Electric Company*, and *Vegetable Soup*. I grew up in the shadow of civil rights and the recognition of America's two hundredth birthday. Our books were premulticultural; they were more melting pot and salad bowl. We weren't compartmentalized, but rather expected to let our watercolors bleed into one another while somehow retaining our own uniqueness. Somehow, the blending always stopped short of sex and marriage, but food was OK, food was safe, food was just a harmless perk after all the centuries of oppression and exploitation we did to one another.

I was addicted to obscure words and dictionaries so big you could use them to see over the wheel, and yet there were words that, had I known them, would have changed my life. *Familiensinn*: German, the feeling and sense of family connection. I longed for it. I cultivated it despite the pain it has often caused me—family is not easy to seek or create. *Toska*: Russian. According to Nabokov's translation of the Afro-Russian writer Alexander Pushkin's *Eugene Onegin*, it is "a sensation of great spiritual anguish, often without any specific cause . . . a longing with nothing to long for." *Fernweh*. Back to German, "a longing and homesickness for a place you have never been." These words explain my childhood weirdness.

Growing up, I read cookbooks to feel connection. My favorite was *Jim Lee's Chinese Cookbook* with its jade-green and black monochromatic drawings and advice like "be your own *dop mah* (sous chef)." *Joy of Cooking* (Rombauer), *The New York Times Cook Book* (Claiborne), the red-checkered tablecloth cover of *Better Homes and Gardens*, *The Silver Palate Cookbook* (Russo and Lukins), *Betty Crocker's Cookbook*—these were our outsources. My grandmother cooked by example, my mother cooked by altered formula. Pre–Food Network, all we had were Saturday afternoons on PBS with Martin Yan, the controversial Jeff Smith (ironic that his cookbook was my first nonkid cookbook as a kid), *Great Chefs of the West*, *Great Chefs of New Orleans*, Graham Kerr, Pierre Franey, Paul Prudhomme, Jacques Pepin, Julia Child, Justin Wilson, and my favorite, Nathalie Dupree, host of *New Southern Cooking*.

My grandmother used Saturday as her errand and chore day, but whenever I got the chance I interrupted her flow by watching Justin Wilson with her. She called him "that bad-talking man," and she was thoroughly tickled by his faux Cajun accent. Nathalie Dupree may have been talking "new Southern cooking," but it was the only half hour during the week where something resembling my food culture and food identity was profiled on TV. I often asked my grandmother if the "white lady from Georgia" got it right or not. Nathalie spoke about beaten biscuits and drew the mental picture of an enslaved child whacking a loaf of biscuit dough a thousand times to get it light and airy, and for the first time, I saw myself in the African American culinary past.

As the years went on, new people took the place of the first generation of cooking shows I religiously watched. Joan Nathan's *Jewish Cooking in America* was in class two and I was hooked. More *fernweh*, more *toska*. New word: *Fressfrumkeit*. Yiddish: to be a dedicated Jew through greedily eating delicious Jewish food. Or to put it in a nicer way, to savor the taste of Jewish spirituality through its food. Old word: *Mishpachah/mishpocheh*. Hebrew/Yiddish: family, clan, tribe, a fellow Jew, a member of the tribe.

MY OWN PRIVATE CONVERSION

When I was seven years old, I declared myself Jewish to my mother. I had seen the movie *The Chosen*, and I had a deep episode of *toska* when Rod Steiger went into a haze of *devekus*, a Hasidic mystical term for cleaving the soul with the presence of the Lord. Every Saturday my breakfast of champions was challah with butter and blackberry jam, but that was the secular pleasure of being in the melting pot. This was a different romance.

My brilliant mother, always the tactician in the war between the will of the child and the will of the parent, let me tarry on with my pseudo-self-conversion. The self-satisfied smirk she wore as days passed was the portent of something sinister to come. On the sixth day—the same time it took the Lord to make the world—she declared we would be going back to the hospital, and I felt an immediate sense of dread.

"What they did to you as a little baby they have to do all over again."

Immediately, the tricorn I had turned into a yarmulke went back into its original shape. The bacon went back on the plate. I was suspicious of challah, as if it had betrayed me. I began to look forward to being Santa's best friend again. My mother had won the battle, but she lost the war.

Yiddishkeit. Yiddish: a distinctly Ashkenazi Jewish term for the warm and fuzzy chicken soup–ness of religious observance and dedication. I taught myself the Hebrew alphabet by the time I was eight. I annoyed my Jewish classmates with little tidbits from Hebrew school and got expressions out of them, and with a little self-push, I began to amass a little library of books in English on Jewish knowledge. Years of guilt that I was not lighting candles, attempts at fasting, and admiring *tallitot* came to a head.

I took classes in black-Jewish relations between Howard and American University, met Dr. Pamela Nadell, took classes in Jewish civilization, and kept reading. A lot. I became an intern and researcher for the Center for Folklife and Cultural Heritage at the Smithsonian, and I wanted to present about Jewish food. She introduced me to Joan Nathan, from whom I learned to make my favorite challah recipe in the world, and then I landed in the Sephardic synagogue in which I converted two years later.

African Americans ate Yiddish food in delis and from the influence of Jewish employers in the North, Midwest, Eastern Seaboard, and West Coast. Pastrami and corned beef, Reubens and—for the brave—matzo ball soup and kugel translated with pickles and lox into a new vocabulary for African American migrants from the South. In my new spiritual world the Sephardic kitchen was much more visions of pomegranate and citron trees and rainbow spice markets than bites of hearty satisfaction just out of reach of the steppe and tundra. The chatter of the women as they stuffed vegetables was as familiar to me as my mother and grandmother cleaning collards. Everything was fragrant and fresh; nothing lacked a story.

My Sephardi and Mizrahi hosts seemed more amused than impressed when I shoveled in *z'hug* and *harissa*, hot sauces they shared with their neighbors in their home countries. Many of my new friends were Moroccan; others were Syrian, Persian, Iraqi, Tunisian,

Egyptian, and from the former Turkish empire. They had spice cabinets like ours, packed to the rafters with turmeric, cinnamon, *za'taar*, sesame seeds, cardamom, and cloves. I developed my own repertoire of Sephardic soul food—*bourekas* (meat-, potato-, or spinach-filled phyllo pastries), dark brown eggs from the *hamin* (Shabbat stew) pot, frothy mint tea, cigars (Morocco's ancient answer to the *taquito*), roasted lamb, and *bamya* (okra), *lubiya* (black-eyed peas) and *selek* (stewed leafy greens.)

I think there is still a lingering sentiment in the culture that sees Jewish food as a mass of things that go on rye bread; cannot possibly be pronounced without gagging or producing mucus; and are blessed by a rabbi and smell like fish, cabbage, harsh condiments, and crotchety old people. Some even read some sort of sinister kabbalistic workings or blood libels into our recipes. I can tell you none of this is true. Jewish food is a matter of text expressed on the table. Entering the Jewish foodscape changed my life.

Jewish food and black food crisscross each other throughout history. They are both cuisines where homeland and exile interplay. Ideas and emotions are ingredients—satire, irony, longing, resistance—and you have to eat the food to extract that meaning. The food of both diasporas depends on memory. One memory is the sweep of the people's journey, and the other is the little bits and pieces of individual lives shaped by ancient paths and patterns. The food is an archive, a keeper of secrets.

One of the reasons I am madly, passionately, head-over-soles in love with Judaism is the unrestrained passion it has for questions, analysis, study, review, revision, and that dance it seems to revel in between tradition and intellectual anarchy. This process is not always done with a book. Sometimes it's lived out through folk and material culture, and with food—the scriptures of Torah and Talmud give a uniquely Jewish life and law to what could just be a means to suppress hunger and, hours later, a reason to read a magazine for ten minutes with your pants down. I love that almost the entirety of the Jewish people will sit down for a seder and discuss and debate the ancient lessons of slavery versus freedom while using an edible Torah to process those lessons in their bodies—through all senses available to the eater.

Passover is, thus, my favorite holiday. Why not? I am the descendant of enslaved people. I take this holiday personally. There is something truly profound about a cultural moment like Passover where this is made manifest, a moment where you are obligated to debate and discuss some of the most important questions and issues of the human condition while debating and discussing the execution of your family's heirloom recipes.

The Haggadah states, "Now we are slaves . . ." Every day I suit up and go out to the plantation kitchens and cook like our ancestors, I live that phrase. I am not enslaved, but by showing the living what the dead went through, I live a scary and unsettling past. I feel like a doorway for all the spirits of the plantations I visit. I feel their souls passing through me as I cook and tell their stories. At the end of the day, I feel like a terminal and less like a man who is breathing and aware.

There is nothing more frightening than looking through warping glass windows and seeing the glimpses of things you were never alive to see, feeling steps just before your own, knowing that they, the enslaved—the nameless, politicized, maligned, commodified ancestors—are around you, cheering you on, doing the ring shout around your body. It's as if by cooking you have crossed a boundary, and the dance of pounding, kneading, sweating, choking, and smelling connects with something timeless, all of the movements that came before you become you. I realize that I'm trying to divine a text from the scatterings which our lives and our civilization as a people with shifting freedoms have presented. Passover was one of my inspirations to go back and fetch the medical, spiritual, emotional, familial, and ethnically didactic texts found in the foods of the continent and the Diaspora, in kitchens high and low.

In Jewish culture, much like continental African and African Diaspora cultures, food is a mnemonic device. Whether it's matzo or hoecake, our civilizations value symbolic food, and passing down foods and food memories from generation to generation, and with them stories as history, pushes us across the globe. In Judaism, memory is a commandment—commands to remember enslavement, to remember the plight of the enslaved, to remember the days of national youth and vigor, to remember through the eating of a sacred meal on Passover, to remember through the reading of the Torah. When I go up to the scroll, I am bid by mystical custom to find a word that begins with the first initial of my name, and once I do the memories of the generations that came before us can be sung; all of this work is about finding myself in the script that has always captivated me. What I'm speaking of is recovering the narratives across time, connecting all of us into one idea—that our food has not just been fodder for our journeys, but embodies the journeys themselves.

In Spain and Portugal the food eaten by conversos, Jews who pretended to convert to Christianity to avoid persecution, could be used to punish them or sentence them to death for heresy. A people's plates could be used against them. In teaching about the Holocaust as a Hebrew school teacher, I found a book by my now friend Cara De Silva, *In Memory's Kitchen*, about the "model ghetto" of Terezin, where Hitler's captured Jews wrote down recipes most were certain they would never taste again. As I cooked a dish or two with my students and led through lessons on the Holocaust/Shoah, my gears started to turn and I asked myself why the formerly enslaved never did quite the same thing outside of the obvious. I got the courage to finally put the two food narratives side by side, and in the meantime

I spent days learning about the intricacies of matzo balls, *sambusak*, and challah decorations, and legal fictions used to cook cholent and *adafina*. For the first time I divided and studied food in two categories, the mundane and the ceremonial, and the parallels started to emerge.

In the script of African and Jewish and American and gay histories, my whole journey could be whittled down to a new word. *Makom*. Hebrew: place, but it's also a scriptural synonym for G-d. Where you are matters. The same scripture that inspired my ancestors in American slavery inspires me with a bit more flavor. Egypt is called, in Hebrew, "the narrow place." When you are all the things I am, it's easy for people to put you in a narrow spot indeed. You have to have a way out.

KOSHER/SOUL: NEW ORLEANS

"Mr. Twitty, you will be meeting with me when you come to New Orleans," said the note.

Mrs. Mildred Covert of blessed memory saw me in the pages of *Southern Jewish Life* in an article about my journey across the South looking for my roots. A prolific food writer, and an inspiration for the title of Marcie Cohen Ferris's study *Matzoh Ball Gumbo*, Mrs. Covert was every bit Jessica Tandy in *Driving Miss Daisy*, fortunately albeit without a drop of the backhanded prejudice. I liked her because she wore a white leopard-print blouse, a vermillion jacket, and smart shoes. Before she introduced herself, the door to the car swung open at the hotel where she and a former Hebrew school student turned successful journalist picked me up, and all I heard was, "Get in!"

Mrs. Covert and her student, Alan Smason, took me on a tour of her New Orleans. Her mother was an immigrant from Galicia, and many of her siblings were born in the old country. Her mother arrived at the docks in New Orleans and tried to feed her children bananas fresh from Latin and Caribbean ports, whole with the skin on. She didn't trust tomatoes and had never seen a hot pepper. Her mother unwittingly had come to the Babylon of *treyf* (nonkosher) food.

"Michael, do you know who we learned to cook from down on Dryades Street? It was the black ladies who lived around us and worked for us and sometimes beside us. My family kept kosher. I went to an Orthodox synagogue that's now a church. But I tell you this much, my family learned how to eat American through the black ladies. They taught us how to cook." Tomatoes, cayenne pepper, okra, more fresh fish, more chicken, rice, and a host of other ingredients became staples. Not everyone kept kosher, but in the South this was not the priority of Jewish life; it was community and the continuity of Jewish identity. There were no alien foods—some Jews created a kosher answer to every Southern dish, others had Hanukah ham biscuits, but they were loyal Jews—traveling miles for bar mitzvah lessons and hiring traveling rabbis.

Mrs. Covert coauthored three very popular cookbooks, the *Kosher Creole Cookbook*, the *Kosher Cajun Cookbook*, and the *Kosher Southern-Style Cookbook*, the latter decorated with a Hasidic rebbe and a Confederate general happily stirring a pot. "Now, when I got married, my husband, he didn't keep kosher, so I tried a few things. But I turned him around. I promise you this, I can make the best kosher stuffed crab you *ever* had!" She held on to my arm tight as I supported her as we walked through her old synagogue. "We ladies sat there, and that's where my papa would sit every Shabbos." She made me happy to be around—it was as if my own grandmother had been brought back to me.

Later, Mrs. Covert sipped on a cup of tea while I had a bowl of matzo ball gumbo at her grandson's kosher café in Metairie. There were stories of sugarcane roofing the sukkah and Jewish Mardi Gras celebrations and her mother's reaction to jazz. It was refreshing because she told me these stories as if I had a share in them, as if they were naturally a part of me, and I felt whole. "I like what you're doing. Just remember to get all the stories you can, but don't tell no tales, you hear?" She tugged on her jacket, gave me a wink, and put her spoon on the table with a clink as if the point had been delivered three times. She and Grammy would have gotten along just fine.

BIRMINGHAM

Temple Beth-El is a Conservative synagogue in Birmingham, Alabama. It's a gorgeous Moorish-influenced building and it has its own mikvah, or ritual bath, deep in its belly. The morning after I brought kosher/soul rolls to the world with Andrew Zimmern on *Bizarre Foods America*, I'm on a plane headed to the city where my maternal grandparents were raised some eighty years ago, a city I'd never been to, to do a presentation on kosher soul food for an audience of sixty. When my grandparents spoke of the "South," their South was not the rustic countryside my paternal grandparents knew. It was the semirural, quite urban, but not really either, somewhat cosmopolitan and racially charged New South city of Birmingham.

Temple Beth-El's Jews walked a fine line in Birmingham society. Southern Jews were famous for their assimilationist tendencies, right down to not keeping kosher. The good news is that the synagogues' kitchens were mostly kosher, including the strictly kosher kitchen at Beth-El, and most of the time it was staffed by black workers working with a mashgiach (the person who ensures the laws of kashrut are maintained while preparing, cooking, and preserving food). "Bombingham" had a particular reputation for a unique form of reprisal to those who stepped out of line with Jim Crow; according to one member, one of the black janitors at Beth-El discovered a bomb here during the civil-rights-movement era and reported it before it could do any damage. In the shadow of the attack that killed four little girls at the 16th Street Baptist Church, synagogue leaders met with local officials and a deal was struck—we won't make a big deal out of this (yank business ties and get litigious) as long as this never happens again (tell your Klan buddies, Hands off the Jews).

"The secret to the Caribbean compote is cayenne pepper and real Mexican vanilla. They dance together," I tell the three volunteers as we hurriedly use gloved hands to stir orange, pineapple, grapefruit, and mango in big stainless steel bowls. Black-eyed-pea hummus with its million eyes is looking at me with scallions and suspicion while we hurry to finish baking hamantaschen. This triangular cookie, symbolic of the holiday of Purim, simultaneously celebrates the execution of the ancient world's worst anti-Semite, Haman, and the spiritual victory of Queen Esther. Though it might be dark in concept, my Southern flavors such as peach, blackberry, apple butter, and benne wafer brighten up the legend. I run out of time to demonstrate the all-peach barbecue sauce for the assembled crowd, so I cobble together the raw materials and put them on a cart to display.

Many of the women here came from at least two or three generations of Southern Jews who by the creativity of their black assistants and domestics, or their own ingenuity, invented a way to thwart the rearing of ancient libels and create their culinary syncretism that forced them into culinary community with their neighbors. After all, the Leo Frank incident had occurred in Atlanta, where he was tried and falsely convicted of molesting and murdering Mary Phagan. His lynching spurred on the founding of the Anti-Defamation League of B'nai B'rith (ADL) in parallel to the way the NAACP was founded a few years before. Although Jews had lived in the South for centuries, with Charleston once being the center of American Jewish life, Southerners had uneasy relationships with the saving remnant of Israel among them, and Jews in the Northeast often wondered in amazement why there were any Jews in the South at all. Jewish eighteenth-century homes and houses of worship still stand in Norfolk, Charleston, and Savannah, and graveyards stand witness with memorial pebbles to the ancestral dead from colonial days to the Confederacy.

Blacks and Jews have had some of their more tenuous and passive-aggressive relationships in the South. Some Southern Jews participated in the South's evils of slavery and slave trading, and supplied the system with its staples. Yet they were nowhere near as represented as their Christian neighbors in the scales of oppression, and others were active in the denunciation of slavery. Some Jewish slaveholders were no more likely to be understanding or humane, and others were deeply different in their approach toward enslaved blacks among them. A cursory look at the "free Negro" registries of Charleston shows a preponderance of mulattoes with the last names of Cohen, Levy, and the like. In New Orleans and Savannah, Levys, Sheftalls, and other families also emancipated and left descendants of color through whose veins the blood of Africa, the Middle East, and Europe flowed. The first kosher/soul cookery might have begun among black women cooking for Jewish families on plantations, or by way of these black/Jewish families in the early coastal Southern cities.

I have always described Birmingham as my grandparents' Poland. It was a place to escape from, not endure in. Their parents came there to get away from the oppression of the cotton field, but it was only a slight step up. I tell the audience, "I never thought I'd get to come back here, to Alabama or to see the city my maternal grandparents grew up in." I don't know what to look for; the people I want to ask about where we came from are gone; I don't know my true place here.

At the end of the program, people volunteered their stories. A Southern lesbian of Scotch-Irish heritage told me about her journey. She was the keeper of the family recipe box, which had belonged to her in-name-only mother-in-law and her partner, who recently died of breast cancer. She converted to Judaism, attended shul faithfully, and became the Jewish culinary memory of her partner's family. She confessed new additions here and there, including beef bones in her chicken broth for matzo ball soup. She and I were both gay, both Southern, both Jewish, both converts, both avid cooks: there was immediate *familiensinn*.

Shortly thereafter, two older women, heavily accented, stepped forward to shake my hand. Ruth Siegler and Ilse Nathan are sisters. They loved the Southern tea cake dough hamantaschen and asked after the recipe.

"We came here after the war from Germany. We were some of the only people in our family to survive. But, you know, we saw what the black people were going through and we did what we had to do: drove people around during boycotts, got them to register to vote."

Ilse chimes in, "We're glad we did what we had to do, because you had to be able to come back to Alabama." She kissed me on the cheek. "You're *mishpocheh*."

I was chilled to my bone. I had to come back to the place my grandmother of blessed memory was born to find my *makom*.

West African Brisket

1 tbsp sweet paprika
1 tsp coarse black pepper
1 tsp cinnamon
1 tsp chili powder
1 tsp cayenne pepper
1 tbsp kosher salt
5 pound brisket or 5 to
   7 pounds of short ribs cut
   across the bone

4 garlic cloves, peeled and
   minced
1 large piece ginger, peeled
   and minced
4 tbsp extra-virgin olive oil
3 onions, peeled and diced
3 bell peppers (green, red, and
   yellow), seeded and diced
1 small hot chili or more to taste

1 10-ounce can diced
 tomatoes
1 to 2 tbsp brown sugar
2 cups chicken, beef, or
 vegetable stock
1 tbsp prepared horseradish
 (chrain/red preferred)

2 bay leaves
1 sprig fresh thyme or 1 tsp
 dried thyme
2 large red onions, cut into
 rings

Preheat your oven to 325 degrees.

Combine the spices and salt, reserving about 2 teaspoons of sea-soning for the vegetables. Rub into the beef the minced garlic and ginger, then sprinkle with the remainder of the spice mixture. Heat 3 tablespoons of olive oil in a large Dutch oven or pot until hot but not smoking. Sear the beef all around, or about 3 to 5 min-utes on each side to an even brown. Remove from the Dutch oven and set aside.

Add the onion, bell peppers, and hot chili to the leavings in the pan. Season with the remaining spices and salt. Sauté until the onion is translucent. Add the tomatoes, mix together and sauté for about 5 minutes. Add the sugar and stock, horseradish, bay leaves, and thyme. Transfer to a bowl and set aside.

Place the red onion rings at the bottom of the pan and sprinkle with the remaining tablespoon of olive oil. Place the brisket on top of them. Cover with the vegetables and stock. Cover tightly and bake in the preheated oven for 3 ½ hours or until the brisket is fork tender.

Remove the brisket. If you wish to serve hot from the oven, allow 15 to 30 minutes for the beef to rest and absorb liquid. Then remove and carve against the grain. If you are planning on serving it later in the day or the next day, cool and then refrigerate. Once the brisket is chilled, you can remove excess fat and slice (always against the grain). You can then use the sauce to cover in a pan or pot, then heat gently for a half an hour or more, until heated through.

Black-Eyed-Pea Hummus

1 15-ounce can plain black-eyed peas, rinsed and drained, preferably organic

¼ cup extra-virgin olive oil, plus more for drizzling

⅓ cup sesame seed paste (tahini)

½ cup freshly squeezed lemon juice

1 tbsp preserved lemon juice brine, or 1½ tsp kosher salt

4 garlic cloves, minced or roughly chopped

1 tsp mild or smoked ground paprika (reserve some for garnish)

½ tsp ground cumin

½ tsp ground coriander

½ tsp chili powder

1 tsp brown sugar or raw (turbinado) sugar

1 tsp hot sauce

2 tbsp minced fresh parsley (flat-leaf preferred), for garnish

1 tbsp sesame seeds, for garnish

Mash or pulse the black-eyed peas in a food processor. Mashing makes for a chunkier mix while processing makes for a smoother dip. If you are using the processor, pulse for about 15 seconds at a time, until the peas are broken down. Continually scrape the processor so that everything gets mixed in. (You may choose to reserve a few black-eyed peas as a garnish, or to vary the texture. A few will work for a garnish, but for texture add half a can of whole black-eyed peas to your mashed or processed mixture.) Mix the olive oil and tahini together with a whisk. Turn the black-eyed-pea hummus into a mixing bowl, and drizzle in the tahini mixture, a bit at a time, mixing between additions until everything is incorporated. Add the lemon juice, preserved lemon juice brine or salt, garlic, paprika, cumin, coriander, chili powder, sugar, and hot sauce, and mix well, adding more of the spice mixture to taste if necessary. Remember, black-eyed-pea hummus swallows flavors—so you may have to adjust to your or your guests' tastes.

Transfer the black-eyed-pea hummus to a bowl. Sprinkle with a bit of paprika, the fresh parsley, and sesame seeds. Drizzle with extra olive oil if you so choose.

5

—

MISSING PIECES

A frican American genealogy is based on the fine art of scaling an invisible brick wall. To genealogists who specialize in this area, the "wall" refers to documents, records, and evidence before 1870. For many African Americans the document trail ends in the lives of ancestors identified on that year's census. It could provide you with information from one to three generations if you know names, places, and people—but only some African American families have knowledge of names, places, and slaveholders that would confirm their place before slavery. Jackson, Freeman, King, Jefferson, and many other names were chosen after slavery by freedmen who wanted nothing to do with their former slaveholders and changed their names after emancipation.

Other families, like those from which I descend, preserved

names, memories, places, and people. Nearly all of the families from which I descend chose to take the names of their slaveholders. The Todds preserved a name from their first slaveholder, the Bellamys, and the Bowens and Twittys from their last. When you have the names, you can dig further because enslaved people were property—they were valuable, and as such their value was often cause to record them in the backs of Bibles, in tax records, in plantation journals and business ledgers. Still, African American genealogy has often proven to be difficult because of the heartbreaking number of destroyed papers lost to war, house fires, burned courthouses, and carelessness.

Then there are the slave schedules themselves. You are confronted as an African American with the extraordinary promise of the blank spaces on the slave schedule. Each enslaved person is reckoned according to their sex, age, and color. The empty spaces stare back at you, and only by inference can you determine if your ancestor is indeed listed on the schedule. The dehumanization never ends.

In the Library of Virginia, my hands drift over the yellowed, ancient records of tithables left from the colonial period. The fading ink on the paper lists Pompeys and Marys and Sukeys and men named Cudjo and women named Phibba. Under King George, we were property with names. When America moves forward with slavery, apparently we lose that critical piece of information that could guide us backward into our past. These are someone's ancestors, and only the very, very fortunate will know who these people were and when and how those people got there.

It was at the Library of Virginia so many years before then that I discovered just how slavery worked on paper. The Todd holdings in Henrico County, Virginia, listed in 1810 an older and a younger enslaved male and a female. I was twelve. The white librarian had a distinctly nasal and pulled Virginia Tidewater accent and he was as helpful as he could be to a twelve-year-old looking for almost impossible crumbs, but he could not help me move past the sick feeling I got when I saw the Todds' enslaved. At the end of the day, I went home with a scribble of a census record that did not separate humans from animals. Horses, cows, Negroes.

What's in a name? Certainly something of a face but not really a full identity. Cudjo and Phibba, names based on names of Akan origin from what is now Ghana, tell us a narrative of persistence or resistance, or even of white accommodation to the folkways of the enslaved. If you are enslaved, your name can change at any point in time. You must be whoever you're told to be, and you must also be your true self—all at once. Slavery was not ripe with opportunities to build rugged individualism and live a free and industrious life as a unique person with a destiny. It was the erasure of that. Not having much more than a name on paper to testify to your existence, or none at all, is painful for the genealogical seeker who wants more.

Above all we were mostly poor. Poor and marginalized Americans, no matter their color, have had a harder time telling their story because they often went unremarked. They had little and were of little value. We might be grateful that our ancestors were enslaved because it gave them some measure of worth by which to merit record. Otherwise they too could have joined the pauper's grave of American memory—and to be honest, many of them did anyway.

Thirty percent of our fathers were white men. They were slave ship crew members, overseers, slave traders, or slaveholders. They were history's largest aggregate of absentee fathers. We began to have a tradition in our families of "parental events"; in other words, for the sake of family stability, we began to claim fictive kin as real. Truths about blood became buried, and with that our trees became adulterated with white lies. Black folks picked up where white folks left off and continued to amend family records to mask adoptions, episodes of abuse and impropriety, and emotional lament.

Compulsory illiteracy damned many of us. We couldn't write down our own stories. We had to tell them to others, and this caused facts and words to be bent. I wonder what our history would have looked like if every man and woman could have written down or passed down a written account of their own lives. This is not in our treasure trove.

And nobody talked; slavery was nightmare fuel and trauma food. Nobody wanted to talk and tell all about their lives in slavery, and those who did usually only gave the barest of details. Sons and daughters shied away from asking questions of their beleaguered parents, and others outright discouraged discussion of slavery and other "old-timey" things, further pushing information into the amnesia abyss. The "burned county" was not the only enemy of our collective memory, we were. We have inherited precious little, thanks to shame, economic discontinuity, and fear.

Our feet were forced across the map by slavery, and in its aftermath, by economic opportunity mixed with economic exploitation and by threats of violence. Many of us moved every half generation. Trails went cold. People were lost, and connections went undefined. We began to disappear from our own family trees even as they branched out.

We know so much, but know so little, and the fine details keep shifting, but unlike any other American ethnic group those details are always hotly debated. We are not allowed the peace of mind of our own self-rumination. Every aspect of our history becomes a contested article on social media, a gospel truth to be disproved by experts at conferences, and a groupthink to be contained. Our cultural myths we design ourselves around are not sacred like other people's myths; our anchors are constantly being pulled up to make white people feel as if they're in control, and because of this we have struggled to come up with a cohesive and empowering narrative of our own.

My genealogist, Toni Carrier of Lowcountry Africana, knows all of this. She's a white woman of Cajun heritage who has worked on black genealogy for thirty years. Alex Haley's saga, Edward Ball's

Slaves in the Family, and the miracle finds on television shows like *Finding Your Roots, Who Do You Think You Are?*, or *African American Lives* are not as common as one would think.

"It's rare, but not impossible, to get back to the ship, but so many circumstances have to be lined up for you to get there that if one or two are missing, there's little, so little, to go on, but you can't lose hope," she said. "On the way, there are many stories to be told and ancestors to find. You can't miss a detail; research the cat.

"This is not a hobby. Look, for many white Americans, genealogy is a hobby, it gets them out of the house, gives them something to enjoy researching. With African American genealogy, it's more about social justice, regaining a heritage denied. Every African American living today is stolen African history embodied, and this is further compounded by the denial of the lived history of Africans in the United States." Toni's degree is in applied anthropology; she started her work by examining the lineages of black Seminoles. This ultimately led her to the Low Country and to found Lowcountry Africana, her genealogy website. "I realized then that there is a large part of our history that either went unrecorded, or has been underpreserved and underemphasized in digitization efforts. Yet the records are there, and that was clear to me. So we started the website and started digitizing records.

"Charleston is the ancestral home to so many African Americans, because it was a major port of entry in the transatlantic slave trade. It has been estimated that 41 percent of all enslaved Africans brought to North America were brought to Charleston. Later, in the domestic slave trade, Charleston and South Carolina as a whole began selling enslaved people as new lands opened to the west. Because of this, many, many African Americans have at least one ancestor who came from, or through, the Low Country. The work brought me here, just as many African Americans' genealogy research brings them here."

The Low Country's importance to African American history and the Gullah-Geechee people who are its heart resonate with Toni. "The Cajun culture is warm, and kind, and just real. Growing up Cajun, I felt like I was wrapped in a warm blanket. We had ways that I didn't realize were different until we moved. Life happened around the dinner table. What I remember most about being Cajun was that life was lived at the table where you ate. I miss that. It's impossible for me to separate our ethnicity from our food. It's woven together." She even made a solid connection with Low Country food: "The moment I stepped foot on Low Country soil I felt at home in the Low Country culture. We cook the same food; we just call the dishes by different names. Our shrimp stew (we serve it over rice) is the Low Country's shrimp and grits. The Low Country's okra soup is what we call okra and tomatoes or gumbo without a roux. Both Cajun and Low Country cooks make rice and field peas. What Low Country cooks call red rice, we call Spanish rice. It's a Creole cuisine, really."

Toni's ancestors, exiled from Nova Scotia, were part of the main branch that went to Louisiana. Many Acadian French settled in communities across the Eastern Seaboard, some returned to France, but a large group found a new home in French Louisiana. As Cajun speech patterns, music, and food suggest, the influence of neighboring Africans and Native Americans, first the maroons (freedom seekers) who greeted them when they settled the bayous, and later in slavery (there weren't that many, but there were Cajun slaveholders), is indelible in their culture. It is this kiss of Africa, whether it is in the twang of the banjo in the Appalachian foothills of Kentucky, West Virginia, or Tennessee, or the sound of the mortar and pestle husking rice in Mamou, that has come down to us in our own time as remnants, adding to the pile of missing pieces of Africans in everyday American culture.

It's all very personal to Toni. She was deeply affected by Hurricane Katrina and devastated by the shooting at Mother Emanuel AME in Charleston. She spent six days providing free water and ice to the interracial crowds that gathered to mourn and heal. Genealogy for her provides a place where she feels productive in her own search to extend justice and goodness in the world. "We worked with Henry Louis Gates on *African American Lives 2*, we traced Michelle Obama's ancestry on behalf of the Obama for America campaign in 2007, we did the research on the Point of Pines slave cabin that was moved from Edisto Island to the Smithsonian's National Museum of African American History and Culture, and none of it felt like work. It felt like we were making light."

For two years Toni helped me to unravel the families of my four grandparents, drawing on my uncle's previous research and my research, and creating new leads by looking into every conceivable document and source, from Freedmen's Bureau records to Civil War records, newspaper ads, census data, cohabitation records, oral histories with my family members, wills, probate records, and land deeds. After months of careful research her first major discovery was the earliest record of my great-great-great-grandmother Hester/Hettie, found in the will of her mistress Elizabeth Hughes, of Montgomery, Alabama. Hester was twelve in 1840, pushing her birthdate to 1828 in South Carolina, also the original home of the Hughes family. That one record took half a year to find.

Then there is DNA, deoxyribonucleic acid, speaking of hotly debated. Can African Americans truly find their heritage using DNA evidence? Is it useful evidence at all? Now we have been offered the promise to glimpse into the deep ancestral past and reclaim the precious piece of information robbed when our names were changed in exile. Toni says, "DNA is the great equalizer in turning around the underwritten history of the African experience in America. A lot of brick walls have come crashing down with the advent of DNA testing, and a lot of family secrets as well."

We thirst for something that will give us a pin on a map, a place we can call our old country like the rest of America, but like anything else African American it's a controversy by default. Arguments over samples, transparency, accuracy, and meaning have clouded the clarity that this evidence is supposed to offer.

Beyond the disputations of the science itself, I have spent my lifetime bombarded with questions: "Aren't we all African anyway?" "What part of Africa are you from?" And my favorite lead question, "Why can't you just be an American?" I live in a country where the mention of the word "African" conjures immediate overtures to race, class, and threat.

The research on the subject, first popularized by Dr. Rick Kittles and furthered by his company with Gina Paige, African Ancestry, is now going on twenty years of development. My first engagement with this was one of our local ABC affiliate's news reporters, Sam Ford, who was given a DNA test from African Ancestry at their genesis. Like a miracle, he was Yoruba, and not only that, but Yoruba with genetic affinities with men from a particular village of Yorubas. This set my imagination on fire. Other DNA services have begun to tell part of the African American genetic story, all to greater or lesser degrees, but few have made the claims of specificity like African Ancestry. I have chosen to test with them and other companies in order to have enough data to make my own conclusion.

The community of seekers who want to know their DNA and roots in slavery has grown immensely since 1977, the year I was born, when Alex Haley's *Roots* became an international phenomenon. He set out to write "a myth for his people," and indeed my uncle and then I became devotees of the idea of seeking our origins despite the challenges and frustrations. Now there are communities of African Americans for whom finding African origins through

DNA has become a cultural tradition in and of itself, with Internet videos of people opening their results, announcements at family reunions, and lively debate over social media over which companies to test with. We have become a nation within a nation of passionate genealogists and heritage fanatics. The curse of not knowing more has been turned upside down by the desire to know all.

And in all of this I still have a mosaic with missing pieces. I am trying to fill in the blanks and create a narrative that goes beyond myth and functions in power. It is up to the individual African American, and always has been, to come to terms with one's place in the world and in the wider narrative of this country, and within it, the American South.

6

No Nigger Blood

When I was thirteen years old, I interviewed Grammy, my maternal grandmother, about her father, the man she and her sisters revered in a way that was so powerful that knock-down, drag-out arguments would ensue for years to come at the very mention of his name. He was a short man with a long face and forehead, and because of his deep, rich color he was nicknamed after a minstrel song, "Old Black Joe." Joseph Peter Todd II, the son of Joseph Peter the First, was brought from the vicinity of Richmond, Virginia, with his mother, Arrye, and brother, Louis, in the 1850s as part of the domestic slave trade. His mother was the mulatto Hattie Bellamy, the daughter of her slaveholder, and to her he was born in 1888, the year that Jack the Ripper rampaged through the dark, filthy streets of Whitechapel. My grandmother quietly believed that I was her father returned, because for all my man-child rage I reminded her of her defiant father, the army and WPA cook Joe Todd.

Joe might have had a biracial mother, but his father must have been the imprint of his African great-great-grandfather. My great-grandfather was very fond of his shotgun, and my grandmother's most fond memory of Old Joe Todd was his cocking his gun at the Klan. Much to my great-grandmother Mary's terror, my great-grandfather did not allow Klan terrorism to affect the comings and goings of his household. Everyone was ordered to the porch; mother to sew and children to play.

While every other black household dimmed the lights and shut the curtains, my great-granddaddy Joe Todd insisted this was his country and that the Klan had no power over him or his woman or his seed. He sat there with a smile as they rode on by in little parades of intimidation, and as they moved on he openly declared, "If they come to kill me, I'll take them to hell with me, but as for me and my house, we shall not live in hell."

Grammy filled my head with stories of his bravado and derring-do. "Once a white man hit Mother as she was walking, in a car accident. They went to court, and when that cracker went 'That nigger gal over there,' they had throw my daddy out of the courtroom. He stood up in the crow's nest—that was where they would put black people—and screamed and lunged and said, 'That ain't no nigger gal that's *my wife* you b——.' Before he could call him a bastard or son of a bitch, his brothers had put their hands over his mouth, and before the gavel came down a third time, Daddy was put in a car to be taken home."

My great-grandfather, for all his toughness, was a permissive and positive parent who got his point across in aphorisms and poetry. "Like Jesus Christ and Abraham Lincoln said to every man, 'A house divided against itself cannot stand! In this family we must all do our part, do it well or not at all, whatever you start.'" He came home from long days at work and helped his son Nathaniel build stilts out of scraps he found along the road, and as he enjoyed a few Camels he would delight in seeing his children pick pecans while balancing themselves in the air. My grandmother never knew a real beating at the hands of her father, and neither did any of her siblings. He would take them into the bathroom and tell them to throw water on their face while he slapped his own knee. Eventually my great-grandmother caught on; even though he refused to lay a hand on his kids, he never questioned the authority of his wife in things domestic: "What Mother said, you must do."

His respect and love for my great-grandmother was rooted in family legend, retold my grandmother's sister, whom we affectionately called Aunt Jo. The story's authenticity is shakier than the bridge of San Luis Rey, but to not retell it would be a sin. My great-grandfather served in World War I. He arrived back in the United States in South Carolina and made his way to Alabama on foot. While in South Carolina, in the only clothes he had to his name—his uniform—he was arrested and accused of raping a white woman. During the First World War the antipathy toward black soldiers in the South was strong, and the sight of so many in uniform led to rampant reprisal on the part of many white Southerners.

Languishing in jail, he was tormented for several days with threats of being lynched. He prayed to Jesus and had a dream that he would be released and would meet a beautiful woman who would become his (second) wife. As with every story that was ever told in this way since the beginning of beginnings, on the third day my great-grandfather was released as quickly as he had been captured and another black man, probably equally innocent, took his place in that cell, and on a tree within the days to come. One day he found himself thirsty and hungry at a colored schoolhouse in Clay County.

He helped himself to a dipper full of water outside the school and he saw the reflection of the most beautiful woman he ever saw asking him if she could be of assistance.

"This is how my mother met my father, a true fairy-tale romance." Well, sorta. 1. My great-grandparents were married around 1915, before he enlisted. 2. Yes, my great-grandfather was an enlisted serviceman in World War I, but that was about 1918, and he was out under honorable discharge by 1919, being known to have "a good character." 3. This is one of the stories that led to loud after-drink arguments and hurt feelings. 4. The other fierce debate circled around whether Daddy bought a cow and who had to milk it. 5. The only thing anybody agreed about was that they met at the schoolhouse in Clay County.

My great-grandparents were a strong couple and had a strong family unit. My aunt Anna liked to repeat the story that during the Depression her grandmother wrote First Lady Eleanor Roosevelt for assistance, namely because the poorhouse was for white folks— not for black people. Eleanor Roosevelt not only responded, a truck arrived at the Todd household in Birmingham with a few packages of bread, crackers, cheese, and other staples, and a few toys for the children. Nobody knows what happened to the letter, but my grandmother and her two sisters told that story for the rest of their lives. Grammy rocked me to the core every time she said, "Many a night we watched Mother and Father go without so we could eat." It made me realize that they went without food so my grandmother, my mother, and I could be here.

Mary taught my great-grandfather how to read and write, and by 1920 he was literate. For her, he stopped drinking. Because my great-grandmother was a busy schoolteacher, Joe brought his cooking talent home from the Civilian Conservation Corps, and to alleviate her burdens he took up half the cooking in the household. He was especially known for his barbecue, done in true Alabama style, full racks of spareribs and shoulders with a sauce full of se-. crets (which my grandmother passed down to me), the rare winter treat of sorghum molasses on snow, pots of soul-nourishing shy-pink butter beans, fresh roasted peanuts from his cousins and friends back in Russell County, and blackberry cobblers (doobie) from when his daughters went picking with their uncle Lane. But the Sunday breakfasts he put out when times were good were the highlight of nearly everyone's week.

My grandmother said, "My father could make some biscuits and Lord, he could fry perch and chicken. He made gravy with the sausage my grandmother knew how to make best at hog-killing time— full of sage and red pepper and other herbs she would grow. Mother would bring us home from church and Daddy would have that table looking so pretty with dishes of preserves and cane and sorghum syrup and fresh butter and the best hot coffee and tea. Nobody made redeye gravy like him, and when he cooked grits they were perfect. If we had it in the garden we knew there would be okra or mustard or collard greens for dinner, black-eyed peas and rice, and cornbread sticks made in the mold. Whatever didn't get eaten at breakfast got eaten up at dinnertime. If we were good—sweet potato pie, pecan pie, caramel cake, and tea cakes."

This feast made almost everyone's week . . . except when it came to his mother-in-law, Ms. Josie, aka Josephine Hughes Hancock, born during Reconstruction. Her husband's family descended from the plantation of Henry Hancock, a fairly successful man in his lifetime who was also his master's child. The Hancocks and the Hughes families were light-skinned, and colorism was a powerful force in their lives. Josephine's mother was Hettie Haines Hughes, a mulatto who was the daughter of a mulatto, who was the daughter of yet another mulatto, who then married a "bright mulatto," Spencer "Plenty" Hughes, described as a "big Irishman," who liked the bottle and loved to tell jokes. Hettie's mother, Nora, was light-skinned, we presume not only from Hettie's color, but also because Hettie did not see her mother as black. She claimed that her mother was a white woman and insisted that she and her mother were free, and later family lore even rendered her an "Indian mistress."

Hettie was not white. Nor was her mother, and for that matter, neither was her daughter. Mary was born "high yellow," and her daughter, my grandmother, was tagged with the slur "China doll" growing up. They were all women of color whose color often reflected only the bare minimum of African ancestry. When Mary married Joseph, even though his mother, too, was half-white, she was temporarily disowned for marrying a dark-skinned man.

The pictures of the Hughes family are remarkable, if only for one reason. Hardly anyone in the pictures looks black, not the least of which was John Henry Hughes, another of Hettie's children and the son of John Clisby, a white man. He could pass for white and often did. His claim to fame with my grandmother was inviting her to sit next to him in the white section of the streetcar and "pretend" that she was "a little colored gal that worked for him." She always declined, not only out of self-respect but because her mother warned her against him for his proclivities with young girls.

Josephine Hughes Hancock claimed loudly, "I ain't got no nigger blood in me." She was the most difficult person to have around the Sunday table when Joe Todd made breakfast because she refused to eat "anything his little black nigger hands touched." Trial and tribulation broke her of this habit, not to mention that she rather enjoyed stealing tastes in the kitchen when nobody was looking, as evidenced by the trail of crumbs leading to her space at the table. She got her comeuppance when my great-grandfather would pretend to be a haint (a spirit) and would call her name and scare the hell out of her by rushing up on her in front of her grandchildren, covered in a sheet.

My mother barely knew Ms. Josie. She was memorialized in a

Cleveland newspaper surrounded by the next two generations, dozens of her grandchildren and great-grandchildren and first great-great-grandchild. My mother knew her as "the Witch," a name she and her sisters gave to her owing to her mean, crotchety appearance, pursed lips, small glasses, and pearls that shone like vampire teeth. Call her whatever you will, she survived my great-grandmother and lived into her late eighties.

So much in these stories fascinated me and repelled me growing up. First, they clued me in to the truth written in the features of my grandparents—that we were not just black (African), but white people were also in the family genes. Second, it was incomprehensible that people would go out of their way to deny any African ancestry and yet still marry people who had visible African ancestry or claimed it themselves. My grandmother and her siblings, like all the families that came before them, were not the same color, nor did they have the same features. That part of being black—having vastly different phenotypes despite having the same parents—was something I rarely saw in other ethnic groups. Nobody walked me through these rules of race. I was pretty much forced to figure them out as I stared at my yellowish grandmother and my brown mother and my reddish-brown self.

Colorism is nothing new to speak of in the African American community. For the most part, lighter-skinned people have benefited from the preference for those who reflected white ancestry. Some faced a backlash, particularly when they didn't subscribe to the belief that they were any different from any other person of color. That would be my grandmother, who loved her blackness fiercely and loved her father and mother for teaching her to be proud of being black.

All of this led to a lifetime of inner searching to sort out my parts. I have sort of almond-shaped eyes, a reddish-brown tone, a broad nose and plump lips, and hair that every year is less nap and curl and more silk and Sicily. The hair on my arms is straight. I am not biracial. I was born to two black parents whose mixed heritage was long before them encoded in their genes. And yet because of all this, it becomes much harder to have a dialogue about what white genes in a black body really mean. I decided, once and for all, to have a confrontation with the quarter of a white man lurking in my body; I went to go dig deep to find my white man in the woodpile.

7

—

"White Man in the Woodpile"

OAK FOREST PLANTATION, NASH
COUNTY, NORTH CAROLINA

Through Richard Henry Bellamy, the father of Sallie's daughter Hattie, I was able to trace my family story to his grandfather, Reverend William Bellamy—my white, fifth great-grandfather—born during the Revolutionary War, who saw the birth of the Cotton Kingdom in North Carolina. In a lonely little corner of Nash County in northeastern North Carolina lie the remnants of Oak Forest plantation. My partner, Taylor, drove us several hours east of Durham to bring me here. Thanks to the miracle of social media, I know what it's supposed to look like because the Big House still stands, a cliché since it hardly resembles the glory that it was to 1840s eyes. Back off the road—pebbly, sandy, and uneven—lie the house and its outbuildings, surrounded even today by crops of cotton and tobacco eerily suggesting the past.

As we arrived, the farm's current owner, a direct descendant of the Phillips family, pulled up in his truck, and his old dog alerted him to the presence of strangers. Before he could ask "Can I help you?" I made my intentions plain and simple. "My people are the Bellamys and this is my great-great-great-great-great-grandfather's house and I've come all the way from Washington to see it." Mr. Phillips gave me a good look up and down, adjusted his cap, and said, "Who'd you say your people were?"

Mr. Phillips is not rude in asking the question, nor does he look too surprised. In fact, he interrupts a phone call to take us around the site. He tells me what I already know—that his family bought the property in the 1860s and kept the old house and buildings. Some were scavenged but the old house was not. It was a classic early-nineteenth-century planter's house. The whitewash, wraparound porch and steps were all gone. The house had a hall and parlor extension to its rear, where the dining area was likely placed and food could be brought in fresh from the kitchen, but a storm had long since knocked down the hall leading to the parlor.

I don't know how to feel about William. Should I be proud of his achievement, a prosperous Tidewater North Carolina cotton and naval stores plantation at the heyday of King Cotton? Forty-six enslaved black people building, cooking, milking, digging, picking, gardening, raising his livestock, and waiting on his family hand and foot made this possible. He didn't have to lift a finger. I guess I came to ask a question: If he was my ancestor and his sustenance is part of my story too, what of it?

Eastern Carolina was full of natural and human culinary resources. The Tar River had eels, sturgeon, shad, chub, catfish, perch, and rockfish. The woods were full of deer and small game. This part of North Carolina was the cradle of its barbecue tradition. From nearby Edenton and Raleigh, special provisions could be obtained: barrels of oysters and other seafood, spices, teas, coffee, tropical fruits and oils, and whatever liquors could not be distilled on-site.

North Carolina in antebellum times was a place of honest, simple country cooking. "Red pepper is much used to flavor meat with the famous 'barbecue' of the South & which I believe they esteem above all dishes is roasted pig dressed with red pepper & vinegar," said Sarah Hicks Williams. She wrote to her parents in New York about their "lovely sweet potatoes and yams," and cornbread and (beaten) biscuit "sent to table hot." Fried chicken, buttered hominy, fresh or salted shad and shad roe, wild turkey, cold country smoked ham, bacon and greens, apple pie, and peas and melons, depending on the season. Wild foods like gulls, skates, bats, sucker fish, and other undesirables were considered only fit for Carolina's "Indians and Negroes."

Mr. Phillips asked me not once but twice precisely who I was kin to. I made it clear that I am a Bellamy by blood. He avoided discussing the obvious connection—that a Bellamy male forced himself sexually on a black woman.

"You ain't the first one to come 'round. There was another fellow said his mother's people were Bellamys."

"Was he white or black?"

He squints and looks at the ground, then looks up with a nod. "He was a white fella. He wanted to see the graves. You want to see the graves? I'll show you, come on 'round."

Taylor, Mr. Phillips, and I went toward the barn, as he removed a barbed-wire fence beyond which lay a little graveyard guarded by a water oak and waist-high rocks. He pointed to a rusted heap of roof and broken bricks. "That was the kitchen. It just fell apart. We used up all the bricks and nails when I was coming up." The part of this place I had hoped to see most was nothing but rubble. The plantation office was standing, the barn, the dairy, the smokehouse, the outhouse or "necessary," but the kitchen was a rusty iron roof that probably replaced a wooden shingled one. Buried beneath snakes and fire ants are any possible archaeological remains of what my planter ancestor might have eaten.

From his probate record, there were certainly chickens, turkeys, geese, beeves, sheep, and hogs. There were also beehives here to put fresh honey on hot biscuits, and apple and peach trees that produced fruit for making brandy and fruit butters. Without question, there was a sizable kitchen garden here where sweet potatoes and Irish potatoes grew. And, if we are to believe neighboring white North Carolinians, it is likely that cabbages, lettuce, carrots, cucumbers, turnips, squash and maybe watermelons, tomatoes, okra, collards, and other things were cultivated as well. With the help of almost four dozen enslaved blacks, Oak Forest was a well-fed and prosperous little operation, and at his death, Reverend Bellamy owed "Negro Luke" for the purchase of "rice and onions."

Martha Katz-Hyman, my friend and expert curator, walked me through the probate record carefully. Martha frequently cautioned me not to say anything I cannot prove; I assured her I wouldn't, but that my imagination might run free. Martha is an expert in early American material culture, particularly that of the American South and the material culture of slavery. "This is a very prosperous man, a very prosperous man," she said. "However we don't know where these things fit into the larger scheme of the house. It seems as though things are fairly grouped together, but it's not as if we can imagine ourselves going from room to room viewing things in situ. We have to use an educated guess."

Reverend Bellamy, the Methodist minister, had many fine things. In my mind's eye I stand with Martha surveying a table of wealth and bounty that I, as a black man, would never have enjoyed in a state of equality with my ancestor. I would never have been seated at his table. His walnut table. When guests retired after a hearty meal they rested on pillows filled with down from his nineteen geese, from which also came quills to make pens to write out bills of sale and keep record of how many barrels of turpentine had been made, or bales of cotton picked.

A peacock pranced around Oak Forest. Was it just for show or would its tail feathers have been used to make a punkah fan, operated by a slave, to cool the dining table at meals? Judging from Reverend Bellamy's probate record, potatoes, dried fruit, peaches, apples, corn, sweet potatoes, onions, turnip greens, vinegar, rice, pork, beef, chicken, and geese might have been just a few of the raw materials of his kitchen. He had a dairy on-site, as noted by the milk pails, strainers, and churns, for the butter and cream and milk brought to the table. There were hot waffles some mornings to lavish the butter on—he had a waffle iron and a device for making beaten biscuits.

There were silver tongs and tea services, cream pots and steak dishes. There were wineglasses and decanters. Enslaved workers distilled peach brandy on his plantation, and there was hard cider, and hot tea and coffeepots (he had a mill) for those "lavish feasts." It was they who gathered the honey and made the furniture. Waiting at the table, they must have passed the time scanning the oddities he collected in his cabinet of curiosities, most exciting of which to me was a sawfish bill. The privilege of living now is that I can seat myself at the master's table—the table of my white ancestor, a slaveholder—and interpret *his* world, and he has no say.

There are no remains of any slave cabins here. Forty-six individuals would have required anywhere from five to eight dwellings, considering that extended families usually lived in units of ten to twelve people, with certain families and individuals enjoying better or more intimate accommodations. There aren't even any footprints of the cabins to look at, meditate over, or imagine life in. At least there is a probate record, with names and ages, but no hint of who is related to whom, and why or what their bonds were. Like so many other spaces in Southern life that used to be plantations, slave graveyards, cabins, all sacred spaces are obliterated. Even if I don't actually come from any of these ancestors, some of their relatives inevitably married into my families in Alabama.

Before Christmas of 1846, the estate of Reverend William Bellamy was dismantled and a sale was to take place. All forty-six of my white, fifth great-grandfather's enslaved chattel were to be sold from Oak Forest Plantation. Ten would become the property of my fourth great-grandfather, William Jr. This must have been the most terrifying moment of their lives. These families had been together for generations. I am almost certainly not related to any of these men, women, and children, but according to my uncle's records, William instructed them to be kept in family units as much as possible. But at the height of the year, when spirits were to be brightest and work was lightest, there was certainly the misery of knowing that for some, the circle would indeed be broken. Some would go to his kin in North Carolina, others to his other kin in Alabama, walking the long road forged by those planters hot with "Alabama fever," the desire for fresh land unblemished by King Cotton.

Christmas in eastern North Carolina was no small thing. It was the occasion of the John Canoe ritual in which drumming, dancing, parading, and processioning in "outlandish" costumes with raccoon tails, bits of quilt, deer antlers, and ox horns brought a bit of Africa to part of the antebellum South. Beating on large drums known as "gumbo boxes," the John Canoe made its way through the classic plantation ritual of "catching Christmas's gif'" where enslaved children would win their gift from the master and mistress by being the first to say the traditional greeting. Christmas meant real coffee, oranges and penny candy, whole barbecued hogs, pecan pies and syrup cakes, black walnut taffy, possum and yams, corn liquor and ham; it was not supposed to mean leaving the people you had always known, forever.

Under a sprawling dark-green-leaved water oak lay the graves of William and his wife, my great-great-great-great-great-grandparents, along with a child that died in infancy. It doesn't sink in. I don't feel like putting a stone on his grave, as is Jewish custom, nor had I brought any flowers. I am startled by the true emptiness I feel toward this man, even as I feel some reverence for the land I am standing on. Mr. Phillips and Taylor look at me for some sign that I've paid my respects. I take pictures with my smartphone; I aim and click, aim and click, but not a single tear or fuzzy moment. Oak Forest is not my good old plantation home, but Mr. Phillips, unprompted, gives me a flat-cut nail and a brick to take with me, both of which he is confident were made by enslaved craftsmen.

The Bellamy legacy has reared its head often, leading to this moment. At one presentation, a senior-age black man asked me if I was going to look up my white people in Europe. I stated, "Not unless I can find any Bellamys!"

His friend chuckled and said, "John, that's your people, right?"

John looked a little ashen. "Yeah, I guess."

Joke's over. I asked Mr. John if his people were from North Carolina; he said yes.

"Halifax County?"

"Yeah, how'd you know?"

All smiles were gone. "Because, Mr. John, my ancestor likely owned yours on a plantation named Oak Forest."

When the Cooking Gene project started, our first stop was in Chapel Hill, North Carolina. The room was packed and so hot that the sorghum syrup in the back was almost melting. In the rush of people passing business cards and asking questions was a senior white reporter, Cliff Bellamy. His Bellamys were likely the cousins of my Bellamys. We likely shared a distant male ancestor back in England, probably a Norman arriving with William the Conqueror's army. He couldn't believe it any more than I could: he was randomly assigned to cover me, and we really were all, in some way, "kinfolk."

NOT LIVING "IN A GOSPEL MANNER"

In the 1840s Levi Pate and William Mungo of Kershaw County, South Carolina, were both censured by their respective churches for "not living in a gospel manner." Both were slaveholders of my paternal grandfather's family, and both were known for having children with their enslaved chattel. Just before slavery's end, Sukey Pate had several children by Levi, including my great-great-grandmother Margaret. Margaret was so angry over her lot in life as the biracial daughter of her slaveholder that she named her son Benjamin Tillman Mungo after the powerful segregationist who was vehemently against "race mixing." Levi was not particularly kind to Sukey or her children, many of whom were his. He sold off one-half of a set of twins because she "stole" guinea hen eggs and cooked them to feed them because they were malnourished. Different branches of the Mungo-Pate family told the same story independently for generations, recounting the deep pain she faced as she watched her child get sold away from her, growing distant as the wagon took her away.

A substantial number of my ancestors were known to many as "bastard mulattoes." I don't believe I have a single picture of an ancestor born into slavery who didn't have white blood, and remember, phenotype can, and often does, lie. They were a mostly bewildered group without any sort of real cultural or social anchor. This disruption—among the many others—is one of several major mutations in our sense of self that restructured Africans into the Negroes of colonial and, particularly, antebellum slavery. As the number of white DNA matches on my genetic genealogy accounts attest, many of these white men had no names, no record, leaving no evidence other than genes.

The kitchen in slavery was a sinister place. The kitchen is where we acquired the eyes of our oppressors, their blood and bones and cheek-blush. The kitchen was, perhaps more than any other space during slavery, the site of rape after rape, sexual violations that led to one of the more unique aspects of African American identity— our almost inextricable blood connection to white Southerners. The end of slavery didn't stop the exploitation of black women, but these incidents were harder to disguise and cover, and the consequences of these horrors had more stakes under Jim Crow than under the lash. As Caroline Randall Williams, co-author of *Soul Food Love*, once told me, we're "rape colored, our trigger is the mirror."

Not all of my white ancestors were male. My paternal great-great-great-grandmother Cordelia Fore, a woman with a crown of curly hair and beautiful ebony skin, was the descendant of a white indentured servant brought to colonial Virginia. My maternal great-great-great-grandmother Hester/Hettie was the daughter and granddaughter of women whose fathers were white, and her father probably also was a white man. She was open about being sexually abused by her slaveholder and by other men she was rented out to for labor. Knowing this, whenever I walk into the space of a plantation kitchen I am confronted with the dual legacy of the Southern food heritage—these were not neutral spaces; these were places of power against the enslaved in the most dehumanizing ways possible.

I am a male who interprets the cooks of slavery, and I cannot say that men were not sexually abused during slavery—in fact, Esteban Montejo, enslaved in Cuba, alluded to male domestic servants being sexually abused, and talked about the prettiest boys being rounded up, sent to the Big House, and "softened up." As a gay man, I don't know what to make of that scenario: I know it was possible, I know it was real, but certainly not as common as the violation of our mothers. Perhaps they saw gay men as eunuchs. All of it fills me with revulsion. I don't know what I would do if I saw the things they saw, knew what they knew. This is what Maya Angelou meant by "nights of terror and fear."

Other stories were more benign than Hettie's. My great-great-great-grandfather Henry Hancock, enslaved in Tallapoosa County, Alabama, was said to be the spitting image of his slaveholding father, James. Indeed, he looks like a white man in his picture—smart, with a well-trimmed beard and perfectly tied cravat. He was raised alongside his white half brother in the Big House, and by oral history knew the love and care of his mistress as if he were her own child. Of course, he was not; his mother labored day after day and another woman raised her child, perhaps out of spite. There was, after all, more than one way to visit pain on the black women who bore a white man's child.

My friend Toni Tanner Scott is a personal chef who lives near Austin, Texas. We share a mutual friend in culinary historian and food writer Toni Tipton-Martin, author of *The Jemima Code*. Toni Scott's roots are in Texas and Louisiana, where her family goes back to old Creole stock living along the Mississippi and its tributaries for generations among the cane and cotton fields. Toni is also an obsessive genealogist and is fascinated by the search for her and her husband's roots. Oh, of course, her husband is my cousin and the answer to a 150-year-old mystery—whether or not a white man named Richard Henry Bellamy is the reason we call each other blood.

Richard had dark blue eyes. He was smart and handsome, with dark brown hair. He came from fairly successful Southern white folks, with his own roots going back to seventeenth-century New England and North Carolina by way of the British Isles, with stones skipping back to the 1400s. Bellamy: "My Good Friend." In his blood were the Norman conquerors of 1066 who made roasting pork dignified and baking a ham commonplace.

He was born in Enfield, North Carolina, in 1829. When his father's relatives and in-laws secured the best of the "Red Stick" Creek lands during and following "Indian removal," they caught "Alabama fever" and settled in the eastern part of the state, right across from Columbus, Georgia, in Russell County, Alabama, the gateway to the Black Belt. He went to the University of Georgia at Athens, where his dorm still stands, and eventually got his law degree and set up practice on the eve of the Civil War. He was a keeper of the secrets of the Tuckabatchee Lodge. The child of the marriage of first cousins, he sought to have transparent children with his own beloved double first cousin but parted company with her, keeping with the wishes of his father William Jr., with whom he would ever have a rocky relationship.

Denied the pleasure of civilized, moonlight-and-magnolias incest, my third great-grandfather caught Texas fever. In Texas, he settled in Panola County, justly named after a Choctaw word for "cotton." He found his yellow rose in a mulatto country girl. She bore him a son named Heenan. Heenan was not quite the carbon copy of his father, but enough of him was there that he was proud of the little yellow nigger he created, so proud he gave him a little land and money to ensure his way in the world.

The word went out that there was a war brewing thanks to the election of Mr. Lincoln. Bellamy returned home to the plantation along the Chattahoochee River and started as a private in the Confederate army, quickly advancing to lieutenant, then captain. Socializing at the neighboring plantation of the Chadwicks, a family that had immigrated to Alabama from South Carolina, Bellamy found his way to the teenage daughter of my fourth great-grandmother, Rosetta Merritt, a fierce woman "of the Afri-kan nation," born and raised near distant Bellamy cousins in Wilmington, North Carolina. At sixteen, Sallie Chadwick bore the second known child of Captain Bellamy, a tough little girl named Hattie who would grow up to marry Joseph Todd, enslaved with his mother and brother on the Bellamy plantation.

Richard immortalized his best self with gleaming sword and gray suit, looking coldly into the eyes of history, defiant against the Union into which he was born. In east Texas, he had a bouncing mulatto boy, and in east Alabama a mulatto girl who was a match for any trial the moment she arrived. He fought valiantly at the Battle of Vicksburg, where his injury and near death are still remembered among the Confederate monuments:

C.S.

ALABAMA BATTERY

STEVENSON'S DIVISION: ARMY OF VICKSBURG

CAPT. J. F. WADDELL

A DETACHMENT OF THE BATTERY, UNDER LIEUT. R. H. BELLAMY, SERVED ONE 6-POUNDER GUN IN THIS POSITION, RAILROAD REDOUBT, FROM MAY 18 TO A LITTLE BEFORE 10 O'CLOCK THE FORENOON OF MAY 22, 1863, WHEN ITS AMMUNITION WAS EXPLODED BY THE FIRE OF THE UNION BATTERIES. LIEUT. R. H. BELLAMY AND THREE ENLISTED MEN OF THE DETACHMENT WERE SEVERELY WOUNDED BY THE EXPLOSION. THE GUN WAS NOT AFTERWARDS SERVED IN THIS REDOUBT DURING THE DEFENSE.

He was never captured but instead was part of a deal where he was sent back home with the sworn promise he would never raise his hand in war against the Union. Of course he did, again and again, until there was no hope. But he spent the rest of his life celebrating his role in the Confederate cause and believing in the Southern cross. I have no reason to believe that although he only had children who were also of African descent that he himself did not believe in white supremacy, the suppression of the black vote, the suppression of the black man and, most important, that no black man should ever be allowed to do to a white woman what he did to my teenage ancestor. The maintenance of this attitude is what burns my soul in regards to the old school racism of the Old South; it was a one-way street, an ailing body pushed to its limits with gaping, open wounds.

If nothing else, I will confess a small amount of connection when I climbed the small hill in Vicksburg, Mississippi, to see where Richard fought. What does it mean to spend your entire life as one of millions of black people whose legacy is not only the white slave-holding aristocracy but people who fought to preserve your people's bondage for eternity? All around us, the Confederate cause is celebrated and revived. We are even given revisions of truth in which black men fought equally in unity with whites over states' rights.

"Mike, I used to see *Gone with the Wind* come on and it used to make me sick." Cousin Alan recounts his experiences. His grandfather was Granpa Heenan Johnson; my great-great-grandmother was Hattie Bellamy. To our knowledge, they never met or corresponded in this life, but looking at the pictures of father, son, and daughter, the imprint of RHB (Richard Bellamy) is unmistakable. "My great-grandfather, your great-great-grandfather, served in the Texas legislature representing Panola County." As he speaks, Toni pulls out a picture of the legislature from the 1870s and there he is, cold eyes and all. "I had to learn that it was just a part of my history, and I still don't like it, but I know where I come from and I want my children to know too."

We have a 150-year-old family reunion. Toni and Alan are in disbelief as they exchange knowing looks as they survey the Bellamys of Alabama. "She looks like Aunt . . ." The glances belie some deeper truths; there were probably other children fathered by white Bellamy men; there were a lot of "yellow niggers" running around, to use the racist parlance of antebellum times. Our black maternal roots were different but our white paternal roots were the same. Texas was, however, a different fate for descendants there.

Alan talks about relatives, my distant cousins in east Texas who made the best tamales and hot-water cornbread and chili and chicken-fried steak and barbecue. Both Alan and Toni are native African Texans drawing on the heritage that enriched Texas with okra, collard and turnip greens, black-eyed peas and other cowpeas, rice, watermelon, hot peppers and other spices, a variety of sweet potatoes, and other staples of the Afro-Creole culinary world that would became key in the vocabulary of Texas "eats." All the things my cousins enjoyed growing up—beans and rice, rice pudding, okra and tomatoes, gumbo, spicy stews, black-eyed-pea caviar, greens, fried poke salad, pickled okra, and watermelon rind—are all signs of the Africanizing presence of blacks in Texas cuisine. Our influence across the South conquered more territory than any Confederate army ever managed.

Heenan, every bit the patriarch, believed in male privilege and educating boys only, and his privilege won him some victories over the women in Richard Henry Bellamy's other life. Eventually Richard married Evalina, his double first cousin (that ridiculously odd fact bears repeating), to the distaste of his father. Written off, he lived his life in Alabama with his true love, herself widowed owing to the war. Hattie grew up partly as an employee and servant to her own father and lived around Evalina's faithful bodyservant Winter (named for the season he was born in) and his wife and Jack Vangue, one of the last Africans brought to America before the Civil War, a Kongo man delivered on the slave ship *Wanderer* in 1858. There were rumors of gifts from her father, like a deed to a house in Charleston, South Carolina, but whatever they might have been, they never really materialized.

Heenan enjoyed some rewards of being the son of the grocer and lawyer from Alabama, and when he was pressed to give up some of his inheritance to Evalina following Richard's death in 1909, he flatly told her to sod off. Hattie would grow up in relative poverty compared to Heenan and became the wife of Joseph Peter Todd the First, the little boy brought from Richmond, Virginia, the grandson of the Asante man of the Gold Coast who passed down from ear to ear, "You are Asante!" until it ended up in the memory of my cousin Vaddie, keeper of the Todd memories, vastly different bloodlines merged. Two black families grew apart over the next century and a half, finally meeting over Tex-Mex food in a crowded eatery in Austin, toasting to a reunion that was long overdue.

It didn't feel natural that over the course of three and a half decades of pondering race that I never considered that black families could be linked through white bodies. On my grandfather's paternal lineage, the mystery of Harry Townsend persisted. He said he was born in North Carolina, but records showed he was sold in Virginia. I guessed he came from somewhere near the border in one of the bright leaf-tobacco-growing counties that cling to I-95 and 85, the old familiar roads that lead me into Carolina.

A few years ago, a Harvard-educated genealogist, Shannon Christmas, heard me speaking on a podcast and invited me to do a cooking demonstration at his family reunion held on the plantation where his ancestors were enslaved in Warren County, North Carolina. I had to decline, but something pulled me, and I never forgot the invitation. Shannon and I became friends via social media, and one day, thanks to the DNA databases, he messaged me and established that we were connected through his paternal grandfather. He pressed me for details, but I already knew—our link was the mulatto or son of a mulatto, Harry.

Shannon is a leader in the genetic genealogy community, especially via African American genealogy. His bloodlines are ancient. Using triangulation—establishing firm genetic links by connecting multiple people to a common ancestor—Shannon is firm in his knowledge of his family's paternal British and western European roots and their maternal Efik and Igbo heritage. His voice is lyrical with clear, almost Shakespearean inflections and crispness.

Shannon told me a little bit about his family history. We were able to deduce a few things: we know our link is in Warren County, North Carolina, and it's probably through a European ancestor of British descent.

"What I can tell you about my family history is skewed in that very same vein. I can tell you more about my European ancestry than my African ancestry," Shannon told me. "The Christmases hailed from England, specifically Surrey County, and came to Virginia in the 1600s. They settled into southern Virginia and eventually came to Bute County, North Carolina, which later became known as what we know as Warren County before the time of the American Revolution, which cost them some lives. My direct ancestor, John Christmas Sr., was awarded for his participation with ten thousand acres of land in Orange County, North Carolina. His sons were established in what is now known as Warren County. His family helped found and ceded land to create the county seat, Warrenton, North Carolina. The Christmas family has been rooted in that part of North Carolina for quite some time.

"What we are not clear about is if our connection is with the Christmas family, the Davis family, Macons, Hawkinses," he went on. "Yes, that Hawkins—the same family as John Hawkins who helped the English beat the Spanish Armada and got Queen Elizabeth into the slave trade—and I'm one of his descendants. I only learned this through DNA. One of the sons of Philemon Hawkins and Mary Christmas fathered a child who became my great-great-great-grandmother Lucinda Davis in the early 1800s. Lucinda and Henry and her children were all slaves of Dr. Stephen Davis; it's very complicated. There are many African American families who are connected to other African Americans through European ancestors.

It vividly illustrates just how entrenched America was in the process of enslaving and the culture of slavery. Not just the business aspect of it, but kind of how there was a creolization process, if you will, that Europeans, Africans, and Native Americans were making a people who were unique and distinct from anyone else in world because of slavery. It brought people from all over the world into a very different context that had never taken place.

"These families don't make it into the official family trees through this process. An awareness emerges that America is a much more multicultural and multifaceted place than people realize. DNA is creating whole new types of intimate encounters that we discover, connections that were made during that time in American history. But you and I are certain on one thing—we are the common descendants of a white ancestor. It's wonderful we are finding our way back to the continent. But just as important is restoring the links interrupted when slavery sold human beings two or three times during their lifetimes."

If finding out those links wasn't enough, there was also the process of combing through the links to the white families. At first, I was asked to show my charts, which were hearsay without DNA. Then a stunning picture emerged. Lore bore out in scientific evidence of white absentee fathers and their legacies. It will take me years to flesh out all of the connections but thus far I have made contact with members of the Twitty, Mungo, Pate, Benton, Crowell, Hughes, and Bellamy families.

I am indeed a Twitty, but by a female ancestor who inherited the blood of the Twitty family patriarch, Peter Wynne. My direct male ancestor who took on the name had an African paternal root. I am indeed a Hughes and all arrows point to Spencer "Plenty" Hughes being free and a part of the Hughes family. I am a Hancock and a Bellamy. And yet there are so many more links—to overseers, men on slave ships, clandestine lovers—that I have not even scratched the surface in understanding the depth of my European American heritage.

One thing is for certain: Knowledge of white ancestors rewrote the script of my family's American geography. I had forefathers of European descent in Massachusetts Bay Colony (1622) and colonial New Jersey and eastern North Carolina (1674). My female W ancestor pushed my timeline in Virginia back to the beginnings of racial politics in American history. Bookers and Twittys went to Kentucky, Bellamy girls married into Mississippi planter aristocracies, and the Bradford kin of Richard Henry Bellamy by his maternal aunt were major slaveholders in Florida, with massive plantations full of enslaved Africans cultivating sugarcane, cotton, rice, and tobacco. The map of our early American journey and Southern heritage keeps getting larger as I gather more pieces of the puzzle.

I have often wondered whether the white people who know we are kin actually see us as family. It's critical for me to think about the possibilities of every Southern white family connected to African Americans on DNA tests truly reaching out and vice versa, to create a dialogue. Would we be better off if we embraced this complexity and dealt with our pain or shame? Would we finally be Americans or Southerners or both if we truly understood how impenetrably connected we actually are? Is it too late?

Maybe I'll just invite everybody to dinner one day and find out.

Beaten Biscuits

4 ½ cups all-purpose flour	a few small pinches of baking
½ tsp sugar	soda
1 tsp salt	2 tbsp lard or shortening
	2 cups cold water

Preheat the oven to 400 degrees. Mix all the dry ingredients. Cut the lard or shortening in the dry ingredients with a fork, a knife, or your fingers, and pour the water in bit by bit, making sure all of the dry mixture is moistened and incorporated. Knead together, work into a big ball of dough, and place on a flat, sturdy surface. The dough should be pounded with a hammer, solid rolling pin, mallet, or the back of an ax for 25 to 35 minutes, until the dough appears smooth and blisters. To form the biscuits, take the dough, pinch it up, and form it into a small ball. Pat it down and prick it in two or three rows with a fork. Bake the biscuits for 20 to 25 minutes or so or until golden brown.

8

0.01 PERCENT

As a society, we have gone from speculative genealogy veri-
fied only through written documents to genetic genealogy,
which, all truth be told, is still pretty speculative. However, we have a far more reliable means to trace our human journey
and individual genetic markers, we hope. The storm clouds of a new
surge in genealogy have gathered nicely. We love shows like *Who
Do You Think You Are?* and *Finding Your Roots* and *African American
Lives* for a reason—we are constantly reassessing ourselves as individuals, as families, and as a nation and human species. Scientists say
all humans are 99.99 percent genomically identical, but it's that tiny
0.01 percent difference that can be used to pick us apart by ethnicity
or race and biogeographical region. But how do you unscramble a
scrambled egg?

Because of this, genetic genealogy has tended toward the democratic. When it was a several-hundred-dollar investment for one direct-to-consumer DNA test for genealogy and genetic ancestry, you hardly heard anything about it. Now that tests can be obtained from any number of services for under $100, the cynicism and disputation is rampant. Most don't have to announce that this is interesting that most of the naysaying is done by the most genetically sequenced group, that global minority known as white people of northern and western European heritage. There is a dialogue between health and genetics that is constant and revealing—the need to make people healthy and healed led to genome sequencing and genetic testing, which now feeds another kind of wellness: the need to belong. And all of it is, in turn, being shaped by market forces and altruistic agendas.

Full confession: I am not dispassionate and unbiased. I didn't come to genetic genealogy services to be underwhelmed or go back to a vague appreciation of my heritage. I'm here to use a developing technology to sort out what has survived history in order to tease out a fuller understanding of my origins and my family's story. I am unapologetic about my enthusiasm, but I'm also cautious because I feel the need to protect the integrity of the history.

All I ever really wanted was a recipe of who I am and where I come from.

Sometime in the early 1990s, Sam Ford, a local reporter in Washington, DC, began exploring his heritage in a series of specials done for our local ABC affiliate Channel 7. In one story, Sam explored his Oklahoma roots, revealing his family's past as black folks who were enslaved by the Cherokee Nation. Sam's journeys also included a meetup with young biologist Dr. Rick Kittles, who as part of the African Burial Ground project and his own research on genetics and cancer had begun creating a database collected from continental Africans to which African Americans' paternal and maternal genetic markers were compared. Sam Ford was determined to be Yoruba, with close relatives living in the heart of Yoruba country in one of its densely populated cities.

From the time of my fourth-grade genealogy report, my family had given me some sense of who we thought we were. But that first report was shaky. I scribbled about twenty "tribal" names on a wide-ruled, torn sheet of notebook paper and prepared a ramshackle report based on my trying to keep up with my young genealogist uncle trying to explain all of his work to me in an hour. I spoke of Hottentots and Pygmies as if I was Dr. Livingstone himself charging through Darkest Africa. Who were they? What did they have to do with me?

When I was a kid, "African booty scratcher" was the worst thing a black child could say to another black child. Yes, black power, Swahili and *Roots* and, yes, Afrocentrism were right around the corner, and we were about to all be poor righteous teachers. None of that mattered. To be African was to be naked, dirty, covered in flies, and starving on TV. For the cost of a cup of coffee I was but little removed from the starving Ethiopians and beleaguered South Africans.

None of this really got to me. I wanted Africa. As far as I understood by way of my family history, we were West African, European (presumably British and Irish) and Native American (tradition said Creek, Choctaw, and Virginia Indian). There were occasional references to our eye shapes; I was often asked where the Asian was in my family. Our light-skinned relatives on every single branch of the tree were all the evidence we needed for white and Native American ancestors. We were a wide variety of types across the families of my four grandparents. It was as if we were a United Nations of black America.

There isn't much to tell between speculation and my first actual test because it was years before I could afford one. The first result, from Ancestry.com, was simple, thrilling, and slightly disappointing:

West African: 70%
British Isles: 28%
Undetermined: 2%

Yay! I'm black!

If this seems ridiculous to you, please consider that your external phenotypical features (i.e., skin complexion, nose shape, hair type) are not always a dead giveaway for your approximate ethnic origins. Many black people who took the DNA test were assigning different parts of their DNA to broader "racial" categories but were actually finding out just how European they were, and therefore not as easily connected to West and central Africa. Most African Americans average about 10 to 18 percent European admixture, and my results put me in the next bracket—a much smaller group for whom over a quarter of our roots were European. Still others, like Dr. Henry Louis Gates Jr., could claim 50 percent or more, even though neither of his parents were fully of European descent (read: "white").

Already embedded in our reaction to these tests was the notion of how much our women were presumed to have been taken advantage of. The other part was the desire, not so much for purity, but for a feeling of connection to the homeland. It is true: The more African in your overall ethnicity makeup, the easier it is to find African parts of your heritage using genetic genealogy. You're able to connect with people who have taken similar tests and understand how you fit in.

In the summer of 2013, I got a call from Gina Paige of African Ancestry. The growing success of the blog prompted the outreach. I was offered, as a professional courtesy, a maternal (mitochondrial DNA) and paternal (Y-DNA) test from African Ancestry in exchange for appearing in a social media video. I jumped at the chance and told Gina that I'd like to have the results read at an event I was doing at Stagville Plantation near Durham, North Carolina.

"Plantation?" Gina said it just like you think she did. Sounded out in disbelief. "Plan-taaay-shun."

"Okaaaaay. I've never been to a plantation before, so this would be the first time I ever reveal at one."

Stagville held in bondage over nine hundred people in its history. It was the largest plantation in North Carolina history. I want to reclaim my identity where it was taken from us.

Several weeks later I took the test at Am Kolel Sanctuary, a Jewish retreat center run by my friend and social justice activist, Rabbi David Shneyer. After he offered me a blessing, I scraped the insides of each cheek with long buccal cotton swabs, placed them in their respective envelopes, and dropped the sample in the mail. I had nothing to do but wait for six weeks . . . except go to Denmark.

René Redzepi, chef proprietor of the restaurant Noma in Copenhagen, invited me to speak at the 2013 MAD Symposium. He felt that my viral "Open Letter to Paula Deen" merited his program, titled "Guts." I spoke about culinary justice, about the lack of access to land, resources, seeds, and means to connect with one's heritage through food if you are among the American oppressed. The log sitting there as a podium saw my fist and palm several times. I preached a sermon as if I was a Gullah-Geechee descendant.

The day of the African Ancestry reveal, I had not slept for thirty-six hours. Making dinner for 150 people outside in the late summer in North Carolina using only nineteenth-century methods will do that to you. Right before dinner, once everybody had been assembled, the reveal occurred. I was beyond exhausted and ready to collapse, but the nervous energy gave me just enough adrenaline to pump me up.

"Your maternal ancestry comes from a small country right on the coast. . . ."

I could barely contain myself. Miss Josie, sorry; Hester, sorry; Nora, sorry . . . you were not white women. You were not Irish, you were from a woman with ancient roots in Africa.

"This country is known for growing rice and that's why so many Africans were brought to this country to grow it."

One week ago I was talking about rice. My third great-grandmother was born in Charleston. She lived in South Carolina for several years before being sold into Alabama.

"It gives me great pleasure to tell you your maternal ancestry (L2a11a) is among the Mende people of Sierra Leone." My mind immediately retraced her history from a village in southeastern Sierra Leone to capture to Bunce Island in the Sierra Leone River to shackling in Sullivan's Island in Charleston Harbor, South Carolina. Within seconds, the combination of historical obsession and genetic hints and oral history led to a narrative my family had been largely denied for over two centuries.

My paternal ancestry was from Ghana and classified as E1b1a, which is one of several common haplogroups (genetic mutations) for African American men. It's found in high frequencies with both the neighboring Akan and Ewe peoples. I lucked out in some ways. About 30 percent of African Americans end up with a European haplogroup barring a lineage from any sort of African discoveries. Just when I wanted to pass out and never wake up until I was damned well good and ready, I wanted to go to an archive and look up statistics from the slave trade, as if that wasn't what I had been doing for years on end. This paternal ancestry test only analyzed my Y chromosome—every male inherits an exact copy of his father's Y chromosome, and he in turns inherits it from his father, his father, and all direct forefathers going back thousands of years. There was so much more to learn.

My goal became consistency. After a lifetime of being fascinated by what different people around the world ate, I wanted to know everything I could about the food of the populations with whom I shared genetic affinity. I was looking for some part of the Southern story, the Southern food story in my body. To satisfy the naysayers I had to be able to demonstrate that my results were believable and realistic. I want to be clear: my dream was to be able to put myself in the evolving narrative of Southern food from its beginnings to now, and to do so I had to be able to do what most African Americans had the most difficulty doing—trace my ancestry to Africa and follow the lineages across the Southern map into the present day.

From service to service, my DNA results were fairly consistent. To decode what genetic services do is complicated business, but here's the simplest version I could wrap my head around. Each of us is a card shuffle of genes. Some are from far back in our origins and others are closer in genealogical time. Genealogical time refers to the past few hundred years, when it might be possible to document the facts and figures of our family histories, or be reliably related to someone else who took the DNA test.

The commercials and advertisements make matters simpler than they are. People have affinities with different populations around the world. They can be identified or inferred by descent or by population. When we take into account oral history, the histories of regions, and social processes, the narrative gets more complicated, but in some cases it makes sense out of what we might consider a bizarre or untenable result. For example, many Latin Americans are surprised they have Middle Eastern ancestry, but given that Spain was part of the Islamic world for almost a millennium and people with Middle Eastern ancestry traveled to Latin America, et cetera, it makes complete sense.

For African Americans, it would be lovely to be able to say I am this ethnicity or that ethnicity. Problem 1: There are more than two thousand distinct ethnic groups in Africa. Good news: Many of them cluster with others with which they are close in language, culture, and biogeography. Bad news: Many haplogroups are not ethnic specific but are shared among many different peoples, and you can share genomic similarities with more than one population on a direct line.

Problem 2: Samples for these populations have not been taken significantly enough to ensure that comparisons are accurate enough to establish definite genetic affinities. Good news: The transatlantic slave trade didn't take two-thousand-plus ethnic groups into slavery. For the Americas it was likely only about fifty to one hundred, and many of these have or are being targeted for genetic sampling. Bad news: The databases are not consistent from company to company.

Problem 3: Nobody actually agrees on who has the answer for African Americans looking for their genetic roots. Good news: Well, you can shop around and if you keep hearing consistent or corroborating DNA results, then you can be more confident in your results. Bad news corollary: DNA testing is slowly getting cheaper (even full genomic sequencing will soon be below $1,000) and it's always political.

For some of my friends, African Ancestry, with its large database targeted at African Americans searching for their heritage, is the answer. I have been pleased with their work, but I have also weighed my results against historical data and any results from other companies. For others, African Ancestry is not the way to go, and they prefer getting results with more commercial DNA testing services and comparing their results with contemporary Africans with whom they match—or have a confirmed genetic relationship that can be proven in relative genealogical time. For some, having a person who is 100 percent African test with a high probability of being related is the only way to be sure that you share a genetic heritage and have thus found your way back to the motherland.

Not all DNA testing services have been equally beneficial for African Americans. Only now, as the African American genealogy community is clamoring for answers, are some companies amping up their database to provide closer resolution hints at where a particular African American's multiple ancestral roots derive. In the case of African Ancestry, it hopes to be able to combine its specificity with the multiple results offered by companies like AncestryDNA, which express ethnicity affinities not in ethnic groups but in geographic blocs of sub-Saharan Africa. My attitude thus far has been fairly unscientific but politely skeptical—consistency with what we know about the slave trade, what is in my oral history, what we know about the history of slavery in the South, and documented historical evidence and genealogical material are what matter. The tests are nothing but a tool—and sometimes tools don't work or are not the right tool for the job.

My solution going forward became context, context, context. If I wanted to live with a permanent shrug I could have done that for free. Why bother? And yet I wanted to have a plausible explanation for the stories that were passed down and the connections I felt in my bones. This is not all in the hands of science, nor has it ever been, or will be. My truth comes out of a fascination with the sociocultural mechanics of how African America was born.

When you get your test done, your DNA sample is placed on a microarray chip, and several hundreds of thousands of ancestry-informative genetic markers (aka single nucleotide polymorphisms, or SNPs) are analyzed in order to give you what that particular testing company considers its most accurate result according to their computing algorithms and proprietary methodologies. Sometimes that erases or negates small amounts of DNA that may actually be there, and other times results may have off-the-wall conclusions we like to call "noise." Good example: Someone who is just about 100 percent demonstrably northern European who is less than 1 percent Melanesian. Not likely. However, you can be part Native, and because it's a small sample that made it into your genomic profile, the algorithm can also throw it out. You aren't getting an exact recipe for who you are, you are getting a give-or-take average version of who you "are."

You should also know many commercial personal genome services offer three types of test. The first test is known as an autosomal DNA test, and is the one you are probably most familiar with now. This test looks at your twenty-three chromosome pairs to determine the DNA you inherited from both parents, and includes an estimate of your ethnicity broken down into percentages, and matches you to real genetic relatives with some sharing a common ancestor with you in the time frame of the transatlantic slave trade. The second test, for maternal ancestry, is scientifically known as the mitochondrial DNA test; this test looks at your cells' mitochondrias' genetic code to determine your ancient maternal ancestry; you inherited your mitochondrial DNA exclusively from your mother and her direct foremothers going back thousands of years to a common ancestral mother; the test is thus used to determine your maternal haplogroup. The third, paternal ancestry test is scientifically known as the Y-chromosome DNA (Y-DNA) test; this one is only available to males and looks at his Y chromosome to determine his ancient paternal lineage via his father and direct forefathers going back tens of thousands of years to a common ancestral father, which in turn is used to establish a paternal haplogroup. Some services offer all three tests for one price, and others offer them separately.

Another issue is that you have to test as many relatives in your direct bloodline as it takes to be sure of how the puzzle fits together. This, you can imagine, gets very expensive very fast. Every one of us is a mashup of our parents, and they are mashups of theirs, and so on. We double in ancestors with each successive generation. What I very unscientifically call your "surface DNA" doesn't always have all the parts and pieces from your genetic past. Some are more forward, some lurk in the background, and others just aren't there. If you're African American, you can reflect literally dozens of ethnic groups from across one to four continents and yet not have much clarity on your origins.

African Americans do have a higher incidence of Native American blood than white Americans, and yet there isn't quite as much Native blood among African Americans as family lore suggests. It's still there, but it's more complicated than anyone ever let on—direct Native ancestors are not, say, as common as those who are partially Native. There are also Asian and Polynesian elements in African American DNA that come as a surprise. Sometimes people think of Native ancestry codes as Asian, but oftentimes these results stem from the small but culturally and genetically significant population brought from Madagascar between the nineteenth and eighteenth centuries, or the Chinese who worked the Transcontinental Railroad in the nineteenth century.

Not all European ancestry was from the usual suspects of England, Ireland, the Netherlands, France, Portugal, and Spain. DNA testing has illuminated the presence of German, Italian, and other ethnic groups we don't usually associate with slavery in the context of ownership and the sexual politics of enslavement. Some find Ashkenazi Jewish and Middle Eastern, which might imply Sephardic Jewish people hiding as Christians (Iberian conversos). Not all white male ancestors were slaveholders—some were travelers, some were sailors on slave ships, others were clandestine lovers. White female ancestors, like my Virginia grandmother's direct maternal ancestor, are extremely rare, to the tune of one to three percent; and true to context they are typically found in places like the Chesapeake Bay area where American slavery had a seventeenth-century genesis with vague racial boundaries.

At the end of the day you have to really want to know your origin story, not only to get into this type of genealogy, but to have a sustained patience for where it will lead you. On the other hand, my practice sits at the crossroads of feeling the experience to your core and a lust for specificity and depth. We live at a time when our ways of knowing have gotten significantly more powerful than ever before. Twenty years ago someone like me couldn't even have dreamed of knowing what we know now, and I hope to be able to correct what I know over and over as the details get refined. I have no desire to be perfectly right. I just love the journey.

Ancestry.Com's AncestryDNA updated results arrived next.

> African 71%
>   Ghana 32%, Congo-Cameroon 19%, Nigeria 8%,
>   Senegal 7%, Benin/Togo 2%, and <1% each of African
>   hunter-gatherers, Mali and southeastern Bantu [*no
>   shit . . .*]
>   European roughly 28%
>   Scandinavia 14%, Iberian 4%, eastern European 3%,
>   western European 3%. Ireland 2%, and Great Britain
>   <1% [remember the last version of this test assigned all
>   of my European DNA to the British Isles]
>   [*Wow, no wonder I felt that link with Scandinavia when I
>   was younger and still do. Damn.*]
> Middle Eastern <1% [Middle Eastern, *hmmm that's cool.*]

Then came the 23andMe results:

> Neanderthal variants 1.3%. [*Hot damn I'm part
>   caveman. . . .*]

Maternal haplogroup: L2a11a [African haplogroup, 55,000 years old, 20% of all African American folks; it is one of several L2 subclades shared among Mende women]

Paternal haplogroup: E1b1a8a [African haplogroup, 20,000 years old; E1b1a is one of the most common for African American men, with 97% frequency among the Ewe]

Sub-Saharan African 69.2%

West African 64.3%, central and southern African 1.9%, and broadly sub-Saharan African 2.9%

European 28.9%

British and Irish 9.7%, Scandinavian 0.9% [remember AncestryDNA gave me 14%], broadly northern European 12.6%, Italian 0.4%, broadly southern European 0.7%

East Asian and Native American 1.3%

Native American 0.7%, Southeast Asian 0.4%, broadly East Asian 0.2% [*Should I be worried about my family's Native American stories?*]

Unassigned 0.7%

Then I transferred my 23andMe raw data file to another personal genome service, Family Tree DNA:

African 69%—West African 67%, south and central African 2%

European 30%—west and central Europe 27%, Finland 3%

How in the living hell did I get so many consistent results from Finland? So I'm still pretty much African and European, but I'm still pretty convinced I'm part Native American . . . I think.

23andMe did what AncestryDNA did not—it assigned me Native American and Southeast Asian ancestry, and according to the most conservative reading of their results, it's still in there. According to my friend, burgeoning genetic genealogist and blogger Terence L. Dixon, "A long segment on chromosome 16 means, yes, at least one parent contributed a Native American DNA segment to you, and thus indicates at least one past Native American ancestor, someone who probably lived in the early to mid-eighteenth century, and by my best guess, according to what you've told me, they were probably in Virginia or the Carolinas. Or both. However the Southeast Asian and Polynesian—along with southeast African Bantu—affinities in your genome point us in the direction of Madagascar."

Mr. Dixon provided further insightful ingredients to my admixture results from AncestryDNA and 23andMe as follows:

"23andMe found 0.7 percent (+/–) of your genomic markers are similar to Native Americans. While this may sound like a small amount or statistical noise, a scientific study using 23andMe customer data found that African Americans have an average of 0.8 percent Native American admixture. On your chromosome painting there are Native American segments, located on chromosomes 5 and 16, with the latter representing a prominent singular segment. Both are adjacent to European segments, and this likely means your Native American ancestor(s) was (were) mixed with them, which means you're looking at a fourth- to sixth-great-grandparent (think early to mid-1700s) who had more significant amounts of Native American admixture, and who may have identified with a particular ethnic group or tribe. Of course the Native American segment on chromosome 5 could be separate—as in from the other parent. You also have a small amount of East Asian at less than 1 percent near your significant Native American segment on chromosome 16. In many 23andMe customers, I observe when there is a showing of Native American admixture, they also typically score East Asian at less than 1 percent. You could add this to your Native American total." TL is right; sometimes Native American ancestry codes as Asian in DNA results. We do however have actual Asian blood in us in some cases.

"There is also a smaller Southeast Asian component at 0.4 percent, but this is separate from your Native American admixture. It is found as small segments on your chromosomes 1, 8, 16, 19, and 23 (known as the X chromosome). On chromosome 16 it is opposite the Native American segment, meaning it comes from the parent who did not give you Native American. Notably you have Southeast Asian on your X chromosome, which you inherited from your mother. This basically confirms that some of the Southeast Asian is at least from one of your maternal grandparents or paternal grandmother.

"Southeast Asian ancestry shows at the most conservative confidence levels on 23andMe. Because your Southeast Asian is adjacent to your African segments, it likely indicates a Malagasy ancestor or two in your past, and likely from your ancestors from Virginia. The Madagascar population is roughly a fifty-fifty admixture of Indonesian from Island Southeast Asia (Borneo) and Bantu from southeast Africa, but this also has variations. Although the few thousand Malagasy purportedly brought to the Americas have appeared in historical records, I speculate many Malagasy were considered Negro especially if they looked more black than Asian. Some Malagasy belonged to free people of color communities and may have been described as 'mulatto' on historical records. Thanks to genetic genealogy and DNA testing, we now know Madagascar ancestry in African Americans is the newest admixture that was hiding in plain sight."

I'll buy that somewhere, either from Europe or from West Africa, there was a smidgen of Middle Eastern ancestry too. I'm thrilled not to be boring, and with each new group I am traveling the globe in my mind's eye, meeting new ancestors experiencing world history all over again. A little part of me was on a Viking ship, or in the tundra, or running through the streets of ancient Rome, or living in the world's first cities in the Fertile Crescent and smelting its first iron in Africa, and even in an outrigger canoe headed east across the Indian Ocean, and for a historian this is glorious. For a cook it's beyond moving. My sense of family has expanded, but so has my notion of my soul foods and heritage cooking.

Most of my European blood filtered through the British Isles, but we are painfully unaware in America just how genetically diverse those islands were due to migration, trade, and war. For example, Scandinavian ancestry wasn't equally distributed during the time of the Viking raids; they can be found all over but are more concentrated in the East Midlands. While it is still speculation, if my European genetic diversity is mostly British (I don't believe it all is), then knowing this can give me hints as to where people came from and why. Scotland has the highest incidence of Finnish and northwestern Russian genes; it's possible that the recurring Finnish ancestry could have come through Scottish ancestors, and perhaps my indentured servant grandmother was from Scotland. Wales has the highest incidence of Iberian ancestry in the United Kingdom, rivaling a similar number in the east of England, which has the highest Italian and French and German ancestry.

Dixon tells me, "From a biogeographical (the regions where your ancestors lived) perspective, you share a genetic relationship with people who share the same genetic ancestry as you, meaning it is likely some of your ancestors originate from these populations who now live in modern-day nations. However keep in mind human migration and mixing is fluid, so some of your genetic match's countries/regions of origin may reflect migrations to and from other regions, as gene flow can be continuous or intermittent. Moreover we often descend from numerous ancestral pedigrees and have inherited DNA contributions from multiple biogeographical populations, often challenging our perceptions, preconceived notions, and social constructs about our ethnic, cultural, racial, and genetic identities. DNA can also contradict even the best paper trails. No two dishes are exactly alike."

In order to be clear about where I came from, I had to run my maternal uncle and paternal grandfather through Ancestry.com and then later upload them to Family Tree DNA for further perspective:

My grandfather, born of South Carolinians, who mostly arrived and stayed in South Carolina, was a great test case. He is also my only living grandparent at ninety-eight years old, and he's only two generations removed from slavery. He was largely Congo at 31 percent, with the second-largest portion of DNA coming from Benin at 20 percent, followed by Ghana and Mali at 7 percent each, Nigeria at 6 percent, Senegal at 5 percent, and southeast Bantu at 2 percent. My grandfather's DNA covered the entire map of the transatlantic slave trade to South Carolina. His European DNA was largely Irish at 12 percent, British at 7 percent, and Italian at 1 percent. Levi Pate's Italian roots had shown through. My grandfather turned out to have a living cousin from the Serer ethnic group in Senegal.

My grandfather did not have any Native ancestry according to any test, so it became unlikely that he was the source of my Native American DNA. He did have trace elements of central Asian DNA, which was interesting to ponder, or it might just be noise. Family Tree DNA posited his ancestry as 74 percent West African, 2 percent south-central African, and 2 percent east African; 17 percent British Isles, 2 percent west-central Europe, and 2 percent southern Europe. What his DNA told me is that we've been in South Carolina a very long time, and our family history was intimately tied to its distinct history as a colony and a state.

South Carolina's slave trade with Africa was mostly active in the eighteenth century. Putting everything I knew about my grandfather's genetic heritage together, it became clear his ancestors were likely arriving in significant blocs from the Kongo from the period of 1720 onward to midcentury, when their numbers were tempered. His Sierra Leone and Senegambian connections likely entered from 1750 to 1775 as that was the highest point for those importations. Finally his Ghanaian, Gbe, Mozambican, and east African connections would have arrived during slavery's last gasp between the end of the Revolution and the early nineteenth century, when importations were rushed to meet demands before the trade was closed in 1808.

It became clear looking at all of the different results, and calculating generations and arrivals, that there was no one arrival, and only a very few African Americans would have that narrative anyway. My people came to America from the seventeenth century to the days of the closing doors of the transatlantic slave trade. Questions of identity and culture were not settled until after the Civil War, for we were still an evolving people, though by 1820 almost all of us as African American people were here for good. It took about seventy years—a contemporary average human life span for black America—to go from more native-born than imported to almost completely permanently living in or born in America.

My maternal uncle is heavily European. He was the only one of my mother's brothers who didn't have a hard time growing an Afro. Africa clustered in him, but he was still showing only 54 percent African ancestry, and his father's lineage through Harry Townsend turned out to western European (which turned out to be averaged to 24 percent of his total genetic makeup), ultimately going back to somewhere in the borderlands of France, Germany, and Switzerland. Given my maternal grandmother's roots among the Hughes, Bellamy, and Hancock families, among others, it came as no surprise that my uncle showed notable Irish and Scandinavian roots, with smatterings of Finnish and Iberian blood as well. Family Tree DNA assigned him the same amount of European ancestry and, according to their algorithm, it amounted to 43 percent western European and 3 percent Finnish.

My uncle's remaining heritage was squarely African with the largest cluster going to Nigeria at 17 percent, with Family Tree DNA centering his roots on West Africa at 51 percent with 3 percent coming from south-central Africa, and a map not so subtly hovering over Nigeria. Because AncestryDNA combines Cameroon and Congo (16 percent), and because Cameroon is next to eastern Nigeria, I surmised that many of my uncle's ancestors were from the Igbo and their neighbors, much as Shannon Christmas counted several matches among his kin. I also believe that like most African Americans, we have central African ancestry (and he has two white cousins named Mozingo, the descendants of an enslaved Angolan from the Mbundu people), so I can't totally say it's one way or the other. Sierra Leone and Ghana (12 percent) made their appearances with numbers pointing in the direction of the Akan and Mende, and some ancestry from Senegambia (5 percent). Apart from my South Carolina connection through Hettie, most of my uncle's ancestors came through the colonial Chesapeake, and to that end they reflected a much more Virginia and North Carolina Tidewater set of African origins.

While no direct relatives from Africa were located on Ancestry to date for my uncle, it is interesting that he shares affinities with several ethnic Igbo on GEDmatch, a free admixture utility that compares your DNA raw data files to genetic relatives from all three testing companies (23andMe, AncestryDNA, and Family Tree DNA). We identified at least one gentleman who traced his ancestry back to the Igbo living in Imo state. Across all platforms

I found that, relative to the slave trade, the statistics from database test results backed up white preferences for workers and patterns of importation unique to distinct areas of the slave trade. Other Igbo relatives matched me on my father's mother's side, which had been in Virginia since the seventeenth century.

There was also the matching across the different tests that suggested kinship and connection across the Diaspora. According to my distant cousin and genealogist Hasani Carter, my results also showed relatives in Jamaica (where most of the black population has roots in Ghana); among Americo-Liberians; and I had African cousin matches, both from Ghana, one Akan and the other of the Ewe ethnic group. When all the African Ancestry tests for available bloodlines were in, this was the result:

Maternal grandmother/maternal: Sierra Leone, Mende/
    South Carolina
Maternal grandmother/paternal: Ghana, Akan (Ashanti/
    Asante by oral tradition)/Virginia
Maternal grandfather/maternal: Ghana, Akan; Virginia or
    North Carolina
Maternal grandfather/paternal: western Europe,
    haplogroup R/Virginia or North Carolina
Paternal grandfather/paternal: Ghana, Akan/Ewe/South
    Carolina
Paternal grandfather/maternal: Guinea-Bissau/Sierra
    Leone Fula, Temne/South Carolina
Paternal grandmother/maternal: Europe, haplogroup W
    (Finland via Scotland?)/Virginia

This is my new truth. Robert Sietsema, formerly the food critic of the *Village Voice*, upon meeting me for the first time, said to me, "Your people are from Ghana." I hadn't told him one story yet. I asked how he knew. "I've seen your face there." I show people pictures of my late paternal grandmother. Nigerians go wild; within seconds they all say she is Igbo. "This woman looks like ladies from my family; she is Igbo without a doubt."

Cooking from a place of heritage, identity, and belonging is a powerful thing fraught with class and cultural politics. The first debate is about authority. The second debate is about authenticity and who is representing what and why. The third is usually about ownership. The fourth, but not the last, is usually audience.

Once upon a time I was just black or brown; you pick the color designation. I was an orphan of the West, the descendant of unwitting and unwilling Americans. Soul food was just that—for a sad people with amnesia and massive Stockholm syndrome trying to cook their way to some semblance of self-understanding and truth. Everything we tried to do was a poor imitation or with faulty memory; nothing was taken on its own merit, left to its own context. No, we were messy and inferior and confused.

And now I know I am not that. I am an obsessive cook with compulsive genealogist tendencies who can point to a map of Africa, Europe, North America, and with it, the South, and guide you on trade winds to tidal creeks leading to ports, leading to roads and to plantations and more roads and more plantations to cities. It's exhausting but necessary. "Who are you and what does the plate of food you put before me communicate to us who you are?" We've all heard the question.

My answer is plain: my food is my flag.

9

SWEET TOOTH

In 1947, when my father was seven years old, my grandfather took him to the Deep South for the first time, to Lancaster, South Carolina, the home of the Twittys since the time of slavery. Daddy wandered into a store attached to a gas station, and as his father pumped, he eyed a jar of candy and asked the white man behind the counter, "Sir, how much is your candy?"

"What did you say to me, nigger?" The white man's voice was loud and strident.

My father had never been called a nigger before. My grandfather, hearing the commotion, walked in and stood at the door.

"Sir, how much is your candy?" Daddy didn't know what to do other than repeat himself.

The white man slammed his fist down on the counter, knocked the big jar of candy over, and charged at my father.

"Now you listen here, boy, you teach your little nigger that down here

the proper way to talk to a white man is 'yassuh.' You hear that, little nigger? Yassuh!"

My grandfather grabbed my father and threw him in the back of the car and sped away to the old farm. My grandfather never really explained to him what happened or why it happened or why the man was so mean. I have heard my father tell this story ten times, and not once does he become emotional, but I do. I cannot imagine someone belittling my father. He was a Marine, he served in Vietnam, he fought under the orders of the commander-in-chief, he was born here and his family had been here since the beginning of this country, but to that bastard in 1947 South Carolina, he was just a "little nigger," destined to become nothing and from whom nothing good would come. I wish there really were time machines.

Candy is the daughter of sugar. It all goes back to a man in New Guinea, or maybe it was a woman, since women were humanity's earliest gardeners and some of its primary farmers. Someone was thirsty and cracked a piece of *Saccharum officinarum* open to slake their thirst, and they got more than they bargained for. It wasn't just liquid, it was the rarest and most special taste in nature. It was quick energy. It was divine. Sugar became part of the genealogy of the tribes of New Guinea, and in one legend, a man having relations with sugarcane begat the rest of humanity. About ten thousand years ago, in some small, dark way, the discovery of humanity's most treasured taste sowed the seeds for my American experience. Without the impulse to find new lands for which to expand the production of sugar, among other interests, there might not have been a transatlantic slave trade.

Sugar bounced across the Eastern Hemisphere. In common knowledge, we massively underestimate the importance of this one crop to the history of race, food, and power. To scholars of food, race, and economics, the work of Sidney Mintz, among others, is a powerful indictment of the way in which taste can become political and sway the stories of nations. Human intervention took sugar-cane from New Guinea to Southeast Asia, from there to India, where it acquired its Indo-European names, owing their existence to *sharkara*, the Sanskrit word brought to us through Persian, through Arabic, through medieval Latin, originally meaning "gravel." From India, to Persia, to the Muslim world, to medieval Europe, where it was as much medicine as confectionary.

As sugar gained popularity, it was grown in the eastern Mediterranean and Egypt, bouncing from Cyprus to Crete, to Sicily, to the Iberian Peninsula, to the Canaries and Madeira, and later to the islands off the coast of Africa. Drawing on models left behind by the Roman *latifundia*, the idea and cultural presence of the plantation was born in the Mediterranean basin. These plantations were worked by a number of "slaves," a word most people are familiar with that may be traced to the word "Slav," of the ethnic-linguistic nations of eastern Europe. Slavs weren't black, but the workers on these early sugar plantations were often a mixture of Slavs, Africans, Middle Easterners, and local peasants. Slavery did not yet have a racial context.

Sugar diffused among Africans as not much more than a snack plant. Meanwhile, the proliferation of beverages that demanded sugar, and the greater democratization of sugar's availability, and its naturally addictive nature meant bad news for my ancestors and many, many more. According to some estimates, about 80 percent of all captives brought to the Americas were brought to regions where sugarcane was the main cash crop. No sugar, no slavery.

Sugar was by no means the only reason slavery began to grow and proliferate. It is spectacular, though, from the viewpoint of a descendant of the enslaved brought because of its power, that the black journey in the Americas is founded on a human sense—the sense of taste. Slavery began with food. We must not forget cacao, coffee, rice, arrowroot, peanuts, corn, wheat, spices, and the other food that slavery in the Americas (as well as the Indian Ocean islands off the coast of Africa) produced—all feeding a particularly powerful need to consume between the sixteenth and nineteenth centuries, continuing into the twentieth with the legacy of colonialism, down to banana republics, pineapple plantations, and the politics of keeping white, Western consumers satisfied.

After consulting with scholar Lorena Walsh, I came to the conclusion that at least some of my ancestors might have originally been brought to the Caribbean for a few months or a few weeks—depending on the time of "seasoning." Although the majority of enslaved Africans brought to North America were direct importations, seasoning and stops in the Caribbean before disembarking in North America did happen with relative frequency, particularly in the earlier years of the trade. It's highly possible that my kin saw a cane field long before they saw a tobacco or rice field. Seasoning—forcing the exiled Africans to yield to the whip, understand their lot in life as inferior chattel, and accustom themselves to the grueling pace of labor on an American plantation—was brutal. Most Africans brought to the sugarcane regions did not live past seven years to a decade; hence, the trade to these areas hugely outnumbered that in Africans brought to mainland North America. The need to replenish the labor and keep the population going meant massive upheaval in West and central Africa.

In the Caribbean and South America, beginning in 1502, an engagement with sugar and the enslavement of Africans led to waves of forced immigrants having to adapt themselves to the New World. On the islands, all of the patterns that would become manifest in mainland North America came to life in the sugar lands. Enslaved Africans engaged with indigenous populations and poor whites, many of them of Irish extraction, even as they had to contend with differences among themselves. Maroon settlements were created in the wilderness by formerly enslaved people taking their own freedom and forming societies on the margins against the plantation system. An in-between class of mixed enslaved people born predominately of European men taking advantage of their power over African women, and an evolving Afro-Creole culture made up of early, middle, and late arrivals.

Because of the similarities in climate, sugarcane was not the only crop to travel from the Old World to the New. Bananas (a word from the Wolof language of Senegambia) and plantains traveled from Africa aboard slave ships, leaving their secondary home after diffusing thousands of years before from Asia via the monsoon exchange. There would be no fried plantains or banana republics to speak of if it weren't for the slave trade dispersing these staples across Latin America. To the Caribbean and South America also came okra, kola (brought originally to make the water on slave ships more palatable), millet, sorghum (Guinea corn), several varieties of yams, cowpeas, watermelon, tamarind, hibiscus or sorrel (also known as "jamaica"), pigeon peas (Angola peas or *guandules*), oil palm (known as *dende* in Brazil, from Kimbundu *ndende*), and sesame. Many of these would later bounce northward on the same slave ships delivering the "leftover" human cargo, or seasoned Africans, to settlements in the colonial Southeast.

To know there is an archipelago of West and central African culinary influence beginning with the diffusion of crops across the Atlantic basin is only as important as the human story it tells. My own DNA results reflect cousin matches from across the black Caribbean and Latin America. I don't know why I was surprised, but I was. To call each other brother and sister was previously an act of ceremonial Pan-Africanism. Now it was official. I had relative matches from Brazil, the Bahamas, Barbados, Bermuda, Cuba, the

Dominican Republic, Haiti, Guyana, Jamaica, St. Lucia, St. Vincent, and Trinidad and Tobago.

Some of these matches could be noise. But more than once, matches from specific countries came up again and again across different tests. Here it was, in front of my face: I was connected to some of these people because we represented families going back millennia in West and central Africa, split apart by the might of sugar. Some of us were split apart at the factories on the coast, others of us split apart during seasoning, others split by the separation of relatives as loyalist planters fled to the Caribbean after the American Revolution—all and any of these possibilities remain open. In one case, a woman with all four grandparents born in Haiti shared kinship with my paternal grandfather. Because he has unusually high genetic affinities with people living in Benin, a country not particularly important to the North American trade, this was striking to me, because it was a major source of enslaved people for Haiti like nowhere else in the New World. I can't help but wonder if our connection to this Haitian family represents siblings or other close relatives separated in the dungeons of Ouidah, the second most prolific port for the exportation of Africans to the Americas during the period (to the tune of one million human beings), with one person going to Port-au-Prince and the other going to Charleston.

THE CARIBBEAN KISS

Although it has been suggested by some culinary historians that the South owes a debt to the Caribbean for bean-and-rice dishes, this suggestion is tenuous at best. Most of the rice-and-bean or rice-and-pea dishes (hoppin' john, jambalaya *au congri*) in the South are essentially African in origin and arrived directly to New Orleans, Charleston, and Savannah via the trade in Senegambians for whom these dishes were staples. What is more likely to be true is that similar ethnic blocs arriving in different parts of the Americas brought with them similar foods. In Virginia and Louisiana, Africans from what is now southern Nigeria introduced black-eyed peas fried into cakes or fried into balls and eaten as a snack. In Brazil, a similar tradition, much closer to the source, emerged with the frying of black-eyed-pea fritters known in Brazilian Creole as *acarajé* fried in *dende* or palm oil. Africans from Kongo-Angola called their mush *infundi*, which cooked with okra became *funji* in Barbados, Antigua, and Barbuda and the Virgin Islands, and is also known by its Senegambian name *cou-cou* in the same places. Enslaved people picked and cooked the fruit of the ackee tree in Jamaica as they had in Ghana, along with a wide variety of tropical fruits they had known in the continent—a luxury their cousins in North America would not really know. Conversely, besides callaloo (a stew made from okra and water spinach) and a few other dishes like *couve* (collards that accompany the Brazilian national dish feijoada), there was a general lack of greens such as those known in the American South. Like their counterparts in the Caribbean, enslaved Africans in North America would make okra soup, oxtails, and pepper-pot soup and sell them on the street and at market along with fritters.

Beyond all of these connections was the presence of the black cook in shaping the eating habits of whites living in the islands. Clearly outnumbered, enslaved Africans instructed in British and French cuisines nonetheless had to rely on local ingredients and the know-how of Africans, and often grew up as charges of African women. Lady Nugent, a white visitor chronicling her time in Jamaica, spoke of eating fish, fried conch, ginger sweetmeats, jerked or "barbecued" hog dressed in the manner of "the maroons," a black crab pepper pot that included okra and hot peppers (likely Scotch bonnets), turtle soup, mutton, duck, turkey, chicken, tongue, ham, chicken, crab patties, and so much food that when the sweets and fruit arrived she said she felt "sicker than usual." Plantains, coconuts, parrot soup, yams, and allspice assaulted her senses; "It was all astonishing as it was disgusting."

Slaveholder Thomas Thistlewood left ample records not only of his own exploits with the women he assaulted on his Jamaica plantation in the eighteenth century, but also of the life and culinary traditions of his enslaved chattel, having been introduced to the ways of Jamaican food by the cook named Phibbah when he lived on the Vineyard Pen estate. His writings are a bizarre and disturbing look at slavery in the sugar islands, but despite the dark and uncomfortable nature of the text, we learn a lot about what made the cooking of the enslaved in the Caribbean distinct. The African Jamaicans he knew were Twi-speaking Akan from Ghana, Igbos from Nigeria, Mandings from Senegambia, and Kongo-Angolans. Consider "*duckanoo*" taken from the Gold Coast, *dokono*, a bit of plantain, green banana, or sweet potato wrapped in leaves and boiled or baked.

The Gold Coast supplied the second largest number of Africans to Jamaica. *Fufu*-like dishes like *tum-tum*, taken from the sound of the long pestle hitting the mortar, made of boiled plantains and fish, make it into his writings, as does the esteemed pepper pot that was popularized by black women hawking it on the streets of colonial and nineteenth-century Philadelphia. In the "provision grounds" (and to this day, food is still called "provision" in the Caribbean) his enslaved workforce grew sweet potatoes and cassava, muskmelons and watermelons. Cassava was a particularly important food used for making *bammy*, or cassava bread, and *tum-tum*. Well known in central Africa, having replaced millet and sorghum as a staple, cassava "badly prepared" led Thistlewood to have "whipped Mirtilla and Nanny" for making themselves sick by eating it. Meticulous about his enslaved workforce's feeding upon saltfish (shad, herring, mackerel, and cod) and scraps, he noted sumptuous meals of roast pork with pawpaw sauce, stewed crabs, oranges and shaddock, shrimp, stewed snook, roast turkey, French brandy, boiled pudding, and cheese for himself.

The islands were very different from what was to come on the mainland. The enslaved black folks there were living in a world of imported rice, hilly garden grounds with Angola peas, peanuts, breadfruit trees and mangoes, and occasional feasts of flying fish. It was the enslaved of the cane plantations who brought peeled sweet potatoes to the sugar boiling house, and dolloping molten hot syrup and skimmings on top of them may well have started the candied sweet potato craze.

In mainland North America there were, to be certain, touches of the Afro-Caribbean, most of them in the colonial and antebellum North. Whether it was master chefs and catering dynasties of Haitian origin in Philadelphia, West Indian–born tavern owners, enslaved Afro-Caribbeans in New York, pooling their money to buy tamarind and being experts in sea "turtle cookery," or chefs who passed down pepper pots, they all spoke to the island heritage of a substantial number of early black Northern communities. Black Northerners often lived in communities built in part by the shipping of foodstuffs (beef, grain, salt cod) to the Caribbean in exchange for sugar that was turned into molasses, which in turn became rum that bought my people from African elites. One hundred ten gallons of rum might purchase an adult; 80 might purchase a child.

In the colonial South, all Southern coastal cities had absorbed elements of the Caribbean basin. New Orleans, the northernmost outpost of the French West Indies, had many of the traits discussed above. In 1791, Haiti, the "jewel" of the Caribbean, began to give way to the spirit of revolution among enslaved Haitians, and in the course of the next decade, France lost the most profitable colony in the New World. Louisiana—a mixed economy with slaves raising tobacco, rice, and indigo—became a slave society based on cotton and cane. Jean Étienne de Boré, Louisiana's first successful sugar-cane planter, produced one hundred thousand pounds of sugar in 1795. By 1803, the whole of Louisiana was producing more than four million pounds of sugar, worth millions of dollars. Sugarcane plantations, considered poorly staffed if they held a populace of fewer than one hundred enslaved workers, began to source workers from the rest of mainland North America. After 1803, when France was forced to sell Louisiana, the domestic slave trade began in earnest, but from the 1820s to the Civil War, New Orleans became the largest slave market in America. King Sugar was the hungriest of rulers.

The American sugar barons were French, German, Anglo, or Spanish. But they were all part of Creole society, changing their names or personas to adjust. Their enslaved workforce was listed—in the case of the Evergreen plantation, men, women, and children were noted—as Creole, meaning Louisiana-born and likely mixed-race versus "Américain," enslaved chattel born on the Eastern Seaboard brought to Louisiana. Some were from Virginia, others South Carolina. There were even Africans, like Pierre, who was in his fifties when the log was created—and he was a "Congo." Some cut cane; some were blacksmiths, others brickmasons; some boiled sugar all night; others were maids, some were cooks—all were necessary.

You cannot mistake fields of sugarcane. They're twelve feet or more at their highest. The tops of the grasses are a brilliant green and the fields are thick and seemingly impenetrable. According to scholar Jean M. West, the average enslaved worker turned a field of sugarcane into five hogsheads of sugar or 250 gallons of molasses. Visiting plantations like Evergreen in Edgard, Louisiana, in what was once Sugarcane Alley and is now "Cancer Alley" thanks to environmental pollution, you can still see the sugar boiling pots and the cabins—built in the 1850s and abandoned in the 1950s or later—that still sit in situ, surrounded by the cane fields of the twenty-first century.

Going to the Evergreen and Whitney plantations, where the story of the enslaved is highlighted in contrast to the narrative of the enslavers, the parallel lives of black Creoles in rural Louisiana come to life. At Whitney, the owners have constructed a wall of remembrance holding the names of every documented enslaved person in Louisiana in the nineteenth century. Like their counterparts in the East they had names suggesting seasons, days, and holidays—names like Noel, L'Hiver, and Samedi. The placid ponds and bayou into which turtles and gators crawl, full of fat bass, are interrupted by the sculpted heads of Africans who recall young men beheaded and displayed on stakes in retaliation for slave rebellions. Here, you never forget what built these massive Greek Revival houses surrounded by banana trees and palmettos.

The enslaved lived on corn mush, field peas, okra, broken rice, mealy sweet potatoes and the leavings of syrup, the greens called *chou vert* (collards), and hot peppers from Mexico. A real treat was crackling obtained at the time of *boucherie* drizzled with cane syrup, and stews made from the backbone and whatever was at hand. They caught crawfish, snapping turtle, gar, and gaspergou, occasionally brightening their lives with sweetmeats like pralines made with the ever-present pecan and molasses. On occasion they caught wild game from alligators to deer to *"bec'rouche"* in black Creole (*bec rouge*, or ibis) and *gros bec*, or great blue heron, what their Gullah-Geechee cousins called "po' Joe."

To understand what an enslaved person went through on a sugar plantation, we go to Solomon Northup, made famous by *Twelve Years a Slave*, his account of being a free Northern black man who was kidnapped and brought to Louisiana to satisfy the need for more labor. Northup had never seen sugarcane before and was unfamiliar with its cultivation until he was forced to cut plant, hoe, and cut cane in the field:

> The ground is prepared in beds, the same as it is prepared for the reception of the cotton seed, except it is ploughed deeper. Drills are made in the same manner. Planting commences in January, and continues until April. It is necessary to plant a sugar field only once in three years. Three crops are taken before the seed or plant is exhausted.
>
> Three gangs are employed in the operation. One draws the cane from the rick, or stack, cutting the top and flags from the stalk, leaving only that part which is sound and healthy. Each joint of the cane has an eye, like the eye of a potato, which sends forth a sprout when buried in the soil. Another gang lays the cane in the drill, placing two stalks side by side in such manner that joints will occur once in four or six inches. The third gang follows with hoes, drawing earth upon the stalks, and covering them to the depth of three inches.
>
> In four weeks, at the farthest, the sprouts appear above the ground, and from this time forward grow with great rapidity. A sugar field is hoed three times, the same as cotton, save that a greater quantity of earth is drawn to the roots. By the first of August hoeing is usually over. About the middle of September, whatever is required for seed is cut and stacked in ricks, as they are termed. In October it is ready for the mill or sugar-house, and then the general cutting begins. The blade of a cane-knife is fifteen inches long, three inches wide in the middle, and tapering toward the point and handle. The blade is thin, and in order to be at all serviceable must be kept very sharp. Every third hand takes the lead of two others, one of whom is on each side of him. The lead hand, in the first place, with a blow of his

knife shears the flags from the stalk. He next cuts off the top down as far as it is green. He must be careful to sever all the green from the ripe part, inasmuch as the juice of the former sours the molasses, and renders it unsalable. Then he severs the stalk at the root, and lays it directly behind him. His right and left hand companions lay their stalks, when cut in the same manner, upon his. To every three hands there is a cart, which follows, and the stalks are thrown into it by the younger slaves, when it is drawn to the sugar-house and ground. . . .

In the month of January the slaves enter the field again to prepare for another crop. The ground is now strewn with the tops, and flags cut from the past year's cane. On a dry day, fire is set to this combustible refuse, which sweeps over the field, leaving it bare and clean, and ready for the hoes. The earth is loosened about the roots of the old stubble, and in process of time another crop springs up from the last year's seed. It is the same the year following; but the third year the seed has exhausted its strength, and the field must be ploughed and planted again. The second year the cane is sweeter and yields more than the first, and the third year more than the second.

The cane was then taken to a mill where it was crushed for the juice:

The juice of the cane falls into a conductor underneath the iron rollers, and is carried into a reservoir. Pipes convey it from thence into five filterers, holding several hogsheads each. These filterers are filled with bone-black, a substance resembling pulverized charcoal. It is made of bones calcinated in close vessels, and is used for the purpose of decolorizing, by filtration, the cane juice before boiling. Through these five filterers it passes in succession, and then runs into a large reservoir underneath the ground floor, from whence it is carried up, by means of a steam pump, into a clarifier made of sheet iron, where it is heated by steam until it boils. From the first clarifier it is carried in pipes to a second and a third, and thence into close iron pans, through which tubes pass, filled with steam. While in a boiling state it flows through three pans in succession, and is then carried in other pipes down to the coolers on the ground floor. Coolers are wooden boxes with sieve bottoms made of the finest wire. As soon as the syrup passes into the coolers, and is met by the air, it grains, and the molasses at once escapes through the sieves into a cistern below. It is then white or loaf sugar of the finest kind—clear, clean, and as white as snow. When cool, it is taken out, packed in hogsheads, and is ready for market. The molasses is then carried from the cistern into the upper story again, and by another process converted into brown sugar.

By the time Solomon Northup found himself in the sugarcane fields, a new system of sugar manufacture and filtration had been developed by a mulatto named Norbert Rillieux, the son of a white plantation owner and a free woman of color. Much like his contemporary Edmond Albius—a black man enslaved in the French colony of Mauritius who improved vanilla production by developing a method of hand pollination—or Antoine, the enslaved gardener at Louisiana's famed Oak Alley plantation who successfully grafted and improved the cultivation of pecans, Norbert Rillieux is the household name that never was.

The black cooks of Louisiana and the Gulf Coast were equally unsung heroes. Some were men sent to be trained in France and brought back to cook in well-to-do homes in New Orleans and Mobile. Others were called "Tante" (Creole for "Auntie"), women in bondage who had cooked for white families. These were the women who turned the Jollof rice of their Senegalese great-grandmothers, brought during the earliest days of the Louisiana colony, into jambalaya; and the *akara* of their Yoruba grandmothers brought during the Spanish trade into the *cala* (*"Tout chaud!"*) made of rice or black-eyed peas sold on the streets of New Orleans. In kitchens equipped with duck-blood presses and African standing mortars and pestles, they took *kingumbo* from their Mbundu parents and made cayenne-spiked okra soup with a roux, taking the meat out during Lent; adding Choctaw filé powder in winter and spring; adding crab, oyster, shrimp, and duck in season. They practiced vodun on the side, brought from their ancestors from Benin, and with vodun came recipes to feed the deities of their religion, syncretized with Catholic saints including recipes for *fevi*—okra; only in Louisiana would okra carry the entire legacy of the slave trade, from Senegal to Angola—with Igbo, Kongo-Angolan, and Fon names.

THE OTHER CANE

Sorghum was an African grass cultivated for millennia, and its seeds and sweet stalk were being grown in mainland North America since the colonial period. Its cultivation was centered around the settlements of the enslaved in the form of "Guinea corn." In the 1850s, experiments with several varieties led to the attempt to popularize sorghum as a cheaper and temperate alternative to sugarcane. While it did not produce a granulated sugar, sorghum did provide a molasses that was widely popular among Southern and Midwestern farmers because it was relatively easy to raise and produced a cheaper, homegrown alternative to sweeten coffee and baked goods, and could be used as a condiment at the table.

Long before coming to America, sorghum was used to make a taffy in the Sahel in West Africa. But some books today have even attributed sorghum to North American indigenes, and in the nineteenth century it was called "Chinese sugarcane." Sorghum seems to always have had an American identity crisis. Whatever story you want to spin, sorghum is one of Africa's more important contributions to plant domestication, and this should be recognized in an era when sorghum is now a hot commodity being marketed as the Southern answer to maple syrup. At least one variety has been traced to origins in southern Africa, a cultivar known as imphee grown in the Zulu empire.

My grandfather once gave me a jar of sorghum molasses at the end of one of my visits to South Carolina, and I didn't even know what the slightly metallic, earthy-tasting stuff was. My maternal grandfather, Walter, spoke of "stealing cane" in Birmingham from his neighbors' yards growing up, and he almost certainly meant sorghum. The South has a sugarcane belt and a sorghum cane belt, and my family tree straddled them both. My ancestors living in the Black Belt of Alabama made sugarcane molasses; my ancestors living in the Carolina upcountry and Virginia Piedmont made sorghum molasses. While the two have slightly different "cooking methods," the traditional method of extraction was the same.

Sorghum time was in the fall. "Making 'lasses" was a joyful time of the year and communities came together to get the job done. Sorghum time and cane syrup time were about black and Southern communities working together and being cooperative and interdependent. Sorghum masters were often, in many communities, older black men. It was one of the few environments where a soft sort of integration occurred with Southern whites and blacks interacting with each other over a foodstuff. Nobody got paid for use of their mules or mill; it was almost always bartered for things the mill owner could not provide his own homestead.

To see this, I went to a Mennonite farm. The sorghum cane

stood tall and was topped with its telltale reddish seeds, standing as a testament to Africa's presence out in the middle of very white eastern Tennessee. Speaking of very white, try being the only black guy amid a large family of Mennonites. I bought lemonade for the first time in my life from a stand run by barefoot Mennonite kids not far from the fields; and I don't believe their mouths closed the entire time. Chickens and goats and sheep crossed little country bridges. People had signs on their porch for sourwood honey, and another sign announced okra, tomatoes, gourd birdhouses, sweet corn, and hot-pepper jelly for sale. And the hills, blue and a green so dark it was almost black, were breathtaking.

"Can I help ya?" The leader of the skimming seemed perplexed as to why I was standing looking at him with a goofy smile.

"I'm not lost. We came a long way to watch you make sorghum."

"OK, what do you wanna know?" He still looked intrigued as to why I was so curious. I took it that the usual onlookers invited to come to Muddy Pond were hipster types and chefs looking for their new boutique ingredient.

"My granddaddy did this and his father before him, but I've never seen it done. Teach me."

Trust gained, Mr. Guenther introduced me to this family and I stopped being goofy long enough to smell the air—it was like being in a taffy sauna, very sexy for a bear who appreciates sweets. Mr. Guenther explained that the cane was cut midway in ripeness, then it was brought to the grinder, which was powered by a horse going around in circles as the cane was fed into crushing gears. The green juice, running through a cheesecloth or two, was then boiled and skimmed until it reached a thick golden brown color. I assure you there is nothing more beautiful than sorghum syrup being poured into a glass vessel, or more heavenly than hot, new sorghum on a piece of pound cake, itself sweetened with sorghum. It is sexy, it is overkill, it is soul-making, it was so good that I bought more and ate them before G-d gave me two more days of life.

The family worked together, manning the steaming pans, and within a very short time, bottle after bottle filled. The mood was happy, and soon a game of catch ensued between the boys. I finished my smartphone videos, bought a jug or two along with some alleged Cherokee herbal potion, and set out for Nashville. I was happy but disappointed. I had seen the process but not the men—I guess I was still hoping to see my grandfather, and his father and his father before him feeding the mill, chasing the mule, boiling the cane, and celebrating with the three Ms—meat, meal, and molasses made by the women into plebeian delicacies. When my paternal great-grandfather, Grandpa Will, died, leaving my grandfather and his siblings orphans, apart from a hundred acres of land he obtained through mysterious means from Dr. Sidney Hinson (I think they were related), cotton seeds, and a few pieces of rusty farm equipment, he left his children salt pork, a sack of cornmeal, and twenty gallons of sorghum molasses. All of a sudden, the jar of molasses made sense. I still have a jar sitting on my desk, unopened, perhaps just so I can pass it down.

SUGAR'S REVENGE

Some stories just need to be passed on. In 1865, my great-great-great-grandmother Rosetta Merritt, enslaved on the Chadwick plantation in Russell County, Alabama, got into a fight with the former overseer who thought he had it in him to overpower Rose and rape and beat her. According to oral history he pulled her into the cellar of the Big House where they wrestled until she got the best of him and dunked his head in a barrel of cane syrup made on the place. Because he was known to be often intoxicated, nobody questioned her when he was found drowned up past the neck. I told you that story just to honor my mother, who told me to retell the story in order to tell the world that her people fought back.

Sorghum Brined Chicken Roasted in Cabbage Leaves

½ cup kosher salt
½ cup sorghum molasses
3 cups chicken or vegetable stock; I prefer homemade of your choice
5 cups cold water
5 pound roasting chicken, whole

Kitchen Pepper (see recipe on page 24)
½ cup unsalted butter, softened; or lard or canola oil
One large cabbage

Preheat oven to 350.

Dissolve salt and sorghum molasses, into the stock. Allow liquid to cool. Add cold water.

Remove giblets. Wash and thoroughly clean chicken, and submerge in brine in a large bowl for 2 to 4 hours. Remove and rinse.

Mix 2 tablespoons of Kitchen Pepper with the butter, lard, or canola oil. Rub the chicken with the mix under and on the outside of its skin, being certain to cover the entire bird.

Put cabbage leaves at the bottom of the Dutch oven. Cover the chicken in the washed cabbage leaves and tie into a loose bundle, layering as many leaves as it takes to cover the bird. Add a little water or chicken stock to the pot, cover tightly, and put into the oven. Roast for 70 to 90 minutes. When the wings pull away from the twine and the juices run clear, the chicken should be done.

10
—

MOTHERS OF SLAVES

How did we come to have an African American food tradition? How did we become African Americans, and how did we get centered in the South? Can we go back in time and collect the story of African American food from Africa to America, and from slavery to freedom, and trace it through the path of an American family in detail? Well, we have to start somewhere, so let's start with me.

If you are of African American descent, your ancestor's journey most likely began somewhere along the seaboard South in Maryland, Virginia, North or South Carolina, Georgia, or Louisiana, and elsewhere along the Gulf Coast. About 389,000 to 450,000 enslaved Africans were brought alive to North America between 1619 and 1860. Although we have the Transatlantic Slave

Trade Database (TASTD), we will never know the exact number of humans delivered. Not all lived to produce offspring, and even when they did some bloodlines were snuffed out by disease, war, violence, and suicide long before they would leave a trace in our genes. If we go by the TASTD numbers, 128,000 of our ancestors were brought to the Chesapeake, 208,000 were brought to South Carolina and Georgia, and 22,000 were brought to the Lower Mississippi Valley and Gulf Coast. Ninety-two percent of our ancestors, as African Americans, arrived in the South.

Almost all of us have an array of ancestral experiences. Because of our diverse gene pool, it would be difficult to say that there is one narrative of how our ancestors got here. Most likely, many if not most of the possible scenarios—from early importation to late illegal arrivals—exist in our bloodlines. Only about 4 percent of enslaved Africans had arrived by 1700. By 1750, the native-born African American population eclipsed the incoming importations from Africa in its population center, at that time the Chesapeake and Tidewater. That same year about 41 percent of all our ancestors had arrived, and by 1776 more than half were here. An upsurge occurred in South Carolina and Georgia and by 1800, it was up to 80 percent. As a result of a last push to import Africans into the Deep South before the 1808 closing of the trade, the rush to import more Africans into Charleston and the Low Country brought more enslaved people than almost any other period.

Apart from minor numbers brought to Louisiana and the Gulf Coast from Mobile to Galveston, almost all imported Africans had arrived by 1820. It is important to understand that they were not perceived as one bloc, but rather as semidistinct ethnic and regional identities. To put it another way, the average slaveholder going to auction in Annapolis, Charleston, or New Orleans had a greater understanding of African ethnic groups than most Americans of any color do today. They were buying a product and were to some degree prejudiced in favor of some chattel over others given assumptions of skill, work ethic, and knowledge base. Africans familiar with certain crops, deemed tractable or reliable, and those who were considered more attractive than others meant that there were different varieties of Africans in different colonies, so that overall the North American African diaspora would be decidedly unique.

This means that the foodways of this developing population that became our families was not a onetime, linear experience or event. There are people whose ancestors arrived from Africa culturally and genetically mixed with Europeans meeting Africans from the interior, who mix with one another to form an African American culture with regional tones that in turn confront other Africans brought from coastal enclaves, and each group gets folded into those who were already here. Imagine these women negotiating the cooking pots of a new life, using their collective knowledge and experience to make something that would soothe their exile—in tongues 3,500 miles apart with different stories of how they came to be irrevocably enslaved in an alien land. All of the negotiations and conflict— between European indentures, Africans and Native people, with one another, and within their own groupings—affected how the food came to be and what we think of us as soul or Southern. Hear the voices of a black boy captured by the Natchez, a couple of mixed African origins that can't get along, a white woman and her black mate, a black concubine to a white overseer, tri-racial groups living in mountains and swamps, and fifty languages—from Ladino to Cherokee to Kikongo to Gaelic to French and Canary Island Spanish and Serer—and you will understand how beautifully bewildering our heritage is, and why it was impossible to birth this cuisine anywhere else on the planet.

CHESAPEAKE

My family's American journey began where roots of American soul food began: among the tidal creeks, coastal plain, and rolling Piedmont hills in the colonial Chesapeake region between the seventeenth and eighteenth centuries. Over time about 90,000 enslaved Africans would arrive in chains from various parts of West and central Africa with a purchase bias toward Senegambia and the Gold Coast, followed by the Niger Delta and its hinterlands, and West and central Africa. Some went south into North Carolina, which had few ports that could accommodate slave ships, with the notable exception of Edenton and Wilmington—opposite poles of the coast that was famously known as "the Graveyard of the Atlantic." About 20,000 would be brought to the Catholic colony of Maryland, predominately from Senegal, Gambia, Ghana, and Kongo.

The largest collective regional group that disembarked in Virginia was composed of people enslaved in what is now southeastern Nigeria. Despite never achieving an all-out black majority as in South Carolina, Virginia would maintain the largest enslaved population in the colonial and antebellum South; it was more the "mother of the enslaved" than the "mother of presidents." Virginia's central Tidewater and Piedmont heartland, known as the "Black Belt" or "New Guinea," where there was a black majority, would eventually seed many of the black communities of the Southern frontier through the domestic slave trade, as slavery, tobacco, and cotton pushed west, furthering the cultural and culinary influence of the first African Americans. The culinary encounter in Virginia was remarkably complex. The indigenous, pre-European landscape was dominated by the Powhatan paramount chiefdom ruled by Wahunsunacaw from a power seat on the James River near present-day Richmond. As it was with their Siouan (Tutelo-Saponi) and Iroquoian (Cherokee and Nottaway) neighbors, the indigenous diet was based on maize, beans and squash, deer, bear, turkey, fish, shellfish, and a variety of supplementary wild plants, small game, fruits, nuts, roots, and flavorings from sap, leaves, and seeds. Indigenous Virginians (Tsenecommacans) provided a culinary parallel to the preindustrial foodways of enslaved Africans, even as European food traditions—brought mostly from southern and middle England, Northern Ireland, and the Palatine region of Germany—mirrored common traditions in the post–Iron Age, premodern Atlantic world that Europeans and Africans shared on several levels of varying power. An emphasis on staple grains and tubers, a wide variety of cultivated vegetables (including those recently assimilated from Central and South America), domesticated livestock, a wide body of herbs and spices, preserved fish and animal proteins, plant-derived fats, salt, and the powerful influence of global trade—all bonded Old World foodways while separating them from those traditions found in colonial North America. It is unlikely that enslaved Africans found themselves in a food environment that was incomprehensibly exotic or impenetrably alien; they would become allies, inheritors, and stewards of indigenous ways, and harbingers of the Atlantic world, as pioneers and frontiersmen in their own right.

ARRIVAL

The spot where many imported Africans arrived at Yorktown is a windy, quiet, and nondescript space. There are seafood joints and a boardwalk of sorts and opportunities to be a good Historic Triangle tourist. There is also a sign honoring the arrival of the majority of incoming African Virginians at the spot—only recently placed. You can look up a little hill, now paved with asphalt, and imagine the boats being offloaded and groups of Africans taking their first steps on American soil while being brought to a holding space where they were prepared for market. Blair Underwood, Arthur Ashe, Maggie

Walker, Tim Reid, Peter Gomes, Wanda Sykes, and me—all of us and virtually millions more African Americans descended from these unfortunate exiles can trace their American journey back to this quiet and nondescript spot on the York River that will never again know as much traffic as it did then.

Each of my grandparents had ancestors who were enslaved in Old Virginia, but only one, my paternal grandmother, had an entire family tree of enslaved chattel who were brought to and never left the state of Virginia. To my surprise, my grandmother's direct maternal line, which I fully expected to be West African, terminated in a white female, putting me in a very special category of African Americans— the 1 to 3 percent with a white European maternal ancestral line. Based on context alone, a white woman making the choice to bond with a black man and having a mixed-race daughter by an enslaved or indentured African, who in turn survived to pass on the genetic and culinary legacy of her parents, would most likely have arrived as an indentured servant in the mid-seventeenth century. During the last quarter of the 1600s, following the lead of Maryland, Virginia passed draconian new racial codes that severely curtailed the number of biracial children born to white women—laws that employed whipping, fines, and enslavement to discourage interracial sex. Coupled with our connection to old Wonder Booker, my Virginia heritage is as old as that moment, and nearly as old as this country.

My white Old Dominion Eve was of distant Finnish descent from haplogroup W. It's worth noting because I struggled to wrap my head around having apparent Finnish ancestry on multiple DNA tests. Through her, I found it. I don't know much else about her life or the fascinating decision she made to love and possibly marry an African. For his part, her mate was either transshipped from Barbados or somewhere else in the Caribbean, or, much more likely, central Africa, one of the many people from the BaKongo or Mbundu ethnic polities that saw the exile of the initial "20 and odd" blacks to Jamestown via the Portuguese and Dutch and would continue to dominate the African population in seventeenth-century America. Given the hints of Iberian ancestry in my genetic tests, he may—and this is completely speculative—have been mixed himself, a *tango-mao*—a mulatto, and he was probably familiar with the Catholic faith, if not a practicing Christian himself as many were. In central Africa, the Portuguese brought Catholic tradition and Portuguese customs, leading to Mvemba a Nzinga, King Affonso I of Kongo (ca. 1455–ca. 1542), converting in 1506. Now a transatlantic empire with an interest in spreading its influence and religion, the Portuguese brought plants and crops from Europe—wheat and olive trees to make bread and grapevines, toward the ends of making the holy Eucharist. Other Eurasian crops followed—peaches, almonds, kale, and colewort (collard greens), and all various vegetables and fruits acquired over centuries of exposure to the Moors—African Muslims who ruled the Iberian peninsula for nearly a millennium. The wheat crops and grapevines faltered miserably, but cassava, corn—known as *masa Maputo*, the grain of Portugal, sweet potatoes, peanuts, kidney beans, chili peppers, and other "American" crops exploded in popularity, owing to their similarity to previously established crops. Cassava quickly rivaled millet and sorghum, the indigenous starches grown before European arrival, and baked into a flat cake, it, rather than wheat, accompanied native palm wine to celebrate mass.

It is clear that long before this particular group of Africans, named by scholar Ira Berlin "Atlantic Creoles," engaged with Virginia, New Netherland, and other parts of the New World, they were living bridges between Africa and the West. Some of my ancestors were very likely among their numbers. They were multilingual—moving between Kikongo and Kimbundu, traditional African spirituality and Catholicism, the ways of Europe leaving the Dark Ages and Africa leaving a comfortable isolation from the West. It was not long before the people of Kongo stopped regarding these strange people as ancestors from across the watery boundary come back from the land of the dead. However, as the desire to capitalize on the desire for sugar ruled Portuguese interests more than the spread of the reign of Jesus Christ and agricultural experiments, Brazil called, and as indigenous people proved unsuccessful as enslaved chattel, it was the people of central Africa who were captured and exiled through inter-ethnic wars instigated and sponsored by the Portuguese and powered by African elites, rulers, and mercenaries bent on destruction.

Affonso I, the faithful Christian, the scholarly, hopeful king who hoped to send more of his people as emissaries to the Vatican and Portugal to study and spread the Word of the Gospel, took note of this growing, insidious terror. No stranger to milder indigenous forms of enslavement, in his letters he wrote:

> Each day the traders are kidnapping our people—children of this country, sons of our nobles and vassals, even people of our own family. . . . This corruption and depravity are so widespread that our land is entirely depopulated. . . . We need in this kingdom only priests and schoolteachers, and no merchandise, unless it is wine and flour for Mass. It is our wish that this Kingdom not be a place for the trade or transport of slaves. . . . Many of our subjects eagerly lust after Portuguese merchandise that your subjects have brought into our domains. To satisfy this inordinate appetite, they seize many of our black free subjects. . . . They sell them . . . after having taken these prisoners [to the coast] secretly or at night. . . . As soon as the captives are in the hands of white men they are branded with a red-hot iron. . . .

Before his very eyes King Affonso was witnessing the birth of the greatest forced migration of humans in the history of planet

Earth, the transatlantic slave trade. He hoped they would send more "wine and flour," not slave traders, guns, alcohol, and cheap cloth. Wars raged, conflicts erupted, and alliances were made; cultures and foods continued to mix. When they encountered the English in Virginia and Maryland, just as the "South" was being born, the Atlantic Creoles, my oldest African American kin, were already fluent in the fluidity and chaos from which a new food tradition would soon be born. Unlike the West Africans who followed them, the Atlantic Creoles were familiar with many Western foods and beverages, European eating customs, and the ways in which the ritual year affected cycles of feasting and fasting. Africans from the interior looked on the Europeans much as the Europeans viewed them—as uncivilized cannibals—whose wine resembled blood and whose cheese were brains—and whose olive oil was actually extracted from the bodies of the newly enslaved.

The Atlantic Creoles took advantage of their unusual world. Whatever else can be said, the early black community of Virginia both set a tone and was completely different from anything that would follow it. Its members were more a blend of Africa and the West than they were purely of Africa. They were also on intimate terms with Native Americans, both as friends and enemies, and they too would mix with some of these first African Americans. Atlantic Creoles owned animals and they grew and sold produce and poultry in a time when the monoculture of tobacco bid some to plant tobacco and little else. They took oaths, had indentured servants, and even enslaved people of their own; they owned tracts of land and occasionally they acted unrepentantly defiant to authority; and if need be, they could testify in court against their slaveholders.

The same laws that regulated my distant grandmother's womb were tightening the vice of racialized chattel slavery around the neck of African Virginians. By 1692 it was illegal for an enslaved person to own their own cow or hog. Slave codes more and more began to curtail food production as a means of upward mobility; whites reasoned that the successful trade by blacks, free or enslaved, was direct competition to their economic well-being and social power. The black population grew by leaps and bounds as thousands of enslaved people began to arrive from the 1680s to the 1720s, mostly directly from Africa, and the slave codes, like a gathering storm of threatening clouds, awaited their landing. By October 1705, as the colony of Virginia instituted the first comprehensive code for the management of people of African descent, every right and privilege that had been extended to the generation before was struck down with the quill:

> And be it further enacted, That all and every other act and acts, and every clause and article thereof heretofore made, for so much thereof as relates to servants and slaves, or to any other matter or thing whatsoever within the purview of this act, is and are hereby repealed and made void, to all intents and purposes, as if the same had never been made.

By the 1720s the slave trade to Virginia was in full swing, and between this time and the Revolutionary War, the majority of enslaved Africans would arrive on ships directly from Africa, drawing on populations reaching farther into the interior. Most African Americans can trace the majority of their roots to an ancestor who arrived in the colonial Chesapeake or Low Country in the mid-eighteenth century. DNA evidence suggests that in the 1720s came at least one Malagasy ancestor, bringing Southeast Asian genes into my genetic record. The Malagasy, descendants of ancient Indonesian immigrants to the island of Madagascar, were some of the most exotic of Africa's forced migrants, and they never failed to be noted in historical records for their unique blend of Asiatic and African phenotypes.

My great-great-great-grandmother, Arrye Todd, noted for her

"long straight black hair," may have been a descendant of one of the women brought on those ships in a journey that lasted five or six harrowing months. Many African Americans would later conflate Malagasy people with the Creek Indians, and indeed Arrye was called a "Creek Indian" in our family's oral history. Only six ships arrived in Virginia from Madagascar during this specific time period, and if she was indeed a Malagasy descendant, that knowledge alone may help us time her ancestors' arrival.

The slaveholding families that bound my enslaved African Virginian ancestors moving forward in history—many of them brought from what is now southeastern Nigeria and southwestern Cameroon (the Igbo, Ibibio, Moko, Efik, and their neighbors) and southern and central Ghana (the Akan, Ewe, and Ga)—were not grandees, but they certainly wanted to be. They came to Virginia with the dream of money, power, and prestige paid for by tobacco. For lack of available claims in Virginia slavery's power center—the peninsulas leading from the Bay to the Fall Line—they moved to the rolling Piedmont where land and the opportunity to expand was still available. Here in Southside Virginia, the hinterlands of the James and Appomattox Rivers and the edge of the Blue Ridge, spread the oldest slaveholders known to my tree. Among them were the Bookers of Prince Edward County; the Saunderses of Buckingham County; the Fores, the Joneses, the Mitchells, and the Hills of Appomattox County; the Bowens of Southampton County; the Woosleys of Lunenburg County; and the Todds of Henrico County and the city of Richmond. They were English, Welsh, French Huguenots, and Scotsmen—and they bought men and women off the boat at Yorktown, Bermuda Hundred, and Rocky Ridge across from Richmond who became, by random chance, my ancestors.

Africans arriving from 1619 to 1720 predominantly disembarked on the Eastern Shore and Tidewater. As the 1720s pushed into the mid-eighteenth century, the center of the enslaved population moved from the area hugging the Bay closer and closer to the Fall Line, and by the 1750s, Bermuda Hundred, not Yorktown, saw slave ships coming up the James to land with enslaved people being sold there at market. By midcentury, with the native black population eclipsing the incoming Africa-born population, the fully African American culture began to emerge at the crossroads of the cultures that had come before it, with doses of African and Caribbean influences with each new pocket of saltwater Africans. My DNA and that of other immediate family showed many affinities with Nigerian populations, and DNA matching further confirmed my suspicions—we had several Nigerian cousins, all of them Igbo, and all of them shared, with other black families, roots that traced back to Virginia.

Sixty percent of the trade to Virginia before 1745 is well documented, and of those, 60 percent were from the Bight of Biafra, homeland of the Igbo. Eighty percent of all shipments of enslaved Africans during the mid-eighteenth century were going to the wealthiest planters living in the heartland of sweet-scented tobacco, along the York River and its hinterlands, and those living along the upper James River. The totals for known importations to the plantations there show that about 54 percent in the York Naval District were from the Bight of Biafra, and along the upper James 40 percent were Biafran. Of those sampled from unknown districts of Virginia, 49 percent came from that region. Overall numbers for the trade to Virginia, studied over the past forty years, demonstrate that of all the enslaved African blocs brought to Virginia, it was the dispersed men and women of the Bight of Biafra and Calabar who represented an unusual demographic plurality at about 38 to 40 percent of all enslaved Africans imported into Virginia.

Igbo-speaking peoples have inhabited what is now southeastern Nigeria perhaps for as long as five thousand years. Their cosmology was based on honoring the sanctions of the earth, and the ancestors (*ndichie*) buried within. The earth mother, known alternately, according to dialect, as Ala or Ani, is the moral center of Igbo civilization, so much so that the Igbo religion is known as Omenala or Odinani—the "custom" or "traditions" of the feminine earth deity. The Igbo cornucopia was already large by the time the Portuguese and Dutch arrived with crops from the New World, but none were more important to the diet and sense of communal identity than varieties of tropical yam (*ji*) they developed and cultivated over thousands of years. Some were indigenous to Africa, others had come across the continent from Asia; in any case, the Igbo believed the yam to have sprung from the bodies of the children of their ancient divine king—yams were part of the family tree of the Igbo people.

For the Igbo, much like their Akan neighbors along the Gold Coast, the highlight of the year was the New Yam Festival, held after two major offerings held during the harvest season—Ite Nsi and Isa Ire. The New Yam Festival, like other preindustrial harvest festivals, demanded the abandonment of broken vessels, a fresh cleaning of the household, and feasting on the new produce while abandoning the old. For the Igbo the yam had a spiritual patron, Ifejioku, guardian of the crop and its cultivation. Until the sacrifices had been performed, nobody could touch the new yams. Held on a market day, ivory horns sounded by the priests called everyone to the rite. Sheep or chickens were sacrificed by the heads of household, with the blood being received in a portable altar to Ifejioku. This sacred time, the Igbo's answer to Western harvest festivals or Thanksgiving celebrations, was known to them as *iri-ji*, the occasion of eating the yams.

From Olaudah Equiano, the eighteenth-century Igbo abolitionist and writer, we learn that by the mid-eighteenth century, yams were joined by plantains, beans, maize, taro, and other crops central to the diet, along with minor crops including spices, "particularly pepper" (native melegueta pepper, Ethiopian and Guinea pepper, and chili from the New World), and pineapples, which he says "grow without culture." He speaks of "a variety of delicious fruits which I have never seen in Europe." According to Captain Hugh Crow, a British seaman visiting Bonny (an Ijo slave-trading port in which many Igbo lived and from which thousands of enslaved Igbo were exported to the Americas), later coconuts, oranges, limes, and the "fig-banana" joined pineapples as common fruits. The Igbo kept native fruit trees near their dwellings as well, including the star apple, African breadfruit, and native "pears" and "mangoes."

In their gardens they had "no want of ocra," and "calavancies" (cowpeas) of which he says, "The Negroes are particularly fond of this bean." Red peppers were "found in great abundance." Igbo gardens also produced several varieties of leafy greens, including members of the amaranth family; and bitter leaf, from which a soup was made. Common vegetable plants were exploited in every way; not only did leaves became greens, seeds were used for oil or eaten as a separate vegetable, such as melon seeds; and rinds, flesh, and stems each had their separate usage including medicinal ones. Many West Africans saw the thickly planted compound garden as a "soup garden" from which foods could be obtained that could enhance the diet.

The Igbo had much in common in their methods of preparing food with their Kwa cousins to the west. Olaudah Equiano described the eighteenth-century Igbo meal as "flesh stewed in a pan. To make it savory we sometimes use also pepper and other spices and we have salt made of wood-ashes." Most meals consisted of a palm-oil-based soup or stew, thickened with leafy greens, heavily spiced and flavored with bits of smoked fish, or fresh fish or meat on special occasions. As G. T. Basden pointedly describes, the Igbo was "not an epicure. For his stock-pot, he has not many opportunities to exercise a preference; he has chiefly to rely on smoked fish and not much of that in interior districts. There is the consolation that a little of this goes a long way! It has distinct and pungent properties!"

Add to this the description of Captain Crow from the nineteenth century:

"The principal dish of which the natives are fond is what is called a 'yam chop'—the word 'chop' being also applied to substantial eating generally. This dish consists of boiled yams and boiled fowl—for here every thing is boiled—served up with sweet palm oil and pepper, and forms a repast which the narrator (who enjoyed remarkably good health) often ate with a good relish."

This soup or stew would be eaten with cooked, pounded yam, the main starch. A roast goat, sheep, or pig might signify a festival, wedding, or a sacrifice for a funeral. Fried yam, roasted maize on the cob, cornbreads, okra soup, black-eyed-pea fritters (known by the Yoruba term *"akara"* in modern Nigeria), boiled beans, goat's head, melon seed soup, bitter leaf soup, and breadfruit pottage were other popular dishes that might have been enjoyed between the time of Equiano and Crow.

The food traditions of others in the region—the Ijo, Ibibio, Kalabari, and Efik had similar leanings with greater reliance on cassava, seafood, and aquatic life such as giant snails, oysters, and periwinkles; crustaceans like crabs and prawns; and finfish like flatfish, shark, jack, mullet, and bonga shad—were frequent items in the diet. Much of the fish was smoked for a condiment as well as eaten fresh, and some meat was smoked and dried and added to stews for flavor as well. Fishermen from the Senegal and Gambia Rivers, and the coasts of Upper Guinea and Ghana, relied similarly on fish and shellfish, many of which had cognate species along the entire South Atlantic and Gulf coasts from anadromous species like herring and shad to drums and croakers, perches, catfish, and eels, as well as mollusks and crustaceans. To the Chesapeake region came expert fishermen from across West and central Africa who had millennia of experience fishing the rivers, mangrove swamps, tidal creeks, estuaries, and coasts of their homelands.

MY "KUNTA KINTE"

Most of my Virginia ancestors had probably arrived by the 1760s, except one of several notable exceptions—the grandfather of my, as Alex Haley would put it, "furthest back person." The family story that fueled my imagination as a child was simple and succinct.

"Jack Todd was born about 1830, possibly in Africa. According to oral history he was captured by slave traders and brought to Richmond, Virginia." Recorded by my uncle the year I was born, this was as close as my web of families ever got to an origin story for how we came to be Americans. Unraveling the myths of my "Kunta Kinte" and reconstructing the truth of his story became my lifelong mission.

This much we know—he came to Virginia, the largest North American colony with the largest black population. Virginia's market for fresh Africans began to dwindle about the time of the American Revolution. My great-great-great-grandfather Jack Todd, born anywhere from 1815 and 1830, was not likely to have been brought to Richmond on a slave ship in the early nineteenth century. Richmond was evolving into the Upper South's most prolific exporter of enslaved workers, all American born, to the Lower South. It was indeed a major capital of the domestic slave trade but not the transatlantic slave trade. Virginia's most profitable "crop," by his time, had become human labor.

According to my genealogist, Toni Carrier, it is common that the arriving generation's story gets confused in some oral histories of African American families. "It was the grandfather more likely than the grandson who arrived from Africa." And in this case, that appears to be clear. The Virginia slave trade officially closed in 1778, at which point, one way or another, this bloodline was on American soil to stay.

My great-grandfather Joseph Peter Todd's brother Lane had recorded many of the stories in a notebook, which, as these stories often go, was carelessly tossed away.

Shortly after my grandmother died in 1990, I placed a call with her cousin Vaddie, who told me all about the notebook and recalled the story of Jack Todd. Vaddie told me the notebook had recorded the names of several "tribes" we had come from. I was an impatient teenager, but after some time she told me, "I don't remember much but I do remember, he said Jack Todd was Ashanti (Asante) from the Gold Coast."

A lightbulb went off. The Asante culture had given us our own kind of tartan, the glowing, richly colored silk kente cloth developed by the Asante and their fellow Akan kinsmen was widely adopted in the late 1980s and early 1990s as a symbol of West African heritage for African Americans. The Asante Confederacy was a cluster of the Akan peoples—Ghana's largest ethnic family, born about the seventeenth century from groups that had long ago migrated south from the Sudanic kingdoms of Africa's Middle Ages. The Asante were builders of an empire that lasted from the seventeenth to the twentieth centuries, enriched from the Atlantic slave trade and the mining of gold and they remain one of Africa's more well-known ethnic groups.

My uncle dismissed it all, saying there was no proof. Still, I made my way to the embassy of Ghana back when teenagers doing research for the hell of it could enter a Washington embassy as if it were a library—with a school ID. A man named Mr. Obuba, himself a member of the Akwamu branch of the Akan peoples, who worked in the passport office, was "assigned" to teach me a few things after the information officer had tired of my questions. I had no idea that I was interrupting their workday or that they had other things to do, I was oblivious. I had a story to hunt.

Mr. Obuba was a patient and enthusiastic mentor. He married an African American woman and they lived with their son in DC, a place where African immigrants founded active and influential communities after the establishment of integration. I often visited him at the embassy as well as his home, and he spent hours teaching me the Akan way and the rudiments of the Twi language—the native tongue of the Akan. He took one look at the picture of my great-grandfather, the grandson of Jack Todd and great-great-grandson of his African forebear, Joseph Peter Todd II, and said, "That man comes from Ghana." Mr. Obuba said something to me that stuck with me despite my own persistent doubt that the story was true: "The Ancestors have sent me to make sure you know the way of a proper Akan man." Eventually I lost touch with him, but no matter where I went, it was that phrase that stuck with me—in spirit, I felt Ghanaian and welcomed into the family whether the story was true or not.

In 2014 my first Ancestry.com DNA test revealed that I was 32 percent Ghanaian. I had inherited the lion's share of Ghanaian ancestry from my four grandparents. Acknowledging that migrations and national borders did not equal ethnicity, I took comfort in knowing that so much of me was in fact from the country that legend and learning had connected me to. If not all, some of the people that gave me this genetic link were certainly Akan if not Asante. African Ancestry confirmed my paternal lineage was Akan-Ewe from Ghana, a 100 percent match, but this did nothing for my narrative through Jack, since he was on my mother's maternal side. I totally gave up any hope of ever definitively knowing whether the story was valid because I didn't have contact with family that could be tested.

A year after my mom passed, a precious coincidence occurred. Her first cousin Terri by my maternal grandmother shared that she did her parental African Ancestry DNA tests long before me. Our maternal ancestry was consistent, further confirming my faith in the process. Terri then revealed that she tested Uncle Lane's line to get my great-aunt's—and grandmother's—paternal line. Several anxiety-ridden hours later, an online message appeared with the test results: the paternal line of Jack Todd was indeed Akan from Ghana—100 percent match.

If the story of an African man brought to Virginia in chains could survive across 250 years and be passed down by his family from generation to generation despite the failures of memory and all of life's challenges, I surmised there might be other elements of truth to the story. Richmond was never really known as a port for the Atlantic slave trade. However, we do know that enslaved Africans were sold along areas up the James River and around Richmond in the late colonial period. In fact, between 1761 and 1774 the enslaved people from the Gold Coast were at their peak as a preferred commodity, just as the slave trade to Virginia was in its death knell throes. Africans from the Gold Coast were always a prime source of labor, but most Virginians lost out to planters from Maryland, South Carolina, and the West Indies to meet their needs—they were considered industrious and strong if not rebellious and stubborn.

The years 1761 to 1774 would be the likely arrival time for the man who would become Jack Todd's grandfather. But was Richmond possibly his place of arrival? In what is now the Manchester section of the Richmond area across the James River at a place called Rocky Ridge, there was a small depot for the arrival of the enslaved at the end of the Virginia slave trade. More and more Africans were being brought upriver to urban sites and Piedmont plantations as opposed to the traditional Tidewater settlements where the trade was centered on supplying the patrician planters before 1750. Very few slave ships came here compared with Bermuda Hundred and before it, Yorktown, but arrive they did—and primarily at the tail end of the trade.

The buyers were Richmond area planters and merchants. George Todd, a Scottish merchant living in Richmond at the time, was likely the man who purchased my great-great-great-great-great-great-grandfather at auction. He was the father of James Todd, their last known slaveholder in Virginia in the early 1800s. The oral history again stood the test of time. My Asante grandfather, despite hard days loading goods at George Todd's store, found the time to tell his children and they told their children, and they told their children, until it came down to me, "You are Asante."

A MIXED MULTITUDE

My West African Virginian ancestors came armed with hot peppers, yam dishes, okra, cowpeas, melons, and a taste for peanuts and tomatoes. Like the western Europeans and Native Americans, their pots were full of stews and soups eaten with porridge, what we today generically call *fufu*. Some had already embraced corn in West Africa, and others were merely experimenting with it—but corn mush, hominy, spoonbread, and corn pone and puddings were familiar copies of grain dishes from home, and sweet potatoes (known in Igbo as the "white man's yam") replaced yams. The Chesapeake saw the blending of West and central African foodways with those of the southern Algonquians, and of the British Isles and Germany, as well as the blending of genes—my genes. Each negotiation was worked out across the generations and was never really a singular cultural event.

First-generation eaters flirted with western European foodways; second-generation ones embraced them as a sign of cultural advancement and normalization. Field mice, snakes, insects, and the like began to decline in popularity, and a taste developed for baked goods, sugar, and food eaten in courses. Atlantic Creoles from central Africa and Senegambia; Wolof, Manding, and Igbo women prepared European food and began to mix everything before them together, Africanizing the food while themselves being changed irrevocably—and this scenario would be repeated along the entire Southern coast pushing west toward the mountains. Meanwhile it became apparent that neither the English diet nor language would be copied wholesale, as Frederick Douglass said about the latter:

"There is not, probably, in the whole south, a plantation where the English language is more imperfectly spoken than on Col. Lloyd's. It is a mixture of Guinea and everything else you please. At the time of which I am now writing, there were slaves there who had been brought from the coast of Africa. . . . Even Mas' Daniel, by his association with his father's slaves, had measurably adopted their dialect and their ideas."

In order to survive and to cook, a language had to develop to accommodate the flurry of cultural and culinary change in the colonial South. In order to make the new recipes of a new world intelligible, the enslaved had to cocreate a language based on the English of their captors that would make the absurdity of their exile bearable. They participated in the naming of species as Americans created a new tongue to understand their world. "Okra" ("*okwuru*" from Igbo), "gumbo" ("*kingumbo*"), "goober" ("*nguba*"), "pinder" ("*mpinda*" from Kikongo and Kimbundu), "yam" ("*nyambi*" from Wolof), "cooter" ("*kuta*" from Bamana), and "poke" (from Luba, "*poko*," sack—later applied to pokeweed, an edible green) joined Creolized adaptations of European and Native American words to describe the new repertoire. The names of their lands were applied to animals and plants— "guinea fowl," "guinea squash" (eggplant), "guinea hog," and "Angola peas." In the mouths of Plantation Creole speakers drawn from the

Guinea Coast, Powhatan and English words changed from *"pasimenan"* and "persimmon" to "'simmons," *"arahkun"* and "raccoon" to "'coon," "pork" to "po'k," and pumpkin to "punkin." In this new tongue, Plantation Creole, recipes and suggestions were shared as well as memories and stories from home.

LOW COUNTRY

South Carolina was easily the largest importer of slaves on the mainland. By 1808, when the slave trade was outlawed in the United States, South Carolina had imported about twice as many Africans as Virginia, even though its slave population was much smaller.
—PHILIP D. MORGAN

No African American language in the United States preserved more vocabulary from West and central African tongues than Gullah-Geechee, spoken on the subtropical coast of South Carolina and Georgia. When they spoke of a hog (*gulu*) or of wine (*mavalu*) or okra (*kingumbo*) or of the types of edible rodents (*gone*) they hunted at the edge of the rice marsh, they used words from Kikongo and Kimbundu. When they spoke of rice (*malo*), sesame (*benne*), and hunted heron, po' Joe (*podzo*), and fished for catfish (*wa maut*), they were using words from Manding, Wolof, Vai, and Mende. They had Akan day names and their English equivalents, and the names of Yoruba gods, and when they grieved they sang mourning songs nearly word for word carried in the hull of the slave ship. Spoken to this day, the Gullah-Geechee language combines a predominantly English vocabulary with elements of syntax from the languages of West and central Africa and selected words, songs, tones, and verbal rhythms drawn from the same region. In the words of Charles Joyner, one of the great historians of Gullah-Geechee culture, the food followed a very similar path as the language developed by the enslaved there. Gullah-Geechee food, part of a larger tradition of Low Country cooking, came from an "African culinary grammar" in which "methods of cooking and spicing, remembered foods, ancestral tastes" defined the flavor of the dishes and the people who created them right down to the carved standing mortar and pestles and the coiled sweetgrass baskets used to winnow the rice.

It was none other than the seventeenth-century English philosopher John Locke whose 1663 plan for the Carolina colony helped damn my ancestors to be among their numbers: "Every freeman of Carolina shall have absolute power and authority over his negro slaves." In 1680 the black population of South Carolina was outnumbered by the white population by 66 percent, and came mostly from resettlement from Barbados with a few introductory shipments from Senegambia, the Gold Coast, and increasingly Kongo-Angola. By 1708 it was "more like a Negro country than a country inhabited by white people" according to Swiss commentator Samuel Dyssli. The population was almost an even split, with a slight black majority. By 1740 the black population had reached a peak and outnumbered the white population: there were 39,000 black South Carolinians to 20,000 whites. By 1775, on the eve of independence, South Carolina was 59.8 percent black and 40.2 percent white.

Go to Charleston and you will inevitably hear about Sullivan's Island, a quiet spot outside the city that people wander through—but mostly for the views of the Atlantic, not knowing its role during the transatlantic slave trade. Historians have had a habit of calling it the "Ellis Island of African America." Four of every ten Africans brought to what became the United States arrived here, a figure comparable with European arrival in the late nineteenth and early twentieth centuries. One group was of people exiled into chattel slavery, another was of willing newcomers from Europe. But that one word makes all the difference and obviates the comparison: "willing." These were not willing immigrants, and the very idea of

Ellis Island—hope, chosen change, redemption, future, opportunity, and the like—was not to be found here.

"We don't call this place the Ellis Island for black Americans. That's their story; this is where the people of Al-kebulan [Africa] were exiled from their homes and their cultures forever. This is where they were sent to work and die—and they knew that." Marquetta Goodwine, a community leader among the Gullah-Geechee Nation, uses the word "nation," reminding me that the analogy is false. "What luggage was there? Did anybody take their names, write them down? No, they didn't. That's why I cringe when I hear that phrase, 'the Ellis Island of black America.' It is easy to get caught up in the fantasy that we are just another piece of the story of the melting pot." It is also easy to become bewildered by the reality that such a small piece of the American South was responsible for seeding black America.

A long-standing narrative exists about Sullivan's Island being the spot where African feet first touched American soil, and that's where most people assume that's where most enslaved Africans disembarked. I thought that this might be the place to start my search, but this work is an act of constant research. I've even prayed at Sullivan's Island, asking for guidance and direction, and for lack of another space at which to encounter the Atlantic and the South Carolina slave trade, I sank my knees into the wet sand and prayed. I even got a response; but according to Nic Butler, historian at the Charleston County Public Library, the place where the slave trade into Charleston occurred wasn't really there—and that does make a difference.

"There are quarantine regulations that apply to everyone coming into the port of Charleston—no matter where you're coming from or what color you are. A ship pilot would go out and inquire if everyone was well or ascertain who was sick. If there was a little bit of suspicion that anyone had smallpox, they would be isolated and sent to the pest house. These are confirmed cases for those who might have smallpox from West Africa, or bubonic plague coming from the Mediterranean. The pest house is active from about 1707 to about 1787 when it's closed and it's converted. But the city of Charleston builds another pest house on James Island, called not a pest house but a lazaretto, at a place they called Point Comfort. The trade was reopened after the war around 1783 to 1787. However only those people who were sick really spent much time at Sullivan's Island—and it didn't matter whether you were enslaved or free, white or black . . . everybody who was sick was quarantined."

I asked Nic, "So why do you think Sullivan's Island has become the symbol, the pilgrimage spot?"

Nic clears his throat: "Having a pilgrimage spot is a worthy goal. Like the Toni Morrison bench by the road, people need places to reflect. That made perfect sense twenty years ago based on the research that was done twenty years ago. The research I'm doing is not to negate the need for that, but to find the historical record that helps us pinpoint the locations that more accurately reflect where things happened."

Truth be told, Sullivan's Island will never cease to be a place of pilgrimage for me even if the knowledge of the history does revise my vision of the steps it took to make me an American. All across the African Diaspora in the Americas, there is a ritual of going to places where the sea meets the land. In these spaces homage is paid by the descendants of those who survived long enough to cross the water and make new lives—and create new life. The association with Yemonja-Olokun—the Yoruba energy of the sea, mother and father—has led to communal seaside rituals honoring the ancestors whose bodies paved the ocean floor from West Africa to the South and beyond. Flowers and other offerings are placed in the boiling surf; people weep and sing and pray.

Sullivan's Island might not even be a place where we could

remember had there not been a plaque and the bench not been put up, or if Fort Moultrie had not existed in the same space. Condominiums are close by; so are the graves of those who didn't make it off the island. Maybe smallpox was a mercy compared with what was to follow. There is no place else to go but down when you are already in hell. Letting them know I haven't forgotten them is worth staining the knees of my jeans.

The greater Low Country is a gorgeous and humid world brimming with life and fecundity. It's what most people imagine the Deep South looks like, even though it's a relatively small portion of the Southern landscape. It's easy to see parallels in the landscape between here and parts of coastal West Africa. Arriving here was a very different experience for my South Carolina–bound ancestors than for those arriving in Virginia. Palmettos and swamps, tidal creeks and vines, constant moisture and heat, and moss on evergreen trees edging grassy savannas—this was their new home. The lowland marshes filled with water moccasins, canebrake rattlers, alligators, fungal diseases, and mosquitoes were said to be "the golden mines of Carolina; from them all our Rice is produced, consequently they are the Source of Infinite Wealth, and will always reward the industrious and preserving Planter." Another South Carolina planter wrote in 1761, "The best land for rice is a wet, deep, miry soil; such as is generally to be found in cypress swamps; or a black greasy mold with a clay foundation." After a time scrambling for a staple on which to get rich, the late seventeenth century brought Africans who knew how to grow rice and viable rice seed. The history of slavery and African America would never be the same again.

The culinary heritage of the Deep South's black population was in line with the origins of Africans arriving in Charleston and Savannah, the Sea Islands, and at docks along the inlets of the coast. Enslaved Africans who did not run away or die during the revolution—like most of my ancestors—would later be part of a westward movement as upland cotton production became more lucrative. Africans arriving in the early nineteenth century joined established black populations in the Carolina upcountry. Many of those whose ancestors had arrived in the mid-eighteenth century were forced west with their slaveholders to western Georgia, Alabama, Mississippi, and Texas. Others, sold to pay debts or liquidate estates, were shipped to New Orleans. The roots of Southern cooking and soul traditions owe their existence to the points where black populations from the three centers of importation coalesced and mixed their traditions—usually making the common denominators between them standard.

The peoples of Kongo-Angola were a clear majority of total arrivals from the 1720s to 1810. There was a lull in their importations for a decade and thereafter; until the final burst of the slave trade, they had steady but lower numbers. Nic says, "During the 1740s, officially, there aren't Africans being brought over partly because of the Stono Rebellion. It's really low numbers if any. In the spring of 1740, South Carolina essentially prohibited the importation of new Africans. They passed a prohibitive tax on newly arrived Africans. They increased the import tax tenfold, in effect killing the trade."

My people were likely here before Stono and they were Kongo-Angolans; the DNA of my grandfather points many fingers in the direction of central Africa. It's probably no accident that my first time standing and reading the marker for the Stono Rebellion was across from my first venture into a Carolina rice field at Clemson University's agriculture field site with Merle Shepard. On September 9, 1739, a group of Angolans and allies met near this spot along the Stono River. Armed with stolen ammunition the Kongo-Angolans played the talking drums, and—by word of mouth and beat—some one hundred gathered in a rebellion pushing toward sanctuary in Saint Augustine, Florida. When they were apprehended and engaged in battle with Lieutenant Governor William Bull (think Bull Street in Charleston), they were seen dancing. Actually, it was another form of the martial art that would come to be known as *capoeira Angola* in Brazil. They were young men trained as warriors speaking mutually intelligible dialects and they were fed up and wanted their freedom. Many of them would end up decapitated, with their heads lining the roads.

The men and women of Kongo-Angola who permeated South Carolina life were in some ways quite culturally removed from the Atlantic Creoles from central Africa who came during the early period to the Chesapeake. However, there were certain affinities owing to the interactions with the Portuguese. They had much in common with their West African neighbors. If the Akan brought memories of *kenkey* and *fufu*, the central Africans had their *kwanga* (cassava loaf) and *infundi* or *funji*, the soft porridge or mush eaten as a base to the daily one-pot soup. Like the West Africans, the raffia and oil palm provided many of their needs—from wine to fruit to oil—and in the Low Country, the fruit and pith of specific palms including the cabbage palmetto, would be fermented to make wine or eaten as a vegetable. The central African daily meal was based on a highly chili-peppered *mwamba*—or a palm-oil-based sauce—not unlike the basis of the Igbo yam "chop." Joaquim Monteiro, a chronicler of nineteenth-century travels in Angola, stated that "cooking is a vehicle for chili pepper," their common "mess" being a stew made with salt fish, beans, and a palm-oil gravy. They were fond of cassava leaves cooked as greens with palm oil, okra cooked with porridge or made into a soup, peanuts, sweet potatoes, melons, cowpeas, and the pigeon pea—known in the West Indies as the "Angola pea." Many of the building blocks of soul food were key to the central African diet and continued in the Low Country unabated and given the similarity of these foods to those found in West Africa—a common tradition could be built across vast linguistic divides.

But the central Africans—whether they were in colonial New York, the Chesapeake, the Low Country, or New Orleans and the

Lower Mississippi Valley—brought with them an intense spiritual and aesthetic culture that was based on the journey of the soul inside and outside the *yowa*—the crosslike wheel of life and death. Married with elements of Christianity, the Kongo-Angolan reverence for the forces of nature—from the river to the forest—imprinted themselves on early African American religion, iconography, and folk belief and especially music. Their food, spirituality, and musical traditions—whether in Charleston or in Congo Square in New Orleans, birthed jazz, a word of Kongo origin, and dances like the Charleston, and signs on the landscape, from the bottle tree to words like "mojo" and "wanga" to the sign of the eternal journey of the soul etched onto the bottom of their bowls charging their everyday meals with spiritual energy, purpose, and symbolism.

Nic continued, "After 1749, once we are at peace with Spain and France, the slave trade recommences. Some fifty thousand arrive in the next twenty-five years, and most arrive in the years just before the American Revolution." The next largest group came from the Rice and Windward Coasts where the Carolina colony's staple was central to the culture, followed by more Gambians and the people from Guinea—many of whom also relied on rice and cultivated cotton, indigo, and tobacco; raised cattle; and were master fishermen—skills indispensable to the pioneer scene of early Carolina and the development of profitable forms of slavery. The much desired Akan of the Gold Coast were the last major group imported in any significant numbers. My paternal grandfather, whose roots are almost exclusively from South Carolina, reflects this pattern—affinities with ethnic groups from Kongo-Angola, Sierra Leone, Senegambia, and Ghana are all to be found in his genetic profile, with most presumably arriving between 1730 and 1775. In Georgia the Rice and Windward Coasts were primary-source regions; planters sought rice growers, then Senegambians, the Akan of the Gold Coast, and Kongo-Angolans.

As we discuss the trade, Nic gives me a sense of how my ancestors were purchased. "Here's my conclusion based on looking at eighteenth- and nineteenth-century newspapers. The newspapers are covered in announcements for the slave trade. On one day in 1773, there are eight slave sales going on. Incoming vessels come up the Cooper River side of Charleston Peninsula, where the wharves are on the east side of East Bay Street. Most likely they are taking people out of the hold and the auctions are taking place on board the vessel on the deck, or on the wharf beside the vessel. The papers will say, 'Will be sold on board the vessel.' For newly arrived Africans it's probably one person sold at a time. It's a different process for people who were brought here versus those who have been here for a while. Very few folks from Africa are being sold on the streets, if any," Nic says. "Then things change when South Carolina sent delegates to the Continental Convention and on October 20, 1774, all of the delegates signed a document called the Continental Association, article 2 of which states:

'We will neither import nor purchase, any slave imported after the first day of December next; after which time, we will wholly discontinue the slave trade, and will neither be concerned in it ourselves, nor will we hire our vessels, nor sell our commodities or manufactures to those who are concerned in it.'"

Africans were smuggled in until South Carolina reopened the slave trade from January 1804 through January 1808. During the long window from the 1780s to the 1820s, more Africans arrived in and around the port than before the American Revolution. Nic says, "In that window, sixty to seventy thousand Africans were brought into the port of Charleston. The only words I can think of to describe the last years of the *legal* slave trade into Charleston is a feeding frenzy. In 1806, one wharf, Gadsden's Wharf, is designated the slave wharf because one ship is coming in on top of the other, and Africans are being sold there."

Gadsden's Wharf will now be the site of a museum devoted to African American history in Charleston. It is a rare moment where the memorializing of such spaces is deliberate and pointed. To stand there is the closest I may get to the spot where my ancestors changed hands and entered "the slavery."

LOWER MISSISSIPPI VALLEY AND THE GULF

In southern Louisiana and the Lower Mississippi Valley and Gulf Coast, about 22,000 people would arrive from West and central Africa, mostly via the French and Spanish slave trades. New Orleans and Pointe Coupee, Mobile, Biloxi, and the Mississippi River port of Natchez—under the auspices of the French, and later Spanish, British, and American authority—had a lot in common with the rest of the South, and yet things were different here. The French Caribbean and Spanish mainland America had an influence on the culture of the region—in particular through Saint-Domingue, Haiti; and Martinique and Guadeloupe and parts of Mexico and Cuba. Although many Africans imported to Louisiana died soon after arrival, by 1731 the African population outnumbered the white population by two to one, and by 1746, Natchez, Mobile, and the Illinois frontier had the same demographic. Like the Low Country, southeastern Louisiana and the rivers that drained into it from the north and west would be a "Negro country," with black minds and bodies shaping much of the folk and food culture.

The Code Noir (Black Code) of 1724, based on codes for enslaved behavior and treatment from the French Caribbean, established a set of rules regulating the treatment of the enslaved and guidelines for rations and the management of recreational time spent on economic pursuits. Enslaved Africans were not permitted to sell produce or other foodstuffs without the permission of their slaveholders and were entitled to a barrel of corn per month. Many slaveholders permitted the cultivation of gardens and allowed time off to fish or hunt. The Catholic faith, though much more assertive than the Protestant church, left much room for cultural adaptations and syncretism, leading to the roots of Afro-Creole religions like vodun and, later, spiritual churches. And this too, as we shall later discuss, was a vehicle for the preservation of African foodways.

The Company of the West, later the Company of the Indies, with its exclusive right of trade at the mouth of the Senegal River, ensured that 4,000 of the 6,000 Africans brought here from 1719 to 1731 were from the Upper Guinea coast, with a large bloc from Senegal and its hinterlands—home of the Wolof, Manding, Fula, Serer, Bamana, and Jola peoples—growers of rice, millet, maize and sorghum, cotton, indigo, and tobacco, with ancient castes of fishermen, cattlemen, blacksmiths, carpenters, potters, and musicians— who might work well in the American low country. Every one of these skills came in handy in building and enriching the colony. The Senegalese women were known cooks, some having served in that capacity in the European settlements of West Africa. The French engagement with the tables of West Africa was a vested part of their colonial presence early on, both in Senegal and the other region of deep importance to French New World slavery, the peoples of the Bight of Benin. African elites and their servants were well aware of western European tastes, and invited European merchants to grand gourmet meals prepared with a mixture of West African and European cooking techniques using native ingredients capped off with bread, wine, and meat. One of the first settlers brought from Lorient, France, was Perrine, a black cook who arrived in 1720, and later a few enslaved Africans would receive culinary training in France and cooked for their slaveholders and trained others in the cities.

The original Africans imported from the Bight of Benin in 1719 were brought with a barrel of rice, with the instructions that Africans with knowledge of how to grow rice were to establish the crop in the wetlands of southern Louisiana. The people of the Fon- and Aja-speaking regions were not predominantly rice growers, but there were pockets of the country where rice was grown, partly for the supply of the slave trade, and a few Africans also arrived from Kongo-Angola in this period as well. Those that followed them from Senegal certainly were, and members of both ethnic blocs could be found migrating with slaveholders up the Mississippi toward the settlement that became Saint Louis. To this day most of American rice is raised in six states, four of which were settled by the French during the colonial period with West African slave labor with rice-growing knowledge.

While rice was raised along with corn to keep the colony fed with some going to the French Caribbean, enslaved Africans in Louisiana were artisans, fishermen, craftsmen, and dock laborers. Indigo and tobacco were cultivated in the plantations along the Mississippi. Among urban enslaved people a mixed-race class developed, taking its name from the term for those who were born in the New World—Creole. Urban and rural Afro-Creole populations developed with diverse origins—Senegambian, Beninoise, Angolan, Choctaw and Chitimacha, French, Spanish, German, British, and Afro-Haitian. They spoke Français Nègre, and much like Gullah and Plantation Creole, the words and sounds of their French were decidedly influenced by the tone, syntax, grammar, and vocabulary of their fairly consistent homelands. Okra was "*fevi*" and "*gombo*," cornmeal mush became "cousu-coush," and a vibrant language developed to describe the rich spiritual world they imported inside their minds. Wanga from Angola, gris-gris from Senegal, and vodu from Benin reflected the sewing together of a belief system across West and central African practices that came to be known as "voodoo." They used Native American words in their Creole too—"*plaqueminier*" for persimmons, "*choupique*" for bowfin, and "*cowan*" for snapping turtle.

Underlying much of the city's culture is a constant theme of Africanization—in music, food, religion, sex, dance, humor, and language. Beyond the borders of the cities was countryside populated by black French-speaking folk whose worlds combined Africa, Native America, and France in a subtropical environment full of familiar ecological elements. This was a mirror image of much of coastal West Africa, and would have been incredibly powerful in the eyes of the Africans enslaved here.

In Mobile, Alabama, a world a far cry from the Alabama of my grandparents, I got to see even more clearly what Creole meant. There were Creole churches, schools, neighborhoods, firehouses, social clubs, and restaurants. Segregation here was Franco-Spanish by design. As America took over southern Alabama it had to agree to preserve the three-tiered social system, with mixed Creoles maintaining their own special status. The last American slave ship would arrive here just before the Civil War, the *Clotilda*, bringing Africans from Ouidah—Yoruba, Hausa, Fulani, Fon, Ewe, Gun—including a Yoruba farmer who was wrenched away from his wife and children and eventually would come to marry a Yoruba woman brought with him on the ship to Mobile.

It started with a bet in Mobile in a bar—a bet to see who could or would be able to smuggle Africans in despite a long-standing ban on the transatlantic slave trade. Of course, there were smuggled Africans arriving sporadically over the years, and they would be quietly integrated into existing enslaved populations—more alone and scared and hopeless than perhaps the first arriving Africans were. The survivors of the *Clotilda* were no different, but because they arrived in one small bloc, they created a community around their unique position as the last arriving enslaved Africans, and created a settlement called Africatown now in present-day Plateau, Alabama. Cudjo Lewis—a Yoruba man given an Akan-Ewe day name; his real name was Kazoola—created a family and built a community around a church that still stands today, and meeting his great-great-granddaughter in the basement of a Mobile church during a pie auction, I was envious that she could look in the mirror and see an African American face with clear links to a specific corner of West Africa, knowing that her ancestors had preserved a great deal of who they were, right down to her almond eyes, gorgeous deep-brown skin, and pronounced cheekbones. She looked like a face straight off the streets of Lagos.

At the same pie auction across the room, I met a very light-brown-skinned man with straight hair and hazel eyes. He was a chef who had brought an amazing charlotte russe. "You can't have a party in Mobile without a charlotte russe that was brought here straight from the days of France." Mr. Henderson was a second-generation chef, and before him there were other chefs in his family going back to their earliest days in Mobile. His father's restaurant, the Best Restaurant, was one of the few establishments that knew quasi-integration—the Jewish businessmen and the Chinese launderers ate alongside black and Creole customers. Like his father, Chef Henderson learned cooking not only in the restaurant but in the catering trade.

"I may not look black, but I am," he said to me over a bowl of gumbo in Mobile in the Wintzell's Oyster House housed in the building that used to be owned by the town's only black physician—the grandfather of my friend and fellow culinary historian, journalist Donna Pierce. Chef Henderson is the tenth generation to live in Mobile in his family. "A Creole here is a black person with Catholic roots and a French or Spanish last name, and a pedigree." With that he unfurled a family tree going back to a woman of color with mixed children who was emancipated in the late eighteenth century.

His family line included Italian, French, and Spanish heritage, and those earliest arrivals of Africans to Mobile and the Gulf in the mid-eighteenth century.

"You know Creole cooks were different. The white man liked them café-au-lait down here, not blackberry black. It was a way of ensuring that they knew the French way and grew up in that culture. And let's face it—they wanted those women and a lot of them practiced *plaçage*—they had a brown woman on the side—and she was in many cases the cook. Many times they would send a man to France to learn to cook or put him under a chef brought from France, but at the end of the day it all was Creole. Creole black people—we were different, we were Catholic, we celebrated Lent, we had our own calendar—we didn't serve the same things at our tables as the rest of the black community, and they were mainly Baptist and Methodist. You never saw a Creole eat no collard greens here, no *chou vert*, because my grandmama said that people liked to grow them where the rainspout dripped, and that's where the dogs liked to pee, so we had turnip greens.

"We had a gumbo for every season and every occasion. Meatless gumbos for Lent, gumbos for duck, crawfish, shrimp, oysters, whatever was in season; filé gumbo when there was no okra, okra gumbo when there was no filé—gumbos for weddings, for funerals—you could know a lot by what gumbo was on the table in front of you. Now you can get anything you want, but back then a gumbo meant something—it told you what time it was.

"You don't just make a gumbo, you build one. I don't just throw everything in the pot at once after the roux—it's the stock I make and the order I put the crab or shrimp or chicken in. You know a good gumbo because it has layers. You can taste each level the chef has put into it. The rice is important too; each grain has to be separate. Everything you make you have to make the presentation count."

I talked to Chef Henderson for several hours, we spoke of the "Cajans" (an interethnic group not to be confused with Acadians) who were yet another complexity to the mix in Mobile, about the superiority of Alabama shrimp, and the importance of red beans and rice. Mobile is a proud community, and everywhere you go there is some ribbing at New Orleans, with Mobile boasting the first Mardi Gras and claiming many aspects of the culture that the Crescent City boasts, including the culinary trademarks. In truth many people traveled between New Orleans and Mobile and Biloxi, and that migration among French Gulf Coast settlements meant the movement of enslaved Africans and their descendants, and with them the food they cooked.

New Orleans and Mobile became, in many ways, the northernmost ports of the Caribbean basin. Enslaved people took advantage of economic lulls and transitions in the economy and engaged in hunting, fishing, gathering, and gardening to produce foodstuffs that would be consumed locally or imported to the islands. Enslaved blacks also sold cooked foodstuffs like gumbo on the streets of New Orleans as early as the late eighteenth century. Native and African cultures merged and influenced each other, establishing various periods of successful maroon communities living on the edge of a plantation society. They would exert a great influence on the folk culture and foodways of the incoming Acadian refugees. Later the mainly Creole black population under the French would be re-Africanized by Africans brought during the Spanish slave trade, during which more imported humans from the Bight of Biafra and Kongo-Angola would arrive. The regional and culinary mixture was further complicated by the influx of enslaved people and slaveholders coming during the revolutionary period in Saint-Domingue in the 1790s, bringing new dishes, varieties of peppers, okras and pigeon peas, and traditions to the mainland.

In 1764 a court document discovered by scholar Gwendolyn

Midlo Hall showed the first written reference we have to Louisiana gumbo. Two Manding women named Comba and Louison had taken freedom—like many in Louisiana's extensive maroon community—into their own hands. They sold "cakes," and had feasts where they roasted turkeys and chickens, barbecued pigs, and made gumbo filé and rice. The streets of New Orleans moved with women and men selling hot food, produce, fish, shellfish, herbs, and sweetmeats like pralines (made from pecan instead of hazelnuts as they had been in France) and *mais-tac-tac* (popcorn and molasses), all of it advertised by singsong chant. These chants offering sweet potato cakes (*pain patate*) and black-eyed peas (*cala aux fèves*) or rice fritters (*cala au riz*), gumbo, crayfish (*crebiche*), and *estomac mulatre*—gingerbread, literally "mulatto's stomach"—were not just part of the food culture, but were woven into the city's rich musical tradition.

Jazz, like the food created here, was no accident. It was born of Senegambian swing, vodun percussion, and Kongo rhythm with French harmonies, and instrumental compositions with wisps of every culture—German, Mexican, Cuban, Choctaw, and Anglo-American—that ever passed through the city. The chants of the city's vendors could be intoned in the tunes of a recently attended opera—indeed enslaved people attended the opera; or it could be in the fading memory of a chant sung as a child saw the coast of Dahomey for the last time. Enslaved people danced Congo Square alive; they attended mass in church; they paraded and processioned in Mardi Gras; they escaped and lived the free life of maroons; they created a world near the mouth of the Mississippi laced with African influence and spiritual power, and from this place—as the others—African American civilization was born.

11

—

ALMA MATER

My first solid human food was cornbread mashed up in pot-likker, the stock left over from a pot of Southern greens. That's the oldest baby food known to black people in America, going back to the days of slavery. Apparently, I loved it and would smack my lips, hungering for more. I grew up with a grandmother who would make cornbread several times a week and take any that was left over the next day, crumble it into a glass of buttermilk, and eat it out with a spoon. The glass streaked with lines of buttermilk and crumbs grossed me out. But when I asked my grandmother why she did it that way, she replied, without explanation, "At least I didn't have to eat it from a trough."

Although I wouldn't know this until many years after she died, my grandmother was referring to a very real thing. When enslaved children on large plantations were toddlers, they were put in the care of an elderly person, usually a woman whose job was to keep them out of trouble and feed them at midday. The midday meal was usually placed in a trough, the likes of which a horse or hog might use to feed from, using the same mixture a hog might be fed, or worse. Frederick Douglass wrote:

> Our corn meal mush, which was our only regular if not all-sufficing diet, when sufficiently cooled from the cooking, was placed in a large tray or trough. This was set down either on the floor of the kitchen, or out of doors on the ground, and the children were called like so many pigs, and like so many pigs would come, some with oyster-shells, some with pieces of shingles, but none with spoons, and literally devour the mush. He who could eat fastest got most, and he that was strongest got the best place, but few left the trough really satisfied.

I don't know who told her, but I know my grandmother didn't read it in a book. And before I read about it from Frederick Douglass, my grandmother told this to me.

It's such a tiny thing, teosinte. The first time I saw a picture in a book of this wild Mexican grass with tiny, tender little green seeds, I really began to marvel at the ingenuity of humankind and our ability to turn the insignificant into a miracle. You might never have heard of it, but you know its descendant, and chances are, no matter where you live in the world, you've been touched by its presence. Just as people have genealogies, so do plants. Teosinte is one of the ancestral grasses of the corn/maize we know today, which was domesticated by indigenous Americans more than ten thousand years ago, and without it African cuisines and their descendant cuisines in the Americas would not be the same. Corn became our "other mother."

Named maize after "*mahiz,*" a Taino/Arawak word, trade and

migration spread corn out of the central valley of Mexico up into southern Canada and down into the kingdoms of the Andes and across South America. The Natchez people of Mississippi and Louisiana, the saving remnant of the mound-builder civilization with their massive earthworks and trading networks across vast distances—which corn, in part, helped to expand—were said to have forty-two different recipes involving maize, from porridges and quick breads to whole ears or porridge cooked with game, fish, or even as meal dumplings cooked with fruit like Choctaw *walakshi*. The Natchez were the last gasp of this great corn-based culture, but it was the Creeks, Cherokees, Choctaws, and Chickasaws, among many others, who rose as distinct peoples after the time of the Mound Builders, whose foodways would ensure that every Southerner went native.

The South's indigenous cultures range from the southern Algonquians around the Chesapeake Bay, the Nanticoke, Piscataway, and member peoples of the Powhatan Paramount Chiefdom, to the Caddo Confederacy of east Texas, Louisiana, and Arkansas. The native peoples of the South were incredibly diverse, from the fishing Calusa to the master potters of the Catawba to the basketmakers of the Chitimacha to the warriors of the Yuchi and Tutelo-Saponi. Apart from a few peoples living on the Florida coasts and other locales who depended mostly on fish and shellfish, corn was essential to the culture of the Southeastern Natives. Although the ancestors of the "Five Civilized Tribes" (the nickname given to the Cherokees, Creeks, Seminole-Mikasukis, Choctaws, and Chickasaws) successfully repelled Hernando de Soto in the 1540s, their descendants were constantly pushed into smaller and smaller territories until the full program of "Indian removal" in the 1830s under Andrew Jackson largely denuded the South of its original people. Land was being snatched up to grow cotton and expand slavery. Ironically among the things that made these tribes "civilized," other than an embrace of literacy and adoption of some "white" agricultural conventions,

was the understanding that black men and women could be property. Barely a century before, thousands of enslaved Natives—many
drawn from these same groups—were targeted in the seventeenth
and eighteenth century and sold to other parts of the Southeast or
the Caribbean, while others acted as bounty hunters and mercenaries and conducted ample trade in deerskins, furs, and the like.

Earthworks were leveled, burial grounds were plowed under, but
white Southerners retained the indigenous names of the land. The
character of the South would not be the same without their presence.
They named the lands where my family began: Alabama ("I clear
the thicket"), Chattahoochee ("painted rock"), Neshoba ("wolf"),
Dahlonega ("yellow money"), Wicomico ("place where homes are
built"), Occoquan ("head of the water"), Atchafalaya ("long river"),
Tallahassee, Tishomingo, Altamaha, Mississippi, Tennessee, Kentucky, Arkansas, Chicora—the names and presence of Native people
are as endless as their cultural impact.

Because of corn, beans, squash, pumpkins, and sunflowers, we
are native. Because of barbecue, we are native. Because of Mardi
Gras Indians, we are native. Because of hunting and fishing and
gathering and maypop drink, hickory nuts, black holly tea, and filé
powder, we are native. And because of so many more things, we
are constantly living in the shadow of the influence of indigenous
Southerners. And beyond that truth is the truth that indigenous
Southerners, like First Nations all across the Americas, are still here;
the Lumbees, the Cherokees, Nottaways, Mattaponis, Choctaws,
Creeks, Piscataways, and Seminoles are still here despite genocide,
removal, broken agreements, and disease.

Only a small amount of my genetic Native ancestry made it
down to me. My great-great-great-grandmother, Arrye, by oral history, was a member of the Muskogee Nation (even though I have my
doubts). Her description, "a (Creek) Indian with long black hair,"
isn't uncommon in black families, and is often followed by the say-

ing, "It was so long she could sit on it." My great-great-grandmother Mary Dunn, born in western Alabama, was said to have Choctaw ancestry; and my paternal grandmother's family, in Virginia since the eighteenth century, spoke often of Native roots; by my best guess, members of the Powhatan chiefdom or the Tutelo-Saponis or Nottaways—the latter were particularly known for positive interactions with enslaved and free Africans. You don't inherit DNA from all of your ancestors, but the stories are there, and a few genetic markers point me in the direction of the earliest Southerners, and with that I am satisfied.

Because of the great pride instilled in me for having Native ancestry, I spent a large part of my childhood studying Southeastern Native culture. Everything they did seemed ingenious. I was impressed with the way my distant forebears hunted deer by masking in their skins; fished by poisoning streams with devil's shoestring; caught catfish with bloody, fresh bison hides; wore dresses of Spanish moss; scratched themselves with gar teeth for spiritual strength before playing the sacred stickball game; and made blowguns from bamboo from canebrakes in the bottoms. Formerly enslaved blacks among the Five Civilized Tribes testified to eating Native foods like *sofkee* (a thin corn gruel spiked with lye), *banaha* (a type of tamale-like food baked in husks) and "tomfuller" (*tanfula*), the Choctaw way with hominy.

And yet, our rebel yell and holler, Mardi Gras Indians, our filé powder, our barbecue, how corn was eaten, and the uses of persimmon reflect a conversation that has been largely lost to us—that Africans and Native peoples did engage culturally, and that there are overlaps in cultural practices. The Native relationship with Africans was complex. Africans engaged with Native Southerners as allies, lovers, tribal members, enslaved people, and enemies. All of those interactions—and this includes Natives who were the heart of the Southeastern slave trade before an upsurge in African importations, as well as relationships based on war and trade—affected the relationship of both groups with each other's food. The culture of pottery-making alone, and the hotly debated nature of whether colonoware pottery was African, Native, or both, shows just how entangled both cultures were. For some, the only acceptable pot to make okra soup, a pan–West African dish, was an Indian-made pot.

Africans certainly influenced the food culture of Southern Natives, just as many of the basic building blocks of Southern food owed a direct link to Native ingenuity. Africans engaged with the foods of the New World before their exile on their own terms. This later determined how they used those same foods and the rate at which they accepted them and incorporated them into their culinary identity. In Southeastern Indian villages, people began to cultivate sweet potatoes, watermelons, black-eyed peas (which they added to their *banaha*), and rice, among other foods. Some of these crops, like sweet potatoes, were less subject to destruction by Europeans. Imagine, for example, fields of maize being burned and proved vital in resisting encroachment. In some Creek and Seminole villages, these new introductions made by African freedom-seekers and enslaved Africans became staples right along with the three sisters (winter squash, maize, and climbing beans, which were the main crops of various indigenous Americans). In Seminole culture many of these crops would be brought into the Florida swamps, where tropical African crops thrived on hammocks with bananas, sugarcane, elephant ear, and the coontie root.

Corn is not just a food to those who grow it, any more than yams or rice or wheat are mere sustenance to cultures of which they have been a part of for centuries. The Corn Mother is life itself. Food was often expressed not as a thing in these cultures but as a *member of your family*. Corn, like sugarcane in New Guinea, was built into a genealogy that went back to the beginning of time. Southeastern Native confederacies and paramount chiefdoms were built on the holy trinity of corn, beans, and squash, with memories growing dim of the days when wild goosefoots and amaranths were staples. Dozens of varieties of each crop, and with them pumpkins and sunflowers and a few handfuls of wild greens, made up the vegetable regimen of my distant seventeenth- and eighteenth-century Native ancestors, cultivated in their summer gardens in the village compounds, newly joined by Africanized crops.

Corn came to Africa via the Portuguese, and black people made it part of their own spiritual genealogies and cosmologies, including Yoruba myths of chickens pecking at corn and creating the universe by scratching out the continents. Its post-1492 spread across Africa was a watershed event, but it was not part of some grand Columbian "exchange" in which there was a sharing of material culture for the benefit of the greater whole. Corn was not just going to revolutionize how Africa ate, but along with other crops, in particular cassava, it would become just the fuel needed to spur on the prolific population growth that would be ample fertilizer for the transatlantic slave trade. Africans were already familiar with sorghum, a grass family cousin, and apart from the end results, sorghum is similar to corn in mature form; it has a head of grain instead of ears. This visual similarity and corn's taste and versatility, making everything from parched corn to corn porridges, breads and ferments, helped it become interchangeable with millet and sorghum in many traditional recipes.

Corn was not always immediately adopted by all African cultures that came into contact with it, and in some cases it was not adopted until the turn of the twentieth century. However, many of the societies that would eventually end up in North America did have some engagement with *Zea mays*. Olaudah Equiano left us one of the most complete descriptions of the transition from continental African to Atlantic African. He spoke of "vast quantities" of "Indian corn" growing near his village in what is now eastern Nigeria. To the west, along the Gold Coast, corn became *kenkey* and *dokono* and *akple*, a type of fermented corn dough steamed in banana or plantain leaves, eaten as an accompaniment with sauces and stews. The very root word for corn *(aburo)* in Akan languages shares with the deeper meaning of "white people" or "foreigners" *(obroni)* as something from overseas. All over Africa, it began to fulfill the same role as any other starch with which to make a relish or soup. In central and southeastern Africa, corn appeared as a thickened porridge that was eaten with foods that would later be found in the South—dried and salted fish, shrimp (think shrimp and grits), cassava leaves or wild greens, chicken, meat, pumpkin leaves, offal, buttermilk, and beans. Maize was eaten universally, roasted in the ashes of the fire or over a grill. Quick cornbreads emerged across Africa at various places and times, none particularly complicated and almost all mirroring the hardtacks of slavery to come.

THE VOYAGE OF NO RETURN

At last, when the ship we were in had got in all her cargo, they made ready with many fearful noises, and we were all put under deck, so that we could not see how they managed the vessel. But this disappointment was the least of my sorrow. The stench of the hold while we were on the coast was so intolerably loathsome, that it was dangerous to remain there for any time, and some of us had been permitted to stay on the deck for the fresh air; but now that the whole ship's cargo were confined together, it became absolutely pestilential. The closeness of the place, and the heat of the climate, added to the number in the ship, which was so crowded that each had scarcely room to turn himself, almost suffocated us. This produced copious perspirations, so that the air soon became unfit for respiration, from a variety of loathsome smells, and brought on a sickness among the

*slaves, of which many died, thus falling victims to the improvident
avarice, as I may call it, of their purchasers. This wretched situation was again aggravated by the galling of the chains, now become insupportable; and the filth of the necessary tubs, into which
the children often fell, and were almost suffocated. The shrieks of the
women, and the groans of the dying, rendered the whole a scene of
horror almost inconceivable.*

—OLAUDAH EQUIANO, ENSLAVED IGBO TURNED ABOLITIONIST

When Olaudah Equiano boarded that ship as a little boy, leaving the coast of what is now Nigeria, he thought he was going to be
eaten when he saw a pot of water boiling on board. He moved from
horror to horror on the journey to becoming a prominent abolitionist in Great Britain. His account of the Middle Passage is one of a
precious few that tell me, from the perspective of enslaved Africans,
what my ancestors endured. Probably not a few of them thought they
were being sold to become food. Little did they know that the movement of their bodies and the movement of food from and to the coast
of Africa represented a monumental shift in the human experience,
the two narratives combining to create the backdrop for the story of
African cuisines in the Americas.

Corn's importance was reinforced by its starring role in the
Middle Passage, the largest forced migration in human history. Giving two crops a year, it proved a very successful means of
outfitting slave ships for both the North American and Caribbean
systems. African food plantations were established to feed the captives of the transatlantic slave trade. Slave-trading empires began to
grow vast quantities of corn, rice, yams, cassava, cowpeas, peppers,
and beans with which to supply both the factors on the coast and the
ships for the several-months-long journey to America. Slave trader
Jean Barbot, writing in the late-seventeenth and early-eighteenth

centuries, said that European traders bought "yams, bananas, corn and other provisions for slaves" from farming villages aligned with the elites controlling the trade.

Corn and tubers would accompany my Ghanaian and Gambian forebears on their Atlantic journey in the form of slabber sauce—the sloppily made slurry meant to appease the West African palate. Using palm oil, starches, smoked and salted fish, boiled legumes, and hot pepper, the mixture was so foul that enslaved captives refused it at the risk of being force-fed through a funnel. Along the coast of modern-day Sierra Leone and Liberia, the slabber sauce eaten by my Mende and Temne foremothers was primarily made of rice. In central Africa, my Kongo and Mbundu ancestors were given a porridge mixture based on corn and cassava. The enslaved people held at Bonny and Elem Kalabari, progenitors of many of my Virginia ancestors, were shipped across the ocean with their staple, the Guinea yam.

The slave trade was timed to make deliveries of enslaved Africans in tune with the agricultural cycle, especially those of maize, rice, and yams. Stephen D. Behrendt's work researching seasonality and the slave trade makes a compelling argument for the connection between food and enslavement, referring to "slave supply and demand linked to the seasonal production of African staples and American cash crops." Slave traders were essentially "shifting farmers between Atlantic agricultural systems." Most enslaved Africans delivered to the Caribbean arrived during the winter months during the time of the cane planting. My ancestors arrived in North America during the height of the weeding and tending of crops—predominantly in the late spring through early fall, when they would be ready to go right into the field and could avoid the immediate shock of colder weather. For many, the waiting period between planting and weeding and harvesting a crop was the time of year they were hunted to feed the trade.

Since yams were "not fit to be taken out of the ground before July and August," ships were advised to be mindful of the yam season, and also to take care to procure them for the journey since "the Calabar slaves being generally better pleas'd with food of their own country, than with any of Europe, except horse-beans which they like pretty well, boil'd with pork or oil." John Grazilhier, another trader, instructed Barbot that it was obligatory for a ship on the coast of Calabar to procure the yams first, then the enslaved. About a hundred thousand yams were used to feed a ship of five hundred slaves, but "not less ought to be provided, the slaves being of such a constitution that no other food will keep them." Boiled yams and water, a sauce made from "a mixed portion of dried, fresh and salt fish, stewed down," cooked in filthy pots was their fare. Whatever else can be said about these unsanitary meals, cooked as a mess and served unceremoniously as filthy hands reached for calabashes or into common pots, these journeys cemented the movement of African crops and animals into the plantation societies of the Americas while introducing the newly enslaved to the monotonous diet that would become the basis of their foodways in the colonial South. Geographer Judith Carney says, "African species were likely put aboard every single ship that crossed the Middle Passage." In slave traders' urgency to pacify and graft their workforce onto new landscapes, the transport of African plants, guinea fowl, guinea hogs, and sheep proved crucial in the Africanization of early America.

Once they arrived, corn greeted them again as they awaited sale, and in one form or another—from ashcake to hominy—probably was their first meal in the plantations of the Chesapeake and beyond. The crop they encountered the most on any given farm was corn—food for humans and livestock.

Corn played backup to rice in the Low Country and southern triangle of Louisiana. Even in South Carolina, corn vied with rice as a staple, with one or both starches starring in every meal. In Louisiana corn preparations reflected the impact of both Senegal and Benin, where maize held its own. It became coush-coush in the hands of Senegalese women, who then passed it on to Acadians. In the rest of the South, a similar dish would be known as "kush." Kush was stale cornbread cooked with grease, red pepper, and whatever else was on hand—a forerunner to Southern cornbread dressing. Most corn was not consumed in porridges and scrambles; instead most corn only knew second life as hoecake or ashcake or hominy, and because of the latter, the black population may well have been spared from massive nutritional deficiencies.

The domestic slave trade, and the resettlement of Tidewater and Piedmont planters over the mountains and south to the Gulf, was largely responsible for pushing corn as a staple across the American South. Corn became the centerpiece of the ration system in most locales. Mark Catesby, an eighteenth-century traveler, noted that corn's "easy culture, great increase, and above all its strong nourishment, adapts it to use in these countries (Virginia and Carolina) as the properest [sic] food for Negro slaves." Hominy, standing in place of *akple*, *infundi*, and other porridges, became the center of the eighteenth-century black diet:

> He is called up in the morning at daybreak, and is seldom allowed time enough to swallow three mouthfuls of hominy or hoecake, but is driven out immediately into the field to hard labor; about noon is the time he eats his dinner, and he is seldom allowed an hour for the purpose. His meal consists of hominy and salt, and if his Master be a man of humanity, he has a little fat, skimmed milk, rusty bacon or salt herring to relish his hominy or hoecake . . . they then return to severe labor, which continues in the fields until dusk . . . it is late before he returns to his second scanty meal.

Hominy's saving grace was nixtamalization—the chemical dehulling process conceived thousands of years ago in central Mexico, with variations through the cultures of the woodlands. Nixtamalization made corn a more readily digestible food, with more of the essential amino acid lysine, taking it from an empty carbohydrate to a complete food when eaten with beans and field peas as it often was. Although nixtamalization was found throughout the Americas, it did not transfer to Africa in the same way that detoxifying cassava crossed the Atlantic.

Sarah Thomas, a formerly enslaved woman from Mississippi, described the hominy-making process:

It was made by putting oak ashes in a barrel wid holes in de bottom and pouring water over dem ashes and what dripped through made a strong lye. Den dey husked de corn and put it in dat lye to boil till it swell up and was tender and husks come off and lef' the corn purty and white. Den dey washed it through several waters till it was clean.

Peter Randolph of Prince George County, Virginia, recalled:

I know my reader will sympathize with me. At nights he would have me to beat hominy. This hominy was beat out of corn. It was beat in a mortar a large piece of timber similar to a water bucket. They had a pestle to beat the hominy with. By the time I would get this beaten it would be about 10:30 o'clock and the next duty I was to perform was to go and wake my mistress up in order for her to see if it was fine enough. Then I would return and next time beat it into meal. Then I would have to go and get another peck of corn and beat it, and by the time I had accomplished this it would be about 1 o'clock I think that was good bedtime.

Nixtamalization, combined with a temperate climate and less lethal labor system, gave enslaved Africans in the Chesapeake a reproductive advantage over enslaved Africans in the Caribbean and Brazil, who were being undernourished by a diet based on cassava. Cassava made you feel full despite very little nutritional value on its own. The custom of allowing enslaved people to cultivate gardens or truck patches, essentially a carryover from African forms of slavery, was an added advantage as it supplied supplements to the hominy-based diet. Caribbean provision gardens grew far more starchy tubers and fruit than leafy greens or vegetables and legumes. Add to this the range of wild foods available in the region, and the diet of enslaved African Marylanders and African Virginians made them taller, healthier, and hardier than their counterparts. Despite this, the everyday fare of the enslaved person on a tobacco plantation or small farm in the Chesapeake and Tidewater seems, at first glance, not one on which a cuisine could truly be built. To quote a plantation mistress's commonplace book from Prince Edward County, Virginia, where my paternal grandmother's family was enslaved:

Allowance of Meal per week for Negroes: 1 ½ peck for each man, 1 peck for each woman, ½ peck for each child.

In addition to this the enslaved workforce was to receive fifty pounds of bacon divided among twenty workers per week or "140 fish," likely salt herring. Men received the most protein, women less, children often none. I'm sure Mrs. Dupuy felt she was being generous. Southern planters often bragged about how much better-fed their enslaved workers were than free white laborers in the North.

Peter Randolph described the ration system from the viewpoint of the enslaved, mirroring Mrs. Dupuy's notes:

The food of the slaves is this: every Saturday night, they receive two pounds of bacon, and one peck and a half of corn meal, to last the men through the week. The women have one half pound of meat, and one peck of meal, and the children one half peck each. When this is gone, they can have no more till the end of the week. This is very little food for the slaves. They have to beg when they can; when they cannot, they must suffer. They are not allowed to go off the plantation; if they do and are caught, they are whipped very severely, and what they have begged is taken from them.

From the Eastern Shore of Maryland, Frederick Douglass's observations on the nature of this ration system from the perspective of the enslaved were echoed by many in his time and beyond:

It was the boast of slaveholders that their slaves enjoyed more of the physical comforts of life than the peasantry of any country in the world. My experience contradicts this. . . . The pork was often tainted, and the fish were of the poorest quality. With their pork or fish, they had given them one bushel of Indian meal, unbolted, of which quite fifteen per cent was more fit for pigs than for men. With this one pint of salt was given, and this was the entire monthly allowance of a full-grown slave, working constantly in the open field from morning till night every day in the month except Sunday. There is no kind of work which really requires a better supply of food to prevent physical exhaustion than the field work of a slave. . . . As a general rule the slaves did not come to their quarters to take their meals, but took their ash-cake (called thus because it is baked in the ashes) and piece of pork, or their salt herrings, where they were at work.

The hardtack of slavery was the ashcake or hoecake. Take white cornmeal, water, and mix. Let set, then bake in the ashes of a fire, either covered up or simply right on top of hot coals, with the provision that you will pick out splinters and dust off or wash the cake free of ash. (Oak or hickory ashes weren't too unpleasant; both impart a slightly salty taste.) In the field, a broad hoe—hefty and solid— might be washed and heated in the fires that were always kept to distract insects; or it might have been made on a griddle, called in colonial-speak a "hoe." Either way, the matzo of enslavement was nearly universal and had little variation from Maryland to Missouri, from Texas to Mississippi to Florida.

Solomon Northup wrote in *Twelve Years a Slave*: "The majority of slaves have no knife, much less a fork. They cut their bacon with the axe at the woodpile. The corn meal is mixed with a little water, placed in the fire, and baked. When it is 'done brown,' the ashes are scraped off; and being placed upon a chip, which answers for a table, the tenant of the slave hut is ready to sit down upon the ground to supper."

"If you wants to bake a hoecake, the old Virginny way /you hold it cross a nigger's head / and hold it there all day," claimed one song. "Bile them cabbage down / bake the hoecake brown / pretty lil' gal stop messing around /you better bake them hoecakes brown," demanded another. Corn was in a part of every aspect of life of the enslaved from birth to death. For my ancestors, corn was not just their food. Cornstalks fed fires and provided insulation, corn husks were a cooking utensil, and corn silks were medicine for earaches.

Corn seed supplied the chickens, guineas, turkeys, and geese that made enslaved people the poultry keepers of the South. Corn husks became dolls, the ticking with which rough mattresses were stuffed, and with time might even be made into rugs. Corncobs found new life as material for smoking meat, served as parts of pipes, and were used to wipe up after defecation.

Corn was also the centerpiece of a unique ritual by which the tensions of oppression and violence were mediated in a late autumn celebration called "corn shucking." Plantations or farms would band together to shuck the dried corn crop and store it in corn cribs. These events included feasting and dancing, and were one of the few times in the year when slaveholders were openly mocked and ridiculed in song by the enslaved. Owners could be criticized, for example, for not providing enough food for the party or for being generally stingy with rations; alternatively, exceptionally generous slaveholders welcomed the occasion as a time when they would be praised before the community.

James V. Deane, formerly enslaved in Maryland, remembered:

> At corn shucking all the slaves from other plantations would come to the barn, the fiddler would sit on top of the highest barrel of corn, and play all kinds of songs, a barrel of cider, jug of whiskey, one man to dish out a drink of liquor each hour, cider when wanted. We had had supper at twelve, roast pig for everybody, apple sauce, hominy, and cornbread. We went back to shucking. The carts from other farms would be there to haul it to the corn crib, the dance would start after the corn was stored, and we danced until daybreak.

The merrymaking at the corn shucking functioned as a sort of courtship occasion for the enslaved. Like the Anglo-American corn shucking, the promise of finding the red ear of corn during the furious competition between teams brought the hope of being able to smooch the girl of one's desire. I have to wonder if any of the courtships that lead to me began this way. For the most part the stories of life in slavery that are passed down hold no romance, no pleasant family memories, no recollections of genuine love. I cling to these stories and make them into my own fantasies to make the ancestors more human.

The girls, for their part, practiced dancing for weeks, doing the pigeon toe and buzzard wing, and "set de flo'" by dancing while balancing a glass of water on top of their heads, showing poise and control. They even used the hominy water in their preparation to starch their petticoats so that as they "played the cloth," pulling and swaying during the dance so that the cloth would pop and snap, they would get maximum attention from the boys. The dance moves of the men imitated agricultural and domestic labors and would trickle down to us as mere entertainment.

Corn was our other mother, and sometimes she committed infanticide. As slavery pulled to a close and sharecropping and the industrialization of food emerged, plain cornmeal and un-nixtamalized corn was consumed in greater quantities out of convenience. The big, pearly, puffy grains of hominy—pasty but filling and nutritious—gave way to corncakes and mush that were empty carbohydrates with little nutritional value. The descendants of the enslaved, caught in the system of debt and poverty, could afford little more than meat, meal, and molasses—the 3 Ms—and these often came from the plantation store, leading to more debt. On such poor diets, nutritional deficiencies abounded, especially the scourge of the South, pellagra, caused by a lack of niacin. Thousands of Southerners, depending on corn for their mainstay and little else, developed the disease, which caused itchy skin, senility, and bowel disturbances. Many Southerners died, including my great-great-great-grandmother, Hettie Esther Hughes, the midwife born into slavery, who lived to be ninety, but died because of a preventable nutritional deficiency founded in Mother Corn.

Trough Mush

4 ½ cups water
½ tsp salt
1 cup buttermilk
1½ cups white stone ground
 cornmeal

bits of greens, potlikker,
 other like tidbits, optional

Let the water and salt dissolve together. Add the buttermilk and bring to a boil. In small amounts, add the cornmeal until it is completely incorporated into the liquid mixture, turn down the heat, and cook for at least a half an hour. When the mush is near its end, add the leftovers. Be sure to add your tears.

Hoecake

1 cup white stone-ground
 cornmeal
½ tsp salt

¾ cup boiling hot water
¼ cup lard, vegetable oil or
 shortening

Mix the cornmeal and salt in a bowl. Add the boiling water, stir constantly and mix it well and allow the mixture to sit for about ten minutes. Melt the frying fat in a skillet and get it hot, but do not allow it to reach smoking. Two tablespoons of batter can be scooped up to make a hoecake. Form it into a small thin pancake and add to the pan. Fry on each side 2–3 minutes until firm and lightly brown. Set on paper towels to drain and serve immediately once all the hoecakes have been cooked.

12

—

CHESAPEAKE GOLD

The table at dinner is always furnished with the finest Virginia ham, and saddle of mutton—Turkey, then canvas back duck—beef—oysters, etc, etc, etc—the finest cellery—then comes the sparkling champagne—after that the dessert, plum pudding—tarts—ice cream—peaches preserved in Brandy etc. etc—then the table is cleared, and on comes the figs, almonds and raisins, and the richest Madeira, the best Port and the softest Malmsey wine I ever tasted.

—HENRY BARNARD, PETERSBURG, VIRGINIA; MARCH 14, 1833

Across four centuries, the seasonal rites of King Tobacco have barely changed. I realized that when my father taught me how to grow tobacco that was essentially unchanged since the arrival of my ancestors in the colonial Chesapeake. Arriving West Africans had a high degree of familiarity with the crop, although we're unsure to what degree this played a factor in the European assessment or appreciation of Africans as laborers among the fields of oronoco (used for snuff) and sweet-scented (used for pipes) tobacco. When Jamestown was founded in 1607, tobacco fields filled the Senegal River valley on which some of my ancestors lived and surrounded African villages and settlements. African villagers were known by one visitor as "born smokers," whom you could no sooner trust with your tobacco than you could a "cat with bacon."

On a farm in Southampton County, Virginia, in November 1762, where some seventy years later Reverend Nathaniel Turner would stage the rebellion that rocked the world of antebellum slavery, the possible forebears of my great-great-great-great-grandfather John Bowen (black) lived with the successive generations of their (white) slaveholders—John the Elder and John Bowen Jr. In the assessment of property of John the Elder there was nine hundred harvested pounds of tobacco, probably the remnant of a much larger crop, along with corn, wheat, and cotton. The enslaved people amid the Bowen farms (say their names: James, Ben, Peter, Ned, Rose, Frank, Jordan, Hannah, Mingo, and unlisted children) performed multiple labors; in addition to raising the main cash and domestic-use crops, they milled grain, made shoes, and made barrels, possibly even the hogsheads in which the tobacco was delivered to market. They sheared sheep and carded and spun wool and cotton. They mended fences, took care of the cattle, hogs, sheep, and poultry scattered around their dwellings. From winter to winter, sunrise to sunset, their calendar was filled with the work of building the Southern world, and in the midst of this, at least one person had their hands on John Bowen the Elder's and Jr.'s cooking pots and spiders.

My forebears roasted in ashes and steamed in shucks, cooked on sticks and used hot rocks. Likely they had Dutch ovens and spiders, and in these implements the roots of proto-soul food were born. Their world of gadgets consisted of wooden spoons and metal castoffs, shells and found objects, wooden bowls and occasional porcelain cups obtained through barter. Nothing fancy was present. They used what they had, held in bondage in what was for a century or so the center of American slavery—the tobacco lands along the Tidewater coast.

Tobacco is known famously as the "thirteen-month crop." The work of maintaining a tobacco farm was constant. For most of my Virginia ancestors, it was not precisely a plantation, but a farm with enslaved workers and probably enslaved hires during planting and harvesting time. Only the Saunders, Booker, and Jones kin seemed to live on actual plantations, the measure being the number of enslaved blacks in full employ. Have fewer than twenty, and you're not a planter; at best you're a prosperous farmer with human capital to his name. Have twenty and you're a planter and you have a plantation. In addition to tobacco, keep in mind that large fields of corn, wheat, hay, and patches of cotton and flax had to be cultivated, along with vegetable gardens and orchards. Trees were constantly being girdled, felled, and moved, then transformed into firewood, fences, buildings, and shingles. There was livestock to care for, oyster shells to burn, and fish to be harvested during the spring run of herring, shad, and rock. There were household duties and specialized work—tanning of hides and milling of grain, blacksmithing and shoemaking, carpentry and coopering and the making of the barrels that actually shipped the tobacco off to market. On smaller farms, the Mitchells likely did some of this work alongside their enslaved workforce while the prosperous Bowens did not, and on larger ones like those of the Bookers and Saunderses there were overseers, and their payment is noted in personal accounts. But the bulk of this labor was done by black hands. A field hand like Elijah's older brother George could expect to maintain one to two acres of tobacco alone; that's equal to 12,000 to 20,000 or more tobacco plants.

In January and February the work begins. You burn the ground in set patches to kill any mold, spores, or extraneous seed before sowing the tiny seeds—ten thousand or so can fit in a teaspoon. You cover the ground with branches and boughs of pine to protect the ground from snow and cold . . . and you wait. While you wait, you prepare the fields, removing debris and tree stumps, making the earth as bare as possible before adding heaps of manure and other amendments. On days of intense sunlight and warm air in March, you let the patches catch light and heat, and the seedlings—first looking like nuclear-green moss, then ever-expanding—grow into little plants. By April you weed the tobacco beds and start to pluck out the weaker seedlings, and by May the transplanting begins after the hills are made—thousands upon thousands of hills made by a grub hoe that, you will remember, was the cooking implement for hoecake, the hardtack of slavery. When rain looms, you move the carefully plucked seedlings into the fields, and for a few days they appear as if they will die and look like hell.

The rain comes, and by and by the plants perk up and exert their weediness, pushing and moving up toward the sun. Competing weeds—often edible greens that are tucked away for relish with the nightly hoecake and herring—are removed from each hill to give the tobacco a fighting chance. The cultivation time for each hill is about a minute or two, and only a skilled worker knows how to chop at the tobacco just right to catch every weed before moving on to the next hill. The "noxious weed" gets taller; the flower wants to come out and bloom, and as they do the plants are topped so that the energy goes to the leaves and not floral sex. A few plants with their flowers remain in the field to provide seed for the next year. More than enough will come from four to six plants left to go to seed.

As they do, the suckers appear—which must be snapped to prevent the plant from sending unnecessary energy into inferior leaves; think about tobacco's cousin, the tomato, which is cultivated in a parallel way. Summer progresses and the tobacco hornworm appears, and in these thick, green, clinging little nightmares comes the nasty task of removing them from the plant, a chore for enslaved children who might be punished with swallowing several if they missed any. According to one person I interviewed, they taste sour and their juicy bodies have the slightest lingering nicotine sting. After the children, speckled guineas and Spanish black turkeys were driven through the fields, pecking off tobacco worms and their larvae, fattening themselves on tobacco's pests.

August comes. Just as ninety-degree days rule, the coopers go into a frenzy making hogsheads to pack the tobacco in once it has cured later in the fall. The lower leaves turn yellow and brown on the edges; these are removed as priming commences. When all else is done and no more successive weedings are to come, the harvest time means every possible hand goes into the field. The waterboy is busy bringing water and persimmon beer to the field for anyone who wants a gourd full. The salt herring and salt pork among the rations become critical as workers expend sweat and calories from sunrise to sunset.

My hands have been gummy with tobacco sap, stuck together with little aphids sticking to my hands. I have had my little tastes of working a tobacco patch, hilling up the soil to make the mounds, and I can testify to this: at the rate of one good mound a minute, being bent over like this would break anyone's back. But imagine hundreds upon hundreds. I never could. My first tobacco worm—horrifying and clinging and mercilessly juicy—made me never want to pick another one off. I've had the loopiness of tobacco's many little narcotic chemicals and felt my hands and thoughts tingle and felt my brow burn. A little 'bacca here and there, and I still can't imagine what my ancestors went through, not even when I have felt how heavy a stake of tobacco was loaded down with sap-heavy leaves.

To figure out just how much work this actually meant for my ancestors, I went into the agricultural censuses just before the Civil

War for the Virginia counties where they were enslaved. George Saunders, a prosperous slaveholder whose family had been around since the early eighteenth century, has 27 enslaved people producing 12,000 pounds of tobacco in 1850, the oldest of whom was born before the Revolutionary War. By 1860 his slaveholdings increased to nearly 50, with 23,000 pounds of tobacco as output. The holdings of the Wootens—an offshoot of the Bookers—went from 12 workers producing only 3,500 pounds to 19 workers producing over 8,000 pounds. On the Ligon plantation in Prince Edward, the greatest amount of tobacco was produced of any plantation on which my ancestors were enslaved, 27 enslaved increased in ten years to 34, and in 1860, 35,000 pounds of dark-fire tobacco came from this farm alone.

The tobacco plants are staked and lifted up into the barns, where they cure. In the colonial period, the oronoco variety was speared and staked whole before it was lifted up into the barns, filling rung after rung; these leaves were cured by natural heat and air. Dark-fire cure, which was what most of my enslaved Virginian ancestors did, relied on heat from an intense fire made in a depression in the center of the barn. In 1839, the year Edward Booker I was born, the method known as flue curing was enhanced by the "accidental" discovery made by an enslaved teenager named Stephen on the farm of Abisha Slade in Caswell County, North Carolina. After falling asleep, he used charcoal to fire the flue, the higher heat resulting in the golden "bright leaf" tobacco that would transform smoking into a milder experience for the everyday person. From West African crops of tobacco predating the arrival at Jamestown to the innovation of bright leaf tobacco, my ancestors' labor and knowledge not only enriched Mother Britain and early America, but itself paid debts to France for American freedom after the War of Independence, and created a billion-dollar industry after the Civil War.

King Tobacco spread up along the rivers that drained the land between the Eastern Shore and the Blue Ridge, the natural high-ways where the hogsheads were brought to market. The anadromous species like herring, shad, sturgeon, and rockfish or striped bass are born in freshwater but live in salt or brackish water, returning to freshwater to spawn. In days past, this meant rivers gleaming with fish by the thousands headed back up the Potomac, Patuxent, Patapsco, Choptank, Rappahannock, York, James, and Appomattox. Thousands of these fish were caught by seining, then were processed by scaling, gutting, and salting for rations—three salt herring a week was typical. Beyond these species, the waterways provided dozens of varieties of salt and freshwater fish, blue crabs, oysters, clams, and terrapin, and the enslaved relished their eels, longnose gar, and muddy flavored bullhead cats.

The oak-, hickory-, pine-, and chestnut-filled forests provided wood for cabins, shingles, barrels, baskets, and tobacco stakes among other useful products in a world where nearly everything was made at the homeplace, right down to the "drunken man" or worm fence that made the vast acres of cleared land into a patchwork of cash crops. Split oak baskets in varying forms for tobacco, corn, and vegetables were also used for fish traps. Broken tobacco stakes were not wasted but coddled together to form rabbit, raccoon, and opossum traps. Pigs and other livestock flourished on the acorns and chestnuts that filled the forest floor by the millions. Oak and hickory also powered the fireplaces of the Chesapeake's plantation kitchens, the smokehouses and the cabin fireplaces where enslaved people would occasionally hang a skinned cottontail rabbit to smoke and dry the meat for later use, as well as its barbecue pits during the laying-by, harvest, and Christmas.

As tobacco swallowed up everything before it, it left tracts of land unfarmable for twenty years or more. In the place of native hardwoods came scrub pine and "weedy" trees that were not as useful for the needs of the plantation—especially not for cooking and smoking meat. The march west and south by planters and their workforce in search of "fresh land" was in part driven by farming methods that didn't conserve the soil or prevent the drying up of natural resources—fish, game, rich pasture, and arable land. Plantations like Thomas Jefferson's Poplar Forest saw the enslaved being forced to turn to undesirable wood, like resinous pine, to fuel their cooking fires, because preferred species were in short supply. The food of the Chesapeake grew legs as the culture of the Upper South was forced to branch out from lower Delaware Bay and the Chesapeake rim to past the Appalachians into the southern halves of Ohio, Indiana, and Illinois; and much of Missouri, Kentucky, Tennessee, northern Georgia, Alabama, Mississippi, Arkansas, and northeastern Texas. In this moment, spread over time from the late eighteenth to the mid-nineteenth century, the canon of Southern food and its African American component gained incredible singularity of character. Turkey with oyster dressing on a Maryland plantation became turkey and freshwater clam and mussel sauce on a slaveholding Missouri farmstead.

Initially, tobacco shared the scene with corn and wheat to meet the needs of both home and market. Later, tobacco prices fell during the time of the War of Independence, and acreage decreased because of worn-out fields and want of new land. Planters turned to increased production of corn and wheat to feed an expanding country and grain-starved, Revolutionary-era Europe. The world of wheat had a completely different seasonal rhythm, and it required fewer workers than tobacco; wheat was sown in the autumn and harvested after the transplanting of the tobacco in June. Wheat helped create the surplus of black workers in the Chesapeake, especially on the Eastern Shore, on the Tidewater peninsulas, and on the northern rim of the region. The shift in labor needs did not bode well for my forefathers and foremothers. It meant that the Upper South's greatest cash crop would soon be human beings.

Before the shift to wheat, my ancestors knew about "seldom," their word for wheaten bread and foods which were rarely consumed outside of special occasions; thus the tradition of Sunday biscuits or holiday rolls. But corn, their adopted mother grain, remained, along with salt pork and salted herring, the mainstay of Old Virginia. George Washington's attempts to convert his enslaved community to full-time wheat eaters failed; they not only preferred the versatility of corn but required it to feed the dunghill fowl—their chickens and other poultry that they depended upon for petty income at market. Black people were the "general chicken merchants" of the Chesapeake region, and none of the homesteads of my African Virginian forebears would have been complete without a poultry yard with hutches for hens. From my grandmother's recollections, the poultry yards were always loud with Dominicker (Dominique) hens, guinea fowl, ducks, geese, and black turkeys—the same birds that pecked the tobacco clean of worms.

Freedom comes in as many forms as resistance; each garden, animal, or fish trap, and hidey-hole, represents a fight against a monotonous diet meant to instill a sense of inferiority and difference. No human could live on that kind of diet and survive, let alone pass on a culture to the next generation. Yet nearly every enslaved person in the Chesapeake was faced with the plebeian corn-based ration system in one form or another. Without their creative ingenuity and the flow of foods and recipes between the Big House and the slave quarter, the world of Southern cuisine as we know it would not have existed. As they were forcibly moved across the Upper South into the northern parts of the Cotton Belt, foodways born in the Chesapeake went with them.

To highlight the difference between the two worlds, Frederick Douglass described in great detail the tables of the grandees as he knew them in the early nineteenth century:

The highly-favored inmates of this mansion were literally arrayed in "purple and fine linen, and fared sumptuously every day." The table of this house groaned under the blood-bought luxuries gathered with pains-taking care at home and abroad. Fields, forests, rivers, and seas were made tributary. Immense wealth and its lavish expenditures filled the Great House with all that could please the eye or tempt the taste. Fish, flesh, and fowl were here in profusion. Chickens of all breeds; ducks of all kinds, wild and tame, the common and the huge Muscovite; Guinea fowls, turkeys, geese and pea-fowls were fat, and fattening for the destined vortex. Here the graceful swan, the mongrel, the black-necked wild goose, partridges, quails, pheasants, and pigeons, choice waterfowl, with all their strange varieties, were caught in this huge net. Beef, veal, mutton, and venison, of the most select kinds and quality, rolled in bounteous profusion to this grand consumer. The teeming riches of the Chesapeake Bay, its rock perch, drums, crocus, trout, oysters, crabs, and terrapin were drawn hither to adorn the glittering table. The dairy, too, the finest then on the eastern shore of Maryland, supplied by cattle of the best English stock, imported for the express purpose, poured its rich donations of fragrant cheese, golden butter, and delicious cream to heighten the attractions of the gorgeous, unending round of feasting. Nor were the fruits of the earth overlooked. The fertile garden, many acres in size, constituting a separate establishment distinct from the common farm, with its scientific gardener direct from Scotland, a Mr. McDermott, and four men under his direction, was not behind, either in the abundance or in the delicacy of its contributions. The tender asparagus, the crispy celery, and the delicate cauliflower, egg plants, beets, lettuce, parsnips, peas, and French beans, early and late; radishes, cantaloupes, melons of all kinds; and the fruits of all climes and of every description, from the hardy apples of the north to the lemon and orange of the south, culminated at this point. Here were gathered figs, raisins, almonds, and grapes from Spain, wines and brandies from France, teas of various flavor from China, and rich, aromatic coffee from Java, all conspiring to swell the tide of high life, where pride and indolence lounged in magnificence and satiety.

Indeed the list of skills, according to author Letitia Burwell, entrusted to these cooks with these various "species of meat and vegetable to be found on a plantation," was the "egg-beating, butter-creaming, raisin-stoning, sugar-pounding, cake-icing, salad-chopping, cocoanut-grating, lemon-squeezing, egg-frothing, waffle-making, pastry baking, jelly-straining," the "flavoring the best ice-creams; buttering the hottest rolls," and preparing "every kind of cakes, jellies, and blanc-mange . . . besides an endless catalog of preserves, sweetmeats, pickles and condiments." The cuisine of the Big House made the cooks among the enslaved a class above the rest. In the words of Frederick Douglass:

> These servants constituted a sort of black aristocracy. They resembled the field hands in nothing except their color . . . so that in dress, as well as in form and feature, in manner and speech, in tastes and habits, the distance between these favored few and the sorrow and hunger-smitten multitudes of the quarter and the field was immense.

This was the world of James Hemings, Peter Hemings, Edith Fossett, and Fanny Hern at Monticello; Charles at Lexington Park; Robert at Riversdale; Emily Plummer at the Three Sisters plantation; Hercules at Mount Vernon; Hannah at Poplar Forest; Henny at Wye House. The biggest and most prominent plantations demanded that guests be entertained, and with them their enslaved workers who transported them and bore their luggage to distant plantations. Access to the best food available and the clandestine economy this created, along with access to news of the larger world, empowered the cooks right along with the knowledge they were self-aware of their monetary value. Even Booker T. Washington's mother, one of only a handful of enslaved workers on a small Virginia tobacco farm, found herself cooking for the thirteen members of her slaveholder's family, plus the enslaved workforce, including her own small family and any white or black workers brought in to assist with harvesting the crops, as well as any guests.

The aristocratic tables of the Carters, Lloyds, Carrolls, and Lees, complete with heirloom porcelain decorated with tobacco leaves to honor their source of wealth, were far less common than those tables that bridged the world of the enslaved with that of the enslaver. As much as some of the people who enslaved my family might have wanted to emulate the wealthiest planters, this scene from famed architect Frederick Law Olmsted's *A Journey in the Seaboard Slave States* might come closer to the mark of what life might have been like on the Todd or Mitchell farms:

> On their plantations, generally, the Virginia gentlemen seem to drop their full-dress and constrained town-habits, and to live a free, rustic, shooting-jacket life. We dined in a room that extended out, rearwardly, from the house, and which, in a Northern establishment, would have been the kitchen. The cooking was done in a detached log-cabin, and the dishes brought some distance, through the open air, by the servants. The outer door was left constantly open, though there was a fire in an enormous old fire-place, large enough, if it could have been distributed sufficiently, to have lasted a New York seamstress the best part of the winter. By the door, there was indis-

criminate admittance to negro-children and fox-hounds, and, on an average, there were four of these, grinning or licking their chops, on either side of my chair, all the time I was at the table. A stout woman acted as head waitress, employing two handsome little mulatto boys as her aids in communicating with the kitchen, from which relays of hot corn-bread, of an excellence quite new to me, were brought at frequent intervals. There was no other bread, and but one vegetable served—sweet potato, roasted in ashes, and this, I thought, was the best sweet potato, also, that I ever had eaten; but there were four preparations of swine's flesh, besides fried fowls, fried eggs, cold roast turkey, and opossum, cooked, I know not how, but it somewhat resembled baked sucking-pig. The only beverages on the table were milk and whisky.

Lucky for us, the white Saunders kin, a prosperous slaveholding family from Buckingham County, were neighbors and business associates of the "Mark Twain of Virginia," George Bagby and his family. Bagby's *The Old Virginia Gentleman*, collected in one volume after his death by his daughter, is replete with references to the characteristic foods of the tobacco belt. For want of a direct primary source tied to the plantations on which my ancestors were enslaved, George Bagby describes the foodscape of the James River basin in the nineteenth century; he's literally describing the food world my Booker, Fore, Hill, Mitchell, and Saunders ancestors knew, from the soil and water to the trees and air and how ingredients from those elements were translated into the delicacies of the everyday Virginia table:

I am tolerably certain that a few other things besides bacon and greens are required to make a true Virginian. He must, of course, begin on pot-liquor, and keep it up until he sheds his milk-teeth. He must have fried chicken, stewed chicken, broiled chicken, and chicken pie; old hare, butter-beans, new potatoes, squirrel, cymlings, snaps, barbecued shoat, roas'n ears, butter milk, hoe-cake, ash-cake, pancake, fritters, pot-pie, tomatoes, sweet-potatoes, June apples, waffles, sweet milk, parsnips, artichokes, carrots, cracklin bread, hominy, bonny-clabber, scrambled eggs, gooba-peas, fried apples, pop-corn, persimmon beer, apple-bread, milk and peaches, mutton stew, dewberries, batter-cakes, mushmelons, hickory nuts, par-tridges, honey in the honey-comb, snappin'-turtle eggs, dam-son tarts, catfish, cider, hot light-bread, and cornfield peas all the time; but he must not intermit his bacon and greens.

Bagby's world—my ancestor's world, the farms and plantations along the James and Appomattox Rivers—seemed to burst at the seams with a diverse variety of crops. The "cornfield pea" that wound its way up the cornstalk as it had in West Africa was the "Grey Crowder" cowpea, still cultivated in Southern gardens today. Different patches of provision grounds were unique to their soil types and microclimates and seemingly observed a form of a shifting cultivation:

Butter-beans, snaps, green peas, beets, cabbage, and a few flowers make up the contents of the garden; other vegetables, such as tomatoes, onions, black-eye peas, cymlings, and "rosin" ears, being grown here and there, first in this and then in that patch, in various parts of the plantation—a curious and peculiar feature of old-fashioned Virginian management.

The commonplace book from the Falkland plantation in my family's homeplace of Prince Edward County, located in the Virginia Library, written in the hand of Mrs. Dupuy, echoes Bagby's semicomical observations. The enslaved workforce cultivated some of the same crops that would have been critical to their health and comfort, and their ability to create a cuisine. The crop list, divided by season, is rich: artichokes, asparagus, beets, butter beans, cabbage, carrots, celery, corn, cress, cucumbers, cymling (pattypan) squash, fennel, gourds, kale, lettuce, (musk) melons, mustard, onion, parsley, parsnips, peas, potatoes, pumpkins, radishes, red pepper, rutabagas, snap beans, spinach, sweet potatoes, sweet potato pumpkin (cushaw), tomatoes, turnips, and watermelons filled the Big House garden. Many but not all of these would have been grown in the gardens of the enslaved along with okra, field peas, peanuts, and ground peas—a curious survivor from West Africa, the Bambara groundnut.

The plantation landscape was divided up into plots appropriate to each crop complex. Sandy low grounds of the Chesapeake swelled with white- and yellow-fleshed sweet potatoes, watermelons, and muskmelons. The watermelon, symbolic of stereotypes and the subject of so many racist images from the late nineteenth century, was a lifesaver for the field worker dehydrated and pushed past exhaustion in the fields. One man formerly enslaved on a tobacco plantation in Maryland noted that he was severely whipped along with a girl for "stealing" a watermelon for refreshment on a hot August day. Of sub-Saharan African origin, watermelons and muskmelons traveled to the Chesapeake both from European and African strains, as they already had diffused into northern Europe by the time slavery was in full swing. Beside riverbanks and tidal creeks, the melon patches flourished, marking the plantation landscape as ships picking up hogsheads of tobacco loaded from dock to dock.

Sweet potatoes—red, white, and yellow, second in importance to corn as a starch—were stored in the floor of the cabins. According to Booker T. Washington:

In the center of the earthen floor there was a large, deep opening covered with boards, which was used as a place in which to store sweet potatoes during the winter. An impression of this potato-hole is very distinctly engraved upon my memory, because I recall that during the process of putting the potatoes in or taking them out I would often come into possession of one or two, which I roasted and thoroughly enjoyed.

The storage pits for sweet potatoes were so important that they are a telltale sign in many parts of the Chesapeake of the presence of the enslaved. Archaeological digs have recovered these pits across the former tobacco belt. Sweet potatoes and peanuts—pilfered foods, along with beads, items particular to and precious to each family and individual—would be stored hidden from plain view in these subfloor pits; some from the earliest colonial period contain the residue left behind by enslaved people pouring alcohol as libation to the ancestors. When enslaved people purchased or bartered for goods, they kept them in these spaces covered by dirt, slats of wood, or their sleeping pallets. These little private spaces were not just practical; they spoke stories about identity, power, and privacy—three things my ancestors were often denied.

The cooks on the Chesapeake plantations shifted between the worlds of the cramped, drafty cabin, and "ruling" the kingdom of the Big House kitchen. My great-great-great-grandmother, Evertine Hill, mother to Elijah Mitchell, was likely one of their numbers—a turkey feather fan, the kind used to bring the coals to life in the morning, remains in my family's possession. With tools in hand she melded Africa and North America. What took place in their hands was a dance of cultural blending and cultural resistance that was almost too civilized and graceful to notice. It was not just the spices, ingredients, and cooking methods that Africanized the diet; it was the spirit imbued in its preparation. Its vocabulary snuck into the language of the South, its flavors pushed the preferences of Britain and Germany to the rear, its manners determined the flow, and its communalizing nature brought the West and central African influence together to allow their touch to masquerade as if Europe still had the upper hand.

In 1800, as my Virginia bloodlines endured, a black preacher near Richmond named Gabriel Prosser convened a meeting of enslaved men to discuss a plot to liberate all enslaved people. His plan was to slaughter slaveholders in the cause of freedom, except Frenchmen, Methodists, and Quakers and, according to legend, one member of the Tidewater planter elite—Mary Randolph, mistress of a Chesterfield County plantation and a mansion in Richmond named Moldavia, whom he sought to retain for her renowned cooking. She would be the "Queen of the Kitchen." Mary Randolph would eventually come to write what is considered the first Southern cookbook, *The Virginia Housewife*, in 1824, three years before her death. Randolph was raised at a Goochland plantation where the food culture and other remnants of West Africa abounded, and her cookbook abounds with the taste and touch of the enslaved, and draws clear connections to the cooking and flavor palate of the planter elite.

Mary Randolph's relations put her squarely in the nexus of the sweet-scented tobacco elite on whose plantations the courtly cuisine of the Chesapeake reached its apogee—she had ties to Thomas Jefferson, the Lees, the Carters, the Custises, and the Washingtons. She was also surrounded by people who shared my eastern Nigerian ancestry—mostly Igbo cooks whose first-and-second-generation children were probably her first playmates growing up. Mary used okra, a word derived from the word "*okwuru*" from a dialect of Igbo, for the same plant. There's no accident there, or that Mary recorded dishes that hearken back to the street foods and celebratory dishes of southeastern Nigeria. Fried chicken, stewed okra, okra and tomatoes, okra soup, chicken stewed with yams, black-eyed-pea cakes, hot-pepper vinegar, barbecued shoat, boiled turnip tops, and catfish curry demonstrate the merging of cuisines of four or five continents, but all bear the unmistakable touch of the people who surrounded her.

Mary Randolph's approach to cooking, based on British food-ways laced with French influences, nurtured by the black women whom she grew up around, became the standard as Virginian/Chesapeake/Upper South cuisine spread across the South with the domestic slave trade. Similar recipe books—most notably *The Kentucky Housewife* (1839), *Domestic Cookery* (1845), *Fifty Years in a Maryland Kitchen* (1873), *Housekeeping in Old Virginia* (1879), *The Maryland and Virginia Cook Book* (1894)—created a canon of cookbooks written by white women whose worlds were populated by black cooks and servants, whose presence can be read across the pages in recipes in dialect, recipes with only first names, or recipes with descriptions of plantation life and its seasons of celebration and rare calm. Each of these books is replete with ingredients, flavor combinations, cooking methods, and food preferences that touch on the contributions of the enslaved, from a recipe on how to cook "co'nfiel' peas," to an admonishment to not let Negro cooks "ruin" cymling squash when they fry it in bacon grease.

In the end it was the white ladies, the "keepers of the keys," and not the black men and women who worked for white slaveholding families and for more than two centuries shaped and processed European, African, and Native American foodways, who got the credit for forging this tradition of Upper South foodways. Author Susan Dabney Smedes gave credit to the butler but only as a machine run by white authority, a widely practiced tradition in reckoning black "help":

> The butler, George Orris, was quite equal to the trust committed to him. It was only necessary to say to him that a certain

number of guests were looked for to dinner, and everything would be done in a style to suit the occasion. George himself was said to know by heart every recipe in Mrs. Randolph's cookery-book, having been trained by that lady herself. . . . George was so formidable in his dignity of office that the timid young wife stood quite in awe of him, and before she learned to know the good, kind heart that beat under that imposing appearance, was actually afraid to ask for the keys to get a slice of bread and butter in her husband's house.

With these men and women running the dining rooms of Chesapeake plantations, Southern hospitality was born. It was an extension of *teranga*, one of many indigenous concepts of peaceful living based upon hospitable treatment of others, in this case, a concept brought from Senegal and Gambia with the Wolof, Serer, and Fulani, ethnic groups often selected to work as domestic servants. Combined with the chivalry that Southern planters tried to emulate, it was the hallmark of Southern culture. Southern food would retain its anchors in Virginia and the greater Chesapeake, but for many the food traveled west and south, spreading the Upper South food tradition far and wide, even beyond the boundaries of adjacent states. From beginning to end, my people were there passing down the cuisine born in the womb of the mother of American slavery.

The Saunderses, the Mitchells, the Bookers, the Joneses, and the Fores shifted cultivation and pushed up hills and down valleys, planting tobacco. The Bowens moved south into North Carolina and then on to Georgia and, finally, Alabama, changing over to cotton, and with each generation they grew in slaveholdings. The Townsends and Woosleys migrated into Tennessee and Alabama, also choosing to grow cotton. The Todds would eventually sell Jack and Arrye and their children apart, and it is this moment in the passage we will visit next—the moment they were separated in the only place in antebellum America rightly nicknamed the "Devil's Half Acre." Another ancestor passed them in time, a little boy brought for sale to Richmond from the tobacco belt of North Carolina, named Harry.

13

—

THE QUEEN

Enslaved Africans had been part of the colony's labor force from the earliest days of settlement. Some were involved in the cultivation of rice as early as the 1690s; however, most were employed in cattle ranching and naval stores. In the 1720s white South Carolinians turned to rice, a labor-intensive crop. During the decade of the 1720s some 8,817 slaves were imported into South Carolina; more than three-fourths of these were purchased after 1724. Thus, it appears that these slaves were destined for work in the rice fields.

It was evident that whites in eighteenth-century South Carolina understood the ethnic backgrounds of Africans sold in the Charleston slave markets. They had a decided preference for individuals from known rice-growing areas such as the Windward Coast. The debate may never be

settled as to who brought the first seeds; however, there can be no question as
to the key role that Africans played in the production of rice.
—WALTER EDGAR, *SOUTH CAROLINA: A HISTORY*

Middleton Place is a gorgeous Low Country rice plantation located just outside of Charleston, South Carolina.
There are sheep mowing the lawn in front of the remains
of the Big House, which was damaged during the Civil War. There
are huge swaths of subtropical wetland where you can see alligators
and turtles sunning themselves with rice birds and herons bouncing on their backs. It's hot as hell in summer, and buggy and mean
and nasty, and all gentility is lost when you begin to think you feel
the mold growing from the inside out. My tour guides are Ted Lee
(one-half of the dynamic culinary duo of the Lee Bros. catalog and
cookbooks, along with his brother Matt) and Jeff Neale, a scholar
and interpreter on the staff.

Ted points out edible mushrooms and the elephant ear you see
everywhere—"The corms were sold on the streets of Charleston"—
and they note to watch out for snakes and snappers. "Rice fields were
deadly. Imagine getting a bite from a poisonous snake or losing a
toe to a snapping turtle, or getting infections and parasites just from
the water. We haven't even talked about yellow fever, malaria, and
the host of insect-borne diseases, or gators or heatstroke. These were
some of the most lucrative and deadliest plantations in the South."
But dear G-d, is the rice pretty and heavy when it's harvest time,
every bit the Carolina gold the legend speaks of. So delicious I feel
guilty when we're treated to lunch at Middleton: plates filled with
red rice, stewed okra, shrimp and grits, benne wafers, fried quail,
and every other delicacy their chef can push out. All I can think
about is the way your feet dissolve in the sludge of the paddies.

"That's where Ms. Edna stayed." Ted points out the living quarters of Virginia-born chef Edna Lewis, who cut her eyeteeth on the

Deep South's foodways here during a stint as the chef in the same restaurant. The landscape around here has gone deeper into interpretive education and further away from romance. Sugarcane, guinea hogs, water buffalo—yes, water buffalo, Sea Island cotton, indigo; it's all here. So are the beautiful Africa-inspired sweetgrass baskets that fanned the rice, and the standing mortar and pestles. I try my hand at it; I have a lot of broken rice but I fan it and separate out the chaff. I would have been a poor worker, but as Jeff says to me, "The middlings [broken pieces] would have been your dinner."

If cotton was the king of the antebellum South, rice was her queen for the three centuries of her engagement with slavery. With the revamp of Carolina Gold rice and other heirloom varieties and hybrids thereof, the narrative of rice in the South has become centered in the rebirth of one of its most important cash crops as a boutique ingredient. The prominence of the rice kitchen is more popular than ever thanks to the vision of Glenn Roberts of Anson Mills, the scholarship of Dr. David Shields, and the work of Chef Sean Brock of Charleston's restaurants McCrady's and Husk. I appreciate their work to restore the respect of the Carolina rice kitchen on the land, on paper, and on the plate, but I don't want to retell their story because they—and others—can tell it better. Contemporary food media have celebrated this renaissance without ever acknowledging the 360-degree change from the roots of rice culture in the American Southeast. At its birth it was all black and depended on the skill and knowledge of black women—women like my sixth great-grandmother, an anonymous Mende woman.

My mother was named Pat, and she was born in 1948. Her mother was named Hazel, and she was born in 1925. My great-grandmother, Hazel's mother, Mary, was born in 1892. Her mother was Josephine, born in 1872, a woman who claimed that she had "no nigger blood" even though she was born to a mulatto woman born in slavery herself. That woman, my great-great-great-grandmother was named Hettie, and she first appears, as far as my genealogist, Toni Carrier, could trace, around 1840 on a document in Alabama. She was held by a family from her home state of South Carolina, and she was twelve.

Hettie's oral history, passed down to her children and her children's children, was remarkably in sync with what documentation can tell us. She lived to a ripe age, though she was snuffed out by pellagra, a disease brought on by a nutrient-poor diet based on empty calories from corn. From her womb came many children by several men, the last being a "bright" mulatto, perhaps even a free man of color she married named Sam Spencer Hughes, known by the nickname "Plenty," a nickname from the Manding of the Gambia. She was the daughter of a woman named Nora (born ca. 1800–1810), and her father's name was Isaac (neither of these individuals survive in any known records to date), and she said she was from Charleston.

It will take me some time to sort through the possible leads that might bring me closure about the origins of Hettie Haines and the lives of her parents. This much I do know—she was so mixed with European ancestry that she nearly appeared "white." She was taken from her mother as a little girl, and protested that she was not in fact born enslaved—or, for that matter, "Negro." This has led us to believe that her mother was also the daughter of a white man and a biracial woman. That biracial woman's name is not known, but this much is likely: Nora's mother was born in the late eighteenth century, and her mother—by the general degrees of separation from Africa by DNA and the timing of the slave trade—was born in Africa at about midcentury.

The period between 1750 and 1775 was the heyday of the arrivals from the rice-growing regions of West Africa. There was an explosion in imported Africans from Upper Guinea—Senegambia to Guinea to Sierra Leone and Liberia, the last two together known as the "Rice Coast." If we were to take these three together, we would have about 40 percent of the known trade to what became the United States. Of course not all came to South Carolina and Georgia, where the rice plantations were centered, or to Louisiana. But the vast majority of those from the Rice Coast and neighboring rice-growing areas arrived in the Low Country. It is no accident that two separate DNA tests show that direct descendants of Hettie have genetic affinity with the Mende. Ground zero for Mende entry into this country was the port of Charleston.

Because I have nothing else to go on and no names to tell you, I've taken a cue from the scholars of ancient genetics who have named the evolutionary mothers of humanity to distinguish their legacies. I asked my sixth great-grandmother, *"Bi Mende beyei?"* What is your Mende name? She answered, *"Nya a la Mame Wovei."* Elders in Mende are all *"Mame."* She reveals herself to me: "My Name is the Elder Woman."

It started with a ship from Madagascar that wandered into Charleston harbor in 1685 that needed repair and a gift of rice, so the legend goes. Some scholars like Judith Carney say that African red rice was already here and was joined by Asian rice. By 1691, a colonist could use rice to pay taxes, and by 1698 ten thousand pounds had been exported. Most of the Africans then were from Senegambia and rice-raising regions of Angola, Ghana, and the like. Then came the people of Kongo-Angola, and it was their labor that transformed more than 150,000 acres of land from the Cape Fear River to northeastern Florida, building dikes and dams, gates and levees necessary for the cultivation of rice on tidal river plantations. By 1770, with the plantations importing women like Mame Wovei, 66 million pounds of rice were produced on the eve of the American Revolution, making Charleston's rice planter elite some of the wealthiest men in America.

Mama Wovei, the Elder Woman, was not an old woman when she was likely captured in a war by a rival ethnic group, or during slaving season when the crops were between planting and harvest. She was anywhere from eighteen to twenty-five years old and her ability to grow, pound, and process rice, and the fertility of her womb, were central to her value in the Charleston market. In the years before the revolution, women like her commanded high prices. She joined other Africans from rice-growing cultures—Manding, Temne, Sherbro, Bassa, Vai, Jola, Kpelle, Gola, Kisi, Balanta, Papel, Biote, and Manjack. I have no idea whether she was married or had children before she was delivered into the hands of the captors who took her to the coast, who took her to Bunce Island, who took her by canoe to the ship that ultimately delivered her to Charleston. I just know that she and another woman with ethnic affinities with the Temne and Fula of Sierra Leone both crossed the ocean in the mid-nineteenth century, and each would pass on their DNA to me from the midcolonial period. From them would come my maternal and paternal lineages.

The societies in which these women lived cultivated rice in a variety of ecosystems, and used sophisticated means of dealing with the crop according to whether they were growing it upland, along river valleys, in swamps, or near mangroves. Gender roles defined who was responsible for specific tasks. Men cleared and prepared the fields; women selected the seed, planted, and weeded the fields; and both sexes harvested and took some role in the processing and storing of the grain. Rice had been a part of West African life in Upper Guinea and the Western Sudan for nearly two thousand years by the time the Europeans arrived, spreading out from heartlands along the Senegal, Gambia, and Niger Rivers. Rice cultivation spread out from the ancient Sudanic kingdoms as my ancestors reinvented themselves, redrew linguistic and clan lines, and migrated from the empire of Old Mali and went south into the lands of the Bullom and others, coming as Mane conquerors displacing the indigenous people and planting up the rain forests and coastal swamps in African red rice, namely *Oryza glaberrima*. This three-thousand-year-old rice would in time be joined by Asian rice, *O. sativa*, from introductions made from both the Islamic and European worlds.

African red rice is a sacred plant to many of the people who still grow it. It is intimately associated with the ancestors; it was even used to start a revolution in colonial Senegal. According to my friend Senegalese chef Pierre Thiam, "a young, handicapped Jola woman named Aline Sitoe Diatta" had a vision during a drought from the Jola Supreme Being to return to the ancient rituals of their ancestors, and to abandon the broken Asian rice given to them by the French colonial authorities during World War II. It was not enough to grow and cultivate the rice; the Jola were to return to traditional forms of land management and respect for sacred woodlands. Aline Sitoe Diatta met her end in exile in Timbuktu, ultimately dying of starvation. Rice has a long history with culinary justice.

African rice was a part of the whole system of how social power, spirituality, sexuality, material craftsmanship, and culinary ability were expressed. Because of this, my ancestors from the Rice Coast developed rich and highly socially regulated cultures where agricultural knowledge, music and dance, and the art of the masquerade flourished for both men and women. Again we are in a world where a single food set the blueprint for an entire civilization. Rice fed the ancestral dead; it was necessary for sacrifices to lesser deities; men sang of their prowess while preparing the fields; and women gave constructive criticism back as they pounded rice. It was the first and last solid food a person ingested from cradle to grave; rice was tied to the flow of the generations. To pound and cook rice was a skill central to everything they knew. According to scholar James McCann:

> African rice . . . produces almost twice the protein content of wheat per unit of land and slightly more than maize. Like other true grains, rice is rich in B vitamins and contains complex

carbohydrates (starch and fiber.) The key to rice's nutrition . . . is its processing and cooking. Processing involves threshing, milling, and winnowing. Unlike the processing of the European grains . . . the processing of rice is intended to produce grains without breakage. Women use a mortar and pestle with a skilled tapping and rolling motion that minimizes breakage of the individual grain and yields white rice by removing the bran and germ from the soft endosperm.

Mama Wovei's value lay in her ability to process and cook rice. African women didn't favor a sticky rice but rather a rice where every grain is separate, produced by boiling for 15 to 20 minutes, pouring off the water and cooking over a low heat, or allowing residual heat to steam the rice, and as with most vernacular rice dishes, a tasty crust develops on the bottom and sides of the pot. What I didn't know growing up was that African Americans—Africans and Afro-Latins—made rice like my grandmother made.

Through Mama Wovei, I am an heir to the legacy of rice growers across the planet. It has been said that if an extraterrestrial wanted a specimen of the world's most common human, they would have to find a poor woman in a rice field. If a Sierra Leonean has not eaten rice, he says he has not eaten. My friend Vietnamese-American activist and advocate Amanda Nguyen says the same can be said in her culture; to ask if someone has eaten today is to literally ask if they have eaten rice, because nothing else satisfies and nothing else is more central to the experience of the meal. It brings to mind the big bags of rice I saw in the corner of my grandfather's kitchen on my first trip to South Carolina, and the constant chorus from my cousins: "I have to eat rice every day!"

The peoples of the Rice Coast weren't Africa's only rice growers at the time of the slave trade. Because rice had been introduced into what is now southern Ghana, Dahomey (modern-day Benin), coastal

Nigeria, and parts of Kongo-Angola, some of the other Africans had some experience with the crop. It not only was a subsistence crop but was produced with the express intent to be used to provision slave ships headed to the New World. Across the Americas the Africans from these regions and Upper Guinea were brought, to some degree, for the purpose of growing rice. In some areas, it helped vary the diet or replaced yams or millet, in others it was a side crop not worth much attention—in southeastern Nigeria, rice acquired the name "the white man's beans."

Rice has since caught on quite well in West and central Africa. Every culture seems to have their answer to rice and beans—a cheap and filling meal. In Ghana, this particular combination is called *waakye*. In Senegal it is a particularly ancient dish, likely as old as Mali and Songhai, *ceeb u niebe*, or rice and black-eyed peas. Rice and chicken, rice and lamb or beef, rice and fish and vegetables, rice with peanut stew, and rice with okra or leafy greens are all seasonal Senegambian specialties, an entire cuisine based around rice.

The movement of Africans across borders in the colonial era has spread a Senegalese dish called "Jollof rice," made with tomatoes and onions, drawing its name from the Wolof empire, but worthy of arguments as to which version—Senegalese, Sierra Leonean, Ghanaian, or Nigerian—is actually the best. Jollof rice has become the transnational dish of West Africa and has accompanied the modern diaspora of West African immigrants across the globe. It has become for them the go-to heritage food that reminds them of home. In West Africa rice becomes fritters, and mashed balls to be eaten with stew; it becomes porridge, part of soup, and a dessert when prepared mashed with honey. Rice is a mother who has bonded wide swaths of West Africa in ways millet and sorghum have not.

In Mende land the husking and cooking of rice was a daily event to Mame Wovei and her compound. Working with her sister, she would pour the rice into a foot-and-a-half-deep mortar made from the wood of the iroko or African teak tree, and working in concert they would take the six-foot-long pestles made of ebony or the wild rubber tree, and beat the rice in turn and tandem with a solid work rhythm as they sang and clapped between leaps of the pestles. They would then fan the rice in large winnowing baskets to take away the chaff. The usual soup consisted of water, red palm oil, smoked or fresh fish, pepper, and onion, and on special occasion meat and poultry. Sweet potato, cassava, or okra leaves varied the sauce, and on other occasions the rice might be eaten with a similar mixture of ingredients with tomatoes, eggplant, and other garden vegetables. Much like the Chinese division between *tsai/fan*—meat and vegetables or fish and the rice that is the main attraction—the Mende likewise call the other food *ndahaing*—the thing that goes with *mbei* (rice).

In her garden, she grew sweet potatoes, yams, hot peppers, ginger, cassava, okra, peanuts, corn, sugarcane, beans, onions, and herbs. From the trees surrounding her village she had a rich variety of wild and introduced fruits, including the *ndoku-wuli* (*Diospyros* spp.), hog plums, berries, oranges, coconuts, papayas, guavas, bananas, and plantains (the latter eaten as a starch), leafy greens, and mushrooms. From the rivers and swamps, women caught catfish, crabs, tilapia, and other fish. Men cutting grass would catch rats, porcupines, bushbucks, duikers, primates, and snakes. The chickens, ducks, guinea fowl, and goats that rummaged around her village would become stews during a feast or would be salted, rubbed with hot peppers, and roasted to celebrate a wedding or the rice harvest.

The societies of the Rice Coast were policed by the Poro and the Sande (sometimes called *Bundu*), secret societies each gender—male and female—was expected to pass through on the journey to manhood and womanhood. Their presence manifests in the dancing of masks—instructive and didactic material emblems of ancestral law. No young woman was allowed to marry until she had passed through initiation with the Sande. Mame Wovei would spend three months in the bush learning the rules of acceptable adult behavior, modesty, beauty, customs regarding sexuality, and cooking in both everyday and ritual contexts. In this respect, she was like many, but not all, African women who went through a three-to-six-month period where they would be educated according to their new responsibilities, complete with the invitation to eat as much as she liked to gain weight so that she might make for a desirable candidate for wife and mother. Part of her tuition was paid in smoked fish, palm oil, salt, onions, and the basic ingredients of the Mende stew, and the women who taught her shared their tips for dishes that would endear her to her future husband and, if necessary, best any other wives he might have.

When you drive along the roads in the alluvial plains of Louisiana and Arkansas in the late afternoon, the fields of rice are a particularly green crop. The water in the fields reflects the color of the leaves, especially after a storm. The plant matures, and over time the heads are pale-golden with the ripe seeds that will be husked to make the product. To go into a rice field, to wade into the water, muck, mud, among the poisonous snakes (in the Carolina coastal flatwoods, that means canebrake rattlesnakes and cottonmouths) and alligators, to face unbelievable clouds of gnats and mosquitoes, is a unique experience. It is hot and hellish, and the thought of doing a "task," an assigned portion of acreage (each enslaved person shifted their attention between quarter-acre portions on up to five acres each) for the day's labor seems impossible and even cruel.

Slaveholders assumed some immunity on the part of their enslaved chattel, and there was a tiny bit of truth to that. Many of the rice cultivators carried the sickle-cell trait and had had bouts with tropical diseases that made them a little hardier than their European slaveholders. (Incidentally, Mame Wovei's direct descendant, my maternal grandmother, was herself a sickle-cell carrier.) However, yellow fever, skin infections, and skin conditions from standing in fetid water were indiscriminate. Many did not survive, though my sixth great-grandmother beat the odds and lived to produce children who lived to produce children whose descendants produced me.

My travels in the Low Country went from Wilmington, North Carolina, where my great-great-great-grandmother Rosetta Merritt was born (family oral history collected by my uncle said she was "of the African nation") to Pawleys Island and Hobcaw Barony in Georgetown, South Carolina, where I met a Gullah woman named Laura Herriott and sat down to a lunch of sweet red rice with beef sausage, a fine okra-seafood gumbo, fried chicken, and iced tea sweetened with pineapple juice. Afterward, she took me to go catch a *wa maut*, and she smiled broadly when she realized I understood she was talking about catfish (unfortunately we caught nothing that day). Laura is there to stay after living elsewhere, and has a little cottage where she hosts ecotourists and sports enthusiasts who come to the Low Country. It's a good strategy for a part of the country that's being eaten up by development and gentrification—where graves become golf courses, old homesteads become luxury subdivisions, and going to the sea for sustenance is off-limits because the beach is privatized.

Georgetown County, South Carolina, was the heart of the rice plantation industry. The richest American slaveholder who ever lived, Colonel Joshua Ward, had 1,130 enslaved chattel on his plantation, Brookgreen, producing for Ward more than 3.9 million pounds of rice per year. From Georgetown to Georgia, the names repeated themselves—Ball, Ward, Alston, Heyward, Manigault, Laurens, Drayton, Middleton, and Doar. According to historian Walter Edgar, "In 1850 South Carolina produced 104,759,672 pounds of rice (74.6 percent of the nation's output); Georgetown District produced 46, 765,040 (44.6 percent of South Carolina's total and 33.3 percent of the nation's)." To visitors from "off," like Basil Hall from England, the subtropical world of the Low Country rice plantation was remarkable, and the process of making rice seemed so magical as to require minute detail:

Our host, who soon joined us, explained that the current we saw, was caused by the flood tide, though the sea was distant full 30 miles. This ebb and flow of the rivers intersecting the level parts of South Carolina, is of the greatest consequence to the rice growers, as it enables them to irrigate their fields at the proper season, and in the proper quantity; an advantage which leads to the production of those magnificent crops with which all the world is familiar.

During our stay at this extensive and skillfully managed plantation, we had an opportunity of being initiated into the mysteries of the cultivation of rice, a staple of Carolina. This grain is sown in rows, in the bottom of trenches made by slave labour entirely. These ridges lie about seventeen inches apart, from centre to centre. The rice is put in with the hand, generally by women, and is never scattered, but cast so as to fall in a line. This is done about the 17th of March. By means of flooded gates, the water is permitted to flow over the fields, and to remain on the ground five days, at the depth of several inches. The object of this drenching is to sprout the seeds, as it is technically called. The water is next drawn off, and the ground allowed to dry, until the rice is risen to what is termed four leaves high, or between three and four inches. This requires about a month. The fields are again overflowed, and they remain submerged for upwards of a fortnight, to destroy the grass and weeds. These processes bring matters to the 17th of May, after which the ground is allowed to remain dry to the 15th of July, during which interval it is repeatedly hoed, to remove such weeds as have not been effectively drowned, and also to loosen the soil. The water is then, for the last time, introduced, in order that the rice may be brought to maturity—and it actually ripens while standing in the water. The harvest commences about the end of August and extends into October. It is all cut by the male slaves, who use a sickle, while the women make it up into bundles. As it seems that no ingenuity has yet been able to overcome the difficulty of thrashing the grains out by machinery, without breaking them, the whole of this part of the process is done with hand flails in a court-yard.

The cultivation of rice was described to me as by far the most unhealthy work in which the slaves were employed; and, in spite of every care that they sink under it in great numbers. The causes of this dreadful mortality, are the constant moisture and heat of the atmosphere, together with the alternate floodings and dryings of the fields, on which the negroes are perpetually at work, often ankle-deep in mud, with their bare heads exposed to the fierce rays of the sun. At such seasons every white man leaves the spot, as a matter of course, and proceeds inland to the high grounds; or, if he can afford it, he travels northward to the springs of Saratoga, or the Lakes of Canada.

Each plantation is furnished with a mill; and in most cases that fell in my way, the planters contrived to make this and everything else, or very nearly everything else which they require, on their own estates. All the blacksmiths' and carpenters' work, for example, was done by the slaves of each plantation. . . .

When I taught at a local synagogue, one of my classes was for tenth and eleventh graders, and innocently enough one of our conversations turned to the subject of race. I was the only African American in the room—the only person of color in the room, period—and the presiding adult. Not long into the conversation I got a slew of corrections:

"My teacher [at private school] told me blacks prefer to live in ghettos, so they just stick to their own kind and that's why they don't get ahead."

"My ancestors came here and worked hard and people discriminated against them; I don't understand why black people can't get ahead."

"Why are you even bringing up slavery? That happened a really long time ago. I mean you shouldn't forget it, but it's really not helping talking about it. In fact, we make racism worse by talking about it."

I stumbled in my words. I could have given them a long history lesson but I couldn't think of where to start. I also realized I was not arguing with high schoolers but with their parents. This is how their parents really felt about race in America, and I was profoundly discouraged. I wanted to leave the room and scream but I had no choice but to face the gantlet. I tried to counter with the narrative of compulsory illiteracy, lynching, targeted redevelopment, redlining, and loss of culture and heritage, but I got choruses of "I don't buy that," and, "That's bullshit." Until Keith Doar piped in.

"Guys, have some respect. You're being assholes."

"What?" Furrowed brow and defensive stance set in from the private-school kid.

"Guys, come on. Don't argue about this," one of the females in the room said, raising her voice in uncomfortable concern—not for my feelings, but for the intuitive sense that her friends could come to blows over what's been said.

Another kid chimes in, "What's up your ass, Keith?"

"Have some damn respect. Mr. Twitty is the teacher, and besides, he's right. You don't know what you're talking about. My father's family had slaves, people like Mr. Twitty's people, so just because yours didn't doesn't mean you don't benefit from it. We had rice plantations in South Carolina."

All the mouths in the classroom fell open. Keith didn't "look" (Ashkenazi) Jewish, and neither do I. He looks like any Carolina boy, although he's never lived there. I've seen his face a dozen times, and he's usually wearing a pastel polo underneath his chin, and I never really noticed that until then. The naysaying young neocons in the room have nothing to say. The class ends on a silent dribble of conversation until Keith's father pops up to bring him home.

The next class, Keith and his father presented me with a book to borrow: *Rice and Rice Planting in the South Carolina Low Country*, by his great-uncle David Doar. Like most rice-planting families, the Doars kept a record of their plantation days—almost like albums of the good old days when they were grandees. A similar book helped begin the journey of Edward Ball with his epic *Slaves in the Family*, tracing the paths of the descendants of the Ball family plantations. To the Doars it was a dusty book worth pulling out every once in a while to say that they had been here a long time. On the long road to returning the book, Keith and I talked about my research on my own family, and I told him about Sierra Leone and how the enslaved Africans' experience with growing rice transformed the land and made the plantations incredibly lucrative.

My friendship with Keith persists to this day. The openness he and his family have expressed negates any feelings of guilt or blame, and that book represented an invitation to share. Keith's mother, who is his tie to Judaism, has even suggested, as if she herself were a seasoned Southerner, "You're probably related." That expression is said with a smirk or flat lips, and it's incredibly sincere and truly meant. It means the past cannot be changed, but the present is here, and indeed many of us are connected because of a broader network of people who existed in the past—in and out of slavery—and there's no point denying, in the words of my friend, writer, and slaveholder descendant Grant Hayter-Menzies, that we have "tangled vines."

One day I hope to take Keith to Sierra Leone so that we can make peace with our mutual pasts as Americans.

Across the Deep South, rice became a staple—and artifacts and photographs bear witness. Rice traveled with whites and blacks, but it was black people doing most of the processing. My white fifth great-grandfather William Bellamy paid "Negro Luke for rice and onions" in Nash County, North Carolina, and most likely "Negro Luke" raised these himself in the bottoms of the Tar River. In the plantations of Kershaw County, South Carolina, in the upcountry, upland rice was grown by several planters and raised as a home crop by most; that enslaved people were growing it for themselves did not merit census-taker records. In Russell County, Alabama, where my maternal grandmother's father's family was enslaved, there are several references to whites there being taught to grow rice by enslaved people brought from South Carolina—one of three areas that drew immigrants to the Black Belt and the wiregrass regions of Alabama. My white Bellamy ancestors' cousins raised rice along with sugarcane and cotton on their northern Florida plantations. Rice was raised all the way from the seventeenth century to the twentieth century. From Wicomico County, Maryland, to the banks of the James River in Virginia, to east Texas, from the Missouri bootheel to the banks of the Suwannee River in Florida, and it almost always came with the word "Negro," somewhere near it in the records.

If it was not raised for export it was raised for home consumption, and some of that rice was African red rice brought from Guinea, a portion of which owed its introduction to experiments by Thomas Jefferson. From Jefferson's distribution of seed, upcountry planters began to grow rice on their plantations, and as the domestic slave trade and migration west pushed white and black Southerners toward other parts of the region, rice went with them. Rice husked in many forms—red, gold, white—was exported from not only the old rice belt of the Carolinas and Georgia, Florida, and Louisiana, but from Alabama and Mississippi as well. It became a seasonal staple and respite from corn, the other mother of whites and blacks, and it established the base of an entire cuisine, as described by Northern visitor Henry Barnard:

> But he served up a grand dinner to a small party—first came a calves head stew as soup—then fish fried or boiled—roast veal and ducks, with Irish and sweet potatoes—boiled rice (an article of which you can form no opinion from what we ordinarily meet with in the North) and fine bread—peas and beets—turnips and salad. Then came the dessert—another fruit—fine large oranges—pineapple—plantain and bananas (tropical fruits which I have never seen at the North but which resemble the richest pear in flavor)—apples—raisons and almonds—prunes and ground nuts and to wash down the whole of each the finest claret, sherry and madeira wine.

Today, the Low Country has seen a renaissance brought on by efforts to resuscitate a particularly rich part of Southern cuisine centered in Charleston. In the upsell are histories of the enslaved and antebellum black heroes of the kitchen like Tom Tully and Nat Fuller, cooks born into slavery whose culinary power was matched by their social power and ability to bring together white and black Charlestonians despite racial and political divides following the Civil War. I had the privilege of meeting Reverend Clementa Pinckney, a state senator and a leader of "Mother" Emanuel African Methodist Episcopal at a dinner honoring the legacy of Nat Fuller, who held a reconciliation dinner after the Civil War to bridge divides. A few weeks after our meeting, on June 17, 2015, Dylann Roof entered Mother Emanuel, waited like a hunter and murdered Senator Pinckney, a forty-one-year-old husband and father, and eight others in cold blood.

Dylann Roof said he wanted to correct history. He frequented the region's historical sites looking for evidence that whites were being maligned, and sought to expose a supposed myth of black agency in building the world he was born into. His ultimate aim was to start "a race war." Charleston has a very complicated history. Mother Emanuel had its doors shut in the mid-nineteenth century because it was where the Denmark Vesey conspiracy leaders met. Vesey, a literate free man of color from the West Indies, working alongside an enslaved conjurer named "Gullah Jack," himself imported by antebellum planter and slave trader Zephaniah Kingsley, had his plan foiled by an enslaved spy who was ultimately not rewarded for his betrayal.

The hanging tree from which Denmark Vesey hung is not far from a restaurant named Nana's. Chef BJ Dennis and I sat down with elders there and talked at length about the recent events, and whether positive change was coming to Charleston. Plates of yams, garlic crab and rice, oysters and rice, red rice, spiced shrimp, macaroni and cheese (macaroni pie) and collard greens sat on the table, although to be honest I was full from Chef Dennis's collard greens, made with peanut butter and coconut milk over rice from lunch. Everything there, just like my first forays into South Carolina as a child, was "over rice."

"Ain't not a damn thing changed. They come hugging on us and talking about how sorry they are. They not sorry for keeping a street named after John Calhoun or having a hanging tree, but they are sorry because that boy lived up to his heritage." The attempt to single-handedly bring back The Old South was not just terrorism, it was an act of war.

"There is two groups of people. People who felt the need to make peace because of politics because that's who the *buckra* [Gullah for "white people"] expect us to be. We always turn the other cheek. It's not enough to bring a [Confederate] flag down off a pole. You got to mean it in your heart."

The conversation was spotty, but wove in and out of the massacre. As special bottles of pepper sauce got passed, many lamented those who had sold city property or family farmland to developers. It was here in the Low Country that "forty acres and a mule" was originally promised. The loss of valuable real estate that is culturally and socially and environmentally important, to make room for luxury, gated communities, infuriates and frustrates those who wish to keep the Charleston and countryside they grew up with alive.

"Where we gwine go to catch fish, to catch swimps, to get crab or oystah? It's like they take the food right out we mouth!" It reminded me of a young black Creole man attending Dillard who told me that the rural Creoles lamented development and laws because "the white man don't want us to eat!" Indigenous rights all over the world include the right to make a living from the land one has lived on for generations, and to get food as one traditionally has. This is part of our ongoing reinterpretation of ethical treatment of indigenous people—but apparently does not include African American communities that have lived in the United States now for four hundred years.

Between candid interviews as friends of Chef BJ came in and out—and he knows everybody—he gave me his own history, and as he did his Gullah accent, full of lilt and sand—grit comes out more and more.

"My granddaddy used to raise sugarcane and show me how to bank it, and they used to dry shrimp and fish on the roof of the house in the hot sun. They would pick this fruit from the palm tree, and it tastes as good as a peach—we would make preserves and wine with it. People had banana trees and coconut trees too. You don't see them much anymore. That's what I want these kids out here to understand, we can feed ourselves. We can run this."

An elderly gentleman came in to get his garlic crab (with rice) order. Garlic crab is just that—cracked blue crabs cooked and flavored with butter and garlic and, if you request, hot peppers and "boil" spices and herbs. It is heady and will make you hungry the minute you smell it. He turned to BJ as he left and said "You tell 'em, we not 'Low Country,' we are Gullah." Two societies still live here with a slight bridge of a historical elite.

Much like New Orleans, Charleston had a three-tiered society among African Americans—they lived in isolation from whites in the countryside, lived with them in the cities, and sometimes formed social units based on being the product of sexual relationships—willing or forced—between white slaveholders and black women. In the Low Country, water and mosquitoes and the threat of yellow fever, malaria, and other diseases kept many blacks separate from whites for much of the year. Overseers might be black drivers instead of white ones. In Charleston, the "tans" had their culture and society, much as the Creoles in New Orleans and Mobile. Just as Louisiana had a culture and language develop among all-black French-speaking communities living in close proximity with the land, so did the Gullah-Geechee.

Mame Wovei's people didn't stay in the all-black factions of Low Country life; it's clear to me that her descendants were urban, or at least spent only so much time in the rice fields. I hope to learn one day if she in fact cooked in a household or was a domestic, which I believe she may have been. This much I know: the culture of cooking and eating rice she found when she arrived at her home of permanent exile would have been very familiar to her, and if she was cooking, she helped shape it. Many contemporary West Africans, from Senegal to Gambia to Guinea to Sierra Leone and Liberia, have marveled at the degree to which the basis of Gullah-Geechee cuisine strongly resembles the leafy greens, stews, soups, rice dishes, and seafood preparations of their own homelands.

Gullah-Geechee people went in and out of these worlds. They certainly had their own lives along the "slave street" of the tidal river plantations and the Sea Islands, cultivating not only rice but sugarcane, sweet potatoes, corn, pumpkins, and supplementary garden crops. The food world belonged to them. According to Walter Edgar, black people not only managed the cattle, tended urban and plantation gardens, and brought food to market on behalf of their slaveholders, they had an informal network of people who had truck gardens, kept hutches for poultry, trapped game, and caught fish, and the market they created fed Charlestonians high and low:

> Ironically, it was black Charlestonians who virtually monopolized the local food market by purchasing produce from country blacks and marketing it to their own advantage. There was a tremendous variety of foodstuffs available; beef, pork, poultry, game, fish, rice, potatoes, and an assortment of fruits and vegetables. The blend of cultures that would be reflected in the colony's cooking began in the marketplace where European produce (turnips, collards, cabbage, broccoli, and cauliflower) could be found alongside African (okra, cowpeas, eggplant, peanuts and yams) and that which was native to the province (pumpkins, corn, squash, melons and beans).

The same could be said of Savannah. A painting from that market shows a black woman surrounded by about twenty varieties of produce, and just as in New Orleans, the hawking of street food like peanut cakes, and the running of alley and backyard taverns for the enslaved, was established practice. Black people were bakers and pastry chefs. They served the grandest meals in the urban mansions of Charleston, with the kitchen in a building back behind the Big House, and they were suppliers of oysters and okra; mullet and elephant ear; or taro, a crop of which Ted Lee told me whose "corms are frequently mentioned of being sold in season at market, as well as wild mushrooms that enslaved people would gather."

In the Low Country, the cuisines of Senegambia, the Rice Coast, and Kongo-Angola joined British, French Huguenot, and German foodways and the remnants of the traditions of coastal Natives. Black cooks moved in and out of their own comfort zone, creating their own cuisines based on flavors and combinations that might be deemed too plebeian for their slaveholders. Actress Fanny Kemble spoke in horror of being told that enslaved people cooked up "fish entrails" because white people didn't want them. Gullah-Geechee folks loved sun-dried seafood, shark, and food drenched in hot pepper, and partook of wild fruits and gator tails with relish and, in the earliest days of slavery, also millet and sorghum brought from Africa and Barbados. However, many whites were themselves raised in the bosom of slavery, and this affected their speech patterns, mannerisms and food preferences. John Davis, tutor to the Drayton family, noted, "It may be incredible to some, that the children of the most distinguished families in Carolina are circled by Negro women. Each child has its momma, whose gestures and accent it will necessarily copy, for children we all known are imitative beings. It is not unusual to hear an elegant lady say, 'Richard always grieves when Quasheebaw is whipped, because she suckled him!'"

The rice kitchens of the Low Country and Louisiana ran on parallel tracks, with a clear bond between the two regions being the sourcing of Senegambians with whom *ceeb u niebe* turned into hoppin' john in South Carolina and Georgia, and jambalaya *au congri* in New Orleans. Jambalaya, the ultimate Southern rice dish, finds its parallel in Carolina red rice—really a tomato pilau (pronounced "perloo") which the Gullah community made complete with green bell peppers, onions, and even a bit of garlic and hot pepper. The same dish, called "Spanish rice" or, by others, "mulatto rice," had been made by my grandmother and her mother and her mother. . . . Take that to West Africa, and they will tell you it's an American version of Jollof rice.

The family of Bilali Muhammad, an enslaved Muslim (about a fifth of all enslaved Africans who disembarked in what became the United States were Muslim), prepared *saraka*, a sweet cake made with honey and rice, in the Sea Island of Georgia, while on the other side of the South, enslaved women sold *cala*, rice cakes often given a touch of spice and a dusting of sugar, both dishes owing part of their existence to *munko* cake in Senegambia and rice *akara* from the Bight of Benin. From the recipes of Sarah Rutledge in her *Carolina Housewife* to Lafcadio Hearn's *Creole Cookery Book* and the *Picayune Creole Cookbook* to the *Carolina Rice Kitchen*, the Afro-Creole rice table is resplendent and plentiful from the Low Country to Louisiana. Between the pages of these books and the hands of Southern elders come chicken pilau, breads, puddings, rice cakes, crab fried rice— rice as the necessary accompaniment to barbecue hash, okra soup, crawfish étouffée, and red beans, as they had in Saint-Domingue/ Haiti—and sugar and rice for a quick breakfast; all come down to us through the centuries as legacies of this heritage. So also have soups made with peanuts or peanuts and oysters, *benne* (sesame seed) and hot-pepper sauces, crab gumbos, and a battery of food with which the only acceptable accompaniment is rice cooked perfectly, with every grain steamed, separate and distinct.

Cowhorn Okra Soup

2 to 3 tbsp bacon drippings, lard, or vegetable or canola oil

2 medium yellow onions, sliced or chopped

3 tbsp flour

2 tbsp finely chopped herbs of your choice (bits of parsley, rosemary, basil, etc.)

½ tsp Kitchen Pepper (see recipe on page 24)

salt to taste

2½ quarts ham, beef, chicken, or vegetable broth

½ cup cooked crumbled bacon

3½ cups Roma tomatoes, chopped, or 28 oz. can, chopped, with juice

½ tsp crushed red pepper flakes

2 pounds okra, sliced into thin pieces

1 cup cooked Southern blue crab meat (optional)

2 cups cooked rice

Heat the bacon drippings, lard, or oil in a Dutch oven until hot but not smoking. Dust the onions in the flour, add them to the pot with the heated oil, and sauté until translucent. Add the fresh herbs and Kitchen Pepper and salt and cook for 1 minute. Add broth and crumbled bacon and tomatoes. Cook for 1 hour on medium-low heat. This will create the stock for the soup. Add the rest of the ingredients except for the rice, and cook for 30 minutes more. Ladle each serving over cooked rice in bowls.

African Soul Fried Rice

2 tbsp canola or peanut oil, divided

2 garlic cloves, thinly sliced

4 scallions with their greens, cleaned, trimmed, and sliced thin on the bias

1 tbsp minced fresh ginger

1 ½ tsp sea salt

red pepper flakes, powder, or sauce to taste

½ cup fresh, thinly sliced okra

1 cup bell peppers (green, red, and yellow), seeded and diced

1 cup thinly sliced (think ribbons!) washed, trimmed, stemmed collard greens

4 cups cooked rice
1 cup cooked black-eyed
peas—*not mushy*, cooked
just till done and tender!

1 tsp soumbala or netetou
powder

Heat 1 tablespoon of oil in a wok or large skillet until very hot. Add the garlic, scallions, and ginger and cook, stirring, for about 3 minutes, until they are soft and release their scent. Add the other tablespoon of oil and add the salt and red pepper. Add and quickly sauté the okra slices, bell pepper, and collard-green ribbons for another 3 minutes. Add the rice, black-eyed peas, and soumbala and cook, stirring, until heated through, about 5 minutes. Stir repeatedly to keep it all from burning, and monitor the heat. If you choose to add cooked proteins, add at this point and heat through another 3 minutes. Send to table hot.

14

—

ADAM IN THE GARDEN

"The rich often have the meat of pigs, goats, harts and cows, as well as of a large number of fowls, from which they even make (stock for) cabbage soup, and several other stews they have learned from the whites and passed on from one to another. Malaguetta (pepper) is always prevalent in all their stews."

—JEAN BARBOT, THE GOLD COAST, 1732

"The Negroes here grow great quantities of snaps and collerds, they have no cabbages here."

—CAPTAIN WILLIAM FELTMAN, UPON VISITING

AN ENSLAVED COMMUNITY ON A HANOVER

COUNTY, VIRGINIA, PLANTATION, 1781

I learned the most about food when I had the least amount of money to spend on it. The years without were not romantic. I just had no choice but to draw on the tradition to get me through. Instead of nightly scrounging to find cents for taco money,

I made a pilgrimage to a hardware store in Orange, Virginia, and bought bulk Southern heritage seeds from jars lodged in a wooden cubbyhole system. If there was one thing my grandmothers agreed on, which wasn't much, it was that they remembered the Depression as a time when even though their families had to make do with less, they were still not as bad off as some urban whites who got comfortable in their power. If there was one thing black elders across the South remembered from the 1930s, it was the sight of white men and women at their back doors looking for something to eat.

Their secret, of course, was the garden. Long before anyone heard of a "victory garden," Africans in America, South and North, were no strangers to the truck patch or provision ground. In West Africa, it was often taken as a right that enslaved or indentured people would have their own ground to raise food for themselves. The wild nature of early slavery, where blacks in lean-tos and makeshift shelters had to create the infrastructure around themselves, lends credence to the idea that early enslaved people in Brazil, the West Indies, and the South were not only coerced to feed themselves, they understood it as a right. Even in federal and early antebellum America we have incidents of the enslaved insisting on ground for a patch.

The garden to the African homestead was the source of "sauce." In other words all the ingredients for soups and stews that typically accompanied the main starch—yams, cassava, rice, millet, sorghum, fonio, and the like—were grown by African women in a midden-based patch or separate ground near a stream. This is not to be confused with other fields in which three to ten crops might grow together in mounds. Like the three sisters, corn, millet or sorghum might support beans or cowpeas while melons and other cucurbits grew on the ground. Shifting cultivation, the uses of animal manure and ashes as fertilizer, using vegetable scraps to enhance a garden's fertility, multiple turnings of the soil, and the modeling of garden spaces after the plant communities of nature—all tips out of the permaculture handbook—came hand-in-hand with Africans to the South.

During those lean times I had to be strategic. Corn was tasty but carried with it too many chances to attract pests and bacterial infestation. Cabbage did too. No Southern garden was complete without either in its due time, but I could not afford to waste space on buggy plants. My father taught me how to dust leaves with fine-sifted ashes to kill aphids, and how to make weak lye-soap sprays. My provision patch would be organic as much as possible, bugs picked off and squashed underfoot, with things grown together to confuse buggy pests, conserve water, and to crowd out weeds.

With a mattock I made large mounds for the sweet potatoes. This one action—mounding up dirt impregnated with wood ash and broken oyster shell—gave me a satisfying feeling of not knowing where my legs started and where the earth ended. I felt at one with all the images I'd ever seen of African men with bent hoes in hand cultivating the soil. In went slips of white yam, Haymans, Spanish Reds, Puerto Ricos, and Beauregards, and the red Japanese sweet potato that most closely resembled the "nigger choker," a type of sweet potato most favored by the enslaved. Within a few weeks, the mounds were luxuriant with sweet potato leaves that I picked every now and then for use as sautéed greens.

On the highest point of those ridges went the cymling squash, a white pattypan type that I ate small and green and squishy. Where space was left I planted cowpeas, including ones that looked like Blue Crowders that I bought dried at a Senegalese market in Harlem and remained viable seed. Every hint and every tip came right out of journal references of travelers in the early South, like Philip Vickers Fithian from Sabine Hall, one of the Carter family plantations in Virginia; and recollections by the enslaved. I spread out herbs like Eritrean basil, sage, lemon thyme, mint, chives, Italian parsley, and rosemary instead of having an herb patch; and placed bushes of long red cayennes and fish and goat peppers on the edges of the garden for pest control. Treasures from former head gardener at Monticello Peter Hatch, Wesley Greene, and William Woys Weaver were dispersed among seed from Orange, Southern Exposure Seed Exchange, the D. Landreth Seed Co., and from elders I had met along the way.

Long before the current movement to taste the past and revive forgotten terroir, it made sense to me that the Caseknife pole bean from Wesley and the Cowhorn okra from Peter and the yam potato from William were something more than just neat relics. They were the very taste of how my ancestors survived slavery. This—the variety, the flavors, the shiny Green Glaze collards and Amazon tomatoes—this was the taste of proto-soul. I filled every cast-out flower pot with different tomatoes—Large Reds and Amish Paste, Cherokee Purples and German Greens—and placed them strategically around my yard. I had a Carwile's southwest Virginia peanut patch; I grew Nankeen yellow cotton to sell as a novelty; I sowed old varieties of lettuce from spring to early winter and planted garlic in fall and onions in the spring, and bought bulk supplies of organic apple cider vinegar and quality olive oil.

On the side of the house I grew yellow squash, and no sooner than I had eaten or given away the last one, I started cushaw, or "sweet potato pumpkin," plants outside in little hills for the late summer and early fall. I planted and harvested by the signs as my Virginia grandmother taught me, and watched the moon and its phases true to my Scotch-Irish surname. Waxing and waning moons, starlight and bright full moons I could use with a piece of lightwood to garden at night suddenly mattered. I grew tomatoes brought from Saint-Domingue during the Haitian Revolution and eggplants from Togo, Carolina black peanuts and maroon pods of Burgundy okra, and Kentucky Wonder beans for my mom, and melons—Anne

Presenting a colonial African American meal to Henry Louis Gates Jr. for *Many Rivers to Cross*. Historic Londontown, near Annapolis, Maryland, 2012. *Photo by Delroy Leon Cornick Jr.*

In a bright leaf tobacco field with Nottoway tribe member Beth Roach. Dinwiddie County, Virginia, 2012. *Photo by Jacob W. Dillow*

Hearth in a reproduction of an eighteenth-century Virginia slave cabin. Colonial Williamsburg, 2012. *Photo by Jonathan M. Lewis*

Picking cotton and listening to work songs recorded by Alan Lomax on my iPod. Chippokes Plantation State Park, Surry, Virginia, 2012. *Photo by Jacob W. Dillow*

Finding out my African ancestry with Gina Paige. Stagville Plantation, North Carolina, 2013. *Photo by Jacob W. Dillow*

Plantation meal cooked on the open hearth. Mecklenburg County, North Carolina, 2012. *Photo by Jacob W. Dillow*

Pounding Carolina Gold rice. Middleton Plantation, Charleston,
South Carolina, 2012. *Photo by Jacob W. Dillow*

Chef and farmer Matthew Raiford with a sugarcane mill.
Brunswick, Georgia, 2013. *Photo by Jacob W. Dillow*

Barbecue at Great Hopes Plantation. Colonial Williamsburg, 2012.
Photo by Jacob W. Dillow

Mammy ain't nobody's name. Natchez, Mississippi, 2012.
Photo by Jacob W. Dillow

Buying cymling squash from an African American–run community farmers market. Natchez, Mississippi, 2012. *Photo by Jonathan M. Lewis*

Cheapside slave auction block. Lexington, Kentucky, 2012.
Photo by Jacob W. Dillow

LEFT In the kitchen at Old Alabama Town. Montgomery, Alabama, 2012. *Photo by Jacob W. Dillow*

BELOW Slave Row at Evergreen Plantation, Edgard, Louisiana, 2012. *Photo by Jonathan M. Lewis*

Arundel muskmelons, Moon and Stars, and Georgia Rattlesnake watermelons.

I never learned to can (I will someday) but I did make sauces and I froze them. I half-assed pickled by shoving burr gherkins into jars of vinegary brine, and faked it pretty good by keeping them in the refrigerator. I learned to cook the old dishes and learned to appreciate the taste of collard sprouts and black-eyed-pea leaves, and made a pretty pale pink vinegar from chive flowers. As I interpreted at historical sites, I dragged my vegetables on the table as props and, one after the other, cooked them up, disappointed by the way the cast iron never seemed to keep their raw beauty going.

History did not let the historical black garden go unremarked. These spaces were little landscapes of resistance: Resistance against a culture of dehumanizing poverty and want, resistance against the erasure of African cultural practices, resistance against the destruction of African religions, and resistance against slavery itself. Garden truck was sold and bartered to buy finery and finer things that set the enslaved materially above their base station. More important, there was capital to be gained from the practice of selling truck to the slaveholder. In my family's case, corn and other crops were sold to George Saunders of Buckingham County, Virginia. For some enslaved people, this meant the purchase of their freedom or that of loved ones.

The gardens were more than just sources of nutrients; they were spaces where the medicinal and spiritual practices could be kept alive. I don't know why, but I felt compelled to hang up drinking gourds on sticks, and on those sticks tie multicolored strips of cloth and to them attach shells. African art historian Henry Drewal and his wife, anthropologist Sarah Khan, visited me during the year of lack and, without prompting, Henry began reading the various juju I had unwittingly put up in my space. In fact, he said, among the Yoruba there was a whole language of blessings and curses attached to the juju placed at the edge of a garden or a field, his personal favorite being an ear of corn with twenty or thirty seeds and one shoe, literally meaning, "If you steal my shit may you have twenty or thirty kids and only one shoe between them."

My gourds were apparently some sort of African American feng shui. Gourds are homes for spirits. The good ones go in and make a home and hover and protect you, and the bad ones get trapped and have to do work for you. I spread around oyster and clam shells from the Bay just to be pretty, and spiraling whelks to symbolize growth and life everlasting. I buried little things of importance to me, and with every humid day the hum of the land and soil grew louder within me, and in that tunnel of time and spirit I went just a little more "native."

Our gardens were the source of our music, spreading over the wattle and picket fences onto the walls and roofs of our cabins, and into the trees grew our bottle gourds, the same ones we ate from, that made well water sweeter to our lips and carried persimmon beer to the fields. We would eat them when they were very young if we were hungry. These same gourds became the enslaved person's orchestra—the banjo—drawing from the edges of the trade, Senegal and Angola, the rattles of the quaqua drum, the gourd fiddle. In the middle of hell, music was made from the sound of the gourds, to the pounding of corn or rice in the mortar and pestle, to the beating on boxes and doors and cutting of bamboo for cane fifes and pulling the sinew of the slaughtered that made strings that made the air sing.

To some, the idea of youth or community gardens might be clichéd, but to the African American community, especially in the South, the movement to grow food where you live is not a trend, it's a necessity. "Growing food is like growing money," said my friend Ron Finley, the gangsta gardener of South Central Los Angeles. He's right, and programs that he, vegan chef Bryant Terry in Oakland, Malik Yakini in Detroit, and Will Allen of Growing Power in

Milwaukee have begun are transforming the way black urban communities eat and seek empowerment. In the South, activist Jenga Mwendo and actor Wendell Pierce in New Orleans, Dana Jewel Harris of Atwood Community Gardens, the HABESHA (Helping Africa by Establishing Schools at Home and Abroad), and Dr. Rashid Nuri's Truly Living Well in Atlanta, and the community gardens stewarded by Hurricane Katrina survivor Fenwick Broyard in Athens, Georgia, are among the many projects I visited in cities from Baltimore to Montgomery to Austin to Charleston that reconnected young people and black communities to the land and to their food and gave them a sense of ownership.

There is a contrast between these worlds and those of the rich and burgeoning farmers market scene in Southern midsize cities. The farmers markets are predominantly white spaces, and it's not without some irony that a significant few are located in areas where enslaved bodies were once sold, as in Richmond, Lexington, and Saint Augustine. The kids at Dana's farm and weekly farmers market get to see African American farmers and chefs and work with leaders in the black food movement. Their elders juice Georgia peaches and warn them away from high fructose corn syrup, and they hear stories from Jamaica, West Africa, and the Great Migration by hanging out with market participants from different walks of life. What's more, they are meeting black farmers and cooking fresh food and they want to be there.

Even for some black adults, the experience of going to a mainstream farmers market can be alienating. As in love as I am with food and growing things, I don't have enough appendages to count the number of times I've gone to farmers markets and have been greeted with presumptions that I needed to be instructed and led by the hand through their merchandise, or just outright been given a cold shoulder while young, white, urban professionals confessing their ignorance have been humored. I've even been told about myself and my work at two markets while wearing sunglasses. Having to open my mouth and prove someone's prejudice wrong is exhausting, and over time I stopped seeking out the kinds of artisan food and beverage others delight in without scrutiny and take for granted.

"Boy, get that dirty water out of here!" a woman in pink with a heavy Jamaican patois said to a teenager holding a commercial ice tea. "Drink this!"

"What is this red stuff?"

"It's called sorrel, hibiscus, and it's sweetened with agave syrup, drink up!"

"I kinda like it." He gulps it down, smiling. "I want some more."

"Pay me what you pay the 7-Eleven for that dirty water and you got a deal!"

"Michael," Dana chimed in, "tell him where it comes from." Now I'm on the spot.

"It's called 'roselle' or 'jamaica' too; it's originally from West Africa and it's probably why you like red drinks today!" The boy nodded and bought another cup.

Behind us, two chefs from downtown restaurants cooked up fresh succotash with a bounty of vegetables obtained from a third-generation farmer at the market who came from Montezuma, Georgia. Beside him was a buddy from Birmingham who spent forty years in New York and had recently come back South to Atlanta.

He looked at my ditty bag. "When I was going up North, my grandmother put one of those around my neck. She called it an asafetida bag."

He squinted and pulled back and gave me a knowing smile, and I knew the story wasn't finished because this was the body language of our elders when a story was about to be told. "I got sent up North with two pieces of fried rabbit, a corn pone, and an asafetida bag."

"Asa-feti-dy! That's what they used to call it!" The farmer from Montezuma cackled a bit and joined in. "Yeah, they swore up and down that would keep you from haints and from getting sick. Whoo! Now you got one." He shook his head hard.

"You ain't got no High John the Conqueror in there do you? He conjure me, and he'll conjure *you!*" The man from Birmingham winked at me. "I drove a bus, then a subway train, put all my children through college, my wife died, and then I decided to come back down here."

He bid one of the teenagers to bring him a plate of succotash. The reward was a tussle of hair and a pat on the back. I got a good feeling from all of this energy because it was positive; tough love was unnecessary, and there were a dozen young black men hanging about being helpful, productive, learning their history, eating and drinking healthy things, and learning how to cook.

"Taste this chow chow. It will change your life, boy!" The farmer from Montezuma gave me a spoonful of chow chow, which I never really liked, but it was fantastic. The table was full of jars of okra and watermelon pickle, chow chow, hot sauce—the country kind— where split hot peppers dance in a glass soda bottle filled with vinegar. "All of this comes from my farm, three generations, going back to slavery." The farmer from Montezuma lamented that he had no sorghum to give me but told me he would come in late fall.

That weekend in Atlanta, touring Truly Living Well, Atwood, and the HABESHA farm, seeing goats and free-range chickens, cage-free eggs and every bit of Southern produce imaginable, plus a few banana trees and pineapple patches, didn't just make me feel proud, it made me feel a fullness, a feeling of being sufficient. For the first time in my life, I was seeing black cooperative economics in full swing. A vegan caterer bought vegetables from the farmer from Montezuma, and she made food to sell at the HABESHA fund-raiser, where every conceivable faction in the new black consciousness movement—from the Nation of Islam to more orthodox Sunni Muslims to Akan and Yoruba and Asaur Auset (Kemetic/

Egyptian) to Baptists to AME to CME to humanists and socialists and Rastafarians—were all rallying around the idea of better food for the black community and making sure young people were educated and empowered to keep the movement going. Her proceeds supported sending young people who had trained in the urban farm to Ghana and Ethiopia where, upon their return, they would train the next class. If this wasn't extraordinary enough, I saw a dollar go from black hand to black hand to black hand.

My boyfriend and creative partner at the time, Jacob, was clearly a standout. "There's white people here y'all, a white man just showed up," someone jokingly blared out on the microphone as we walked in with Dana. Dana didn't know what to say, but Jacob did: "I figure it's my turn to be the minority and just deal. Besides, how many times is the narrative, 'Young, white activist wants to come in and save the black people from McDonald's.' It's OK, my feelings aren't hurt, I get it."

We ate spicy raw kale wraps and had collard-green ice cream in recycled paper cups. We decided the latter was basically a garden smoothie with honey that had been frozen hard as a rock, but it wasn't bad. The idea isn't new, this is the savor the Black Panthers knew—and why the most dangerous thing they did, according to J. Edgar Hoover, at least—was feed the next generation. Pan-Africanist leanings have come to the soul food table, and for good reason; economic disparities are out of control. This taste in my mouth is the flavor of black folks taking their country back.

The feeling of being around a predominantly black food scene where black people were addressing chronic health disparities and food access challenges for themselves was exhilarating. Earlier that summer, I had been in Donaldsonville, Louisiana, where during the time of Jim Crow black farmers and landowners got together and decided that sharecroppers in the cotton and sugarcane fields had enough trouble to not be in debt to white planters, so they created a community farm where all who were hungry could get produce. That was 1912. The year of my travels was 2012, and somehow, without black Twitter, without Facebook, without Instagram or Snapchat, black farmers in a time of Klansmen and lynch law solved the problem of food insecurity. Thankfully, the secret weapon, the garden, had not been forgotten.

BUCK SWAMP

Matthew Raiford is a leader in that regard. His Gilliard Farms, near Brunswick, Georgia, is named after his third great-grandfather, Jupiter Gilliard, born in 1812 in South Carolina. He is there to showcase his attempts at re-creating the foods of the old days. "The only thing I learned in culinary school was how to say what my grandmother taught in French. I paid a lot of money to learn how to cook like my grandmother in French."

A jarred barbecue sauce made with watermelon molasses was in front of me. It was the "CheFarmer"'s, and it was perhaps some of the best barbecue sauce I've ever had.

Under live oaks strewn with Spanish moss, Matthew told me about his and his sister's operation. Here, Carolina Gold rice was already growing in a seedling house and Bradford and Georgia Rattlesnake melons had taken over part of his acreage. Scuppernongs and muscadines had come back to the family homestead's grape arbor. Georgia Red sugarcane was set to be grown for seed in the hopes that the grinding mill and sugar boiling pot would be put back into operation in the next few years.

"This is the Buck Swamp community. Church, school, we did for ourselves for 150 years and that's what Gilliard Farms is all about, taking what we have always done and showing the next generation just how special that is.

"I remember Friday was fish day. You know, growing up, we

didn't rely on the supermarket here, we went out to the tidal creek. Shrimp, blue crab, mullet, whiting, oysters, drum, big ole sheepshead, snapper, grouper, gafftopsails—you know, sea catfish; we had nets and cane poles. I lived for a grouper fish sandwich, and when I started cooking, white people went crazy for them. You know these little country fish sandwiches with mayonnaise and mustard and hot sauce with paprika in the batter. That was one of the tricks we had brought from slavery on down, put that paprika in there to make that gold in the crust pop. That way they can't say it's underdone."

Matthew's farm grows many of the same crops his family has always raised. He had a letter from his great-grandmother from the 1940s to a relative up North recounting how the crops are doing; cane, corn, watermelon, and potatoes get a mention.

"We grow everything they grew—turnips and turnip greens, peanuts, collards, onions, field peas, watermelons, sugarcane, cabbage, rice, tomatoes, okra, hot peppers, corn, potatoes, sweet potatoes, figs—you got hogs, chickens, deer, rabbit, squirrel, possum, and coon. What more do you need in life?" The ground is littered with live oak acorns and huge pecans. Matthew was chosen to represent the United States at the global Slow Food event in Italy, and food from Gilliard went with him, including the delicious barbecue sauce made from watermelon molasses.

My own grandfather, Gonze Lee Twitty, earned his way into the Cooperative Hall of Fame by being a founding member and lifelong activist with the Federation of Southern Cooperatives, founded in 1967. Black farmers have struggled to hold on to their land and have had to sue the government for past grievances, including denying equal protections and privileges given to white farmers that put them at a disadvantage. The loss of black farmland and farm ownership is dramatic. Where Matthew Raiford is in the Georgia low country, it's downright tragic. This was the land no white man wanted once upon a time—the American tropics, where African culture and traditional foodways thrived. Now black churches and graveyards are bulldozed to make room for golf courses and luxury resorts. Projects that combine the know-how of those from "overseas" with those who know how to promote local, historical foods like those of Dr. David Shields, like the efforts to raise sugarcane again on Sapelo Island with respected elder Cornelia Bailey, will hopefully go a long way toward retaining black ownership and stewardship over the land.

The cost of not having access to the land and water, and not being able to grow or appreciate the taste for homegrown traditional foods, has a deeper cost. Washington, DC–based nutritionist Tambra Raye Stevenson, originally hailing from Oklahoma City, came from a family with deep roots in the all-black towns of Oklahoma and Texas. "My people were cowboys, cattle farmers, and former slaves. My people got more than just forty acres and a mule; more like seven-hundred-plus acres—until the government pulled an eminent domain in Oklahoma to create a lake." Her "furthest back person" was a woman the white family named "Mammy," Henrietta Burkhalter, born a slave in Baltimore. Sold as a young girl to the Burkhalter family in Georgia, "Mammy" trekked with the white family and her sons to Mississippi, then Texas, and finally rested her soul in McIntosh County, Oklahoma, after the Emancipation Proclamation, with her son Jiles Burkhalter. A DNA test via African Ancestry reveals Tambra shares ancestral affinity with the Fulani people of Nigeria and Niger—known then as Hausaland. "Mammy's" rape in Mississippi by former Confederate soldier and banker George Washington Speed and the subsequent history of her family has always deeply impacted her work.

Tambra takes a sip of her homemade hibiscus drink, then continues, "History is the missing piece. Once you begin embracing your own heritage and culture and you interweave it with what you're doing; it transforms into a soul completion journey of 'Finally

I am home.' I am coming back to Africa, coming back to love, coming back home, and most of all coming back to a place of healing. From there, I began looking at my identity through food. I finally made the trek back home to the Fulani *rugas* [homesteads] of northern Nigeria. There I learned and enjoyed the traditional dishes and drinks. I even had a renaming ceremony in Kano, Nigeria; I am 'Muallayidi,' meaning the 'one loved by God' in Fulfude, and shared my family's journey in America with the help of a Fulani translator to the community of men, women, and children. I could really begin looking at an ethnic group—the Fulanis—and the spirituality of a people matters so greatly. My main question for myself was, How does that identity become realized in terms of food?"

Tambra's effort, NativSol, meaning "New African Traditions Including Values of Spirituality, Oneness, and Love" (also "Sustainability, Organic, and Local"), seeks to teach black folks how to navigate the complex waters of diet and lifestyle. Once she knew something of her African roots, she began to look at the diet and identified foods that were better for her health, from millet to coconut and spices. She now gives nutrition lectures and cooking classes across the country and the globe. In building a grassroots movement in Africa and the Diaspora, she created Women Advancing Nutrition, Dietetics and Agriculture (WANDA) to encourage black women and girls, in particular, to be the harbingers of a new awareness of their value and foods. "My food, my plate, and my kitchen serve as a healing space. When we grow our own food, we own that process and we know what we're putting into our bodies."

Tambra is an evangelist for healthy African food: "Nutrition has been taught from a Western perspective, post–Rene Descartes, based on a separation of body and soul. We know that many African people believe body and soul are deeply connected. The soul of the food and the soul of the people go hand in hand. When I joke with my audiences and say 'If it's white it ain't right, but if it's brown let it stick around,' I'm not talking about race, but rather so many of the foods we've come to rely on aren't good for us. We have one of the lowest gluten tolerances, as descendants of sub-Saharan Africans; we can't keep putting refined sugar and other highly processed poisons into our bodies.

"Diabetes and heart disease and hypertension are the chief culprits. They're going to, in essence, bankrupt countries; they keep enslavement going. They're bankrupting black America right now. Your heritage foods are your health and your wealth. Genetics feed into that. Look, most of the genomes sequenced aren't ours, so medical advice is based on bodies that don't have our stories. When it comes to the way the food is made, produced, processed, prepared, all of that will impact the microflora of your gut. Your gut is your primal brain; all the intelligence of your ancestors is in your gut and genes. Your food and environment are like fingers on a light switch turning the genes on or off."

It's an interesting concept. When you look at the traditional power objects of many West and central African peoples, like the Kongo, the belly of the object is where the medicine is kept. One of the more devastating losses in the transmission of African foodways to the New World was eating as a form of healing. Much like Indian and Chinese cuisines, there was a deep connection between everyday health and everyday food and using certain ingredients to fight off ailments, inspire alertness, and overall well-being.

"With the whole notion of Africa rising and Black Lives Matter, the question is, What is it rising to? Once we know our lives matter, what are we going to do with them? From a food perspective, Western food imperialism is a new kind of Trojan horse, all in the name of job creation and development. We're hooked like a fish. Just like the 'hood, Africa is now being invaded by plastic rice, instant noodles, soft drinks, and fast-food chains like KFC and Johnny Rockets and Burger King. People on the continent are being affected by a social desire to relate to anything in the West as the 'best' at the cost of their own heritage.

"Food, racism, power, and justice are linked. What I'm trying to do is dismantle culinary nutritional imperialism and gastronomic white supremacy with one cup of *zobo* made from hibiscus, one bowl of millet salad with groundnuts and dark green vegetables, and one piece of *injera* at a time. The next wave of human rights abuse is in the form of nutrition injustice when we don't have access, can't afford and lack the education of our nutrition-rich heritage foods due to food gentrification, discrimination, Western food subsidies, and cultural food appropriation. Yes, Africa's rich heritage foods were labeled once inferior and forbidding foods like her people. Change the plates, you change the palates, then you will change the future," Tambra declares.

Sweet potatoes and collard greens, turnip greens and fresh seafood, lean meats and healing spices have always been part of our tradition. Everything in our tradition is not fried. Some of soul food's glories come from the freshness in the ground. Long before white America became health conscious, the enslaved had an idea that not all the master class ate was good for it. Frederick Douglass even noted that most of the gout and other conditions went to slaveholders, not to the enslaved. In communities where health disparities, lack of economic opportunity, and food deserts are rampant, we would do well to keep greening our neighborhoods and, as Tambra suggests, make our grandmothers' gardens bloom again.

Sautéed Greens

6 tbsp olive oil
1 large red onion, sliced
thinly
2 garlic cloves, or 2 garlic
scapes sliced thinly
1 very small hot pepper (try
the Maryland fish pepper)
or a pinch of red pepper
flakes
1 ½ cups vegetable stock

2 pounds Green Glaze
collard greens, or 1 pound
collards and 1 pound kale;
washed, stripped from the
stalk, and very thinly sliced
into long strips
1 red, 1 yellow, and 1 orange
bell pepper, all seeded and
thinly sliced
kosher salt to taste

Heat the olive oil in a large pan. Add the onions and garlic and sauté until translucent. Add the hot pepper and one third of the stock and cook for 1 minute. Add the collard and bell pepper slices and cook over low heat for about 5 minutes. Add the rest of the stock and cook over medium heat. Season with salt to taste, mix, cover, then cook for 20 minutes. Serve on its own or spoon over cooked rice.

15
—
SHAKE DEM
'SIMMONS DOWN

Possum up a 'simmon tree
Raccoon on the ground
Raccoon say to the possum above,
Won't you shake dem 'simmons down?

—"BILE DEM CABBAGE DOWN"

Dey laid 'im under a 'simmon tree,
His epitaph am dar to see;
'Beneath dis stone I'm forced to lie,
All by de means ob de blue tail fly.
Jim crack corn and I don't care, Old Massa's gone away.

—"THE BLUETAIL FLY"

On April 9, 1865, when the Albemarle Pippins and Hewes
crab apples set south-central Virginia in riotous bloom, my
paternal great-great-grandfather Elijah Mitchell and his
older brother George accompanied their slaveholder from Clover
Hill to the area around the Appomattox Court House, just a bit
down the road. They must have been stunned at the sight of two
thousand armed black troops in their suits with shining buttons—
men from places as close as the tobacco factories of Richmond and
sailors from as far away as China. Elijah, the teenage house servant
at the Mitchells' small tobacco farm house, pretended not to know
about what he had been hearing about for weeks as he stood beside
the Mitchells' table fanning them—that the possible end of slavery
was moments away.

Exiting the courthouse was a defeated Robert E. Lee and a tri-
umphant but weary Ulysses S. Grant—and at that moment, as the
Confederacy's 150-year mourning period began, my great-great-
grandfather and his brother counted themselves among the first black
people to find out that the long nightmare of American slavery—
nearly three centuries in the making—was over. Their slaveholder,
Blake Mitchell, immediately declared them free—even as they still
held his horse in place, waiting for whatever was to come next. They
laughed and cried and couldn't wait to spread the news—the day of
jubilee was here—and they, unlike many, had lived to see it. Gone
were the days of pulling the punkah for Elijah, and that night hard
cider and persimmon beer drowned out the fears and worries of the
many unknowns to come.

Their world was so connected to natural rhythms and seasons
that children were often named or nicknamed after the season in
which they were born, or the time of the year when a harvest or
planting time occurred. Few plantations were without their fruit
trees, especially in central Virginia, where apple and peach trees
were an established custom since the days of the British colonies.

The quince, pear, cherry, and plum trees followed close behind, some going wild as farmsteads were moved and civilization changed around them.

As I moved across the South from Maryland to Texas, there was always the familiar grape arbor covered in scuppernongs and muscadines (my grandmother said her father called them "muskydines") and other foxy grapes. Every elder smiled at the mention of black walnuts, hickory nuts, pecans, chestnuts, and chinquapins, many recalling the taffy pulls passed down from slavery time, when the delicious meat would be added to molasses for candy.

We left behind centuries of tropical fruits and nuts for temperate ones, although some came with the Portuguese, like peaches and grapes, giving us a small taste of things to come in the South. We learned to make preserves and jellies and jams through acculturation, and added our own knowledge to the making of leathers and liquors and dried fruit saved for the lean times. Plants were not just plants to us; they were homes of spirit; they were parts of our familial makeup; they were part of our genealogy. Palm trees and acacias and fruit trees all had their prayers and spells, cosmological lore and proverbs, and we in mainland North America lost much of this in the Middle Passage, while some of this knowledge was preserved in the more tropical regions of American slavery in the Caribbean and Brazil.

When our ancestors first arrived in North America in the sixteenth and seventeenth centuries, they found themselves in search of familiar plants with which they could capture semblances of the natural world they were forced to leave behind. I will never know the wonder and mixed expressions of sadness and joy that those enslaved Africans experienced as they encountered flora similar to those that they used in their homelands. All of my grandparents spoke of being walked through the woods and edges of fields by their elders from the time they were very young, learning which things were good to eat and which things were "pizen." They learned a few healing traditions. Black boys and girls in the American South became the predominant gatherers of wild fruits, nuts, seeds, leaves, herbs, greens, mushrooms, and wild spices, just as children fulfilled a similar role in West Africa. White chroniclers often spoke of these wild foods as "only eaten by Indians and Negroes."

Everywhere I traveled in the Deep South, I saw elephant ear growing around where black neighborhoods were. It's a type of taro plant, the cocoyam of West Africa. In the jungle surrounding the Kingsley plantation near Jacksonville, Florida, where Madigene Jai (she was part of the N'diaye clan, a common name among the Wolof and Serer), an African woman from Senegal, held sway as plantation mistress, elephant ear, water yam, and African red rice grow as "invasives" today. In the shadow of oyster tabby shell cabins formerly thatched in grass and palmetto, erected by Africans drawn from Nigeria, Congo, and East Africa, African plants recall a time when Zephaniah Kingsley, slave trader and polygamous husband to three black women he imported himself, brought plants from Africa and the Caribbean to satisfy the taste for home held by his laborers working fields of indigo, Sea Island cotton, and rice.

Very little of this came down to us once oppression forced us to be on the move. Riots and the burning of black towns, lack of opportunity enforced by racially based classism, and the move to cities began to divorce our people from the land. In the contemporary food scene, the world of foraging has, by default, become predominantly middle-class and white. I remember a childhood full of strangers squinting, wincing, and squealing, "Ugh, don't touch that, you don't know what *that* is!" But I did know because my grandparents and my father taught me about mullein and senna, rabbit tobacco and poke salad, honey locust and my personal favorite, the persimmon.

Our elders frequently explained to us that once upon a time you couldn't go to the doctor or the grocery store. As "CheFarmer" Matthew Raiford told me about his ancestral property at Gilliard Farms near Brunswick, Georgia, "I'm not cutting down these huckleberry bushes—that's gallons and gallons of doobie [berry cobbler], there are persimmon trees and pomegranates and peaches growing all over this property, we don't cut those down. My folks always said look before you cut, and don't just cut things down unless you know what they're good for." He pulled me over to his ancient grape arbor. "One thing I learned from my elders was to put shells down at the bottom of the vines, we just go right to the marsh and the beach and get shells and crush them up like tabby and put them down. We learned since then the calcium keeps the nematodes and other things off—now, my grandmother didn't know that, but some things they just knew from wisdom and experience."

Rare was the elder I interviewed in any part of the South who didn't recall that poke salad or pokeweed—the plant with the beautiful, lusty, deep purple poisonous fruit—was good for "cleaning you out from your head to your feet." The same words occurred over and over as though they were printed on their genes. In the days when many people had intestinal worms and other parasites, slightly toxic plants were good "spring tonics" to clean out the bugs. One of the largest categories of healing herbs in the enslaved community consisted of vermifuges. If you haven't guessed, that word derives from the Latin "*vermis*," meaning "worm."

Like many other plants, poke had botanical cognates in Africa, and food from nature almost always doubled as medicine. Purslane, mulberries, senna, *Rubus* spp. berries, cresses, chufa, passionflower, peppergrass, *Chenopodium* (lamb's-quarters), dock, wild onion, and others did as well. Pawpaw trees reminded them of similar fruits they gathered, and indeed they were called the "poor man's banana." By knowing and using the plants, my ancestors got on intimate terms with the world of their exile; for some African Americans like myself, there has remained this bit of lore suggesting a chain of knowledge going back to the beginnings of black history. One of the species key to this botanical memory bank has been the persimmon (*Diospyros virginiana*), the king of Southern foraged fruit.

My father and I didn't always have good times with each other. As I got older and more precocious, we were less and less buddies and more and more adversaries. Our knowledge base diverged so much we became strangers. Until I didn't speak to him for more than a decade, I returned in my mind to the moments when I was a teenager and he would climb up a ladder for me and help me gather persimmons, even though he was scared to fall and even more worried about being caught trespassing—but all with the chirping chuckle of a laugh that let me know that Daddy was happy.

"Put the drop cloth down and help me by holding the ladder." My father was purely didactic when in focus. "Now, son, with your other hand, gently shake the tree as I use the broom for the falling fruit." To my complete rush, bunches of blushing ripe fruit clunked on the canvas below. Hours later we would tumble into my paternal grandmother's home. "Ma, you're never gonna believe this," he said, peeling back the layer of the bag. My grandmother happily said, "Oh, 'simmons!!" I took half and, under my father's instruction, made the same persimmon beer that Elijah and George toasted their freedom with in 1865. My grandmother, who used to use the unripe astringent ones in place of pimple cream, turned her 'simmons into a spicy, molasses-laced persimmon bread, drawing on a recipe from the newspaper to back up her memory of a treat that had been eaten in her family for at least three generations.

About a year before her grandfather was born, an enslaved community in Prince Edward County, where she was born, engaged in a "persimmon tree dance," recorded by a chronicler in the *Farmer's Register*. The lead musician "rang" the "banjor" while sitting in the middle of the dance on a barrel of persimmon beer, and the assembled clapped and sang along with him. At times young men stood by the door, freestyle rhyming commentary to the constant throb of the room, not unlike hip-hop:

"Dick had'nt no business dancing with Nance; he ain't a man of gumption. I tried him, and he can't be made to understand the duramatical part of the function, the function of the fundamental, and the imperality of ditrimental things. Gabe? Dick's a fool, and you may tell him Sambo says so: he is knock-knee'd, and ugly enough to eat *Gumbo*."

"Well. I know that; sing on Sambo."

As two women baked loafs of "heavily larded" persimmon bread in the fireplace, the musician kept plucking away in the middle of the floor:

A long white cow-tail, queued with red ribbon, ornamented his head, and hung gracefully down his back; over this he wore a three-cocked hat, decorated with pea-cock feathers, a rose cockade, a bunch of ripe persimmons, and to cap the climax, three pods of red pepper as a top-knot. Tumming his banjor, grinning with ludicrous gesticulations and playing off his wild notes to the company. Before him stood two athletic blacks, with open mouth and pearl white teeth, clapping Juber to the notes of the banjor; the fourth black man held in his right hand a jug gourd of persimmon beer, and in his left, a dipper or water-gourd, to serve the company.

And they sang!

"Juber up and Juber down, Juber all around de town, Juber dis, and Juber dat, And Juber roun' the simmon vat. Hoe corn, hill tobacco, Get over double trouble, Juber boys, Juber.

Uncle Phil, he went to mill. He suck de sow, he starve de pig, Eat the simmon, gi' me de seed, I told him, I was not in need. Hoe corn! hill tobacco! Get over double trouble, Juber boys, Juber.

Aunt Kate? look on the high shelf, Take down the husky dump'in, I'll eat it wi' my simmon cake, To cure the rotten belly-ach. Hoe corn! hill tobacco! Get over double trouble, Juber boy Juber.

Raccoon went to simmon town, To choose the rotten from de soun', Dare he sot upon a sill, Eating of a whip-poor-will. Hoe corn! Hill tobacco! Get over double trouble, Juber boys Juber."

We washed the persimmons to remove dirt and debris, then we took hours upon hours to remove the seeds. The seeds of *Diospyros virginiana* have been found in the quarters of the enslaved across the entire South, providing a sustained record of use from the seventeenth to the nineteenth centuries. The seeds were used as game pieces, roasted and eaten like pumpkin seeds, or even roasted to make a fake coffee. The fruit was fermented into vinegar, or boiled down into molasses or dried into a fruit leather. However, the most important and endearing use was brewing persimmon liquor.

I grew up with closets full of folk wine, of which Grammy was the queen. Strawberry wine, apple wine, blackberry wine, and dandelion spirits all in scummy jugs on the floor smelling yeasty, tied with cheesecloths and rubber bands. I never got any unless I was sick, and even then it was mixed with honey and herby things that made it ever unappealing to my young palate. And yet, I grew up to add to those jugs, making the 'simmon liquor the way it always had been; honey and a bit of yeast, a squirt of lemon and sugar and mashed up 'simmons covered with water. The red pine straw set atop of the mash was there not for color or flavor, although it did add a beautiful autumn glow to the bottle; its main job was to strain the liquor.

Daddy said to always open the tops, lest the bottles blow up. Sometimes I listened, sometimes not. When I heard the sound of a bullet and shattered glass, I knew I didn't listen hard enough. From then on, I knew to mind my father's old ways and I never lost another bottle. Persimmon beer became my social lubricant of choice, even with a whole troop of Confederate soldiers.

Closing down an event with Confederate reenactors is never really easy for a black guy. Let's face it, the Confederates lost the War Between the States, but they won a different type of war. Here I am, playing an enslaved cook, and the reenactors, the home army, looking for a meal. It's hours upon hours of uneasy stares and curiosity bounded by walls of code. Every now and then, a group of reenactors peeks in with a pot looking for food for a "bunch of poor soldiers looking for a hot meal from home."

"A home?" Really? I didn't mind the polite way they asked for my cooking, but it was the assumption that 150 years ago I would have heard anything more than, "Nigger, fix me up a plate and hurry up!" that threw me for a loop. I didn't buy the bonneted white lady who walked alongside me saying at a whisper, "I'm worried to make sure all of our people here on the farm have substance that we'll get through the winter . . ." The whole ritual of playing nice master and nice slave unnerved me; not my drag and not my scene.

Interpreters and reenactors are not exactly the same tribe to begin with. One refers to itself as a profession, and the other a hobby. "The hobby" is largely staffed by more conservative types, and predominantly white and male; the profession is still mostly white, but more female and more interested in questions of diversity, social justice, and new narratives about the forgotten people of the past. The reenactor culture and interpretive culture have their Venn-shared space, namely intense independent scholarship and a dedication to authenticity and detail. There were two cultures at play that afternoon, and they weren't just black and white.

As the day's presentations came to a close, one of the reenactors saw my bottles of persimmon beer, and within minutes a call was sent out to share the liquor and all were best friends. People who had not bothered to talk or say hello all day were pushing cups in my face and chatting me up about my work. One asked if I knew about "locusts and 'simmons," and I told him I'd never made the famous combination of honey locust pods and persimmons but eventually I would, and I pointed out that down by the James was a stand of honey locust trees, long pods, thorns and all, yet another piece of the puzzle found in the archaeological remains of the enslaved people's quarter.

For my other ancestors, Native Americans living in the Chesapeake-Tidewater and the Southeastern cultural region, the persimmon was one of the most important wild fruits available to them. The very word "persimmon" is suggestive of the role of Native Americans in introducing the use and popularity of this fruit. The word comes from southern Algonquian languages, including Powhatan—"putchamin," "pessemmins," and "pasimenan" suggesting a fruit that is meant to be dried. According to scholar of Southeastern natives Charles Hudson, "after squeezing persimmons into a pulp, they spread the pulp out in flat loaves about half an inch thick; when dried in the sun it made a sort of candy that would keep for weeks or even months, depending on how dry they made it."

The fruit was added to meat stews, eaten fresh when overripe, or added to cornmeal among the Natchez in Mississippi and Louisiana to make a persimmon bread. It is not impossible that persimmons and other wild fruits were made into alcoholic beverages in the Southeast; however, there is no evidence that suggests that before the introduction of rum, the fruits were utilized in that way.

Europeans and Africans might ultimately have been the ones who brought the fermentation of Native American fruits into Southern culture. Given some of the connections between indigenous foods and those found across the Atlantic, it might be more in the lap of West Africans that we owe the existence of beers made from persimmons mixed with honey locust. In any case, it's clear two ancient strategies merged.

Trading facts and figures and avoiding all other subjects, I had never felt so close to a group of white Southern men with guns who outnumbered me in my entire life. As I traveled more, I noticed kinship with strangers based on knowledge of the old plants. Sour faces turned to smiles at the mere mention of a pawpaw or discussion of techniques for breaking black walnuts and the like. I felt as if I was among a family of people keeping a flame alive—a university of volumes written in the understory and canopy and marsh and streamside that could not be relinquished, but desired, and for our survival's sake, to be savored. I took a picture with those reenactors that day, for in a small way, we made peace.

As I looked for the roots of the house wine of old Virginia and beyond, I found that along the 3,500-mile coast from Senegal to Angola are several ecological zones that historically supported about forty varieties of Ebenaceae, many of which have fruits that have edible and medicinal properties. The most important, *Diospyros mespiliformis*, occurs in savannas and mixed savannah-forest regions along the entire West and central African coast, from which the majority of enslaved Africans brought to the United States were drawn. They would all have had prior experience with *D. mespiliformis* as a source of timber, food, beverages, and medicine. It was known by many names across this huge geographical range: Wolof (*alom*), Manding (*kuku*), Fulani (*nelbe*), Hausa (*kaiwa*), Bamana (*sunsun*), Asante (*okusibiri*), and Igbo (*onye-koyi*).

None of these terms apparently crossed the Atlantic and survived the acculturation process.

Much like *D. virginiana*, the *Diospyros* species of West and central Africa can grow in several different soils—though many grow best in loams—and also enjoys life along the forest edge and bottomlands. It can grow from about twenty to eighty feet. Its greenish-yellow fruits, which turn a purplish color as they ripen, have a similar but more downturned calyx, and are also beloved by local wildlife. Wild hogs, antelope, baboons, and birds all exploit the tree. For this reason, the gathering of the fruit often competes with the seasonal rhythms of other members of the biomass.

Along with many other varieties of *Diospyros* fruits, *D. mespiliformis* was exploited in a variety of ways. J. M. Dalziel, an early twentieth-century ethnobotanist, states, "Near villages it is often in a state of semicultivation, being spared on farms and kept for shade and fruit." Ebony fruit was often gathered by children, and this particular fruit was highly valued by Wolof children in Senegal. Fruit that was not eaten fresh was mashed to a pulp and dried (known as *baro* among the Hausa), and incorporated into sauces and porridges. Among non-Islamic groups, the ebony fruit was distilled or fermented into a brandy or beer. It was also made into a sort of preserve or molasses, known as *ma'di* or *madya* among the Hausa of northern Nigeria. As a medicine, it was used to cure dysentery, skin eruptions, and as a wash for sores. Among the Mande-speakers, it was known as the *sunsun*, or "tree of abundance," and a home for the spirits; meanwhile, in the enslaved community, the 'simmon tree was often noted for being a tree where "haints" like to hover and hide.

When I was younger, I used to like to walk the woods and look for the things my elders spoke of. I admire them for healing themselves and feeding themselves, for stories of dewberries and agaritas, prickly pears and crab apples during the Surrender and in the

Depression. I long for the hand of my Grammy leading me in the picking of honeysuckles—and the yellow ones were always better. I cannot walk the grounds of the plantations without calling out the trees and plants the dead once used and now nourish with their bones. We were Americans and Africans all at once—tied to two worlds through a bewildering love of the land.

My Mother's Apple Crisp

6 heritage or heirloom apples (large, peeled, cored, and sliced)
1 cup white granulated sugar or vanilla sugar
¼ cup cornstarch
1½ tsp Ceylon cinnamon
1 tbsp vanilla extract or homemade steeped vanilla

1 pinch kosher salt
1½ cups flour
1 cup light brown sugar or ½ cup Muscovado sugar mixed with ½ cup white granulated sugar
1 stick cold butter or margarine (unsalted preferred)

Preheat the oven to 350 degrees.

Mix apples with sugar, cornstarch and cinnamon, vanilla, and salt. Bake for 30 minutes in a 9 by 13 ceramic dish on a cookie sheet covered with foil. Mix ingredients for topping by cutting together in flour/sugar mixture until you get the dough to a consistency of peas, or until it is well blended and, when squeezed by the handful, it will stick together, then break apart into a crumble. Sprinkle over apples. Bake for 30 minutes on the middle or low rack, making sure to put something under the baking dish to catch any spillover. The topping should be a light golden brown.

Quickie version: Microwave the apples with plastic wrap on the top to steam them for 10 minutes or so until soft, then stir. Bake for half the time at the same temperature as above.

Fried Apples

5 or 6 apples (Pippins,
  Jonathans, McIntoshes),
  cored and sliced
¼ cup raw sugar or brown
  sugar

A few pinches of cinnamon,
  allspice, mace, or nutmeg
Lard, oil or bacon drippings
  or butter
A splash of cider

Take apple slices and roll in a mixture of the sugar and spices. Fry until tender and juicy in oil until soft. Lower the heat, add cider, stirring occasionally until soft and sautéed, about 15 minutes.

Red Straw Persimmon Beer

10 cups wild persimmons
1 gallon water
Clean, dry red pine straw

1 cup sugar
½ cup honey
1 tbsp yeast

Boil the persimmons in a gallon of water in a large pot, stirring and breaking up the fruit. Remove from heat. As the water cools, mash the persimmons in the water until the pulp is freely flowing. Then strain the pulp-laden liquid several times into a bowl, being careful not to allow seeds in. In the bottom of an empty wine jug, place a few strands of clean, dry red pine straw. Pour in the sugar and honey. Pour the persimmon pulp liquid on top of that and add the yeast. Cap loosely and make sure that you air the liquor several times. As the pulp and yeast form a thick loaf in the neck of the bottle, be sure to keep watch over the fermentation. After a few weeks, strain the entire bottle, removing the mash, and remember the volume will be reduced once you remove the mash. To keep the fermentation going, add a small amount of sugar to the reserved liquor each week. After several months, the persimmon beer should be ready to enjoy. Allow to ferment for a longer period of time to develop a more complex, light, fruity flavor.

16

ALL CREATURES OF OUR G-D AND KING

THE SOUTHERN MENAGERIE

I traveled to every aquarium in the South from the National Aquarium in Baltimore to the Audubon in New Orleans, from Tampa to Chattanooga to Newport News and Virginia Beach to the Outer Banks, Charleston, and Atlanta looking for "bream." Cut off from the free access to the water as in days of old, and not being a great swimmer, I went from tank to tank looking at blue crabs in Chesapeake Bay environs, and Low Country rice impoundments, and Tennessee River depths, and Louisiana bayous, and Florida swamps, and Appalachian Georgia trout streams, looking for the aquatic world of the Old South, and also just to discover bream. Everybody thinks that they know what "bream" is, just like everybody thinks they know what jack, snook, mullet, and redfish are.

Bream, pronounced "brim," is not the same fish of note in England or western Europe. In the South it refers to several bony species of small fry that make it into the frying pan or deep fryer after you catch "a mess" on a good fishing trip. The most mesmerizing tank of them all is the Nickajack Lake exhibit at the Tennessee Aquarium in Chattanooga, complete with the South's crowning glories—the largemouth bass, the longnose car, and the humongous blue catfish and buffalo (one of my maternal grandmother's favorite fish). I ask a score of boys what "bream" is. The clear winner is the redear sunfish.

Cracking the code of the vernacular is just half the battle. Fish are as seasonal as birds or fruit. Their world is invisible to us unless we are on intimate terms with it. I felt nauseous writing about this part of the foodscape because unlike my father and ancestors before him, I had never spent any measurable time "gone fishin'" in my life. I felt deprived of a harmony robbed of me by pollution, fear of nature, overpopulation, and poor stewardship of water and air, but something in me felt healed knowing the explorers of the next generation could identify bream and its habits, getting knowledge passed down from the generations gone fishin' before.

Meeting Bradley Taylor in his element in southeastern Georgia was a key moment for me to understand the importance of knowing every part of the Southern food chain. A techie with an extensive property used for raising Southern heritage breeds, Bradley is me if I was white and I really liked having a menagerie all to myself. He has a thundering herd of timid Gulf Coast sheep and Pineywoods cattle that appear like magic out of the dust when summoned to feed, and Muscovy ducks, Cotton Patch geese, guineas, Dominicker roosters, and Choctaw hogs. Even the dogs he relies upon to help him keep all the flocks and herds and broods in order are older breeds made for protecting the stock. To get to him you have to take that ancient road from South Carolina into Georgia that goes through a wasteland of dead motels. Roadkill here are armadillos; the only thing living I saw on the way was a mutty longhorn in someone's front yard.

"I studied the path of the yeoman farmer and stock herder in the Old South. That's my lineage." Bradley is as deep into this as I am. He sprayed the kitchen table with his source books, noting a people and a time when white slaveless farmers and herders kept animals out in the piney woods. Go a little farther south in Georgia (and believe me, you don't have far to go from Bradley's) into northern and central Florida and this becomes the Cracker culture, and there are indeed Cracker cattle. (Don't be offended, "cracker" comes from cracking the whip, which if you are looking at this from the enslaved person's perspective, isn't such a good thing, but the cracking often involved pushing the cattle along.)

His books tell the story of the folk culture of what one author nicknamed "Dixie's forgotten people." Poor whites. They lived on sweet potatoes and salt pork and grew cane and tobacco and had stills deep in the woods. They were also an enterprising and innovative people of their own making who often lived on the margins of plantation society, taking what they would and leaving what they refused from both the planter class and the enslaved blacks who, in many communities, outnumbered them. Bradley's work through his animals is very similar to my work through food; he is trying to understand himself.

"Don't be afraid to touch 'em; they won't hurt you." Bradley encouraged me to meet his Pineywoods cattle face to face, big horns and all. He has a story about every breed, including the wrangling he had to do to get his heritage-breed hogs. "We had to go to this old black gentleman's farm time and time again and finally he sold us these guys." As he points to his hogs happily lying in a mixture of muddy water and Spanish moss, I get Old Yeller flashbacks of bristly razor hogs living in the Southern backcountry. I don't hesitate to turn my recorder on just so I can hear what the Old South sounded like in its faunal soundtrack, and I close my eyes so I can hear all the animals sing together, freely running around acres and acres of enclosed land happy and cageless. His wife looking on dishing us up homemade peach pie while their son gets ready for practice, Bradley talks about the days when they provided heritage breed meat for buyers.

"It was a hassle, and we weren't even breaking even sometimes. Everybody wanted heritage pork or turkeys or beef. Sometimes we couldn't keep up. We still provide meat every once in a while to some restaurants or buyers, and we keep the breeds up. They are all a part of our big family out here." We finish our pie, we keep talking shop about heritage breeds, and then Bradley surprises me with a Muscovy duck in a cooler to take to my next cooking gig. He doesn't look like the hugging type but he surprised me with that too; in our mutual weirdness, our obsession with the roots of the culture we love, we found kinfolk, the descendant of yeoman farmers and the descendant of the enslaved.

The food world today is populated by people who find themselves both conservators and consumers of domestic and wild animal life. A new archetype has emerged of the nurturing omnivore both petting and stroking something he (it's usually a he) hopes will later make the perfect ethnical, compassionate entrée. Ecology and biology come into play—enthusiasts make passionate arguments to preserve and protect the land and seascapes from whence their calories come. Calls are made to reserve the rush to pollute, spoil, cut, and deface the planet. And rarely are any of these faces of color, and by color I really mean black.

It's a strange turnover, especially considering that enslaved Africans were masters of the subtropical Southern wilderness. It was they who captured sharks and alligators for food and hauled in massive dredges of shellfish, schools of fish, and thousands of crabs, and crawfish. Many were indispensable experts, drawing on generations on the coast and millennia of experience from West and central Africa. More than one enslaved person served as director of the local fishery or helped whites hunt and track game in the woods. We were the cowboys in the Carolina frontier, having been Fulani pastoralists for thousands of years in the African savanna.

The loss of access to the countryside, rivers, and coastline, and our migration North and to the Southern cities, meant a steady loss of connection not only to the earth but to its creatures. It was the African American who minded the field, empowered by a gun—a rare position of power during enslavement—whose bullets brought in rice birds and small birds that threatened the corn. It was our ancestors who carved sacred signs of Kongo-Angolan origin into the shells of turtles and the scales of fish and sent them back into their elements as prayers—animals no one would dare to harvest or keep. Our presumed association with the wild, albeit less than savory or sane, was reinforced by the number of animals in the New World named after our ancestral homeland—guinea fowl, Angolan chickens, Barbary sheep, guinea hogs, guinea pigs, Congo eels, and the list goes on. Somehow, someway, the African wilderness had merged with the American wilderness—and nights were never again the same.

It is hard to appreciate all of this in a time where I have seen so many schoolchildren damn near break out into tears at the sight of a worm, or squeal in abject terror at the presence of a snake. Our ancestors had no lack of stories about the animal world, through their antics, their peaceful wisdom, and hard lessons detailing the laws of nature. Snakes and worms became living avatars of lightning and ancestral forces. Rabbits and hares and wolves and foxes and manatees (the fish horse) became characters in a divine drama related in terms a child could comprehend, but in a tone and depth that made lifelong impressions on the tellers and told from the cradle to the grave. Br'er Fox and Br'er Rabbit to Aunt Nancy, the American and West Indian incarnation of Anansi—the Spider—himself emblematic of the secret hand of the Creator, refused to die in chains; and in the case of Br'er Rabbit, lived long enough to be appropriated by Joel Chandler Harris of Georgia.

There was nothing in the animal kingdom that did not speak to us. Buzzards, owls, doves—even the ill-fated Carolina parakeet, which was one of the few birds with any striking resemblance to the brilliantly colored fowl of tropical West Africa—all held their place in the folk beliefs of the people, announcing birth, death, calling trouble, and scratching out buried power objects meant to harm and curse, such as the frizzle-head chicken. When a person died, a white chicken would be sacrificed, but nobody remembered why; and a generation later the white chicken became a graveyard symbol, but nobody remembered why. The yard bird was the preacher's bird, and nobody recalled that the chicken brought down on a golden chain from heaven had scratched the dirt making the land form, and it would ever since after be a line of communication from the Creator to his created. In the yards of enslaved, "the general chicken merchants," Dominique chickens—"Dominiker hens"—"made eggs that were turned into barter for old dresses and cast-off porcelain, buttons and trinkets, giving the enslaved tastes of a human life."

We told stories for generations of our animals by name. Ned the hog was more than six hundred pounds and gave my grandfather meat for almost a year and a half in the South Carolina upcountry. Ida and Henry were my great-grandfather's main transportation and led the plow and wagon in his tobacco fields. Buster was my grandmother's cat in Alabama, the one that kept the mice from making it into the jar of molasses; and Frieda, the collie, was her dog, provider of rabbits. On my first trip to South Carolina as a little boy, meeting the Java chickens, peacocks (nobody ever called them that—they were peafowl) and guineas and Muscovy ducks, rabbits, free-range cats and dogs and geese and Brahma bulls and bristly red hogs was, in a way, like meeting family. These were the creatures that sustained black country life and told stories about our lives that they did not tell about our neighbors.

I hear my mother's voice again: "The squirrel is a funny little thing / he got a bushy tail / steals away old Massa's corn / and puts it on the rail / raccoon's tail is ringed all around, the possum's tail is bare / but the rabbit ain't got no tail at all / just a li'l wee bunch of hair . . ." Another "slave song" immortalized on a record, but passed to me from my mother from the generation before her, teaching me about the four food groups: squirrel, rabbit, possum, and coon. Squirrel time is summertime, rabbit time is springtime, coon time is fall time, possum time is wintertime. With this little critter, we had a longer ride than others, even though we had only known it since 1526 or 1619 . . .

"Slaves as a rule preferred possums to rabbits," said "Parson" Rezin Williams from Prince George's County, Maryland, interviewed by the WPA in the 1930s. Fellow interviewee James Deane said, "Yes, I have hunted opossums, and coons." George Jones remembered, "When hunting came, especially in the fall or winter, the weather was cold; I have often heard my father speak of rabbit, opossum, and coon hunting and the dogs." There seems to be a consensus among the enslaved elders who left us the stories of their lives that wild game was important to their diet and a seasonal delicacy. If that doesn't bring it home, listen to Charles Ball:

During the whole of this fall and winter, we usually had something to roast, at least twice a week, in our cabin. These roasts were rackoons, opossums, and other game—the proceeds of my trapping. All the time the meat was hanging at the fire, as well as while it was on the table, our house was surrounded by the children of our fellow-slaves; some begging for a piece, and all expressing, by their eager countenances, the keen desire they felt to partake with us of our dainties. It was idle to think of sharing with them, the contents of our board; for they were often thirty or forty in number; and the largest rackoon would scarcely have made a mouthful for each of them.

In a culture that was not averse to eating members of the rodent family, such as the cutting-grass rat (*Thryonomys swinderianus*) of Lower Guinea; the marsupial Virginia opossum (*Didelphis virginiana*) was a real treat. My great-grandfather was fond of it, as were many in his generation and before. Hunting and dealing with the wild was the concern of men, and this trait, brought across the Atlantic, helped preserve the manhood and brotherhood of many an enslaved man. When the "'simmons" were ripe and the frost and light snow had descended on the land, the possums were considered to be at their fattest and most delicious. Typically they were caught with dogs, kept alive a week or two, and fed cornbread and persimmons until the cook felt that they were "cleaned out." (Possums eat carrion in addition to fruits and nuts.) They were then killed, bled, and cleaned out of their entrails. The possum was soaked overnight in cold, salted water. Roasted with sweet potatoes ("taters"), they were considered the height of the harvest feasting.

To cook a possum (according to my research, at least), you must first soak the son of a gun in apple cider vinegar to kill the rest of his gaminess after the brining. Please do not think you can do this with roadkill. The possum must be culled alive. Grease down the possum with fresh butter or lard, rub salt and red-hot pepper into the possum, and sprinkle all over with flour. Place the possum in the pan, add a cup of water, and bake for an hour. Place sweet potatoes around the possum and drizzle with sorghum molasses. Bake for another 45 minutes until the potatoes are mush and the possum is brown. Remember to add a little flour and water mixed together to thicken the stock in the pan to serve as gravy. Apparently I was going to finally have my rite-de-passage and cook a possum once, but when I discovered it had been the zoo possum at a plantation where I was interpreting, I turned down the offer to singe, skin, gut, and bake the thing—out of respect, of course—and it went back into repose in their coffin of a freezer. But if the occasion should ever arise . . .

It wasn't just the four food groups, it was our relationship with the dogs that caught them that marked our lives. These were the same dogs that Washington and Jefferson had assassinated in an attempt to curtail assumptions of thievery. Puppies with their brains blown out because Old Master thought the dogs were being set on the sheep, or were too protective over Ned or Eggleston or Juna or Mary as she was hauled off to be whipped. Our dogs had been special to us since Africa, when they helped us hunt and guarded our villages. For this, they got bones and scraps of meat and plantains grown just to keep them fed and satisfied. In our Master and Jack folktales, we told of our love of dogs—memorialized by wrapping their skin on our hands—"Love I see, Love, I stand, Love I holds in my right hand." To this day, I have the tooth of one of my late dogs in the pouch I wear around my neck. Some things don't change.

Our animals became bones and remnants. We wore coon and possum bacculi (penis bones) around our necks. A coon bone around a man's neck was a sure sign he was a perfect lover. We harvested the pubic bone of our game and strung them for vitality and fertility. We carried chicken bones in our purses and wallets, and snakeskins and desiccated frogs and shells. Then we became urban and we left behind our country ways—except for the chicken bones; that's something my grandmother did to the grave—and if I am honest I will too. Feathers, shells, scales, teeth, corpses, feet, claws—all of it portents and power and prophylactics against the dark side of death, loss, and sexlessness.

Our leftovers might mean nothing if not for our having left precious few other records of our lives behind in the scurry to not be oppressed. Walking into the zooarchaeology lab to meet Steve Atkins, Joanne Bowen, and Ywone Edwards-Ingram, seasoned Chesapeake-region archaeologists, I found out just how profound those leftovers were at telling the story of the black dead and their soul food. Before me were millions of fragments from meals left behind from slave quarters across the Chesapeake Bay area.

The bones represented a remarkable diversity of wildlife taken in to fill out the rations and garden truck available to the enslaved. It's not just that they fished—they fished at particular times of year, in specific circumstances at lengths close to or far from the scrutiny of their slaveholders. Sometimes they were free people of color making a living for themselves. Some of the fish were not eaten but rather thrown away or sold: landscape architect Benjamin Latrobe was told by an enslaved man in Virginia that he "wouldn't feed shad to a whore's dog." Sturgeon were better sold than eaten, and gar and the muddier cats—bullheads included—preferable to the white and blue cats. The bones told stories of the thinking and moments in the lives of the African Americans of old, as eaters, as fishermen, as entrepreneurs.

Without much survey of the displayed collections came croaker, catfishes, eels, herring, shad, gar, sturgeon, sheepshead, white perch, yellow perch, suckers, sunfish, silver perch, weakfish, mullet, spot, scup, striped bass, gafftopsails—sea catfish and even stingrays. Blue crab and oyster shells, mussels, clams, scallops, and shells from terrapin and box turtle and snappers; the entire ecosystem bent itself to the will of the hungry, exiled African and her children. Apart from the aquatic life, the archaeologists lovingly displayed pig and chicken bones—making up most of the mass—followed by cow and sheep and goat bones, which unfortunately are difficult to tell apart. If we could tell them apart, we might have a very different narrative on whether goat survived as the main red meat of Africans and their descendants, or bowed in weakness to pork. Without much trouble there were raccoon bones, and the other food groups, but also deer, Canada geese, wild turkey, small birds, and even snakes and field rats, without question eaten by the earlier groups of enslaved as they had eaten cutting grass in their homelands for generations.

By the time our ancestors were marched all the way to Louisiana, Arkansas, and Texas, the larder was thick with critters that "only Indians and Negroes" dared to touch. We relished baby alligators and fleshy, red swamp crawfish, and Texas diamondback terrapins were hunted almost to extinction for soup. Pronghorns and jackrabbits joined the usual game roster. Bobwhite quail and beaver made room for these new game, as well as armadillo, wild hogs and peccaries, prairie chickens and bison. Cichlids similar to those in West Africa swam in the waters of the southern Rio Grande, and canebrake rattlesnakes from the Brazos, carefully caught, were relished when stewed in their own gravy.

And yet, despite years of digging beneath cabins to assert a more diverse diet on the Southern coastline, the move into the central cotton country severely curtailed the diversity of our ancestors' plates. The pig ruled even more supreme in central Alabama and Mississippi than he had in Maryland, Virginia, or South Carolina. The rituals of the year were punctuated by his sacrifice. If they were lucky they roasted him in barbecue form in the summer or at corn shucking. The winter meant eating fresh guts and lights that could not be salted or smoked, and the rest of the meat was eaten in preserved bits until it ran out. What was true of enslavement bled into the rest of the lives of black folks through to the Great Migration.

Now, most Southerners had hog killing time, and for the most part, it was done pretty much the same way. What made these traditions differ from place to place is the meaning and investment each Southern culture has added to the tradition. Acadian people and the Creoles in Louisiana had the *boucherie* (the butchering) which could occur any time, but mostly at times requiring a fresh supply of charcuterie. Appalachian people usually did their hog killing between Thanksgiving and Christmas before mountain snows made each hill and holler its own island. In the Deep South, hog killing time may not occur until the very dead of winter, usually between Christmastime and February. In the days before refrigeration was common, an extended cold snap was a necessary element for the fall and winter killing time.

Hog killing was a very intricate ritual no matter where in the South you lived. You can still attend an occasional *boucherie* here and there, but it's not the same as the days when one farm and then the next would shift operations from place to place, with a small feast for all those gathered to do the work of slaughtering; bleeding; singeing and boiling to remove the hair; scraping the hog; hanging it up by the flap of flesh behind the feet; making the cut from the bung to throat; catching and cleaning the guts; tending the head; and then finally processing the meat and lard into distinct portions—the hams, the bacon and belly, leaf lard for baking, shoulders, side meat, feet, headcheese, sausage, and the bits that could either be preserved or left behind—the chitlins or chitterlings (the small intestine), spareribs, the chine—the backbone, feet, neckbone, tail, and brains. Some people made blood pudding, and others eschewed that and let it seep into the ground. Anything left over was given to the dogs that surely gathered for the leavings.

Invariably there would be tables set up where mostly women would process the fresh pork, which they would chop or grind with pieces of fat into sausages. Others would be engaged in rendering crackling, which miraculously appear from the cooking down of fresh lard. In Louisiana, these would be soaked in cane syrup to make an irresistible rustic meat candy. Backbone stews, fresh cooked neckbones, pigs' ears, and junk pot stews of leftover bits and pieces and fresh roasted spareribs were part of a normal hog killing meal. Rounded out with hot cornbread, wheat bread, cabbage or kraut, greens, potatoes, sweet potatoes, applesauce or fried apples, and other seasonal dishes, the little feast rewarded the families gathered to help cull the hogs. Sometimes it was several hogs, other times it was one very large hog; and during slavery on the largest plantations, dozens of hogs and in some cases a hundred or more would be killed and put up.

From Asia came the pig, from Eurasia came the methods of curing and smoking its meat. These American hogs were raised on a new larder of corn, pecans, peanuts, hickory nuts, peaches and wild fruits, tubers, and roots. From Native America, Africa, and Europe came ways to prepare the pork, and from the South came the greatest expression of pork consumption in American culture where these three massive cultural elements came together in the dawn of American history. And yet the greatest irony is that for much of its history, fresh pork was a luxury for most Southern people.

Most meat was cured with a salt-based blend, usually but not always including salt, saltpeter, sugar, and pepper. Regardless of what flavor these ingredients might have imparted, their inclusion was first and foremost practical. Meat went through several rubbings of salt and saltpeter, which helped to dry the meat and stave off rot. A rotten ham or other cut was improperly salted, so it was essential to get salt into every crevice. The meat sat in boxes of salt for six to eight weeks and was then rubbed with pepper and other things like hickory ash to keep off flies that invariably infested the area in meathouses. Red pepper helped keep out skipper fly larvae. For several days, the hams or bacon would be smoked using hickory, oak, apple branches, sassafras twigs, corncobs, or whatever else was available, usually giving priority to consistency. In other words, you picked a source of smoke and stuck with it for a given set of meat. Apple, peach, pecan, or other fruit and nut woods were typically from broken branches and fallen trees which were gathered by young people in anticipation of the smoking process. Later on, hams and bacon would be bagged after smoking to prevent further infestation. The meat would get moldy on the outside, but the mold was merely scraped off and soaked overnight to rid it of two-thirds of its saltiness.

PORK-UTERIE

Italy may have its prosciutto, but the South will always have her country hams—first strictly of sweaty Tidewater summers, then later of crisp Kentucky and Tennessee falls. For generations the masters of these hams were enslaved men each said to possess a special savor to their particular "cure." The recipe books of the turn of the twentieth century, like the *Blue Grass Cook Book*, assure that "Marcus" (that's all he's known as) knows the magic of how to preserve a genuine Kentucky ham. It even poses him doing the work of preparing them for the smoke. But nothing could compare with the skill and art of a black man charged with the art of barbecue. And nothing is today more controversial than identifying the roots of barbecue and what that means to the history of Southern food.

Cooking over sticks and saplings was known to both early indigenous Virginians as well as the indigenes of the West Indies, where the word "*barbacoa*" was supposedly encountered by the Spanish in the sixteenth century. The word "barbecue" also has roots in West Africa among the Hausa, who used the term "*babbake*" to describe a complex of words referring to grilling, toasting, building a large fire, singeing hair or feathers, and cooking food for a long period of time over an extravagant fire. In West Africa, unlike early America, the roasting of fowl, game, goats, and cattle in the savannah and Sahel was associated with celebrations, funerals, and the like. Animals might also be half-smoked en route from the bush to the homestead and rubbed with specific herbs and spices to ensure against spoilage or insect infestation. Absent from both West Africa and the West Indies was the pig (*Sus scrofa*), the Middle Eastern immigrant domesticate that quickly became popular across Eurasia. The Eurasian tradition also drew on the practice of smoking meats. Barbecue coevolved in the New World, but certainly bears specific markers showing its West and central African roots.

Highly spicing meats; the roasting of whole goats; the use of peppery sauces or pepper vinegar; parboiling in some cases; the use of the wooden grill framework; the long and slow cooking process; sauces that utilized tomatoes, onions, peppers, and the like; and the social context of barbecue—as a tool to promote social conviviality and community—hearken back to the culture's African roots. Even as barbecue certainly has roots among Native Americans and Europeans, it was enslaved Africans and their descendants who became heir to multiple traditions and, in turn, incorporated those traditions into a standard repertoire known as Southern barbecue. I recognize barbecue as a multicultural, coevolved culture rather than the sole product of any one of the individual ethnic blocs to which we owe its existence. However, we must cease efforts that would divorce barbecue from its African roots, connections, and narratives rooted in slavery and the African Diaspora.

The barbecue was always inherently political, as a "gift" to enslaved people that bought goodwill, discouraged resistance, and rewarded people pushed beyond their limits. An old, sick, injured or surplus animal (there may not have been enough grain or fodder to feed it) was culled and divided up. In this example, we barbecued spareribs, chines, tails, and other parts, and whole chickens, demonstrating the culinary divisions between the planter's family and the enslaved. As a tool of political coercion, barbecues were used in early

Southern culture to foment connections between planters and their families, and later became a critical ingredient in the performance of political rallies and the selling of candidates. Again, enslaved men were in many cases the early pitmasters, and their "wok presence" is felt both in the documentary evidence left to us as well as in the recollections and memories left by Southerners of generations ago, as well as those for whom this is a living memory. It is black men, not bubbas, who lurk silently and shadowlike in postcards and woodcuts depicting Southern barbecue. Their stories are mostly gone because they were just considered "the help."

As early as the eighteenth century, Peter Kalm was describing pepper vinegar as a popular ingredient for the seasoning of roasted meat. Pepper sauces were most commonly described along with the culinary preference of Africans and their descendants for the "bitey" taste. Rich, red, *mwamba* gravies from central Africa, colored by palm oil, and tomatoes and hot peppers and anything else on hand seasoned fowl and other animals grilled, roasted, or cooked in pits. Today, *peri-peri* roasting as practiced in central and southern Africa, where meat is rubbed and dipped in a spicy mixture or sauce, recalls the Portuguese's spreading of chilis from the New World to Africa, where birds spread the seed and Africans adopted the pepper alongside their own repertoire of spices, using them to give flavor and spicy intensity to almost every savory dish. In West Africa, *suya* cooking is practiced by the Hausa, Fulani, and their neighbors in the savanna and Sahel, using a spice rub that is liberally applied to brochettes of meat roasted over flames. The roasting of bush pigs and other game undoubtedly added to a knowledge base that was easily transferred to two other cultures for whom roasting over a wood fire was a common and popular way of preparing meat, fish, and other foods.

In the West Indies, allspice and pimento wood were adopted from the local Arawak and Carib populations as the key wood for barbecue. These woods give flavor and character to the meat, much as oak, hickory, pecan, apple, sassafras, cherry, and other woods season North American barbecued meats. The coevolved tradition of "jerking" meat, as known in Jamaica and other parts of the West Indies, might have influenced American barbecue. At any rate, early Afro-Caribbean, West and central African, and early African American cultures brought together indigenous, African, and western European elements to create and develop a uniquely Southern art—barbecue.

On the third leg of the Cooking Gene project's Southern Discomfort Tour, my former partner and I engaged the Colonial Williamsburg Foundation to do an experiment in re-creating barbecue history at Great Hopes Plantation, a model middling tobacco farm of the late eighteenth century, where visitors can see the layout that most black rural Virginians—including my own ancestors— lived in for give or take a century and a half. Everything is called a "house"—a corn house, smokehouse, master's house, the cookhouse, the slave house. Between the corn house and the smokehouse, in spitting distance from the cookhouse, we asked to re-create a barbecue as known to the enslaved community. We would be the first people in a living history site of that period to orchestrate the effort.

The plan was not without controversy. The site was short-staffed and the question came up more than once of, "Who is actually doing all this work?" It was suggested that maybe we could just use a gridiron and do it smaller scale, or use a spit. We resisted. It was 108 degrees in one of the most blistering summers we had ever known, and we asked for a deep pit used for making bricks and said we would take on the rest of the work. Before another person could naysay, Jacob rolled up his sleeves, put his hair into a ponytail, pulled out a roll of lipstick, gave his lips a rich ripe crimson sheen, and took his pale ass into the woods with an eighteenth-century reproduction hatchet and felled one tulip poplar sapling after the next. The counterresistance stopped once everyone caught sight of him dragging eight trees across the parking lot.

As he gathered our saplings and set them into bags of cold water to stay green, we realized the meat had to be seasoned. The seasoning is proprietary but included red peppers and salt; and the mop, using cider vinegar, butter, onions, salt, sage, water, and red pepper, was continually dipped, soaked, and dabbed on the roasting meat as suggested by a 240-year-old Virginia recipe. It is difficult to say where exactly this method of using the stick grill started. Some might say the most ancient cooking traditions of Africa, and in most African market places today, bits of wire or grates, much as in the rural South, have replaced the traditional stick frame. In Jamaica, the maroons—West African men and women who escaped slavery and went into the hills to live a separate existence—often cooked using the barbecue method, enjoying their jerked pork, fowl, and game. From Jamaica to Virginia to Louisiana, the Carolinas, and Maryland, early forms of this roasted meat tradition began to evolve. Eastern Algonquian, Muskogean, Siouan, Senegambian, Akan, southeastern Nigerian, Kongo-Angolan, British, Scotch-Irish, and German traditions began to combine with French, Spanish, and mixed Afro-Creole traditions from the West Indies and Latin America. Over time, as Caribbean people migrated back and forth from the islands to the mainland, and as enslaved people were moved across the Southern landscape and sold from Baltimore and Norfolk down to Natchez and New Orleans, barbecue traditions spread and took on regional forms.

Kentucky lamb 'cues hearken back to English tastes brought from the upper Chesapeake, and the granddaddy of 'cue—pepper/vinegar 'cue from the southeast Virginia–northeast North Carolina hearth—spread out through the eastern Tidewater. In South Carolina, other forms, tied to the Afro-Caribbean culinary heritage and high volume of enslaved Africans directly from the continent, developed that would penetrate the Deep South during the spread of the Cotton Kingdom. Where these recipes matched, they rubbed off on one another, where they did not, regional boundaries were drawn, as in Texas, Tennessee, and other places where barbecue culture cooked long and slow into the forms we know today. Barbecue specialists recognize eastern North Carolina, western North Carolina, Memphis, Texas, Kentucky, and sometimes Alabama/Mississippi schools of barbecue. I would include Maryland "bull roasts," and other regional traditions as well, in a larger historical reach to show the variations the culture has taken. We need to recognize the blurry lines between contemporary practices and what was actually known in historical periods. In other words, we have to be careful not to be too anachronistic in our lens on the past.

The next day, veteran interpreter and solid wise man Mr. Robert Watson built a tall fire by 8 a.m., and over two and a half hours the collection of half logs and twigs and sticks—which we continually freshened up with blocks of hickory and oak wood—burned down into a rich, deep and oppressively hot bed of coals. Robert Watson was the man I saw in the colonial Virginia book, the nineteen-year-old who inspired me to be . . . me. Robert grew up in King and Queen County, Virginia, and knows his craft from the ground up, but he's also a polymath of the library of early American knowledge. He measures time in tobacco seasons; his face is ageless; his mentees many. In many ways, I don't think I trust anybody else to lead me through this adventure. Robert to me is the voice of the ancestors.

By 10:30, we set to put the meat on—ribs, chine, and tail; chickens; forelegs; nothing representing wholeness, just fragments of celebration and reward. We quickly sorted the poles into place with some error, but we got more pain from facing the smoke and heat head-on and placing the meat on the carefully arranged poles, praying that no falling pieces had to be retrieved from the deep, fire-licking culinary pit of hell we had created. "Michael, you need

316 The Cooking Gene

to mind these poles now, keep them wet. I don't know who's going in the hole to retrieve the meat when it falls in." Robert turns stress into smiles. We sort it out as I choke down smoke.

The meat remained on the fire for five or six hours, finally coming done in the late afternoon. The results were mixed. Some of the meat was drier because the heritage varieties were different—Ossabaw ribs are not modern hog ribs—and therefore cooked more quickly, but the staff enjoyed them just the same. These needed repeated bastings to ensure moist meat. They were moved to the outskirts of the pit—dug about eighteen inches deep—where the smoke would penetrate but the meat would not burn over the fire. The fire flared as the drippings and fat fell into the pit, and they were doused by sprinklings that eventually re-erupted as the morning went on. After an hour or so, the flaring ceased as the meat was moved to ensure the most even cooking possible and to avoid overheating certain spots. The saplings themselves began to get thin over several hours and several had to be removed and replaced, but most of the sapling grill weathered the five-hour process.

Because the saplings were thick and sturdy, meat doneness was an issue for the chicken—some areas were perfectly done, others were underdone. Many enslaved communities may have practiced some form of parboiling. Parboiling in central Africa was essential for the consumption of the meat by elders, because of the issue of early dental health and even doneness in meat, but we ignored this step in our experiment.

Those parts that were not done were sent to a cook pot over steady heat, where the meat baked for about thirty minutes, retaining moisture but cooking to bone-doneness. The meat was chopped and divided according to preference and dietary need, something that might not have been too different for early African Virginians who carried with them a host of dietary and cultural taboos from West and central Africa.

A challenge to the experiment was coming up with other foods that might have been consumed by an enslaved African Virginian community and were in season. Roasting ears—green corn ears roasted over a fire—was an easy pairing, as were roasted white potatoes, freshly dug from the end of the spring crop. "Dressed" raw cabbage and cucumber, while not necessarily representative, recalled the frequent notion that "pickles and relishes" were enjoyed with early barbecued meats. My colleague, Colonial Williamsburg chef-interpreter Harold Caldwell, prepared roasted peanuts, boiled greens, and quick-roasted chops of Red Devon beef and Ossabaw pork over gridirons. The vegetables were procured on-site and from staff members' gardens. About 90 percent of the meal was locally sourced. Missing from the menu was hot "lightbread," which could have been a part of such a celebration, or any sort of Brunswick stew—which would have been too early for the late eighteenth century—and cakes, pies, cobblers, and the like. While these might have been appropriate for a nineteenth-century antebellum affair, I felt it best not to include these elements, for the sake of time and visual accuracy.

For the visitors, the chopping of the meat proved almost as theatrical as the cooking itself. The cleaver blade split up bits of meat and chicken, releasing a sweet but acrid-laced steam, and gave up pink-ringed meat impregnated with the essence of smoke. A light sprinkle of salt, and the meat went away in wooden bowls to await the dinner after the workday. When fifty interpreters got their plates and walked down the line to enjoy the first eighteenth-century-style plantation barbecue in more than two centuries, the heat didn't matter as much, and the protest subsided. Biting into the chicken, I inhaled all the rustic sweetness and peppery goodness in a day that for the lack of sports drinks would have killed me. The meat tasted incomparable to anything else I ever had or ever would have, and this was satisfying, but not as satisfying as seeing all of us come together, like a family.

Mr. Wesley Jones's Barbecue Mop

This is my adaptation of a barbecue mop innovated by Mr. Wesley Jones, a barbecue master interviewed by the WPA, and who cooked during antebellum slavery.

½ stick butter, unsalted
1 large yellow or white onion, well chopped
2 cloves garlic, minced
1 cup apple cider vinegar
½ cup water
1 tbsp kosher salt
1 tsp coarse black pepper
1 pod long red cayenne pepper, or 1 tsp red pepper flakes

1 tsp dried rubbed sage
1 tsp dried basil leaves, or 1 tbsp minced fresh basil
½ tsp crushed coriander seed
¼ cup dark brown sugar or 4 tbsp molasses (not blackstrap)

Melt butter in a large saucepan. Add onion and garlic and sauté on medium heat until translucent. Turn heat down slightly and add vinegar, water, and the salt and spices. Allow to cook gently for about thirty minutes to an hour. To be used as a light mop sauce or glaze during the last 15 to 30 minutes of barbecuing and as a dip for cooked meat.

Fried Rabbit

½ cup flour
½ cup cornmeal
Salt
Coarse black pepper
Red pepper flakes

1 young rabbit, cleaned and cut up into pieces
¼ cup oil, or its equivalent in lard or shortening

Mix the flour and cornmeal together and season with salt, black pepper, and red pepper flakes. Coat the rabbit pieces and add to a cast-iron skillet with hot (but not smoking) oil. Cook until done and tender, about 20 minutes, turning halfway through, making sure both sides are crispy.

Catfish Stew

A few thinly sliced wild onions or green onions
1 cup salt pork, cubed (you can substitute pieces of country bacon)
1 cup diced potatoes
2 or 3 chopped ripe tomatoes
1 crushed fish pepper or long cayenne pepper
1 tsp Kitchen Pepper (see recipe on page 24)
Salt to taste
Vegetable stock to cover
1 cup bell pepper, cubed, optional
3 catfish, skinned and cleaned, or fillets cut up into 1 inch pieces

Fry the wild onions and salt pork together until the onions are soft and translucent. Add the potatoes and tomatoes and keep sautéing a few more minutes. Add the crushed pepper, Kitchen Pepper, and salt and add the vegetable stock to cover. Add the bell pepper if you wish. Stew together for 30 minutes. Add the catfish and stew together for 10 more minutes until the meat flakes.

17

THE DEVIL'S HALF ACRE

To inspect was a plain matter of business. Purchasers and spectators were about as indifferent to the nudity and the sex of ordinary slaves as everybody is to those of small children. To be otherwise indicated pruriency or hypocrisy rather than virtue.

—FREDERIC BANCROFT, *SLAVE TRADING IN THE OLD SOUTH*

ON THE BLOCK

The domestic slave trade was the largest forced migration in American history, and during the antebellum period enslaved African Americans could expect to be sold or transferred as property two or three times during their lifetimes. The black body was the single most valuable commodity in the American marketplace between the years 1790 and 1860. Most of the movement of enslaved people focused on what some have called the "second Middle Passage," the movement from the old colonial South—Maryland, Virginia, parts of Delaware, and eastern and northern North Carolina—to the cotton and sugar plantations of the Deep South. Those living in other areas of the Eastern Seaboard South were more likely to move on foot with their slaveholders who caught the "Alabama fever," searching to gobble up the lands opened up after the Trail of Tears and "Indian removal."

By the time of the Civil War, three-quarters of my family were imprisoned by King Cotton. One ancestor, Thomas Reeves, was sold from Virginia into South Carolina probably as early as the 1820s. Thomas's descendants would join those who would have the surnames Pate, Mungo, and Twitty, all of whom had roots in the Low Country. Later, my great-great-great-grandmother Hester would be transferred at a young age from the same South Carolina Low Country to Montgomery, Alabama, in the 1840s. Another great-great-great-grandmother, Rosetta Merritt, would be forcibly relocated to Alabama from Wilmington, North Carolina, sometime after.

On banks of the James River in Richmond, second capital of the Confederacy, I can see where one of my African forebears first arrived, where his children were enslaved, and where his grandchildren were sold away to Alabama—the first few chapters of enslaved life in the American South in a nutshell before my eyes. The city's red brick feels haunted in the way the cobblestones of New Orleans feel haunted. And that connection, among many, is no accident—Alexandria, with its infamous slave jails owned by Price, Birch, & Co., and Richmond and Norfolk all functioned as important funnel cities for the domestic slave trade, with many of the captives ending up in the New Orleans slave market and the auction block of the Saint Louis Hotel.

That auction block still stands; it is an exhibit in New Orleans's Cabildo, the courthouse building that functions as a museum dedicated to Louisiana history. Given some of my uncle's research, it is possible that my great-great-great-grandfather Jack Todd stood on that auction block among the many in the slave-trading district of New Orleans. When he was separated from his wife and children, Jack may have ended up in Arkansas, according to the 1870 census studied in my uncle's research. If this is the same Jack Todd, the likelihood that he was sold through New Orleans is high. New Orleans was the leading Deep South center for the domestic slave trade, with auctions taking place at a furious rate to feed the plantations of the Lower Mississippi Valley, where a hundred people working a sugarcane operation was considered a light workforce.

Two to three feet high—just a box of wood echoing with the countless footsteps of doomed enslaved people, and one of a very few of these artifacts remaining to tell the story of the people who wore those shoes. The greatest fear of the enslaved people of the Upper South was to be sold to a "Georgia man" or to be sold "down the river," a phrase with multiple interpretations; it essentially meant to end up being worked to death on the plantations of the Deep South, separated from family, kin, and ancestors, from familiar environments and semblances of home. If you don't shudder looking at the auction block you might need to be checked for the presence of a soul. If that is my Jack Todd in the census record, and if this is his auction block—I may never know, but it will remain for me a symbol of family lost and with him, stories, memories, and the flow of the generations.

HOW I GOT MY NAME

The Twittys, Stewarts, Cauthens, Masseys, and Blackmons—white families tied by cotton, marriage, geography, and Negroes in homesteads in Lancaster County, South Carolina—shifted black people from property to property. They were money on foot within their circles. Not all enslaved people went very far from their homes. Some were part of the dowry package; others were inherited, while others were sold to pay debts and used as insurance:

Likely Negroes for sale:

> Exparte, J.T.K. Belk, Guardian of Jno. H. Stewart. Petition for sale of Negroes belonging to John Stewart, minor. Under decree of court of equity, offer for sale at Lancaster Court House on 1st Monday the 7th January 1861, three choice Negro fellows: William, Wash and Ben., the first two named are young, stout and likely and will rank No. 1 in any market. Ben is somewhat advanced in years, but full of life and vigor. J.S. Witherspoon, *Lancaster Ledger,* 1860.

Then on said day, three Negroes were sold. In the handwriting of the day, all flourish and curl, Jacob located in the archives of a South Carolina ledger a record of the sale of "Negro Washington," my great-great-great-grandfather ($1,200). Also sold that day were his younger brother William (and the source of my middle name, my father's name, his grandfather's and great-grandfather's name) ($1,350) and Old Ben ($525), who may have been Abney Cauthen, their father according to Wash's birth certificate. That same year in the spring he would be given for a wife Adeline Blackmon. Having changed hands more than once, he would leave slavery with my surname, Twitty. I am pretty convinced he never saw his father and brother again.

TOLERABLE COOKS

My friend Chef Kevin Mitchell, who along with Chef Benjamin Dennis and Professor David Shields brought to life the cuisine of Nat Fuller at McCrady's weeks before the shooting of the Charleston Nine, shares with me twenty pages of advertisements he gathered by scanning antebellum Charleston, South Carolina, newspapers advertising cooks for sale. At the Old Slave Mart Museum, one of many places enslaved people were sold, visitors in the mid-twentieth century were treated to sweetmeats on order. Charleston benne biscuits, peach leather, pecan pralines, black walnut pralines, groundnut cakes, benne brittle, benne wafer, and monkey meat cakes (made with coconut) helped sell the quaint curiosity and historically important *building* where men and women like the following might have been sold:

For Private Sale, A young NEGRO FELLOW, a complete cook as any of his colour, an excellent waiting man, and in short, as good and useful a servant as any in the state. Price 1000 dollars, cash. Wm Marshall. *Charleston Courier* (January 16, 1810)

G. B. PIRRIER. 4 prime BLACK BOYS, one of them a complete cook in the French style, the others good house servants. Apply at No. 13 Champneys' street. *Charleston City Gazette* (June 16, 1813)

For Sale, A Negro WENCH, about 33 years old, a complete Cook in the French and English style, a washer, ironer and clear starcher; and her 2 Sons, one seven, and the other five years old. All warranted healthy, And no runaways. Price $1400 cash. Enquire of Dr. MORE, No. 50, King-street. *Charleston City Gazette* (March 18, 1818)

At Private Sale. A valuable young NEGRO FELLOW, about 25 years of age; a complete cook and butcher; belonging to an Estate. For further particulars, apply to THOMAS OGIER, No. 3 Broad-street. *Southern Patriot* (March 30, 1820)

Valuable House Servant. By M. H. Deleon. To-morrow, the 26th inst. Will be sold before my store, without reserve. A valuable middle aged NEGRO WENCH, a complete Cook, and Pastry Cook, can make Preserves and Pickles, very handy about house, accustomed to attend on Children, a good Nurse in Sickness, Sober, honest, and no runaway. A servant possessing so many rare qualifications, is seldom offered for sale; those in want of one of this description, would do well to benefit by the present opportunity. Conditions cash, or an approved endorsed note at 60 days, adding bank discount. *Southern Patriot* (September 25, 1820)

A French Cook. By. A Tobias. This Day, will be sold before my store, at half past 10 o'clock, without reserve, being the property of a person going to France, A Wench, about 36 years of age; An excellent French Cook, and capable of plain Washing. Conditions at sale. April 12 *Charleston Courier* (April 12, 1825)

The same could be said for New Orleans, Savannah, or Mobile. These were the dressed up, polished enslaved sold in full livery and dresses with new petticoats. They were often like me, stocky and full bodied. They were the children of slaveholders, treasured "members of the family" who were gently disposed of. In those advertisements we learn 1,001 things about the lives of enslaved cooks who knew the terror of the auction block. They were pastry chefs, butchers, fermenters; they were trained in the French and English and American styles, and they could nurse white babies at the expense of their own. They could power a dual kitchen and laundry or serve the food they cooked as waitstaff, and most of all they were obedient and reliable property.

HARD TIMES IN OLD VIRGINIA

In Richmond, the Upper South's leading slave-trading center, the Todd family held in bondage a family of six. Jack, the grandson of an

African brought from the Gold Coast, and his mixed wife Araminta or Arrye, and their four children—my great-great-grandfather Joseph, his brother Louis, their sister Mandy, and another sister whose name has been lost to time. At some point around the fever pitch of slave sales, around 1852, the family was liquidated, with Arrye and her two sons being sold to Alabama and Mandy being sold to Tennessee. The youngest daughter remained unaccounted for, and Jack either remained in Virginia or was the individual located in Arkansas whose census data matched the biography of the great-great-great-grandfather.

Richmond's Shockoe Bottom is a very old part of the city, dating back to the eighteenth century when the capital was moved from Williamsburg to Richmond. It was the crossroads of Richmond's commerce, from tobacco warehouses to shipping and international trade, and finally the center of the Upper South slave trade. Its Victorian-style train station looms above the area where hotels and jails once furled bloodred flags announcing the sale of the enslaved. The area has come into the news for promises of development despite the efforts of activists to preserve the area and markers designating the positioning of the slave trade. There, not far from where the farmers market is today, public auctions were held and human beings sat in cages and in basements and backrooms, chained and awaiting sale. It is little wonder this section of Richmond was called the "Devil's Half Acre," where ten thousand people were sold per month during the 1850s. The irony of the farmers market being the site of the former slave auctions would be novel if it were not something I encountered again and again across the South, from Lexington, Kentucky, to Saint Augustine, Florida—the spot where healthy, local, organic food is now pushed once housed the "Cheapside Market" in Lexington, where slaveholders could literally get enslaved workers for a bargain.

MARCHED ON FOOT

Edmund and Samuel, the Townsend brothers, had long since marched their chattel from Virginia and North Carolina to northern Alabama and southern Tennessee, where they had no fewer than eight prosperous cotton plantations centered on the "Home Place" plantation at Hazel Green in Madison County, Alabama. The only part of my bloodlines that did not leave the Upper South or southern seaboard was my father's maternal line, who were fortunate to remain with their families relatively intact in Virginia's undying, fire-cured-tobacco belt west of Richmond and east of Lynchburg. The constant of living in Virginia the entire time shaped their lives and food as much as leaving and winding through the South did those who were forcibly moved. The regionalization of African American foodways was as much a story of who remained as of those who left and how they were resettled. Then again, my Virginia ancestors must have lived in constant fear of being sold into the Deep South, and I can only imagine that every meal might have felt like the last one they thought they would eat together as a family.

> One was recommended as a "rattlin' good breeder," because she had already given birth to two children at seventeen years of age. Another, a mulatto of very comely form, showed deep embarrassment when questioned about her condition. They brought good prices. "Niggers is high" was the general comment. Who bought them, where they went, whether they were separated from father, mother, brother, or sister, God knows.
>
> —JOHN SERGEANT WISE

The human cost of this event is beyond comprehension. More enslaved people were traded in the domestic slave trade than disembarked from Africa to the United States during the Middle Passage.

Communities of people that had been established for a century or, in some cases, two, were uprooted and families were broken apart. Southern roads knew the clank of chains as whole gangs of husbands, fathers, brothers, and sons were marched to distant plantations in the canebrakes, pine woods, and prairies of the South's most fertile soil.

Women and children, loaded on wagons and train cars, would know the sound of constant crying and horrific scenes where women were raped in sight of their children. Hester, a very fair-skinned mixed woman, often spoke bitterly of the frequent rapes she endured from her teenage years onward, and it is almost certain her mother had the same life as did her mother before her, as did the African woman from whom they descended. The value of a female enslaved person was almost incalculable, as both marriage and forced breeding could be used as a means to ensure a self-sustaining population of free and cheap labor. In the words of Bancroft's *Slave Trading in the Old South*:

It was both less common and less essential thoroughly to inspect the women and the girls, although it was not rare to do so. In any case, it was considered important to know how many children a young woman had borne and what the probabilities were as to the future. If a girl was more than 18 or 19 years and had borne none, it lessened her market value. Such perfectly natural and inevitable incidents of slave trading—were often regarded by travelers as outrageous. Charles R Weld, an English barrister, illustrated this in describing what he saw: "Personal examination (of the women in public) was confined to the hands, arms, legs, bust and teeth. Searching questions were put respecting their age and whether they had children. If they replied in the negative, their bosoms were generally handled in a repulsive and disgusting manner." A matter of fact New Yorker reported his impressions as follows:—"In those days, all frocks were secured in the back with hooks and eyes, so that is was an easy matter to go to the woman and unhook their dresses and examine their backs for any signs of flogging. In fact such signs made a woman unsaleable. As all purchases were warranted, if any trader, after a sale, was suspicious of a diseased condition, he took the woman upstairs into a private room where she was subjected to a physical examination.

All I have are accounts written by other people about what they saw and experienced from the vantage point of privilege that comes with never having to be sold like an animal. From their words to those formerly enslaved interviewed by the WPA, it gets clearer and clearer to me why infanticide could and did occur within the enslaved community. This is why enslaved women designed such "remedies" as cotton root tea to terminate pregnancies. A healthy baby was worth $100 on the Charleston auction block in the mid-nineteenth century and, at the same time, after that child was worked half to death, an enslaved fifty-year-old was worth less than $50.

The auctions themselves were a perverted food event. The same potlikker so greasy it would wink back, in which greens and snap beans swam, was sometimes smeared on the faces of the enslaved up for sale, and others were even bathed in it. To be shiny, a little fat, and machine lubricated equaled the picture of health and good care. Enslaved children might be given an apple as a treat or other fruit to make the task of aging them by teeth easier. If nothing else, it made them feign a smile, illustrating their tractability and compliance and ability to play happy.

I have no idea how little Harry got to the Richmond market from his home in what I have identified as Warren County, North Carolina, on the Virginia border. I don't know who was with him or if he was sold alone or was in the presence of a sibling or kin at the time of his sale. All I know is what the following receipt can tell us:

Richmond, February 11, 1835

Received of Samuel Townsend, twelve hundred and five dollars, being in full for the purchase of three Negroes named Harry, Susan and Jim, the right and title of said slaves I warrant and defend against the claims of all whatsoever, and likewise warrant them sound and healthy. As witness, my hand and seal,

JOHN B. WILLIAMSON.

John Sergeant Wise can clue us into what Harry might have experienced when he was interrogated and physically examined and prodded:

"The most careful buyers kept informed as to new arrivals and went to the jails to inspect them, then, and when the slaves were brought to the auction-mart, they were plied with such questions as: 'How old are you?' 'What can you do?' 'Who raised you?' 'Why are you sold?' 'Anything wrong with you?' Hands were open and shut inside and out. Arms and legs were felt up as a means of deciding whether they were muscular and regular. Backs and buttocks were scrutinized for the welts that heavy blows with a whip usually left. Necks were rubbed or pinched to detect any soreness or lumps. Jaws were grasped, fingers were run into Negroes' mouths, which were widely opened and peered into. Lips were pressed back so that all the teeth and gums could be seen. This performance closely resembled that of an expert reading a horse's age. If there was any suspicion that one eye might not be good, a strange hand was clapped over the other and the slave was asked what object was held before him. The hearing was likewise tested. All such inquiries were made with equal freedom whether the slave was man, woman, boy or girl." The descriptions of many observers substantially agree with what Chambers saw: "About a dozen gentlemen crowded to the spot while the poor fellow was stripping himself, and as soon as he stood on the floor, bare from top to toe, a most rigorous scrutiny of his person was instituted. The clear black skin, back and front, was viewed all over for sores and disease; and there was no part of his body left unexamined." Anybody that was interested—or merely wished to appear so, as some always did, for they thought it gave them importance—might join in the inspection. When scars or any irregularities or signs of disease were found, there were significant nods and an exchange of knowing glances.

And then after he was washed and dressed, made to look well fed, tractable, and happy, John Sergeant Wise says:

> Out of the beautiful grounds and past the handsome residences we went, tuning down Franklin Street towards the great Exchange Hotel . . . As we proceeded the street became more and more squalid and repulsive, until at last we reached a low brick warehouse . . . Over the place was the sign, with the name of an owner and the words AUCTION HOUSE conspicuously painted. At the door hung a red flag with an advertisement pasted on its side, and up and down the street a mulatto man walked with another flag, ringing a large bell, and shouting "Oh, Yea! Oh, Yea! Walk up gentlemen the sale of a fine likely lot of young niggers is now about to begin."

The center of the Devil's Half Acre was Lumpkin's Jail, named after Robert Lumpkin, the city's most infamous slave trader. Lumpkin's complex was compared to a "chicken coop," with many dying from being packed on top of one another or from disease or starvation. From holding facility to holding facility the sanitation was unbelievably inadequate. There were no chamber pots, no fresh air.

Precious objects accumulated in these places were left behind or lost. Someone was always screaming, crying, weeping, or sobbing.

The room was stuffy and dark and hot, candles flickering, little bits of light coming through the window. Harry must have been scared to death and clinging to whoever was with him with everything he had. Before too long, he saw his fate—the auction block. All of his life he overheard grown folks talking about the whips, the diseases, the heat that lasted almost all year long, and being worked to death.

> We moved cautiously through the dark front of the building, and came at last to the rear where a small platform occupied the centre of the room, and chairs and benches were distributed about the walls.

He turned his head and saw the auctioneer, whose fast-moving lips and booming voice would turn him from flesh to dollars:

> A large man, with full beard, not a bad-looking fellow but for the "ratty," appearance of his quick, cold, small black eyes acted as auctioneer. A few Negroes sat on the bench by the door, them being the first "lot" to be disposed of. The purchasers stood or sat about, smoking or chewing tobacco while the auctioneer proceeded to read the decree of a chancery court in the settlement of a decedent's estate, under which this sale was made.

Harry ascends the block, an eight-year-old boy; his head is down and his face covered in hot, fast-shedding tears. The auctioneer says he is *"a real, genuine nigger, well-mannered, respectful, obejunt, and willin."* The other children he was sold with got a nod and the auctioneer says, *"You kin look over this whole gang of niggers an' you won't find the mark of a whip on one of them."*

That day was like any other day for the enslaved in the Devil's Half Acre, a day on which the auctioneer,

> Having thus paved the way for good prices, he announced the slaves to be offered were good carriage drivers, gardeners, dining room servants, farmhands, cooks, milkers, seamstresses, washer women, "the most promisin' growing, sleek and sassy lot of young niggers" he had ever had the pleasure of offering.

Some sent buyers; others had "Mississippi" or "Texas" fever. Others planned to hit the Natchez Trace and resell their lot for double the price in Louisiana to sugar planters aching for black labor. Fifteen years later it was the time of my great-great-great-grandmother Arrye and her children to be sold away from her husband and their father, Jack. First he was put with the lot of young men:

> The sale was begun with some "bucks" as we facetiously called them. They were young, unmarried fellows from eighteen to twenty five. Ordered to mount the auction-block, they stripped to the waist and bounced up . . . Cautious bidders drew near to them, examined their eyes, spoke with them to test their hearing and eyes, made them open their mouths and show their teeth, ran their hands over the muscles in their backs and arms, caused them to draw up their trousers to display their legs, and, after fully satisfying themselves . . . bid for them what they saw fit.

Then Arrye came up just as Martha Ann ascended the block before her.

> "I am now goin' to offer you a very likely young childbearin' woman," said the auctioneer. "She is puffactly healthy, and without a blemish . . . Get up here Martha Ann!" . . . She

gazed for a moment at her husband and at her children and then looked away once more, her eyes brimming with tears.

Martha Ann is bid off. *"I congratulate you, you have bought the cheapest nigger here to-day . . . Will you take Israel and the young'uns with her?"* The answer is no. Today a cleaving will take place, a rupture among the generations, a break with the past.

Just like Martha Ann's slaveholder, Arrye's new slaveholder says no. Today Jack and Mandy and the unnamed girl will not go with Arrye and Joseph and Louis to Alabama. The family is split apart. Every three minutes on average, a gavel falls and more bodies are sold and more families are destroyed.

Martha Ann stepped down from the platform, walked to where he was, the tears streaming down her cheeks and there, hugging her children and rocking herself back and forth, she sobbed as if her heart was breaking. My companion and I looked at each other in disgust, but neither spoke a word.

Arrye will leave her girls behind and her man. Poor little Mandy, destined to be a motherless child. Someone must know where she's headed in Tennessee, someone overheard, because years later her brothers went to find her and found her living with a husband and children there. The other daughter was gone, and nobody knows her name or where she went. Her husband, Jack, may have ended up in New Orleans on his way to being sold upriver in Arkansas. In an instant, their little family was no more.

The old creature who had bought the woman lugged out his hoarded money in sundry packages of coin and paper, and as he counted it, "Martha Ann cheer up, you'll find me a good marster and I'll get you a new husband."

Arrye did receive a new husband, a man named Willis, and they raised nineteen children together, bits and pieces of other families, some of their own, half siblings to her boys. No stories ever came down about being sold, the women especially never revealing what happened in the dark, or of boys' faces being smeared with salt pork or being made to jump and run and smile. Harry traveled to places he'd never seen before, traveling shoeless through mountains and gaps in the hills of southwest Virginia, down into hilly eastern Tennessee, ending up in the middle valley, where he spent much of the rest of his life on a northern Alabama cotton plantation, owned by some of the richest men the state of Alabama ever knew. He could not recollect the name of his mother or father, and he never saw them again.

18
—
"The King's Cuisine"

"Cotton is king!"

—JAMES HENRY HAMMOND, SENATOR FROM SOUTH CAROLINA, 1858

The modern adage—"Cotton is king" that one often hears in reference to the influence this little plant gives to the planter, in home and foreign trade, is, in the richest sense of the world, true.

—ANSON DE PUY VAN BUREN

Soup—Cowpea

Boiled—Bacon and Greens

Roast—Possum

Entrees—Tripe and Cow-Heel

Dessert—Fritters and Molasses

Fruit—Persimmons, Chestnuts, Goobers

—MENU OF THE WETUMPKA HOTEL, ALABAMA;

JOHNSON JONES HOOPER, LOCAL COLORIST, 1859

RECORDS

When he was a teenager, Harry Townsend ran away, presumably north to the Ohio River with a fellow enslaved male named Henry. Harry was caught, put in jail, and held there by a man named Mr. Frasier, to whom $5 was paid for his return. After his slaveholder, Samuel Townsend, died in 1856, Harry was enslaved to the estate, maintained in part by a Mr. Cabaniss, an attorney who oversaw the Townsend holdings and whose legal maneuvers led to the emancipation and portioning of inheritance to Samuel Townsend's children, who were mulatto. They went on to Wilberforce University and west to Colorado. Harry was not so fortunate. In 1858 he was still property, worth $1,000 on the Jackson County plantation of Samuel Townsend's estate, where 38 other enslaved people were held. Samuel Townsend's "Home Place," the plantation next door, held about 85 enslaved people, including a blacksmith who made more money for Townsend by being hired out, bringing Samuel to a startling sum of 123 enslaved people.

Samuel had about $25,000 in assets in 1850. His brother Edmund was even more successful, with about $60,000. Both men, born in Lunenburg County, Virginia, (incidentally the origin of the Woosley line that married into the Townsend line), decided to strike west for northern Alabama in the 1820s with their brother Parks. They bought land, expanded their holdings, and with the labor of the enslaved, planted cotton, corn, wheat, and oats, and raised hogs (more than 2,100), sheep, dairy cows, oxen, mules, horses, and cattle. All of the caretaking and the domestic labor, dairying, and production of cloth was done by the enslaved, at the "Home Place" plantation, whose Big House was once shaded by pecan trees and oaks. Samuel had a bumper crop. Fifty-seven bales were made, at about 400 pounds each, or, if you will, 22,800 pounds of picked cotton.

So if you're lucky, and lucky is relative, you will, as a researcher of African American genealogy, have an ancestor who retained the name of their last slaveholder and wasn't sold—and had a slaveholder who died before 1860. Though Harry rebelled by running away, he was caught, punished severely, and released back into the cotton fields. He was a strong and highly valued worker, and his second duty to Samuel Townsend was to make babies—for this reason, Mas' Townsend rarely sold his chattel. He wanted a strong, vibrant population fathered by young men and women he bought as children and could extract a lifetime of work from for the most conservative amount of care and calories. In 1860, Harry fathered my great-great-grandfather Harry Townsend, who in the year of the Centennial married a girl named Laura who was born into slavery herself on the nearby Woosley plantation. For seven generations, we have had this white man's name. Harry probably had wavy hair, because it got passed down to my grandfather's fathers, his brothers, and my uncles—his father or grandfather, it appears by DNA, was also a white man with roots in continental western Europe. The preponderance of genetic and historical evidence to date suggests that his mother's roots—like those of many enslaved Africans in Virginia and northern North Carolina—were in southeastern Nigeria.

To find out more about the world of my ancestors, I went to the agricultural census (nonpopulation census) and slave schedules. These records paint for us a picture of what the properties looked like, from how many chickens ran around to how many dwellings the enslaved occupied (on the Bellamy plantation in Russell County, Alabama, there were seven cabins inhabited by forty-one people), to how much land was made of woods (unimproved), to land that was cleared for planting (improved). The slave schedules have no names even though there is plenty of space for the names to have been recorded. Enslaved people are estimated ages, colors (mulattoes were noted), and genders. Sometimes those of advanced age are noted by name and whether they were born in Africa, but they are rare. It is not possible to know these people's family connections by the slave schedules. They are as nameless as the livestock.

If you have never encountered these types of records before or really felt the impact of their meaning, it does me no good to expound on the numbers here. That any names are assigned at all is due to years of research, as is the volume of cotton picked. This is what America looked like for over four million people in the decade before the Civil War. They were numbers, human machines with a measurable output. They almost completely disappeared into history after building this country and creating their own unique American civilization:

Tallapoosa County Alabama-Samuel Hancock farm-1850

7 enslaved people including Rachel, my great-great-great-great-grandmother and her son Henry, Samuel's mulatto son.

100 acres improved

220 acres unimproved

4 horses, no mules, 6 cows, 2 oxen, 5 other cows, 30 swine, 1,000 bushels in corn, 200 in oats, 5 bales of cotton, 2,000 pounds of cotton picked

1860

120 acres improved

200 acres unimproved

2 horses—2 mules, 3 cows, 2 oxen, 15 cattle, 4 sheep, 20 swine, 78 bushels of wheat, 560 bushels of Indian corn, 200 pounds of tobacco, 17 bales of cotton, 6,800 pounds of cotton picked.

Butler County, Alabama-Edward Bowen plantation, 1850

54 enslaved people—including my great-great-great-great-grandfather John, my great-great-great-great-grandmother Izabella, their children, including my great-great-great-grandfather Needham

Edward had a grain mill

400 acres improved land

3,000 acres unimproved

3 horses—8 mules, 13 cows, 14 oxen, 20 cattle, 5 sheep, 80 swine, 2,500 bushels of corn, 46 bales of cotton, 18,400 pounds of cotton picked.

Russell County Alabama, William Bellamy plantation, 1850

My white great-great-great-great-grandfather

24 enslaved, including 10 brought from Oak Forest Plantation, Nash County, North Carolina

300 acres improved, 200 acres unimproved, 4 horses, 5 mules, 10 milk cows, 5 oxen, 40 cattle, no sheep, 80 swine, 6 bushels of rye, 3,000 bushels of Indian corn, 300 bushels of oats, 8 bales of cotton, 3,200 pounds of cotton picked.

1860 . . . 41 enslaved people in 7 dwellings. By 1860 he held in bondage my great-great-great-grandmother Arrye, and her two sons, Louis and his older brother Joseph; my great-great-grandfather, whom he had acquired through the domestic slave trade, purchased after 1855. Joseph would eventually marry the illegitimate mulatto granddaughter of Mas' William, Hattie Bellamy.

795 acres improved, 150 acres unimproved, 4 horses—7 mules,
5 milk cows, 4 working oxen, 26 other cattle, 100 swine, 4
bushels of rye, 2,800 bushels of corn, 25 bushels of oats, 82
bales of cotton, 32, 800 pounds of cotton picked.

Kershaw County, Robert Reeves farm, South Carolina-1860

10 enslaved, including my great-great-great-great-
grandfather Thomas Reeves, my great-great-great-
great-grandmother Kizzy Reeves, and their son, my
great-great-great-grandfather, Church Reeves.
55 acres improved, 370 unimproved, 3 horses, 1 mule, 6
cows, 1 ox, 18 cattle, 20 swine, 24 wheat
300 bushels of corn, 4 bushels of oats, 4 bales of cotton,
1,600 pounds of cotton picked.

Kershaw and Chesterfield Counties, Levi Pate holdings South Carolina, 1860

My white great-great-great-grandfather
17 enslaved people, including my great-great-great-
grandmother Sukey Pate and her daughter, my great-
great-grandmother Margaret Pate.
60 acres improved
440 acres unimproved, 2 horses, 2 cows, 5 cattle, 20 swine,
2 bushels of wheat, 200 corn, 2 bales of cotton—800
pounds of cotton picked.

THE WOOL PLANT

I am still convinced cotton is something only the Lord could have
made. What good is its fiber to anything else in Creation, but hu-

mankind? While the oily seeds can be processed into an edible prod-uct for livestock, it's not a plant that humans should eat, its lint being pure, indigestible cellulose—the crown of the "King."

We all know enslaved people planted, cultivated, and picked cot-ton in antebellum America, but the crop was truly woven into every fabric of their lives. It served as rough wicks for lamps slicked with game or pork fat, its fluffy dregs were used to set fire to kindling for cooking, its seeds were boiled for their oil to add to cornmeal, and the roots were used in a medicinal tea. Blacks from South Carolina, like my ancestor Wash Twitty, were even mocked as "cottonseeds" by enslaved people from other parts of the South, recalling the practice of their enslavers feeding them cornmeal adulterated by the cheap trash leftovers of the crop after the lint was ginned.

In 1861, as the Civil War came to Alabama, my great-great-great-grandmother Sallie, a teenage girl, likely considered using the secret recipe for cotton root tea that floated among enslaved women living in the King's grip. It was a special tea, meant only for the most vile and disastrous situations; and so well guarded that its use was never told to slaveholders on pain of death, namely because it could literally kill their business of breeding new workers. Cotton tea was a potent abortifacient. It terminated pregnancies, namely those that occurred when white males forced themselves on enslaved women, or when those same women were forcibly bred by close relatives. "Drinking the tea" might just be the solution for a stolen moment in the night or behind a barn when a woman, paralyzed with fear, had to relent or be sold away. This was Sallie's story even as the man who impregnated her, a young lawyer and planter named Richard Henry Bellamy, marched off to war as a private, soon to be a captain, in the army of the Confederate States of America. Faced with the choice to drink the tea or not, she chose to bring her child into the world, not knowing—and never knowing—that miles and miles away in Texas, her daughter's half brother had been born to another enslaved woman. Though they looked almost like fraternal twins, the two infants would be forever strangers.

King Cotton's sordid and greedy nature is why I've confronted it over and over again, trying to understand exactly how a plant could so complicate American history and condemn America to an ongoing entanglement with the race question. More than that, the planters of this wonderfully inedible, beautiful plant—the snow of the Southern fall—were responsible for a dire change in eating habits among enslaved African Americans. Drawn from varied environs along the Southern coastline, my ancestors were packed into the landlocked Black Belt, where cotton prospered in a sea of malnutrition and fomented a monotonous diet befitting its permanent underclass. King Cotton had its own way of eating; and in contrast to the diversity of foodways from the mid-Atlantic to the Lower Mississippi Valley, the stars of King Cotton's cuisine were maize and oversalted swine, swallowed down with rancid molasses and spoiled leftovers.

In the King's grip, a killer diet was born.

CHIPPOKES PLANTATION STATE PARK, SURRY COUNTY, VIRGINIA

Damn, I hate picking cotton. I wish to G-d I could stop, but every fall I find myself in a Southern cotton field for sixteen hours, alone, picking cotton until my hands bleed and my back gives out. I used to shake my head in disbelief at Shi'a and Catholic penitents who mortified their flesh to prove their faith and their distrust in the corporeal form. Now it appears I have joined their ranks in my solitary, twenty-first-century flagellant way, lashing my body with slave narratives and history books until I truly understand those that "wore the shoe." One basket is about fifteen pounds of moist, raw cotton. Based on one overflowing basket, my work is not done until twenty-three of said baskets have been dumped on a cloth at the edge of the field.

At the end of the day, there will be nobody there to beat me if I haven't made my quota of 350 pounds. I will not have had to pick for the pregnant, the young, the sick, or the elderly in addition to my own load. I will not be cut by the whip in the field. All of this makes my experience very "history lite."

I didn't, however, come to learn just what it was like to pick cotton. I need to understand how an entire crop affected my family's story and those of the majority of African Americans. Cotton would eventually come to shape an entire body of our food culture. To know why—and I could be in no better place to do it—I am on the land of the oldest working farm in America, definitely one of the first to use some of the "20 and odd Negroes" who first landed at Jamestown in 1619.

Wanna make a quick joke about slavery? Talk about picking cotton. Nothing symbolizes the nadir of the black experience than this one crop. Something grips you when you go through the Deep South and you encounter it for the first time growing en masse in a field. It's endless and beautiful and horrific. By itself it's a curious, little exotic flower whose creamy blossoms only last a day and change from virgin's blush to full-on sin and scarlet letter before cascading to the ground. Bees descend, and the pollinated flower, now all sexed out, morphs into a pregnant boll. The cellulose inside becomes fibers that are exposed when the boll bursts about two months after pollination. Then the edges of the boll sharpen into the prickly Pinkertons that surround the lint, ready to jab untrained fingers.

Riding down Route 460 in southern Virginia, known as "Dixie below the James," you get your first taste of King Cotton at the northernmost edge of his kingdom. The pattern is quite predictable for most of Southside Virginia into northeastern North Carolina—cotton, peanuts, soybeans, corn—each taking its turn in a cycle meant to stave off soil depletion. Right out of your antebellum night-mares, a "Revival-style" dream house sitting at the back end of a sandwich made of a heavy wrought-iron gate and two small cotton patches pops up as you ride toward Petersburg. Any sense that I have just seen a quaint or charming illusion of the past is replaced by an overwhelming dread washing over me, and my hands tighten as if they are shackled together and this is my last stop; here is my American "Arbeit macht Frei."

The only thing that makes you feel good after having an ancestral flashback like that is washing your eyes out with a bottle of spring-water, hoping you will forget what you saw and to ensure yourself it's the twenty-first century. And, of course, a slice of Virginia pea-nut pie. The Virginia Diner makes some of the best. It is a burned golden, flaky, crusted gem—think pecan pie, but it's only peanuts. Peanuts or "goobers" or "pinders" were brought to Virginia in the eighteenth century from West Africa, and in the mid-nineteenth century the first commercial crops—read "plantations"—were estab-lished in this area of Virginia. The collard greens spiked with hot pepper, sugar and fatback, fried chicken, Virginia country ham (yes, you have to specify that it is indeed a Virginia country ham), sweet cornbread, biscuits, string beans that swim in potlikker that is so greasily reflective that it "winks back," candied yams, and black-eyed peas all serve as appetizers to the peanut pie.

The comfort food of the Deep South, much of it influenced by the presence of enslaved cooks and enslaved people, is especially well known for its salt, sugar, and fat content. But to the discerning eye there is something markedly different about the way food is prepared in the old Cotton or Black Belt versus Appalachia, southern Louisi-ana, the formerly rice-growing Low Country, and even the tobacco belt. The molasses-born sweet tooth finds its way into damn near candied baked beans and collard greens here, and even into maca-roni pie (the traditional Southern, and Caribbean, name of macaroni and cheese). Fat and fatback are amped up, and there never seems to be enough salt. If you live this way for a century and a half or so, what does it do to you?

Better question: Why do we eat this way at all?

Part of the answer lies in picking cotton, which alone would make even Sisyphus throw in the towel. There's nobody here—this is not a solitary activity. When I cook, I usually feel the spirits of people who prepared the same meals long past and I never really feel alone. This is different. My self-exile leaves me as singular as that stupid Zen tree we keep listening out for. I have wooden cups, a tin plate, well water, buttermilk, a "glug" of molasses, cornbread—correction, ashcake—and a piece of salted meat . . . the classic "plowman's lunch" of the antebellum slave. I immediately feel connected to the past, but I'd much rather be back at the diner.

Looking at the tin plate, I wonder what to do next. Growing up, the ultimate moment of horror for a boy who didn't like his food to touch on the plate was watching my grandmother crumble her skillet cornbread into the glass of buttermilk. I can still see the streaks and crumbs lining the glass, and then I remember the troughs. Now, this is exactly what makes the most sense. For enslaved children, the analog was far worse: This mixture was placed in an animal trough, with each child bringing anything he or she could to scoop up the mush. It's clearly the reason that the number one medicinal cure among enslaved people was vermifuge teas to eliminate intestinal worms. For myself, I hate everything I'm eating—even burned matzo tastes better than this crap.

This is the land of Egypt. Now we are slaves.

For example, ashcake is not the sweet, cakelike cornbread thing that is everywhere today, half flour in form and invitingly golden and paired with jelly, honey, chili, or chicken. It's white cornmeal mixed with water, and (if you are lucky) a pinch of salt, molded into a ball that you press flat into a cake. Then you find a leaf of the tulip poplar tree (coincidentally also called the "toilet leaf tree") or perhaps a large maple or, failing these, a cabbage or collard leaf, and wrap that around and have a fire of embers and coals ready to bake it. Twenty minutes later, or when it's capable of destroying your dental health permanently, presto! You can now enjoy the hardtack of life under King Cotton.

Grossed out as I was, the idea of crumbling the ashcake into a cup of buttermilk now made perfect sense, and I asked my grandmother's posthumous forgiveness for turning my nose up to her lifelong habit. Using my "glug" of molasses—so called because it was measured in terms of the number of times it made that sound—I used my right hand to scoop up some ashcake and 'lasses and licked the mess off my fingers. The salted meat—deliberately allowed to pick up some dry aging, let's call it—turned out to be the only thing to relish on the plate. And it's the only thing keeping me from passing out, for now it's replacing the salt I'm losing by the second through my sweat.

"Back to work!" my imaginary Simon Legree whispers in my ear. At first the "raggedy ass spirituals" of *Raisin in the Sun* fame come on in my head like a store tape soundtrack, and pretty soon Paul Robeson is fixing to come down from heaven and smack me for singing off-tune. Cue "Go Down Moses," "Follow the Drinking Gourd," "Michael Row Your Boat Ashore." An hour later, bored shitless, working at an even slower pace than when I was picking to the repetitive hit tune of "Why the hell are you picking cotton when it's the twenty-first century?" I decide to do what any self-respecting antebellum slave would . . . I pop in my earbuds and listen to music on my iPod.

Into the earbuds pour folk music recordings from the chain gangs of Mississippi, Texas, and Louisiana as recorded by Alan Lomax, some of the most haunting music ever captured—and the closest we will ever get to the contours of slave work songs. Into that are other recordings of field hollers, ring shouts, and call-and-response chants. Joined by a sonic gang, my work pace increases, my singing comes back into tune, and I'm wailing about the Grizzly Bear and singing for Berta to come back. My foot movements start to line up with a distinct drag, and basket after basket becomes full as I work-dance my way into the heart of America's "original sin."

A group of ring shouters from Georgia start calling: "God called Adam / Adam! Adaaaam! / Where have you gone? Why you shamed? / Lord I'm ashamed! / Lord I'm ashamed! / Adam's in the Garden, picking up leaves! / Picking up leaves! / Picking up leaves! / Adam's in the Garden and he's picking up leaves!"

This one particular ring shout, thumped out on a wooden floor and further given percussion by the clapping of hands, has me working at a furious pace. The words are jarring as G-d discovers his first human creation has broken his covenant not to eat of the Tree of Knowledge and a frantic Adam is gathering leaves to cover his naked body, his "shame." The first time I heard that shout in a praise-house (Gullah for church) on Beaufort Island, a place dominated by Sea Island cotton, I saw a hobbling man come back to life, and as I matched the claps of the other hundred people in the room and the thump of the cane on the ground, I started to silently sob. Bringing that feeling back gave me visions.

My hands hit a snag on a burr, and within seconds I blink and I see the ancestors gathered around me, picking. I blink again and they are gone. The words of the song evoke the worship of the Lord at once with the pace of field work, while also commenting on the evils of the chattel system—this is the genius I was born into—a sermonic critique in plain sight of the whip.

I wish you could see the cotton fields. The bolls are just opening. I cannot compare their appearance to anything but fields

of white roses. As to the cotton picking I should think it very
light and pleasant work.

—SARA HICKS WILLIAMS, PLANTATION
MISTRESS, NORTH CAROLINA

When you pick cotton, especially in the hot, bright sun, you
lose all sense of the leaves and stalks and detritus. All you can see is
white—it is as blinding as sunlight on snow. Without enough water,
or in my case sports drinks, it's easy to see people fainting, dropping
dead, backs giving out, others rushing to do their quota. The number
one law is stay down and make no sudden movements upward—stay
bent. My knees are sinking deep into the sandy soil, and the reaction
within me is so deep that I fear it will never end. . . . I begin to panic.
As I struggle not to retch and release the ashcake and its "relishes," I
think I'm beginning to understand what this was all about and why
we can't let it go. This scene—repeated from the birth of Whitney's
gin in 1793 to the rise of the mechanical picker in 1947—has never
let *us* go.

Gossypium herbaceum found its way into humanity from many
directions—Asia, Africa, the Americas—and eventually found its
way to Europe. Herodotus, the Greek "father of history," gave the
West notice of a plant with fleece surpassing that of sheep; an image followed up by Sir John Mandeville in 1350 of a plant both cute
and terrifying—full of squirming tiny sheep begging to be pulled
off their plant mother and culled to make a cloth fit for the gods.
In West Africa, no such mystique existed, as cotton grew in many
locales and was a long-established crop with which many ethnic
groups had millennia of experience. In many cases, slave ships de-
parted the West African coast with enslaved people and local cotton
as cargo.

Gossypium herbaceum is also, in part, the little plant with the
beautiful lint flower that helped cause the continuation of slavery

long past its seeming post-Revolution death throes, the Civil War, and between the two and beyond, decades of sociocultural evils for the African American culture and community. The horrors of being sold away from your family, being severely punished, zealous retribution for any sort of resistance, and being forced to migrate against your will were clearly endemic from slavery's start. A couple of treaties and the ceding of land, and the stage was set for seventy years of upheaval. If we are honest about American history, there's no way that the Southeast was really going to be left to the so-called Five Civilized Tribes and their neighbors to remain undeveloped, and rich land unfarmed. The land was there, the people could be exiled, but it begged for a cash crop and a cheap labor force to make it a lucrative landscape.

Eli Whitney wasn't quite the genius he has been made out to be. Primitive rolling "gins" and combing methods were used in West Africa, and his "Yankee ingenuity" probably was married with a healthy dose of appropriation from similar technology he saw in use on a Georgia plantation in 1793. It is a mouse-crumb comfort that the man who spearheaded the American industrial revolution and gave it a raison d'être was himself ripped off to the point where he had no real control over his patent. By the time the first hand-cranked gin, capable of cleaning fifty pounds in a day versus only one pound by a skilled hand, made it onto the scene, my ancestors' fates were sealed . . . the money to be made outweighed the value of their freedom.

Cotton's critical value to American life, culture, and the economy cannot be underestimated. Not only was the generic canon of soul food born in the region's Black Belt, but the roots of blues, jazz, the spirituals, and gospel were seeded there, and with them a long tradition of black humor and sociopolitical commentary. The tropes and tones of black literature as known in America from lyrics and field hollers to folktales told at the end of a weary day grew just as much as the King. Even my grandparents were told the Europe-meets-Africa Raw Head and Bloody Bones stories—horror stories told to coerce enslaved children to sleep so the adults might enjoy clandestine meals of pilfered or contraband food and drink to offset that disgusting ashcake. Yet cotton was not just a black thang—indeed Northern immigration only begins to eclipse African migration to the New World when sustainable population growth and the closing of the slave trade made that system virtually stop in the 1820s. By then, Yankee mills were importing Southern slave-grown cotton, with new immigrants working within.

To put it another way, cotton gave English, Scottish, then Irish and German immigrants a reason to come to an industrializing, modernizing, postcolonial nation. By the 1840s the trickle was a flood, and the North was nearly slaveless and full of conflict over natives versus immigrants. And though they had started outlawing slavery altogether in their nation in 1833, Britain still enjoyed slavery's benefits as its mills became almost completely dependent on the cotton my ancestors grew. Two-thirds of America's nineteenth-century export value came from cotton *alone*. Compromises, arguments, agreements, riots, revolts, Civil War, Reconstruction and its forced close, sharecropping, lynching, segregation, migrations, civil rights, and ghettoization—all of these have been the fruits of King Cotton.

The domestic slave trade was more than just the largest forced migration in American history; it was a turning point for the development of Southern food and in the way African Americans ate. For Chesapeake, Tidewater, and Low Country blacks, living on the coast near ports and between ecological zones afforded them an incredibly varied diet compared to the Cotton Belt. Not only were the environments very different, but the mentality of King Cotton was far more industrial and dehumanizing. On many cotton plantations, time away from the monocrop was heavily regimented, and the gardens that seaboard slaves had depended on gave way to large communal gardens maintained for the enslaved population, usually by the elderly. The crops produced were fairly limited and monotonous: seasonally reliable, cheap to cultivate, and requiring minimal extra cultivation. Collard or turnip greens, sweet potatoes, and cowpeas were usually the lead items. Beyond that, red pepper, tomatoes, and okra might make an appearance, along with peanuts brought from the East.

Seaboard plantations often needed a "trustworthy" (I hate that expression) enslaved person who could shoot birds or deer or other animals that might destroy a valuable plantation crop such as rice. Many of those varmints ended up in the enslaved community's cooking pots. Not so with King Cotton. Apart from the four food groups of rabbit, possum, squirrel, and coon, the presence of such a rich variety of protein was nil, and guns in the hands of enslaved people were absolutely verboten. Fishing—if possible—was not nearly as rich as what could be found along the coast. Muddy-flavored blue and bullhead catfish, buffalo, and bream—a catchall term for small fry perch and bass—became the central surf to the salt swine turf if access to the often slow-moving and stagnant aquatic environment was even available or permitted.

Southern planters also became far more dictatorial about how and what their enslaved people ate. As far as the nineteenth-century planter was concerned, a peck of meal, a pound of bacon, and a pint of molasses was a sufficient weekly ration for a hardworking laborer. Gone were the days where corn was given unshelled for each family to process. Cotton had no time for that. "Jimmy crack corn and I don't care," as the slave folk/children's song goes, "Old Massa's gone away," indeed. Stone hand-mills broke down the corn that was dispersed to workers in the field. The same hominy that had rescued their grandparents in the Upper South from the fate of other nutritionally deficient enslaved populations was no longer to be had.

From pellagra to scurvy to iron deficiencies, the enslaved individual was the only type of person on American soil with a mandated diet that was just as much killing him as it was keeping him barely alive.

Protein was also much harder to come by. Hog killing time in the Black Belt was never quite as cold as that experienced in the Upper South, slavery's former heart. With more urgency, then, were lights, livers, chitterlings, feet, and other offal ever ready to spoil and, thus, eaten with gusto. The hams that Upper South enslaved people relished made way for roasted possum (a carrion eater) and sweet potatoes at Christmastime. Corn was everything, right down to bits of dough fried and drenched in molasses, and whatever was wild and freely available were the snacks—wild persimmons, hickory nuts, and goober patches made for quick energy. We forget just how long much of the antebellum South was still a wild frontier right up to the second of the Civil War. The diet of the "peculiar institution" was forged along the margins and the periphery of the bounty of America's antebellum era.

The "Wetumpka Hotel" menu at the start of this chapter, presented as satire by a local colorist, is thus quite a serious joke. The inside joke is that the tavern guests are eating food fit for slaves, likely prepared by the enslaved, or in the words of the nineteenth century, redolent with "the taste of the nigger." The flavors of the Southern frontier were largely shaped by the tastes and preferences of black cooks and black people, who in many areas of the Black Belt—named for its soil and its people—were the clear majority. For one example, during the Civil War, when the foods and luxuries of my planter ancestors were few and far between, it was the lowly, evasive cowpea brought from Africa in the seventeenth century that General Robert E. Lee praised as the "only unfailing friend the Confederacy ever had." Elite and poor whites were exposed to the unique culinary perspective of the black majority—in slavery and in war—and would in turn pass these traditions down in their own families, further complicating the story of "who owns what" in Southern food. The contemporary reclamation of barbecue, offal, hoecakes, wild foods, black-eyed-pea cakes, and other plebeian fare by white chefs with the capital to promote and popularize these foods is one of the cornerstone issues of culinary justice.

In the black community, arguments and stigmas about soul food as slave food continue with us to this day. The Nation of Islam originally taught its followers to shun and avoid sweet potatoes, black-eyed peas, and collards, along with pork and the like, hence the popularity of white-bean pie in the Nation. Yet these would have been some of the healthiest foods enslaved people had access to at the time, although their preparation became increasingly enhanced by salty, sugary, and greasy flavors to make the monotonous diet more palatable.

Just after the Civil War, my great-great-great-grandfather Needham Bowen, along with many of his family members, signed a contract with their X marks to stay on the land of their previous slaveholder, Edward Bowen, in Butler County, Alabama. Toni Carrier found it in the Freedmen's Bureau records and transcribed it carefully:

Bowen Edward, contract with Freedmen

State of Alabama
Butler County

Be it remembered that Edward Bowen of said County on the one part and the following named freedmen former slaves of said Bowen on the other part to wit Billy (60) years old; Needham (45) Peter 41 Dave [?] [Partially obscured in spine of journal] Jack (35) Anderson (35) Lewis (33) Linn [?] (36) Jones (22), Frank (20) Cynthia (35) Hannah Phoebe

(39) William (20) Reason (45) Cytha 49[?] (19?) Jim (50)
Mariah (40) Clarissa (37) Jinny (28) Addison (40) entered
into the following contract, to wit; for and in consideration
of the labor of the above named Freedmen from the 25th day
of May last until the 25th of December next 1865 the said
Bowen agrees to provide food, clothing, medical attendance,
fuel and houses for said laborers during said period, he
also agrees to make some provision for the families of said
laborers, consisting of twenty children one old [woman?] in
part consideration of their labor and to divide the corn that
is now growing on twenty five acres of land among them
according to [illegible], he agrees not to require them to
labor Saturday afternoon except in cases of emergency. Said
laborers agree to work faithfully obey all orders, and perform
everything required of them by said Bowen or his wife or
any person that said Bowen may employ 27th Jun/65 witness
Billy, Needham, Peter, Dave, Jack, Lewis, Lemuel, Jones,
Hannah Phoebe, William, Reason, Cytha, Clarissa, Jane,
Jinny, Addison, Jim, Mariah

[illegible] Thigpen

[illegible] Thigpen

By 1880 he farmed forty acres of improved land, and had one
horse, one ox, one cow, nine pigs, seven chickens, two other types of
poultry, forty bushels of corn, and seven bales of cotton to his name.
With a little more freedom, sharecroppers and tenant farmers could
plant a garden ranging from an acre to four of vegetables and fruits—
and take up canning to provide food for the year round, a practice
that was not common in antebellum slavery. Some had the time and
the labor to have self-sufficient homesteads where tomatoes, string
beans, cabbages, hot peppers, collards, okra, white potatoes, squash,
onions, cucumbers, muskmelons, watermelons, and the like joined

field peas, ribbon cane, and sweet potatoes to round out the diet. Others subsisted only on the three Ms of meat, meal, and molasses, and if they were lucky, sweet potatoes, field peas, and an occasional meal of greens. Many families went into debt with the plantation store, trying to feed themselves when their own resources ran short.

After slavery, lard, white sugar, table salt, and white bread were more greatly consumed, along with domesticated animal flesh, eggs, and dairy. Freedom was celebrated by the full acceptance of and dependence on foods that were mostly unavailable in precolonial West and central Africa, and largely out of reach for more enslaved people during slavery's long duration. The diet of emancipation—limited by money, power, and access—set the tone for the life of sharecroppers and tenant farmers after the war through the postwar period in the twentieth century. Many people hunted and many had a garden, but not all were able to, and health issues based on nutritional deficiency were rampant because of lack of access and lack of time to devote to varying the diet. It is clear that we don't work twelve to sixteen hours doing hard labor anymore, and that sedentary or stationary work, combined with reliance on processed food—initially a symbol of freedom and attainment—and excessive use of fat, sugar, and salt have been some of the more insidious legacies of King Cotton, both under slavery and during the near century following it in tenant farming and sharecropping.

If slavery had phased out around 1790 and gradual emancipation had spread, the whole history of America and her foodways would be markedly different. Instead, cotton ensured the growing and complete racialization of what it meant to be of African descent. African ethnic groups became the early Afro-Creole culture that began African America. If King Cotton had never reigned, we African Americans might be like any other ethnic group—stories might be passed down; names remembered; songs, words, religions, prayers, perhaps, even one might say, a sense of pride. Instead, names were changed again and again and again, as people were sold, further commoditized, dehumanized, and abused. Understandings forged between African and European cultures over centuries were dismantled, and the industrial spirit in the hands of those early African Americans was crushed for the sake of compliance and submission.

The disruption of the black family, the interruption of an important community-driven ethnic economy, the engendering of a poor diet, an urgent desire to suppress learning and education, and a culture of unrelenting violence—these and all the dependency, instability, and toxic thinking that went along with them were the fruits of King Cotton, none of which black America has been able to fully purge from its system.

DOWN SOUTH/UP SOUTH

All of my mother's families ended up in the heart of Dixie, the Crimson Tide state of Alabama. Her father came from the line of Harry Townsend and the Woosleys of northern Alabama and southern Tennessee, and they would in turn marry a daughter of the Bowens and the Lewises. In the Black Belt, in Russell County, in March 1862, Sallie's child came to term and breathed life as Hattie Mabry Bellamy. Her future husband, more than ten years her senior, was Joseph Peter Todd, sold South from Richmond in 1852. By and by, black families would be formed this way—families picked apart from across the southern seaboard would lace together, and over time stories were lost and memories became dim. But the foods remained.

My mother's memories of dinners in Cincinnati, a barely Northern border city during the 1950s, could have been drawn from the slave narratives, and nothing rekindled them better than the sacred act of washing greens with her. It's very complicated and it's as close to being a mashgiach or kosher specialist as my mother will ever be. She washes each leaf three to four times and has taught me this ritual since I was a little kid. You rinse, you dip it in a sink filled with water and a tiny drop of soap, you dip again, getting all the grit and sandy soil that makes green grow so well off the leaf, and you look for bugs. When that's done, you take out the stem and roll them and slice them and rinse one more time before putting them aside as the smoked meat boils and bubbles with onion and pepper on the stove.

"I don't know why those people from the South always seemed to like bitter or sour stuff. Lemon juice and lemon zest in pound cake and sugar cookies. Mama loved buttermilk, you remember that?" my mother said.

"Yes! With cornbread," I replied.

"And she would crumble it in the glass with buttermilk and eat it out with a spoon and drink the rest. It was gross . . ."

My mother smirked at me and blurted out, "Even you used to eat that!"

"I never ate that stuff."

"Boy when you were a baby, that was your baby food—potlikker and a little bit of greens and cornbread and buttermilk—you used to smack your little lips and smile when Mama gave you that." (With us, stories always got repeated, not once, not twice, but three times, and then a million more until we could recite them.)

My mother continued to sort greens and told me more. "Yeah, when I was a little girl, Mama and Daddy would buy big sacks of crowder peas and black-eyed peas. I hated that because Cookie [her sister] and I would sit on the back stoop shucking them. You know you only got three or four bags of what you get in the store today from those big sacks—sometimes not even that.

"We bought carrots, cabbage, celery, and onions in the store but we got the rest from men who used to come with trucks and wagons. I liked the rag man—he'd say, *'Rag Man. . . . Rag Maaaaan . . . I'm the Rageddy Man!'* Sometimes Daddy would try to get us to eat sugarcane off the truck and he'd get us watermelons and Mama would buy collard, turnip, and mustard greens; sacks of peanuts, sweet potatoes and corn. All that stuff from down South—Kentucky, Tennessee, and Alabama—would come up on old pickup trucks in piles and the women would go buy it and make it for Sunday dinner.

"If we were lucky we'd get barbecue. . . . Daddy cover it with chicken wire and cook over wood and charcoal in the old washtub and it was damn good!"

My mother's memories of up South meals cooked just across the Ohio River remind me that there is something of an unbroken chain left behind despite King Cotton. The Black Belt revealed itself like a memory capsule of foods brought from and through Africa to America, surviving the numerically greatest cultural upheavals in early American history. Little bits of stories mixed with recipes and techniques, treats, and tips come out as she rehearses the family dead in her mind: how to wash collards, sorting through field peas, the right way to chew sorghum and sugarcane, how much salt to put on a watermelon, and, out of the blue, the name of the syrup they poured on their cornbread by the glug—Alaga (Alabama/Georgia) cane syrup! Special meals of Sunday roasted or fried chicken and barbecued pork and fried fish, and bottles of hot sauce made from hot green and red peppers grown in little pots shoved into old "pop" bottles, as they say in the Midwest, the tops pricked to let the spicy, winey dew trickle over greens and chicken.

HEATH SPRINGS, LANCASTER COUNTY, SOUTH CAROLINA

Cotton's final act in my family story was the migration of my grandfather from the South Carolina upcountry at the end of the Depression. His father passed and left him an orphan to an ailing stepmother and his sister, who had already migrated to Washington, DC. The land, one hundred acres, his father's prized possession planted in cotton up to the roadside, was now my teenage grandfather's land to farm. He had had enough.

Bored and restless, the lusty Gonze Lee Twitty grew a last crop of cotton. He made a nice thousand-pound bale of cotton, gathered in croaker sacks dragged along rows in the bloodred Carolina clay. His younger brothers and sisters helped out, but he picked like a machine. He took the cotton up the road to the gin, where he sold it and used the money to buy three things—a suit and a hat, a photograph in his new outfit, and a one-way ticket to his sister's residence in Washington, DC. When he arrived at a job office in red clay–stained overalls, the lady behind the counter nearly shooed him away, but she had never known the Twitty charm.

"'Now, Mr. Twitty, you seem like a nice young man,'" she say, 'but you cain't come here dress like that.' So I pulls out this picture of me in my new suit and hat, silk tie, just so. Taken down in the country. When that lady see me like that, whooo!! She say, 'Come back tomorrow and I give you a job.' That's how I met your grandmamma."

Gonze Lee Twitty would eventually come back to the South Carolina upcountry to participate in the change sweeping the South in the 1960s. In the same county where his great-grandfather Wash was sold to the Twitty family just over a century prior, he would help found the Federation of Southern Cooperatives to help black farmers who had recently abandoned cotton for sweet potatoes, peanuts, soybeans, and corn stay on their land and make a living. In 1991, he was inducted into the Hall of Fame of the National Cooperative Business Association.

In his nineties my grandfather relies on a cane made in China to walk. He directed my ex-partner Jacob and I to drive him down the road to the cotton gin. "All these trees wasn't here back then, it was all shacks with colored people and white folks living in them, and cotton, cotton cotton, cotton. Nothing else. Little gardens, and that's it. Stop here. Stop here. There go the gin, I got to make water . . ." (Yes, I too thought that was just something they made up to say in *Driving Miss Daisy.*)

Cotton has not been grown in Lancaster since the 1960s. Now even the cotton and textile mills are closed, for the most part. If you don't work for the service industry or local government or city services, chances are you don't work. Farming is mostly soybeans and cover crops these days.

My grandfather peeks in with us. "You see that? That thing scoop up the cotton and suck it up and the gin pull the seeds out and then it pack it down and you gets a bale, see?"

He grinned with a few missing teeth and cloudy eyes, and led us over to the scale. "Yessir I puts my cotton bale right here, gets my money, and I left on the Southern railway the next few days! You know why I did that, boy? So you could write this down in the book. You go on and write this down in the book. I picked cotton so you could pick up a book."

Our patriarch is always one to seize the opportunity to make a moment; he grabs my shoulder and tells Jacob, "Take a picture of us, and know you part of the family now." He reminds me about how we went to the Obama inauguration—with tickets. "Yessir, Reverend Jackson—what he say? Hands that picked cotton picked the president? That's us, boy, that's us."

Jacob is tearing up, but it's not emotion, rather that there is a full deer carcass rotting nearby in the heat of a South Carolina July. Wiping his eyes and smiling, he squints and takes a few shots of me standing in front of the gin where G. L. Twitty, seventy-five years ago, made a bale, way down South, in the land of cotton.

We made our way back to the last remaining acreage of the farm where my aunts were tending barbecue and roasting sweet potatoes under the black walnut and pecan trees. They were also frying bream and catfish pulled from the pond near the church where my great-grandfather is buried. Fresh green tomato slices were being fried in the kitchen, and so was chicken coated in seasoned flour mixed with cornmeal—adobo seasoning and seasoned salt, to be exact. Fresh garden cucumber slices were marinated with onion, sugar, and vinegar, while little half-wild peaches from the trees by the house became a sticky, golden cobbler. Humongous yellow and crimson watermelons got broken and distributed. I still didn't like watermelon so I gave my hunks of heart to Jacob, who ate them as fast as I could pass them. My aunt looked at me and then him; squinted and smirked and said, "This buckra—he eats his watermelon—he a Twitty; you don't eat watermelon—you ain't no Twitty!"

Sweet Potato Pie

2 large boiled sweet potatoes
  (orange, yellow, or white)
2 tbsp spiced rum
3–4 eggs
1 cup of sorghum or light
  molasses

dash of salt
¼ cup freshly churned butter
pinch or two of nutmeg
  (optional)
1 9" pie shell

Preheat the oven to 375 degrees. Mix all of the ingredients for the inside together and pour in to fill the crust. Bake for 45–50 minutes or until the knife or fork comes out clean.

19

—

CROSSROADS

Our food was never just food. It was medicine and a gateway to good fortune, and a mystical lubricant between the living and the dead. In West Africa the ancestors were always the first to be fed at a meal, a small portion being placed on the ground for their consumption. We kept this alive with bits of food and libations of liquor poured from a bottle on the street corner, a practice now mocked by some as "for the dead homies." Graves and hidey-holes from slavery time show evidence this was so, and until our own times, libations and offerings conferred with prayer have been the centerpiece of the revival of traditional and New World African religions. Our faith was confirmed by the act of stretching the communal aspect of the meal so that it reached our dead; my mother remembered Memorial Day as a time where meals were consumed in the cemetery as fresh wreaths were laid and hymns were sung.

When someone died in the Georgia Sea Islands, a white chicken would be sacrificed near the cabin door. Black-eyed peas were thrown in the middle of the crossroads for good luck, or scattered about so a barren woman would conceive. My great-grandfather of blessed memory once carried the fabled John de Conqueror root in his pocket, as he did wishbones and black-eyed peas. All of this was passed down to me through my grandmother, and at the stroke of midnight on New Year's Day, I would put black-eyed peas into every wallet and purse in our home.

I never saw fallen salt that I did not throw over my shoulder. I learned to plant forked sticks in the ground as I walked on by my garden's edges to protect and hang up the hollowed-out gourds and make of them homes for purple martins, but mostly to keep in the good luck (spirits) that rode in on the wind, just as horseshoes were the chargers for our fortune and opened and closed the spaces of the rural world. Both of my grandmothers planted basil by the front door for good luck, but neither one knew it came from Kongo. Grammy had a small vial filled with mustard seed, symbolic of her faith, and there were always little bags of salt.

I grew up steeped in the old religion. My grandmother spoke of spiderwebs for bleeding and corn silks for earaches and mullein for coughs and red cedar for sprains; sassafras for spring tonic, green persimmons for acne, plantains for fungal issues, poke to clean you out; and garlic, raw honey, nut-grass, and ginseng—the old religion was nothing without its healing methods. At age twelve, I frantically wrote down everything she could tell me. There was rabbit tobacco and red pepper tea, and nobody lived without aloe growing all over the house, or had a pantry without lemons or ginger, and even cinnamon sticks had their place. The little plastic pots around her garden housed thyme, sage, mint, and balm, just like Gilead.

One spring season when I was six, I was sick for a week with the flu. My grandmother's solution was to steep thyme in hot honey and add rum to it, and maybe a dash of this or that, and something spicy but bitter. It eased my congestion and helped me sleep, but I hated the taste and did everything I could not to spit it out. Finally, I had enough. I hid the jar of weird, yucky stuff in my piggy bank.

"Where did the cough syrup go?"

"I don't know, Grammy," I said, lying my ass off.

She knew I was lying, and she loved me so much that she was not going to tolerate my dishonesty. "Where did you put it?"

"I didn't put it anywhere, Grammy, I just don't know where it is!"

"Fine. Why you a lie?" ("You a lie . . ." is a very serious way to call someone a liar in black elder-speak.)

"I'm not a liar." Yes I was.

"OK, I'm going to go in that room and make all your toys talk, and then I'm going to make your toys tell me where you hid it, and they gonna tell me, and when they do, not only am I going to make you take your medicine, but I'm going to go make you cut a switch."

I was afraid more of the talking toys than the switch. I pranced out of bed in my precious red robe, tied at the waist, mumbled and cried and retrieved my cough syrup from my piggy bank. She made me gulp an extra glob down, and as I struggled against alcohol-induced coma, my grammy smiled at my defeat. On the night-light went, and when I woke up I found a note waiting for me next to an ice-cold ginger ale.

"Don't do that again. The pig tells all."

I still don't like piggy banks but I do crave ginger ale when I get sick. My grandmother's powers confirmed, I never tested her again. When she was alive, I had no idea she was part of a larger world where people divined from reading random passages of the Bible, where beads were not just beads, where pictures of saints and candles kept off the dark side, and children wore pierced coins and little bags filled with bric-a-brac or asafetida. There were rabbit feet and crab claws, sagebrush brooms hung over doors or in trees, and dead trees in the countryside covered in empty blue and brown and golden and clear bottles and, once in a good moon, a red one. When the light hit those bottle trees, the spirits inside them assumed a garb of light and took form and flight.

Our old ways came from a confluence of the largest influences in African American spirituality. There was the Upper Guinea Coast—Senegambia, the Western Sudan, and the Rice Coast—and then there was West and central Africa, societies without pantheons of gods and goddesses, as one had in Cuba, Brazil, Trinidad, and Haiti. In these places, owing to the influence of the Catholic Church and a mixture of Yoruba, Fon, and Kongo-Angolan religion, a far different paradigm developed. The Yoruba and Fon brought with them the family of gods and sacred narratives and sacrificial prescriptions revealed by Ifa/Fa, a divination system par excellence made for a complex and coherent spiritual system largely unknown outside of New Orleans during the time of slavery.

The Kongo-Angolans were especially important shapers of New World black spirituality. Their worldview and ideas about the cosmos, shared by many of their enslaved brethren, focused on healing, sacred medicine, and the concept of the crossroads—the dividing line between the living and the dead, those who were born from the underworld and those who would return to it, an eternal cycle expressed by the movement of the sun and moon and phases of light, darkness and transition. Fused with gleanings from Christianity, which dovetailed nicely with the symbol of the cross as crossroads, and buffered by the practices of Muslim-influenced peoples, the old religion took the Kongo-Angolan path of the African Atlantic and married it with similar practices from upper West Africa, various Christian elements, European folk beliefs, and Native American spiritual practices. When I was growing up, nobody knew any of this; it was just backward country talk whose death could not come fast enough.

The old religion was all about good luck, protection from white folks, keeping off snakes and beasts, loss, fire, water, and disaster. It was a religion of love-seeking and -keeping, and it had its rules, dictated by tradition, about food. Chickens got served to preachers because chickens had always flounced in the hands of African priests, and nobody remembered why. The food served to the dead never had salt, and *saraka* cakes were given to the young children of enslaved Muslims. Mothers said "Ameen, ameen," and nobody passed on the stories explaining why.

We took our feasts and made them religious. Funerals meant a parade of fried chicken to the house of the bereaved. We made an art of church and Sunday dinners, then Friday *jummah* and Shabbat, to African *bembes* and *akoms* (gatherings where ceremonies and dancing take place) where the priests and attendees needed to be fed. The act of baking pies and cakes and roasting meats and stewing vegetables became a form of prayer, and before the gods of Yoruba and Akan religion, Judaism, Christianity, Islam, and beyond, the banquets of the spirit were set.

The old religion wasn't just the customs, it was the thought behind them, that they were inviolable. Our Sunday dinner and holiday table had to be set with white tablecloth and candles, and that was my favorite part. "Hazel, do you think we're born of the purple?" My grandmother ignored this and kept setting the table. I continued the tradition with Shabbat, making an altar of the table as it always had been, setting a place, as it were, for my Creator.

Dictated by the old religion, black-eyed peas were eaten on New Year's Day, along with the heads of things, with greens for cash and peas for change. Nobody knew that in Kongo, greens symbolized life and vitality, even as the Creoles added new greens to their gumbo *zherbes*, each one representing a new friend in the year to come. The Manding call the cowpea *"soso,"* and the Wolof call them *"nyebe."* An ancient staple of the diet in Senegambia and its hinterlands, the black-eyed pea grows well in hot, drought-conducive conditions and is a symbol of resilience, mercy, and kindness. *Nyebe* are the kind of cooked food one gives as *sadaka*—righteously given charity—to beggars on the streets of Senegal.

Black-eyed peas represent fertility, the eye of God, and they are associated with the force of change and wind, the Yoruba goddess Oya. They were a spiritually potent food long before our arrival in America. Leftover peas are even used to repair the cracks in the outer walls of the great mosques of old Mali. "Black-eyed pea" in Yoruba is *"ewa."* Change the tone and it's the word for "beauty" and the word for "tradition." To ingest black-eyed peas is to become filled with beauty, and ancestral tradition.

Every time my grandmother opened her purse, they would spill out along with her wishbones and bits of roots, to my mother's great embarrassment. It was a minor point of contention between the two, but even long after my grandmother died, my mother shook her head in annoyance and disbelief, and yet my mother left this world with black-eyed peas in her purse, too. No one remains untouched by the old religion. I am the next generation, and I know it will not die with me. The conjure-bag around my neck assures it.

The old religion manifested itself in love potions, and this was where it got very tricky and too close for comfort. One neighbor of my grandmother's brought a beautiful pan of meat to share with my grandmother, which she accepted and later gave to the dog. The woman believed in using a bit of her menstrual blood in her husband's coffee and food to keep him loyal. Apparently, even my grandmother had her boundaries, even when it hurt to give up food for a family of nine out of fear of bad hygiene.

In the old religion, the ancestors are never far away; it is as if they are just on the other side of the looking glass. Before my great-great-grandfather died, he warned his children to behave, and once when they did not they were chased by a vicious dog that they reported, as it got closer and closer to them, had a face that resembled that of their deceased father. In my dreams and those of my mother and grandmother, we visited the recent dead and sometimes those who had gone on long before. As I chased bones and records across the South, not one night went by when a visitation in my sleep did not occur.

In 2012 as the Cooking Gene project's Southern Discomfort Tour wound through South Carolina, we met a white genealogist named Lon Outen, who had responded to my query from a few months before. He dug up an enormous amount of material on the Twitty and Mungo families, and was able to show me where the Twitty slaveholdings and Mungo slaveholdings were in Lancaster and Kershaw Counties, respectively. He also knew a great deal about my great-great-grandfather Terrill Mungo, a member of the Chesterfield County militia after the Civil War. Terrill Mungo married the daughter of Sukey Pate, young Margaret, the daughter of Levi, herself a descendant of a woman from Sierra Leone. He would eventually buy a portion of the small cotton plantation he worked on as a homestead when his former slaveholder, William Mungo, fell on hard times. Terrill Mungo, by any measure, lived an extraordinary life, beginning it as the bodyservant to "Young Marster," William Mungo's son, and ending it as a man of some prominence.

After hours of poring over deeds, census records, and histories of each of the white families, Lon volunteered to take us on a little field trip: "I talked to an old woman who lived out Kershaw way who knew where all your people were buried. So we can go out there and see if there's anybody left. It's in the sandhills, and we have to go to a hunt club property where I believe the Mungos and Pates are buried. I haven't been there in twenty years so we will see what we can find. I don't know what's there, so I can't promise anything."

When we arrived we found ourselves looking at a red chained gate across a closed road. We had to trespass. One of the great indignities of having enslaved and postslavery dead is that their graves are not protected; they are often covered up by asphalt, condominiums, golf courses, and hunt clubs. Stories are buried with bones and memories and records. I came this far, so looking into a South Carolina shotgun was a small price to pay to meet my great-great-grandfather, who knew his way around a shotgun himself. The three of us pushed on.

The sandhills are a particularly strange ecosystem in the bosom of the Carolinas. They are nowhere near the coast, and yet the sandy soil and dunes reflect a time during the Miocene era when the coast was indeed here. It's all scrubby oak and pine with pitcher plants and other carnivore flora lurking for insect prey. This is not cotton-growing land at all. There are little cacti. The bugs here sound as if they are made out of metal. You see small patches of broomcorn sorghum and corn planted for the benefit of the game—deer, turkey, quail, squirrel, coon, possum, and woodcock—and nothing else but searing heat and beetles for miles around.

We walked for about twenty minutes, hoping not to get shot, and Lon just about gave up. "I don't think it's here anymore; I'm so sorry. I don't see anything anywhere." Before my heart could break, Jacob noticed something glimmering, and then there was a bright yellow line of police tape. The glimmering came from purple and green glasses and vases on the ground; there was a broken plate or two and a doll. We found the graves, some of them facing east—toward the sunrise, and Africa.

In the Old South, especially in South Carolina, Georgia, and Florida, people were buried in ways traditional to West and central African custom. Quarry rocks, soaring loblolly pines symbolizing evergreen life everlasting, all of this paled in comparison to the last effects of the dead, from medicine bottles and the cups they last used to clocks and toys. It was said in Kongo in the late nineteenth century, "The natives mark the final resting-places of their friends by ornamenting their graves with crockery, empty bottles, old cooking-pots, etc., all of which articles are rendered useless by being cracked, or perforated with holes." The Kongo spiritual expert Fu-Kiau Bunseki noted that "the last strength of a dead person is present within the objects." In order to keep the dead placated and the living at peace, what belonged last to the dead stayed with the dead.

The grove of graves silenced me as if my tongue had been taken out. That beautiful porcelain, the lavender-colored glass, clear as if some force had polished it. Loblolly pinecones littering the ground, knots of wood where headstones might have been, the face of the doll—all of it was remarkably satisfying. I knew that these ancestors, at least, had been buried in a way in line with the traditions I had always heard about but until that moment had no idea had anything to do with me. This was powerful. They lived and died with the old religion.

Nobody said anything for the duration of the visit. There were fingers pointing, but no words. Lon looked pleased, but not happy. He seemed more grateful than I did that nothing was moved or bulldozed or changed.

"You're really lucky. Usually they'd just as soon plow it all up and smooth it out. Somebody decided to keep this a gravesite. Officially, you should be able to visit it as you like."

I stopped and noticed a woodpecker that had been following us, hopping from tree to tree, drumming its presence into our ears. The old religion was clear. These were the sentinels, the guards. The birds were the living manifestation of the guardians of our dead, from screech owls to woodpeckers to the frizzle-head chicken—indeed in some black graveyards you see the motif of the bird, resident of heaven and earth—like the ancestors.

This is what it meant, to be at the crossroads. I had a bottle of water with me, and I poured a little bit at each tree and quarry rock and the four or five headstones that were there. I wish I knew what they loved to eat most. I would follow the custom of bringing a plate of their favorite food and leaving it at the grave, as was done in the days of old. This is how we remembered each other—by what we ate.

GRIEF

Often when you embark on big life journeys, sometimes the ones who have been with you the longest leave you. It's almost a cliché. My mother died as I was writing this book. I sought solace in the unfolding of my research. "The loss of your mother is the hardest loss of all," I was told by historian and interpreter Wayne Randolph, "because she is the person who has known you the longest." The genes that were passed down to me and to her live on in me as a living connection to an ancient past. In that past I began to create a space for safe healing.

"When you hear the death wail at the crossroads, that's when you start crying. That's how they do it in Sierra Leone." Dr. Edda Fields-Black, a friend and expert on the Low Country rice connection, starts talking to me about grief and the dead. She's lived in the rice-growing countries of West Africa, and now she's trying to understand her own heritage as an African American of both Carolina Low Country and Caribbean immigrant descent.

"You get out of the car, the taxi, the bus, and you start rolling and stumbling toward the center of the village. Your grief joins everybody else's grief. Everybody is crying, even the children who don't know why they are crying. People's hands are in their faces, on their heads, everybody weeps until it becomes one sound."

Dr. Fields-Black's description of the grief ritual gave me vivid, difficult dreams. I saw myself on the rusty roads of the Sierra Leone backcountry, exiting a crowded vehicle, rolling my body to the village, bloodshot eyes and dust-stained clothes, only to find out the dead was my mother. I found myself enslaved and alienated by aspects of the Western death ritual—funeral homes, phone calls, informing creditors, legal paperwork, family discord—and in the end my mama didn't have much of a homegoing at all. I quietly laid her to rest in the presence of a friend and nobody else. Given how my grandmother left the world, I could not have been more heartbroken at how lonely her passing was and how unbearably silent her interment was. Even the manager at the cemetery could not believe we were "it" given the usual size of black funerals.

I poured libation. I cried a little, I prayed. I went to the car exhausted and empty in the cold spring air. I felt like I had not loved her enough—and maybe none of us had.

The Mende have a very interesting grief narrative of their own in African American culture. In 1989, a documentary titled *Family Across the Sea* highlighted the relationship between the Gullah-Geechee of the Low Country South with the people of Sierra Leone. Rice, the Krio language, and Gullah, the heritage of slavery from one coast to the next, and the remarkable nature of an entire culture built on memories of a distant homeland made the film something of a quiet cult culture classic. From the moment a woman named Kadiatu meets her American cousins for the first time through a sweetgrass rice basket used to fan and winnow the grain to the look on her face as she is told their story—something she's never heard before. The film is powerfully emotional. Joe Opala, an oft-quoted expert on the subject—a white Oklahoman who has lived in Sierra Leone and taught there for many years—helped make the connection between the descendants of Amelia Dawley and the Mende through a song the great African American linguist Lorenzo Dow Turner recorded years ago. It was beaten against the walls of time, but the tune and the words were faintly intact, like the words on palimpsests. Amelia Dawley was singing a Mende grief song.

The next documentary, *The Language You Cry In*, came many years later. Amelia's daughter, Mary Moran, and her descendants came to Sierra Leone, to a remote village where the song had been preserved. Opala and a team spent years struggling to arrange the reunion despite the horrific civil war that plagued our ancestral homeland. Finally, when the smoke cleared, they went back to the place where the song began. On the other side of the ocean was a woman who clung tight to the same song that her mother had entrusted to her. She wept bitterly when she met Mrs. Moran; for both women the song about laying the dead to rest was in fact their source of resurrection. The documentary took its title from a Mende proverb that says that you can believe someone's sincerity when they speak in the language they cry in.

My mother was not too impressed with the idea of us being from Sierra Leone at first. The Sierra Leonean girls at her British boarding school said that she and her sisters were "too proud." The very thought of being from the same stock as them annoyed her more than anything else. She coughed and hacked, suffering from COPD and bronchitis. My reveal moment to her was less than Hallmark. I reminded her that the Mende were the main group on the *Amistad* and that they tried to turn the boat around.

"Well, I can get with that, then. At least I know we didn't just take shit from anybody. We fought back, but I always knew we came from strong people. We had to." She was too sick to hear the rest, and Mama drifted off on her couch end, a semireluctant daughter of a warrior people. It was in that same British boarding school on the Isle of Wight that my mother had slapped a British girl across a table for daring to call her a "nigger." My mother was no stranger to fighting back when injustice was at hand.

How bizarre it was for me then, after she died, to be a part of a culture that took the relationship with the ancestors and the dead very seriously but was also known for its resistance to enslavement.

You never really know it all, how to respond, how to cope, as Dr. Fields-Black reminded me: "I thought I knew what this was all about until I went to Colleton County and a distant cousin took me to the family graveyard. It was in really bad shape: lots of flooding, lots of earth being moved around. One of the graves was open, and I looked down and there's water, and floating in that water, a skull. A skull of one of my ancestors—and you know what, Michael?—I knew then I didn't get it. I had been all over Africa and I thought I knew what this was all about—but I didn't. That's when I started learning what this connection was really all about. That skull and that grave was where I had to start."

The grave is not an unusual place to have a conversation about food in our culture. My mother spoke of graveside picnics on Memorial Day and trips on Mother's Day. There was a time when the grave was full of food offered to the dead in our culture in the rural South. A white chicken was slaughtered upon the announcement of death in the South, just as it had been in much of West Africa. Even when the chickens weren't killed anymore, the white chicken icon remained in many black cemeteries. Our funerals were chock-full of fried chicken sent by relatives to feed the relatives during the week of mourning. I love fried chicken, but I told my father that when my maternal grandmother had passed I was introduced to "fried chicken hell," there was so much chicken.

But maybe all I longed for in my sadness was the familiar ritual of gorging on fried chicken, or perhaps the Mende rituals where the ancestors come out to dance with the living. I felt, as an only child, incredibly alone. Toni Carrier, my genealogist, had a Mende doll on her mantel. "That's the dancer that comes out when the ancestors show up," she said. Leopard skin and red and black and white—the African colors of life and death and transition and mirrors adorn the body-length costume. "You see those mirrors?" she said. "When the ancestors come out and go toward you, when you look into their face, you see yourself."

Macaroni and Cheese the Way My Mother Made It

SPICE AND SUGAR MIXTURE:

1 tbsp light brown sugar
1 tsp seasoned salt
1 tsp garlic powder

1 tsp onion powder
1 tsp coarsely ground black
  pepper

2 sticks (1 cup/227 grams/
  8 ounces/16 tbsp) butter,
  unsalted, cut into small
  pieces
8 ounces cream cheese
1 cup whole milk
1 (12-ounce) can evaporated
  milk
3 eggs
1 pound cooked elbow
  macaroni

2 cups sour cream
8 ounces (2 cups) shredded
  sharp Cheddar cheese
8 ounces (2 cups) mild
  Cheddar cheese, cut in
  cubes
4 ounces (1 cup) shredded
  mild Cheddar cheese
Paprika to taste

Make the spice and sugar mixture: Combine the brown sugar, seasoned salt, garlic powder, onion powder, and black pepper, and blend well. Set aside.

Preheat the oven to 350°F. Spray a 9 by 13 baking dish or casserole dish with nonstick vegetable oil spray and place it on a rimmed baking sheet. Set aside.

In a mixing bowl, using a sturdy spoon or a handheld mixer (or in the bowl of a stand mixer fitted with a paddle attachment), combine the butter and cream cheese, and mix well until completely combined and softened. Add the milk and eggs, and mix until the ingredients are fully incorporated and the mixture is smooth.

In another large mixing bowl, combine the cooked macaroni, sour cream, shredded sharp Cheddar and cubed mild Cheddar, and mix to combine.

Pour the egg mixture over the pasta mixture. Add the spice mixture and gently stir to incorporate and coat the pasta with sauce. Pour or scoop into the prepared baking dish.

Bake for 30 minutes, or until the top is lightly browned.

Remove the dish from the oven and turn the oven off. Sprinkle the shredded mild Cheddar and paprika on top, and return to the oven (which will still be warm but will cool down) for another 10 to 15 minutes, to allow the cheese to melt and create a crust on top.

Funeral Potato Salad

3 pounds red potatoes, washed, peeled, and cut into ¾-inch cubes
1 cup sweet pickle relish
4 large hard-boiled eggs, diced fine
1 large sweet onion
1 medium green pepper, diced
½ cup bell peppers (yellow, orange, and red), seeded and diced

1½ tsp seasoned salt—add more if needed
1½ tsp garlic powder
1½ tsp sweet paprika
1 tbsp brown yellow mustard
4 stalks celery, finely diced
1½ tsp celery seed
½ tsp lemon juice
2 cups mayonnaise

Cook potatoes in salted boiling water about 5 to 7 minutes. Drain well and let cool.

Combine pickle relish, eggs, onion, peppers, seasoned salt, garlic powder, paprika, mustard, celery, celery seed, lemon juice, and mayonnaise in large mixing bowl and mix well. Add potatoes and mix until well coated. Refrigerate for two hours.

New Year's Day Black-Eyed Peas

1 pound dried black-eyed
peas
1 ham hock, a piece of salt
pork or bacon, or smoked
turkey
1 cup chopped onion
(optional)
Salt to taste

1 crushed fish or cayenne
pepper or 1 tbsp fish pepper
sauce
1 tsp Kitchen Pepper (see
recipe on page 24)
a few tsp of molasses
(optional)
fresh herbs of your choice

Sort your peas, making sure you check for pebbles or bad peas. Soak the peas for several hours or overnight, or if in a rush, soak them in boiling hot water for 30 minutes before cooking. Prepare a stock of salt meat and onion and season with salt, Kitchen Pepper, and a hot pepper. Boil these together for 15 minutes and add the black-eyed peas. Add enough water to cover. If you like you can add some molasses for more flavor, or the fresh herbs. Cook for an hour and a half. Pair it with corn pone.

20

—

THE OLD COUNTRY

What does an African American who knows he's "part white"—or to be more accurate and maybe a little too clinical and boring, shares genetic affinities with European populations—do when he goes to Europe? What is my role and what is theirs? Or does it even matter?

The basic imprint of my family's life for two centuries—the English language, English and European and biblical names, the gloss of Christianity, the clothing we wear, and a world shaped by white hegemony, Eurocentrism, and the primacy of the Western Civ experience—were the kinds of things James Baldwin said had nothing to do with him, and by extension, us. Now post-Baldwin, peak-Breitbart, science says the average African American is 15 to 25 percent European, or more. Can I compartmentalize?

Does 28 percent of me come home? Where does the rest of me go? Can I see myself in the great culinary traditions of Europe as much as those I seek in Africa? Am I an extension of British cuisine's evolution via the American South? I'm not really prepared to answer any of these questions, but I must ask them. Now.

Fate has it that I have visited the heartlands of my western European component—Scandinavia, England and Ireland, and France. As a child, drops of whiteness didn't matter, they were remote. I was just me, nothing more. Only later did I start to note how un-dark I was compared with other diasporans and continentals, and even some stateside people in the Low Country and Lower Mississippi Valley. I was a mulatto more than I knew. My beard did not rug on my face but rather crackled and crinkled out from my chin. My hair did not form a helmet but rather soft, ever-straightening wavy locks that over time began to fail to fro as they did generation after generation before me.

The first round of DNA tests was both disturbing and a relief. Graduating from a childhood where I wanted the "bluest eye," I cowered in the corner as I waited seconds to find out how black I am. I don't want to be mostly them—I want to be mostly us. I'm worried until the last second that I have spent too much of my life wishing myself white. Then the first outcome came—71 percent African, 28 percent European, the rest ambiguous and uncertain. Many tests later, I am still just that; a little over a quarter European, and in a rare bracket of black people who have more than the average 10 to 15 percent European ancestry.

Loving world history, and unsure of my place in it, I grew up much like James Baldwin's "Stranger in the Village," a presumed outsider to the great, white West. Now rumors and stories of connections to places that are not black, not African, are confirmed, bloods having blended long before I or my parents were, in the Southern expression, "a thought." According to my DNA and the family histories of my white folks, my European story was apparently northern, western, southern, and eastern, stretching to Finland and Russia, south to Italy over to Iberia and up to Norway and Iceland. I could see myself not only in Viking invasions, but Roman children, serfs on manors, and Norman nobles. Everything I had learned about the food of the past focused on them—and until now I felt that I was learning about an alien people with slight glimmers of insight into my own world.

But these were not aliens. They were my ancestors. Finnish women traded as human chattel and Irish warriors and Scots herdsmen. I am little bits of Spain and Portugal, probably more the latter, and Germany and central Europe lurk in my body, as does Ukraine. I don't understand why so many people scoff at this notion of black people with white roots, as if our European ancestry was moot. I have been told, "You can't be everything." "You're not really British/ Irish/French." "You can't march in that parade." But our ancestors had complicated relationships across color lines, or were violated. It's not our responsibility to make people feel comfortable with this fact or to rationalize the rules of cultural inheritance.

On the other hand the apparent silliness of African Americans reaching back to Europe is complicated when African Americans assert their Africanity. The usual pattern in contemporary public race discourse is that African core identity is asserted, and then we are reminded that we aren't "pure," as if that was the original assertion. It's a verbal assault against an attempt to put the African part of our bodies and faces and names in a primary role, defining who we are. It is a microaggressive assertion of white supremacy. Interethnic rape as violence against a people and their women, and of relationships founded in power imbalance that created the phenotypical and genetic diversity that sits at the crux of the Atlantic world.

Being here to reclaim something left of me in Europe as African American is no small thing. It is an act of war against the idea that I am fatherless. No, I am no cultural orphan of the West; I can now identify some of the stories and narratives of western European history and its diaspora that I fit into as a descendant. Cooking and claiming specific European foodways feels less like appropriation and more like repatriation.

In America, whiteness is a founding idea. In Europe, ethnicity among "Caucasian" types still matters. "I don't dare tell anyone my gran is Irish," says an English friend of mine. I was astounded that even in the early twenty-first century, ideas persisted among millennials about the conflict between Irish and English, and the cultural, religious, and social distinctions between the two. To some twenty-first British I encountered, the Irish were still "scum," a people who Oliver Cromwell, my distant relative, "needed to civilize." So many echoes but no clear lines of sympathy. I wanted to weep for the Irish. I have seen the bullet holes in the columns and walls all over Dublin. And yet it was the Irish buying into whiteness that gave birth to the minstrel show, draft riots during the Civil War where black people were lynched, and violence over school busing in South Boston. There are no heroes here, just varying levels of power and responsibility.

The Irish I met harbored a simmering dislike of the English and of the British role in Irish history, and a distrust that was something akin to the way black folks felt about white people. The Irish language, in beautiful glittering seaweed neon green, greeted me at the airport. I took pictures of every sign in Gaelic I could find, including my personal favorite warning pet owners to curb their dog and scoop the poop. Celtic speech ways were resisting death by venturing into the mundane. The church and the folk religion were everywhere—these two failed to die. And then there was food.

My Irish host, Connor, made it plain that the English meddled in the Irish diet and that English colonization of Ireland meant that certain foods and seafoods were reserved for the Anglo-Irish, or were exported and not consumed locally. There were two cuisines, and ethnicity and class defined them. His sketch history of British control was only reinforced by the history of the potato and potato varieties in the Isles. The "yam" potato joined the "Lumper," and various types of cabbages, kale, onions, leeks, turnips, carrots, parsnips, and skirret joined a few herbs here and there to form the bulk of the Irish vegetable diet. According to my friend and heirloom variety expert William Woys Weaver, the "yam" was not a sweet potato, but rather a little potato named so by the enslaved of South Carolina. It was brought by the English to plant to feed their lessers on the Ulster plantations; food for black laborers became food for white laborers and because they kept growing it, a small piece of African American food history was preserved across the Atlantic in Europe.

Dublin's little farmers market was not the most inviting place. I found myself drawn to something called "spring greens" that looked a lot like collards. It's no secret that the colewort spread from central Asia to Europe and was widely consumed. Regardless, my thumbing of the leaves led to a pointy and abrupt "Can I help you, love?" that was not sweet or welcoming. I quickly learned to not play privileged tourist and kept my hands off everything, and even started walking about three feet away from each stand so as not to incur the look that said, "Shit or get off the goddamned pot." "Fish, love?!!" was the last thing I heard as I shook my head no and walked away.

Across the street there was an African and Caribbean market. A quick walk inside gave me whiffs of stockfish and crates filled with yams, sweet potatoes, and peppers. Next door there was a jeans store specific to women with wide hips, and around it examples of possible hair braids and weaves. Beneath the altar, a picture of President Barack Obama, placed near the dummy booty that was so pronounced in the window display. I found myself in a real tug-of-war over what a real semblance of home was and what it was not.

Our meal that night at a popular Dublin restaurant was simple, but it was delectable and familiar. There was *boxty*, a type of Irish potato pancake, my personal favorite; *champ*, a mixture of potatoes, green onions, butter, and buttermilk. Connor had salmon, which has its own place in Celtic mythology, and I had chicken, not the most Irish of meats if you think of lamb or pork or even beef, but seasoned with Irish sea salt, pepper, savory, tarragon and parsley, it was probably the most delicious combination I had since visiting the British Isles. I had cabbage too, and all of this was familiar and potent and heavy in narrative. I told Connor that Americans thought Irish food was corned beef brisket, cabbage, and potatoes and that was pretty much it. His reply: "What you think of Irish food over there is pretty much shite. I mean, c'mon man, this is fuckin' Ireland!" The comment received no further elaboration, and I took another bite with a smile as if to say I understood what he meant.

Although the failure of the Lumper potato crop in the 1840s had next to nothing to do with the colonial era Irish Americans from whom I descended, I decided to grow it one year in one of my heirloom garden projects. It was a delicious and filling potato, and I could imagine the parts of me that were Irish peasants dipping boiled potato into buttermilk three times a day. Growing it was chilling. I imagined the plant dissolving into goop and causing a failure of every crop around it. The Irish potato famine is perhaps modern Western history's most powerful and blatant example of the intersection of class, ethnicity, power, and mismanagement of the food supply, and of the significant ways food can shape a people's destiny.

On the bus, people in Dublin were curious about my origins, and after ascertaining that I was American, and not African or Caribbean, they mentioned cousins in America and Canada, England, Australia, and elsewhere. They were descendants of relatives who made the passage in the 1840s, and to this day money flowed back to Ireland from people who sometimes barely knew their present-day cousins. Not really having an equivalent in the African Diaspora, it seemed like a bizarre codependent relationship, but I was jealous. For a little bit of dash, the Irish Diaspora had a sense of where it came from and why they existed. Not even the fall of the Lumper potato could destroy the families it dispersed, or permanently bury the dead on whom it reaped an incalculable harvest.

My friend Richard Cameron is a British nurse and photographer originally from Yorkshire. He is tall and redheaded and every bit the Viking descendant, with a family that traces its roots deep into central Britain's history. We are both gay men, members of the Bear tribe, and I think it's funny to see us walk down the street together. He's imposing with his piercings and leather gear, but he's a warm and fuzzy man. It seems like I've spent half my real-time friendship with him walking down Oxford Street, the heart of London off of which there is Soho, London's gay neighborhood, where the pubs are full of bearded, bellied men readying up for a club or commiserating over darts.

Richard and his husband, a British Jew raised on salt beef sandwiches and herring in the crucible of Stamford Hill, lead me through the streets of Brixton, perhaps one of the most well-known of London's culturally black neighborhoods—and by black we mean folks from the British Caribbean. "Behold a pale horse," a phrase from the book of Revelations (Rastafarianism is very much interested in biblical prophecy) rendered as ghastly as possible in graffiti, was my welcome mat into the market. A Saturday in Brixton finds the streets—including the "Electric Avenue" of Eddy Grant fame—filled with people buying cows' feet, fresh saltwater fish, stockfish, and Scotch bonnet peppers, yams, cassava, plantains, and sugarcane. There are collards and callaloo, and I get handsy with the produce and compare notes with the women on what looks and tastes the best. *"Don't care where you come from / as long as you're a black man / you're an African . . ."* blares Peter Tosh from a stereo.

Richard's husband interjects, "You know that 'Electric Avenue' was where the community here fought the police over being harassed during the 'sus[picion] laws' in the 1980s. To you guys it was a party song; to us everybody knew it was a protest song." Not only in the Brixton section of London, but Toxteth in Liverpool, Moss Side in Manchester, Handsworth in Birmingham, and Chapeltown in Leeds felt the backlash of a revolt against police overreach as the sons of Britain's white working class sought to club into submission the descendants of enslaved Africans looking for opportunity. It was the enslaved Caribbean upon whom their Empire was built, and the colonized African and Indian upon whom it once depended.

Black Britain only mildly absorbed my family in the 1960s. During their brief stay in England, my mother and her sisters attended the Greylands school on the Isle of Wight. They were perhaps the only African American girls there. The rest of the black girls were from Africa, the daughters of diplomats and potentates.

In London my grandmother found their time there difficult to navigate, starting with the laundry. Sending out laundry that would take a "fortnight" to return was infuriating enough, and it would have been worse had my grandmother known that the shop owner did not mean "four nights." Her youngest children quickly shifted from Mama to "mummy." It was all too much and too fast—she had never lived in any place as big and busy as London. From my grandmother and mother came many stories of the first visit to Westminster Abbey. Walking hand in hand, they could barely contain their awe, looking around completely unaware that they were passing distant relatives, locked away for eternity in those crypts.

When I visited for the first time in 2010, I came to present a paper on culinary history at the Oxford Symposium in Food and Cookery. I spent as much time as I could in London and ended up making it a three-week tour of bits of England, Ireland, and France. I walked into Westminster Abbey with the image of my 1960s family, pertly dressed and pressed, walking into one of the most historical cathedrals in the West, my grandmother in tears because she had never seen anything that was so beautiful. I also walked in with a mission . . . to find the grave of Cromwell, my distant relative. The Crowells of North Carolina had a story of tossing the M into the sea as they sought to run away from Oliver's influence in the seventeenth century on their way to America. The Cromwell/Crowell story was a staple of this particular branch of white family—but in my heart of hearts I don't question it; who in their right mind would want to claim descent from a man who was so hated?

On the walls of Westminster Abbey there are fading paintings of kings long dead and murals with odd-looking lions and elephants that the artists themselves had never actually seen in person. Elizabeth rests in effigy, her stargazy pie-eyes fixed on salvation in heaven, conveniently forgetting her Elizabeth Berkley/ *Showgirls*-like ascent to power, executions and all. Then there is the room holding Mary Queen of Scots interred in a room holding her mother and grandmother, decked out in silver and gilded gates, a tribute from her son James I. Remembering that it was my mother, already beginning to suffer from kidney failure, who put the money together for my trip, I broke down and cried. In all my years I would not be able to give my mother this—a love letter grave for all eternity.

Cromwell's grave marker in the floor told me a different story about family. Oliver Cromwell successfully wrested power out of the hands of the English monarchy during the English Civil War. Charles I was tried and beheaded but the Protestant ascendancy was brief, and after Cromwell died in 1658 and received a funeral befitting a king, he was infamously disinterred during the Restoration and "executed" postmortem. If Cromwell was indeed my distant relative, the controversy of having him in my family tree might not be worth the trouble. To Connor, Cromwell might as well have been the devil himself.

It's probably safe to say that none of this ancestry talk ever worried my grandmother's head while she was living there. She was not wondering about her white cousins or genes; the science of DNA was still in progress, and furthermore, why should she care? Her first problem—a culinary one—was difficult to resolve. England was not exactly the place where an authentic Southern meal a la Alabama could be prepared. My grandmother found British food revolting, giving black pudding, a popular ancient sausage made from blood, onions, and flour, the starring role in her disdain. At best, the English roast dinner with rib roast, Yorkshires, carrots, potatoes, cabbage, stuffing, and the like was the closest thing to edible anybody in my family would eagerly consume.

It was the West Indians who came to the rescue. In some ways the West Indian immigrants to Britain were not much different from my grandparents. Using the impetus of movement and economic change following World War II, Southern blacks went North, and so did many Caribbean and Latin American blacks. Other Caribbean blacks, many of whom served in the British army, chose to go to the mother country, so England absorbed thousands of black Caribbean subjects between the 1940s and 1960s. These worlds did not develop in isolation—the Caribbean Diaspora interlocked with the Islands, and America produced a powerful revolution in music and culture and philosophy that shaped the black Atlantic. Minds and bodies traveled from Kingston to London to Brooklyn fomenting new narratives established in the days of King Sugar.

The Caribbean blacks who came to Great Britain had similar dreams of England in the way that African Americans thought the North would be a paradise of golden streets and freedom. They took low-end jobs, drove buses, became nurses, did menial labor, and were ghettoized. Housing discrimination was real. The National Front developed to "Keep Britain White." Others arrived—Pakistanis, Indians, Bangladeshis—and similar prejudices emerged in response to an increasingly browner Britain.

My grandmother's culinary repertoire necessarily expanded in this new world where black food meant Caribbean food. She was around women very much like herself, born in Jamaica, Barbados, Antigua, and Dominica. They had common stories of slavery, distant touches of Africa, colorism, and childhoods where going to the country and the farm for the first time in centuries felt like an exotic experience. Oxtail stew and jerked chicken, and rice and peas, curry and samosas, lentils and naan, and new hot sauces to spike it all came into the Townsend family palate. I grew up with some of these foods, never really fully understanding their historical and cultural context until now. I had no clue how complex a narrative it took to move my family table beyond the foods of sharecropping and slavery.

Along Electric Avenue was a stand for the healing herbs—*cerase*, *chaney* root, and dandelion. I bought a chart of West Indian healing herbs and foods from a vendor from Barbados who had, for a spell, lived in Virginia. He said he missed the cornbread. Coconut milk and sugarcane juice ran from a machete at a juice stall; kids bounced a soccer ball on the playground of a nearby community center. Some of them, I realized, had never seen the Caribbean—or for that matter had any thought of going to Africa. Some families hadn't been back to their home islands in a generation or two. I didn't know what to make of that shift in worldview.

My friend the culinary historian, cookbook author, and BBC radio personality Rachel McCormack is a short Scottish lady with a lot of will and a loud voice. I'm late, and I meet her screaming at me with a kiss on my cheek as she grabs my hand and drags me onto the train headed southeast of London to Somerset, to the inn of her friend Nick Robinson. "What a strange sight we must be!" she says as we plop into our seats, the train just beginning to move away from the station.

Most of my time in the UK had been in London; I'd never seen the countryside, except from the air. The word "enchanting" is easy to reach for to describe it, but it's really the only word on the shelf. The land was divided up patchwork style just as I had seen in books—hedgerows and orchards and pastures and fields, neat and ancient-looking with old varieties of cattle and sheep en masse, and more wood and stone and thatch as we inched toward Somerset and the West Country—the rural world of some of my English ancestors.

The West Country was not quite "The Shire" of Tolkien fame, but it was as if the world shrank. Rough rocky streets and stone buildings, flower boxes and narrow country roads without lights made a world plunged into darkness and superstition easily conceivable. The trees, the slate-colored sky, the flow of the land—there was nothing here that reminded me of the South in any way. Maybe the apple trees did. The apple trees and orchards and little stands of fruit plants on the southern farmstead, like the kind you see in central and western Virginia; but the rest, I kept grasping for something here that would bring me back to the South, to give me some hint of the English roots of Southern food.

We bought samphire, a type of green, edible wetlands succulent that tastes like asparagus; and a rock crab that put up a fight from the minute he saw me eyeballing him from the other side of the tank. Their rock crabs are British muscle bears compared to the spindly beautiful swimmer blue I was used to along the Chesapeake. None of the fish on ice were Southern: haddock, plaice, cod, hake, pollock, sole, John Dory, turbot, and brill—not a bass or trout or gar or catfish in sight. Nick and Rachel set about to make some headcheese, and a whole hog's head appeared, along with two small chickens and several types of cider. "Somerset is known for her hundreds of apple varieties and her cider," Nick reminded me. The beef behind the counter was rich and bloody, and there were sausages made not only of pork but of venison and duck and wild boar.

And yes, the market had pig parts and a few chickens, but clearly beef and lamb and gentlemen's game won out over pork and chicken—the two lead proteins of the Southeast United States. Puddings, savory and sweet, were available for sale, along with pork pies and Scotch eggs, but I couldn't remember the last time I saw a pudding on a Southern table that didn't come from a box. No corn, no sweet potatoes, no okra, no hot peppers, no string beans or heaps of tomatoes and greens. None of the markers of home were here.

The South was more apparent in the market in Brixton than it was here, although there were chitterlings advertised on the outside sign in seventeenth-century poetry:

> Gloria deo sirs proface
> Attend me now whilst I say grace
> For bread and salt, for grapes and malt
> For flesh and fish and every dish
> Mutton and beefe, of all meates cheefe
> For Cow-heels, chitterlings, tripes, and sowse
> And other meate that's in the house . . .
> For all these and many moe
> Benedicamus domino.

—THOMAS HEYWOOD, 1602

Nick laughed heartily at every one of my novel moments, from praying I wouldn't die on the medieval country roads of Somerset to gasping at the thatched roofs around me, but this was the England we were taught about in literature class that I swore I'd never get to see. He walked me around his inn. His orchard had over a dozen types of local apples, fruiting citrus under little greenhouses, and quinces and old fruits like medlars and pears and bushes full of raspberries and blackberries. Their two pretty, emerald-eyed Bengal cats skulked about with a sexy prance while I selected apples to fry in butter with sugar and spices, Virginia style.

We had hoped to cook in the oven, which was older by a century than the inn surrounding it. The hearth and oven were built in the 1400s, making them the oldest part of the building. Nick's son shined a flashlight inside the chimney: "Apparently a murder of crows had made the oven a bit too much like home!" It would have required extensive cleaning before we used it, so we abandoned the fantasy. No matter what, the historical cook in me was thrilled to see something so old that could still be used for cooking and baking, and I touched it with reverence, looking for the energy of cooks before me.

My Virginia-style fried apples elicited requests for seconds and "the kinds of *h*erbs" I put into the dish, emphasizing the "h." My medieval-style chicken and mushroom pie with pepper, mace, cinnamon, nutmeg, and ginger that was initially destined for the ancient oven; and potatoes roasted in duck fat, steamed samphire with butter, and the mean-ass crab with the finger-cutting claws; and a stuffing made from English bread, heavy on sage, thyme, and pepper, rounded things out. The dry, crisp ciders of Somerset were our beverages.

I warned Nick's son about the temptations of bombshell Southern cheerleaders and spent dinner talking American politics and waxing poetic on Southern food, which won me more raised eyebrows than requests to come make another meal, the hit fried apples notwithstanding. Southern food was perceived as only fried and cheesy for some reason, and steeped in grease. I explained that while fats were an important flavoring in our food they were not a mainstay, certainly not traditionally. Nobody had heard of collard greens ("Is it like lettuce perhaps?"), and okra was more associated here with Indian cuisine than anything else. Going back to London with Rachel, my head filled with more questions. The African cooking gene was looking more prominent in the Southern cooking gene than ever before. We took English breads and cakes and made them lighter, took tea and put tons of sugar and ice in it, and ate meat with our hands after roasting over a hole in the ground, covered in hot spices.

It was a $200 trip to Liverpool by train, but it was one I had to make. No farther than DC is from Philadelphia, I couldn't believe it cost that much to hop from city to city. At Merseyside Dock within the Maritime Museum was another museum space, the International Slavery Museum, dedicated to the translatlantic slave trade and its legacy. Liverpool was the single most powerful European port in the history of the trade, followed by London and Bristol. From these three places came the financial backing, the boats, the supplies—beads, cloth, manillas, tobacco, liquor—and the sailors responsible for ensuring the transport of my West African ancestors to the Southeastern United States and the Caribbean.

Liverpool gives you nothing of London, which magically becomes "*Loon*-duhn" in the mouths of the Liverpoolian populace. The lilt and creaks of their speech were disarming, and they seemed a few tablespoons nicer than Londoners; they were overall a more pleasant species of British, not unlike Midwest blue collar to East Coast white collar. It was hard to believe that from these people came the exporters of African exiles to the New World. I wanted to dislike them, from the outside looking in; they didn't quite have the nasty twang I had experienced in the South when I knew that I was not among friends.

As you ride down the streets, you see names associated with the slave trade and slave traders; Earle Street, Cunliffe Street, Great Newton Street. Penny Lane (of Beatles fame) is named for James Penny, one of Liverpool's most famous and prolific slave traders. Signs for Jamaica Dock, the Goree Piazzas, and others point us in the direction of the central position of the slave trade in the building of eighteenth-century Liverpool, once merely a fishing village on the west coast of England. The first commercial wet dock in the world was built here—to help launch the largest forced migration in history. The human cost was translated into luxury goods, Georgian mansions, and banks, exchanges, and buildings built on that wealth announcing the power of Empire.

Adam, one of the educational advisers, agreed to meet me. Adam was short, ginger, adorable, and kind of reminded me of John Lennon. He was very open about Liverpool's past; there was no sugarcoating in his words. He spoke of not only remembering the past but dismantling racism; he spoke of injustices done to black Britons before the sus laws and after, and the interplay of class and race. I didn't know how to not hug him; everything he spoke of with passion and conviction about racial injustice were words I never heard expressed in quite the same way in the United States.

My hotel, a five-minute walk to the museum, was on the Albert Dock. It's brick through and through. It didn't take me long to figure out what this place was. It was an eighteenth-century warehouse—a warehouse big enough to be retrofitted as a twenty-first-century hotel. I asked the timid girl at the front desk about the building's history. She looked down and in a lilting Scouse accent told me it was a warehouse for rum and shipping supplies and maybe spices. I knew it was more than that—but I didn't have time to interrogate her before meeting Adam. Besides, I figured she had never had that question brought to her by a guest. I ran away from the baked beans over toast to get a serving of truth.

"I don't really like where I'm staying; it's a nice hotel but I don't feel right staying there," I told Adam. "The halls are long and brick and even when they're lit they feel dark. I don't think I'll sleep well there. I asked the young woman at the front desk and she said the building was used for various trade and shipping items in the eighteenth century." I confessed my misgivings to him, thinking he might tell me it was haunted.

Adam didn't blink, nor did he take a deep breath before blurting out the truth. "The hotel you are staying in was one of the warehouses where the chains and barrels of supplies were kept." The black-and-red eighteenth- and nineteenth-century ships bobbing outside my hotel window did not give me any feeling of nostalgia, comfort, or a sense of the grandeur of the seas. These were the kinds of boats that took us away from our homelands forever. They were powered by avarice and Empire. All the quaintness had been snuffed out, and everything I saw just seemed packed to the rafters with dread. "You have to see the bank. Carved into stone are two enslaved African boys with chains around their ankles."

If this were America, Adam might be the descendant of an overseer or a member of the slave patrol, or even a descendant of a slaveholder himself, bearing his soul to the descendant of someone who had been enslaved. Instead he was a descendant of Liverpoolian people who, if they had not built or provisioned the ships themselves, certainly invested or had some stake in them and the trade—with middle-class tradesmen investing in voyages. Adam seemed to be painfully aware that, without his education and compassion and interest in social justice, he might have been a National Front member throwing rocks at protestors in Toxteth, or a lad ready for his first voyage to the malarial coast of West Africa where he heard with salty and morbid cackles, "Beware and take heed of the Bight of Benin, where few come out, but many go in." In this young white man's hands was another part of my history, and I was at peace sharing it with him.

Going through the museum, Adam pointed out the attention the exhibit drew to correcting the narrative of African involvement as an exchange of elites across cultures, and the inherent value of African societies as they were without European conventions. The museum exposed me to the fact Haiti had to pay reparations to France for throwing off the yoke of slavery and colonization. "We have a historically black community of Toxteth; here's a man who was forced out of school because of racism, and a woman who was taunted because she was biracial. We encourage black Liverpoolians to tell their stories as part of our narrative, just like we want people to know that your president, Barack Obama"—I liked that he pronounced it as "O-*ba*-ma"—"is part of the story too. The legacy of violence and corruption is a living reminder that the slave trade isn't done taking victims all over the African world."

London, Liverpool, and Bristol are sprinkled with reminders that the power behind the eighteenth-century slave trade was Great Britain, which until American independence fueled the trade to North America. The Georgian townhouses and massive banks are not monuments to English ingenuity or cultural or intellectual power. In the eighteenth century, Britain ruled the seas, and on the seas between Africa and America were hundreds of vessels crossing from coast to coast with the bodies of millions of West, central, and southeastern Africans. On those boats, powered by the British Empire's mastery of mercantilism and colonial capital, were the people who led to me. All I can think about on the train ride to London is how powerless I am to go much further than knowing that in all of these places at that time, an exact path to my family tree lay needle-in-haystack, probably many times over. "The slave trade isn't done taking victims," said Adam.

Back in London, Jago Cooper, curator of the Americas at the British Museum, took me through the crowded halls which were full of tourists angling to see Assyrian palace walls and the Rosetta stone. The glass ceiling and marble reflect a glowing coppery orange twilight that only the English autumn can produce. I'm determined, so we push through forests of hands and arms ending in smart-phones snapping shots.

On the way Jago shows me an artifact from the Captain Cook

expedition. In an instant the conflict of cultures is brought to life. "This is a shield from Botany Bay, collected by Cook around 1770. It is as if a split-second decision has been preserved through time. An Australian indigene made a desperate effort to keep the strange invaders off and he ran away leaving this behind. It's rare that you have an object tied to such a specific and exact moment when history occurred. We've had Aboriginal delegations come and perform ceremonies over this object."

We get to the North American hall. Tucked among artifacts from the Southeastern Native Americans is a drum collected by Sir Hans Sloane in the eighteenth century from the colony of Virginia. To any music enthusiast with a passion for African drums, it's evident where this drum came from. It's an *apentemaa*-style drum from what is now Ghana, the former Gold Coast. It has enjoyed some notoriety in scholarly books about the history of black music and black folk art. I thought it was huge, from looking at the books, but it's small. I remark on this and Jago agrees. The drum is almost toylike. At one time it was believed that the drum was American cedar and the skin of a whitetail deer, an artifact completely African in design but North American in material construct. It is now known that the drum is made of wood native to the Ghanaian rain forest, and the skin is American white-tailed deer. The Akan Drum is one of the most well-known "American" artifacts in the British Museum. The body is African and its cover is American. The drum was "found," half-buried in a sacred, secret place until it was stolen.

I ache to touch it. I just want to look at it until oblivion. That drum is an attempt at survival, persistence, memory. That drum brought to Europe almost three hundred years ago was read as a Native American artifact. Now we know it's African American. When we take leave of it, sitting among objects it has no real relationship to, I lament that a delegation of African Americans of Ghanaian descent haven't come here to bless it, or with them Akan priests. I kiss my fingers and press them to the glass. If nothing else I know this—the drum is me.

Like the shield, the drum captured distinct moments in time. The movement of the drum from an Akan town to a slave ship, the beating of the drum to make the enslaved dance and exercise for an hour each day. The drum likely clutched by a youngster as he was sold from an auction block somewhere along the Rappahannock, York, or James Rivers. And the moment the antelope skin wore through and the American deer had to suffice. Then there was the moment it was half-buried to conceal its use as a communication or religious device, and the moment Sir Hans Sloane dug it up and confiscated it. Behind that glass is perhaps even the moment the bearer knew his sacred drum connecting him to home was gone forever.

21

—

SANKOFA

*Before he can get others to respect his past, the African in the Dias-
pora must first discover his authentic heritage.*
—MONICA ODINCHEZO OKA, *BLACK ACADEMY COOKBOOK*, 1972

I came into the world with the dream of reconnection with Africa.
Black America reached back to the motherland between 1970
and 1980 like never before. From Afros on Howard homecoming queens to dashikis and classes in Swahili, a yearning emerged
after America's second reconstruction. In came reggae and the Ras-
tafarian vision of return to Zion (Africa), the cross-pollination of
Afro-Latin and Afro-Caribbean cultures in the cities of the North,
and the final thrills of African independence and the fight against
apartheid. Our music was re-Africanized by conga drums, mara-
cas, and cowbells, and blossomed into new electrified soundtracks
of disco, hip-hop, house, and go-go; African cookbooks went on the

shelves in black households; and artifact by artifact, black America started redrawing the lines of its understanding of its own ethnicity. This was the decade I entered my family story, two and a half centuries after the first of my African ancestors arrived in the American South.

Before we could call ourselves African Americans for the first time since the late eighteenth century, the United States had a birthday, 1976, a year that always fascinated me more than the year I was born. My childhood was surrounded by reminders of a yearlong birthday party that saw my conception but for which I was fashionably late. There was one gift that kept on giving, and for all of its controversies it would shape my life for the better: By the time I was born, just about every black household and many others had a copy of a hardback book from Doubleday Press that purported to tell the story of a black family from its genesis in a Gambian village to a porch in a small Tennessee town. Alex Haley's *Roots*, a book born of mythmaking, "faction," and aggressive marketing, told the epic story of black people in saga and miniseries, and none of us were the same again.

Because of "Haley's Comet," slavery became a story to tell on the terms of people of color. The dream of finding Africa and claiming a piece of it to connect to a place and a people became the holy grail of black genealogy. In the shadow of the disillusionment after Watergate and the close of the violent Vietnam experience, the Bicentennial was nostalgic, patriotic, and sunny; it was a return to what Americans believe made them American. Meanwhile, the civil rights revolution settled into a decade of hashing out what the consequences of integration truly meant. An epic recounting of where we had been and how far we had come was overdue, and my main inspiration told in color TV what woodcuts never could.

Who would we become once we confronted the Africa we longed for? How would we deal with the results of the silent plague of sexual assault that reigned over us, from slavery's beginnings to the jailings of black women during the civil rights revolution? Would we be able to return to the plantations of our ancestors in pride or in shame? What did the South mean now, under a liberal peanut farmer named Carter for president? And as for soul food—the cuisine of racial distinctiveness, the memory cuisine of the great-grandchildren of the last generation born in slavery—would it become a cuisine of ethnicity, a bridge to the past, and a road to new possibilities for the black food of the future?

Meanwhile, the South welcomed back streams of returnees from the Great Migration to Atlanta and Charlotte; the South became the heart of the Sunbelt; Jimmy Carter put a new face on Southern identity just as the South became the heart of the conservative elements of American culture. The South began to reinterpret itself in a time of uneven upsurge and decline. Slowly but surely, a food culture emerged from different corners of the region, and the influences that meant anything at all were remixed into a new narrative largely spun by white Southerners about how the South came to be and what it meant *now*.

We have come to this strange cultural moment where food is both tool and weapon. I am grateful for it. My entire life I knew, and many others knew, that our daily bread was itself a kind of scripture of our origins, a taste track of our lives. It is a lie that food is just fuel. It has always had layers of meaning, and humans for the most part despise meaningless food. In America, and especially the American South, "race" endures alongside the sociopolitics of food; it is not a stretch to say that that race is both on and at the Southern table. But if it is on the table alone we have learned nothing; we continue to reduce each other to stereotypical essences.

It is not enough to be white at the table. It is not enough to be black at the table. It is not enough to be "just human" at the table. Complexity must come with us—in fact it will invite itself to the feast whether we like it or not. We can choose to acknowledge the presence of history, economics, class, cultural forces, and the idea of race in shaping our experience, or we can languish in circuitous arguments over what it all means and get nowhere. I present my journey to you as a means out of the whirlwind, an attempt to tell as much truth as time will allow.

Make no mistake, I am now even more defiantly African American than ever before, and I am black, but I am not just black. If I was, I could not adequately tell the stories locked in my body or cook the food that connects to them. In American culture, black is too often viewed as a bubble in which individuality and variation are often seen as destructive to the integrity of the whole structure; we depend on these essences, we depend on these stereotypes for immutable, ready, off-the-shelf ideas about what it means to be a person of African descent in America. This has made it easy to disregard and smudge the names and identities of the cooks and the eaters who came before us, and to mute the music of the tradition they passed down to us.

The real history is not in the food, it's in the people. We are working against the loss of our cultural memory; against the consequences of institutional oppression; against indiscriminate and flagrant appropriation; and against courts of public opinion that question our authenticity, maturity, and motives in the revolutionary act of clarifying and owning our past. It is my belief that the very reason we are here in space and time is deliberately connected to our journey with food. The only question I've ever wanted to answer for myself was, How was my destiny shaped by the history of Southern food?

That's why the book you're holding now took nearly four hundred years to ripen. This was not a story that the status quo could afford to have told. We were just not worth the narrative others received. We were not romanticized as pioneers or as mothers, as Old World craftsmen or as entrepreneurs; we labored under the shadow of the label of property. The world of food writing has long talked about "African words" and "slaves," "plantation cookery" and the like, but we lost the crown of mammy- and unclehood when the Confederacy lost its kingdom.

We are not living in the past or for the past. Recognition, credit, acknowledgment, and the learning and transmission of the old ways are all critical. However, we need the best of our food culture as African people in America to move forward to give us opportunity in areas where there is blight, to bring alternatives to a wilderness of food deserts and plagues of chronic illness and nutritional deficiency. A heritage that is only self-congratulating and masturbatory is not a heritage at all but rather insipid nostalgia. We cannot afford that; everything must be put on the table; our food is not just food for us, it is a way into an alternative history and a new vision of who we can become.

What you read in the previous chapters is the account of my stumblings through these legacies to find my location in the now. And yet in forty years, the ultimate destination has not changed. The future is also the past. The reunification with Africa, mother of black America, mother of the Old South awaits me, and I don't have a choice in the matter. I have come to a place of overdue reunion with her—and I look to those who have made the journey before me for inspiration.

CULINARY *SANKOFA*

Joseph "JJ" Johnson has been executive chef at The Cecil and Minton's in Harlem. He's made the journey I need to make, the reverse Middle Passage to West Africa. He's originally from Pennsylvania, the Poconos area to be exact. "My parents were from New York, my mom is of Puerto Rican and Bajan heritage, and my father was born in New York, but my grandmother was from Rocky Mount, North Carolina, and grandfather was from Mississippi." JJ has lived in New York City since 2002. "I could never get out of New York. I was never 'good enough' to get that new step. No one would ever give me the reasons why I couldn't make the job and move up the ladder.

"But then I was at *Rocco's Dinner Party*, I met Alexander Smalls, he started talking about Afro-Asian cooking, and that's when the search ended. Everywhere he's traveled he has studied the ways enslaved people have impacted the food culture in Italy, Peru, and Brazil. He started realizing Africans and Asians have crossed each other's paths as diasporas, especially migrant workers. So he reached out to me to work on implementing his vision of Afro-Asian—and American—cuisine. It changed my life, it opened up my eyes, it made the lightbulb click; it did it all for me.

"Alexander is originally from Beaufort, South Carolina. He lived across the street from the head of the local KKK but went to school with his son, and he was friendly with him, and that's one of a few things that made the son not turn out like the daddy. He knew what the Diaspora was and traced how it influenced white folks, whether it was the Gullah Islands or elsewhere in the plantation South."

REEDUCATION

Chef Johnson went to learn about African cuisine in Ghana, frequently the first stop for African Americans exploring West Africa. "I loved history as a kid. I was educated wrong. When I have kids I will make sure they are properly educated about their heritage." JJ brings up stereotypes of African food being "third world." "Everybody is poor, there's no table; and then you go there and there are people who are rich and poor and in between, and the rich eat with their hands not because they are backward or uncivilized but because it's the culture. You eat around the table, you only use your fingertips, and your food does not touch your palm. You're expected to have clean hands, clean breath, smart clothes; it's nothing like what you learn here about Africa."

African cuisine in America is predominantly the expanding Nando's *peri-peri* chicken chain and Ethiopian restaurants. Somali, Eritrean, and other Horn of Africa restaurants can be found in the Twin Cities, and in and along with Ghanaian cafés around Washington, DC, as Nigerian spots are in Texas or Senegalese in New York. African cuisine is still a cuisine of immigrant communities, and some have speculated that it has had a failure to launch. My own feelings are that it hasn't had a white savior yet, a translator. My friend Tunde Wey is owning the preparation of Nigerian foods and conducting dinners like my own that discuss race in America. But we both wonder if African cuisine is not lying in wait for someone white whom a "mainstream" audience will trust to lead them, just as the African role in Southern cuisine had its translators. Tunde's response to the issue of racial politics and Southern food in his *Oxford American* piece with John T. Edge, director of the Southern Foodways Alliance, mirrors my own sentiments:

White privilege is an obscene thing. It takes everything, quietly, until there is only silence left. Then it takes that too and fills it with noise. Southern food culture—which, to its corrupted credit, is more honest than "Northern" food culture, where "modern" is mostly a euphemism for appropriation—is the perfect lens through which to observe this phenomenon. Southern food culture has openly appropriated black food culture and then prescribed the proper feelings the appropriated should possess regarding their hurt. Through kind concern, dispassionate reportage, and open quarrel, this privilege invalidates black folks by suggesting their experiences of prejudice are nothing more than overactive and hypersensitive imaginations at work.

Culinary appropriation is about as dirty a phrase to those cynical about so-called identity politics as "reverse racism" is to the progressive- and racial/social justice–oriented. My own displeasure over the crowning of Chef Sean Brock as (African-influenced) Southern food's savior has nothing to do with Sean as a person. Sean and I spoke by phone and broke the silence. I admire Sean and know he is my cousin rather than my combatant. He says he agrees with my main point and is wary of how he and his work are portrayed in the media. I take him at his word, but I still wince at a food media that has asked me more than once in the past, "What do you know that Sean Brock doesn't?" It's complicated by the fact that Sean was touted as a culinary Dr. Livingston in an article on Mediaite.com, "Sean Brock Finds the Origins of Southern Cuisine in Africa":

In his mission to revive traditional Southern cuisine, Sean Brock decided to take things one step further: as recounted by *Food and Wine*, the Charleston chef decided to board a plane to Senegal and trace his cuisine's roots back to Africa. Pulling the white chef version of Henry Louis Gates Jr., Brock had realized that Southern cuisine is fundamentally defined by the food of West Africa, which was brought to the Americas via the slave trade, and decided to visit Senegal to find the ur-cuisine of the South. To his surprise, he discovered hundreds of parallels between the food he cooked and the food found in Senegalese kitchens—hoppin' john, collard greens, cornbread, et cetera—as well as infinite spinoffs from centuries of culinary evolution. And even better, he ganked some Senegalese cooking steez for his own kitchens, finding inspiration everywhere—and learning some things that could veer him into completely unexplored territory for a Southern chef.

But in truth, Sean's extraordinary and laudable work to translate Southern heritage ingredients into a fuller contemporary cuisine that keeps Southern producers busy, buffered by such products as offered by Glenn Roberts of Anson Mills and the scholarship of prolific and sincerely motivated culinary historian Dr. David Shields, is not the first effort made to understand these connections. They all recognize that, but some in the larger food media in search of a great white hope of African cuisine have seriously overreached in their breakdown of the next chapter of African and American cuisines in dialogue. Since the mid-twentieth century, people of color have been trying to make sense of our food heritage from Africa to America from slavery to freedom—and chefs like JJ have not really received the appropriate attention for trying to make connections ruptured by centuries of repression. Tunde directly confronted this in his conversation with John T. Edge and put it the way I have not been "allowed" to: "White privilege permits a humble, folksy, and honest white boy to diligently study the canon of appropriated black food, then receive extensive celebration in magazines, newspapers, and television programming for reviving the fortunes of Southern cuisine."

JJ says, "They aren't even teaching history anymore—they are saying Africans migrated here. I feel like these days African Americans are becoming more aware and open about the impact of slavery the way the Holocaust has become a part of our awareness of how historical events impact us all." To the end of all of this, I have piggybacked on the notions of food justice popularized by Afro-vegan chef and activist Bryant Terry by calling for culinary justice. Culinary justice is the idea that a people should be recognized for their gastronomic contributions and have a right to their inherent value, including the opportunity to derive empowerment from them. Today, this widens the lens of food justice, which centers around increasing access to healthy food and helps amplify how culture, food, and power interplay and amplifies the agents leading the revolution.

Yes, Sean had to go to Africa. It was important, and while he was not attempting to abscond with our heritage, a heritage which he as a white Southerner inevitably shares with us and is indeed a product of, the fuss made over his noble effort is hot compared to the relatively cold reception given African Americans working toward self-knowledge and cultural repatriation. As Tambra Raye Stevenson and many others I met on my journey have made clear, the traditional African diet of fresh vegetables, including fiber- and vitamin-rich tubers, legumes, and leafy greens and fresh fish and interesting spices and limited fat, meat, and sweet intake, provides an outline that is a powerful model for positive change in African American health. This isn't a discussion based on limited notions of cultural ownership—a notion mainly trumpeted by the "mainstream"—it is about what a full embrace of our African heritage can mean for our mental, physical, economic, and spiritual health, while improving the way we relate to our neighbors, with whom we have shared our heritage for almost four centuries. Some of the healthiest diets on earth are found along the 3,500-mile coast from which our ancestors derived.

It is also clear that structural racism is beating back the black chef. It started with segregation; black chefs in the South were either poorly paid shadow figures (often women) working for all-white establishments, or were locked into their own neighborhoods in Jim Crow. Nashville Hot Chicken wasn't a pan-Nashville dish; it was locked behind the walls of racial separation. Now gentrification, denial of loans to open brick-and-mortar restaurants, and lack of community support are the demons—economic stability utilizing our cultural capital is at stake.

The pessimism doesn't end here, but the news is not all bad. There is an inflorescence of black culinary activity and its ability to turn inward and reach out to continental and Diasporic cuisines is really its true saving grace. In some ways we descendants of the enslaved are held back by the push-pull of "race relations." Conversations centering on interethnic dialogue, while important, do only so much for understanding our own journeys. Intra-ethnic self-care is at stake from the narratives we tell the next generation, from sustainable best health practices to our relationship with the environment and protecting spaces of cultural memory. We have to tend to our own healing, not just work at assuaging the tensions born of slavery's racially divisive nature.

That's my very polite way of saying ongoing racial tensions in reaction to flashpoints and indignities may make white people nervous and uneasy or even annoyed, much as the fantasies of revolt and revenge did centuries ago, but this is not about proving to white people that black people are "cool," in the sense of being long-sufferingly patient or interesting and trendy. This is about food being a tool for repair within the walls of black identities. When you are oppressed, how you survive your oppression is your greatest form of cultural capital. In the case of black people worldwide, the cross-pollination of African cuisines and the exchange of knowledge among cousins, this capital is limitless.

A PAN-AFRICAN CUISINE

Ghana's appeal to African Americans is partly based in being an English-speaking country, owing to the British colonial past. But its modern father, Kwame Nkrumah, was not only a revolutionary but a devout Pan-Africanist. Nkrumah attended Lincoln University in Pennsylvania, a historically black institution of learning. He read Marcus Garvey and got to know his cousins in the Diaspora.

When Ghana became independent, Martin Luther King Jr. and his wife, Coretta Scott King, were in attendance; and the year of the March on Washington, W. E. B. Du Bois was buried there, having moved to Ghana for his sunset years. Nkrumah wanted this, a place that African Americans could return to recapture something of their past.

Ghana's coast is dotted with slave castles; JJ said the fact he hasn't been to one yet is the most important reason to return. British, Danish, French, American, Portuguese, and Dutch, among others, traded in enslaved people, not all of them from the Gold Coast. Millions of human beings poured out through Elmina, Cape Coast, Anomabu, and other sites. Ghana's heritage of kingdoms built on gold and prestige enhances the narrative, and so does its relative stability in post-independence Africa. It doesn't change the fact the complex cultural and political foment was in many ways shaped by warring ethnic groups jockeying for power in order to obtain European trade goods and weapons. The end result was that the Gold Coast became, along with six other regions, a major source of enslaved Africans.

My four bloodlines tell exactly that story: Africans from different Akan and Ewe groups caught up in the world's largest forced migration. As earlier discussed, the Gold Coast was a unique place where cultural mixing and fusion between the African, European, and Islamic worlds took place early, beginning in the late fifteenth century. Before there was a Columbus crossing the ocean blue, my ancestors' lives were already being affected by forces beyond their scope of understanding or control. Now African Americans are taking advantage of the open door policy and coming back to Ghana, becoming part of Nkrumah's dream of healing the wounds created so long ago. Other African nations in my bloodline, like Senegal and Sierra Leone, have also sought out these connections with African Americans due to the presence of historical sites related to the slave trade, established cultural links, and the growing body of black Americans who reconnect to the continent through DNA.

"When I went to Ghana I was there just to cook American theme dinners," says JJ. "You know, stuff like barbecue, American Thanksgiving Southern-type dinners, but then I started to see the influences on the African Diaspora and the South. Before you even get to the ingredients or the cooking you feel the energy. It's alive, it's communal, it's vibrant, but nobody's telling you in school where that commonality African peoples comes from. It was all in the body language—I felt it was like I was on the yellow brick road. Everybody was friendly, everybody was hugging me. Seeing children on their mothers' backs, carrying food on their heads, and people buying food right there that day, always fresh from the field, from the water, from the trees, from the bush."

Ghana's culinary introduction for JJ was abrupt and fiery. "My first moment was when the cook made me *peri-peri* prawn, the whole kitchen started laughing at me; I started to tear up and sweat. That was my first lesson. I remember going to the fish market and seeing the fish go from the water to the restaurant. And everybody knows how long the fish or shrimp have been out of the water. When I talk about *peri-peri*, I'm talking about from the birthplace, not Portugal. I'm making the birth of *peri-peri*; you're making a variation.

"Many people don't understand the difference between the colonial gloss and the African beginning. *Fufu* is the original, *mofongo* is the variation. I saw all the connections. The number one thing I learned in West Africa—I don't think anyone will believe me—is that West Africa is the birthplace of everything west of it. Those traditions merged with similar foodways in the Americas and American ingredients, and then come the Asian migrants from India, China, Japan, and beyond, and this ties it all up. That's why we have this explosive cuisine in Peru, Brazil, the United States, Canada, Jamaica, Trinidad and Tobago, and all over. I never made feijoada—but then I made it—I had never been to Brazil, but I had these black beans in Ghana with braised meat and cinnamon sticks stewed down. Brazilians were amazed, they thought I had been to Brazil."

JJ, as a professional chef, defends the ground on which he stands. "When we were promoting the cuisine of The Cecil, I got into a little argument with one sister. I said our cuisine is the celebration of the food of slaves. She winced. 'How can you celebrate the slaves?' No, I'm not celebrating slavery, I'm celebrating how they survived, and you have to know the source and what happens when people from that background met incoming migrants from Asia. But that's the part I really need to know. I never made it to the slave castle and that's why I need to get back. I'm going to learn more about our cooking, the way our ancestral grandmothers cooked because at the end of the day, your goal as a chef is you want to cook like your grandmother."

SOURCE

Take me to Senegal and Gambia, where my Serer fathers left the trading port of Saint Louis, bringing with them the food values of *teranga* (hospitality), *moun* (patience), and *set* (a commitment to cleanliness and order). Give me *ataaya* (green tea) with rock sugar and mint, and I will tell you how my Virginia grandmother made iced mint tea every summer. They say in Senegal that the truth is a hot pepper and *ataaya*, which keeps you up all night long and will surely help you release the truth. For this reason, we would be wise to learn from the value of *kal*, the joking relationship where everybody says their piece while keeping the peace in a humorous but thoughtful manner with no hard feelings.

Let me see the Doors of No Return and weep for what was lost. Soothe me back into peace with *ceeb u niebe*, rice and black-eyed peas; *ceeb u ginaar,* rice and chicken pilau; and *ceeb u djen,* rice and dish. Bring me *soupakanja,* okra soup. Let me taste the one and only true Jollof rice, red with tomato and palm oil, spiked with "the truth." Finish me off with chicken *yassa,* but let me learn to eat with my cousins, sharing from a common bowl.

Take me to Sierra Leone, where the values of the Sande and Poro societies reign. Teach me about working together and brotherhood and sisterhood and cooperative effort to work and support one another to keep the community going. Take me to Benin, where the *dokpwe* does the same things and fields are cleared in a matter of a day. Give me healthy *plasas* greens and rice; let me hear the Mames talk about wisdom and beauty and modesty as the ways of the great cook.

I need to hear the bumping of pestles making percussion with sunrise and twilight. I need the scratch of grating tubers and the grinding of spices on stone. I need the sonic world of the ancestors, lullabies said while babies are fed, bawdy songs as the land is smoothed for planting. I need to understand the sound of the wind in the rice and the complexities of the yam mounds intercropped to save space. I need the rustle of the oil palm fronds so I can hear the generations speak.

In Ghana there will be yam *fufu* and Ashanti chicken, *akple, kenkey, waakye,* more rice and beans, more Jollof rice (Ghanaian style) and the ubiquitous groundnut stew, *nkantenkwan,* a place where family means the people who feed you. There will be thousands of proverbs swirling around about the value of sharing stomachs, and the Creator bringing life and food from the earth, and ancient stories about the days when people ate heaven and wiped their hands on the clouds until the Creator drifted away. In Nigeria, my Igbo and Yoruba cousins will feed me *isi ewu* made from the head of the goat; *ogbono* soup and *egusi; akara* from fried black-eyed peas, *moi moi,* a bean pudding; and *ofe okwuru,* the mama of gumbo. They will talk about the merits of hard work and personal achievement and the importance of balancing reliance upon spirit with self-care. I will go to Cape Coast and Anomabu and Ouidah, where my ancestors ate the soil as their last African meal.

The Yoruba will tell me my new names with food, just as they do with newborns. They will put water to my lips to speak the truth. Then honey for a sweet life and sugarcane for good luck. There will be hot pepper to teach me to weather adversity and be fruitful in this life, and salt to remember to live life with flavor. Palm oil will give me a life with ease, bitter kola a life of great length, and red kola a life free of the influence of evil.

The Yoruba say that the world is a marketplace. Their babies learn from the ceremony where they meet themselves that the world is a marketplace full of tasty things. To get what you need to make your feast you must keep your cool (*itutu*), have good character (*iwa*), and be full of creative fire (*ashe*). The key is to be selective. Not everything is meant to be eaten and not everything should be tried. Fried plantains and *piri-piri* sauce, *babbake*, and Angolan *mwamba*; there are many good things to eat, but the rest of the world marketplace doesn't know it yet.

I will go back to my cooking pot of humankind. The cooking pot in West Africa is a symbol of the womb. The world itself is a womb and a pot, a cooking pot supported by three stones, precariously hovering, stirred by the great hands of the universe. If the stones work together, the world will always stand; if they do not, everything will fall apart, and the feast will be lost. If the cook is not loving and careful, the fire will cease, and if the fire ceases, we will all go hungry.

Se wo were fi na wosankofa a yenkyi, a Twi proverb: "It is no sin to go back and fetch what you have forgotten."

AUTHOR'S NOTE

—

The Cooking Gene is a work of narrative nonfiction intended to weave together elements of genealogical documentation, genetic genealogy, first-hand accounts from primary sources, the most recent findings of culinary and cultural historians, and personal memoir. My aim has been to give a sense of the bric-a-brac mosaic that is the average African American's experience when he or she attempts to look back to recapture our cultural and culinary identities obscured by the consequences of racial chattel slavery. If it were possible to give a linear, orderly, soup to nuts version of my story or any of my family's without resorting to genre gymnastics, I would have considered it. Instead, I am pleased with the journey as it has revealed itself to me.

Toni Carrier of Lowcountry Africana devoted two years to this project. Unfortunately this is not the space to divulge all of her notes and findings, which consisted of thousands of pages of wills, cohabitation reports, censuses, and nonpopulation agricultural reports, birth certificates, lists of enslaved individuals, as well as recorded oral histories from family members. My uncle Stephen Townsend's thirty-plus-years body of work was also an invaluable source, but I tended to rely upon the original documents he cited rather than his conclusions about what the data tells us, which were sometimes different from my own. Where appropriate I have directed the reader to the general source or type of documentation used.

A further note on genealogy: I realize that genealogists are a very proud people, as are culinary historians, historical interpreters, and the rest of the confederacy of popular humanities. I would like to absolve

Toni of any responsibility for conclusions drawn from the data which may seem too far-fetched for some, because Toni simply provided documentation when she could find it, less so interpretation. The majority of the conclusions drawn from the data collected by her, my own searching, or my uncle's previous research, are mine. I'd like to preemptively state that this is much more an issue of checking feelings than facts.

Another element to consider is that my knowledge base on the topics listed above spans my entire lifetime. As an autodidact it can become difficult to tease out all the pieces that have impacted my thinking and direction. To that end, I have provided, in the bibliography, an extensive listing of source works that, taken as a whole, give the reader an idea of the scope and breadth needed to pursue such an ambitious and unusual project as this. It is really difficult to write outside of your own headspace and to remember that your reader may, in many cases, be unfamiliar with elements of the subject matter. In these notes, I hope I provide something of a road map in case you may want to pursue your own journey into Southern food's impact on your family history and identity.

CHAPTER 1: NO MORE WHISTLING WALK FOR ME

Fannie Berry's narrative can be found in the extraordinary volume *Weevils in the Wheat* (Purdue, 1992). It consists of the narratives of enslaved Virginians far and beyond those collected in *The American Slave*. References to West African social metaphors for cooking are well discussed in Fran Osseo-Asare's *Food Culture in Sub-Saharan Africa*. My references to still-life art as symbolism are inspired by the gorgeous work of Phyllis Bober (1999) and her discussion of still life as a vehicle of religious symbolism. The work of many of the people who have taught or inspired me on the way, like Dr. Weaver or Wesley Greene or Peter Hatch, among many others, is detailed in the bibliography.

CHAPTER 3: MISE EN PLACE

The quote about the punkah, "It was natural to ask for a drink of water," is from Letitia Burwell's narrative in *The Plantation South* by Katharine M. Jones (1957, page 57), which is a treasury of the literature celebrating the Old South. I pulled many quotes from this book to illustrate the

perspective of the white planter class and those that visited the antebellum South.

CHAPTER 7: "WHITE MAN IN THE WOODPILE"
Filling in the blanks on early North Carolina eats was made possible by
the beautiful volume *The Way We Lived in North Carolina* (Joe Mobley, ed.).
The reference "not living in a gospel manner" is from the extensive work
of expert genealogist Lon Outen (2012), who before he knew me was following the path of the Mungos and Pates for twenty years.

CHAPTER 9: SWEET TOOTH
The suggestion about the Caribbean being the main sources of rice-and-
pea dishes comes from *Serious Pig*. Lady Nugent's journal is available
as open source on the Internet, and is a fantastic source about Jamaican
plantation culture and cuisine. *In Miserable Slavery* is a study of Thomas
Thistlewood's journal, and I am grateful to Emily James for introducing
me to the book. Solomon Northup's *Twelve Years a Slave* is one of the key
emancipatory texts and provided the best examples of what it was like for
an enslaved person working in the sugarcane fields, especially given his
position as an outsider, a free man of color from New York. Any and all
texts in this chapter and the following regarding botanical exchange are
rooted in the growing volume of work of Judith Carney (2001, 2009). Dr.
Carney has extensive lists of crops in the New World with an African or
Africanized heritage, and source material on origins.

CHAPTER 10: MOTHERS OF SLAVES
The opening statistics are drawn from the foundational opening chapter
in Henry Louis Gates Jr.'s *In Search of Our Roots*. I felt it was important
that readers be aware of the temporal framework of the early African
American journey. The *Atlas of the Transatlantic Slave Trade* is my go-to
source for rounded numbers regarding the slave trade to North America,
with the caveat that those rounded numbers are the average, not necessarily the exact number of people brought, traded, and moved, but the
approximate number based on documented individuals. Nevertheless,
we can draw some inferences by the numbers and what they have to tell

us. The goal is to find out the sources of the food and what those sources mean for the definition and destiny of the cuisine.

The work of Professor Linda Heywood and her husband John Thornton (2002, 2003, 2007), along with Joseph Miller (1999), are vital for understanding both the Atlantic Creole story and the theory's progenitor, professor Ira Berlin. His *Many Thousands Gone* and *Generations of Captivity* provided my road map for how I wanted to explore this history as a matter of migrations and morphings of culture, rather than a subcultural backdrop. Basden, Crow, Equiano, and other voices of the Biafran past helped to elaborate the Igbo past, but the work of Douglas Chambers really brought to the forefront the critical importance of understanding the Igbo and their neighbors in the development of early Virginia, the earliest center of enslaved American life. Charles Joyner and Peter Wood are mainstays of scholarship around the Low Country, and Philip Morgan's idea of the two main Southern windows—the Chesapeake and Low Country—also helped shape my vision of early African American foodways as essentially a seaboard cuisine. But the work of Gwendolyn Midlo Hall and Daniel Usner helped us all to remember the critical role of Louisiana, the Gulf Coast, and the Lower Mississippi Valley. This chapter is really about the effect that nearly a century of scholarship devoted to the cultural history of African America has had, and how it should be recognized for, changing how we view black history and the black experience. As Mechal Sobel put it so beautifully in her signature work, it was a "World They Made Together."

I want to personally thank Nic Butler for hours of interview time where he gently led me through the critical moment when many of my ancestors were brought ashore. It was a moving and extraordinary experience to get the level of detail needed to re-create the moment my African ancestors were forced into American realities.

CHAPTER 11: ALMA MATER

The corn chapter draws on the words of abolitionist Frederick Douglass, whose tireless memory gave us so much of what we know about black life in Maryland and the Upper South. Charles Hudson's classic study, *The Southeastern Indians*, and Robbie Ethridge's *Creek Country*, should be read along with *Black Indians* by William Loren Katz and *IndiVisible: African–Native American Lives in the Americas* by Gabrielle Tayac to truly understand the impact of Native traditions on the South and the relationship between African and Native peoples. La Fleur's work (2012) and that of James McCann's *Maize and Grace* not only examine the impact of *Zea mays* in Africa, but the former is of the few works that actually begins to tease out the transatlantic effects of African and European culinary fusion on the coast of West Africa, my ancestral homeland, the Gold Coast. Stephen Behrendt's masterful discussion of trade and seasonality frames the wider picture in which humans, crops, foods, and commodities traveled, giving us another layer to the narrative.

CHAPTER 12: CHESAPEAKE GOLD
Here we return to the work of Frederick Douglass and narratives from the anthology of Katharine M. Jones (1957), specifically those of Letitia Burwell (page 63), Frederick Law Olmsted (page 54), and Susan Dabney Smeades (page 27). George Bagby's *Old Virginia Gentleman* is available as open source or in print, and is the source of the quotes about bacon and greens and the crops of the central Virginia Piedmont.

CHAPTER 13: THE QUEEN
Walter Edgar's *South Carolina: A History* is a fantastic, thorough state history showing the movement and culture of black South Carolinians against the backdrop of the state's economic and political history. Pierre Thiam's *Senegal* is the source of the story about Aline Diatta. See Judith Carney (2001) and Edda Fields-Black (2008) for African influences on the culture of rice in the Low Country. The Sande initiation process and what it meant from a food perspective is perfectly outlined in Sylvia Boone's amazing work, *Radiance from the Waters*.

CHAPTER 15: SHAKE DEM 'SIMMONS DOWN
"The Persimmon Tree and Beer Dance" is from the *Farmer's Register*, volume 6, by William B. Smith, 1838.

CHAPTER 17: THE DEVIL'S HALF ACRE

Bancroft's *Slave Trading in the Old South* was my primary source for this chapter, followed by *Soul by Soul,* and the narrative of the Richmond slave market sale by John Sergeant Wise in Jones (1957, pages 68–77). Special thanks to professor Isabela Morales, who studied the Townsend plantations for her expertise on the body of records around the Townsend family for this chapter and the next. Her invaluable kindness and generosity opened doors to my family history I never knew existed.

CHAPTER 18: "THE KING'S CUISINE"

The records at the beginning of the chapter are intended to be as alienating as a Bertolt Brecht play. They are directly pulled from the agricultural censuses/nonpopulation schedules from 1850 to 1860. Sarah Hicks Williams's comment about picking cotton being "light work" is a quote from Jones (1957, page 47).

CHAPTER 19: CROSSROADS

See Newbell Niles Puckett's *Folk Beliefs of the Southern Negro* and the work of Robert Farris Thompson, particularly *Flash of the Spirit,* for references to spiritual practices and beliefs; also see *The Way of the Elders.*

CHAPTER 21: *SANKOFA*

I encourage the reader to explore more about West African cooking through the work of Fran Osseo-Asare, Rosamund Grant, Pierre Thiam, and others. The cookbooks in the bibliography are not just cookbooks, they are important sources of knowledge regarding the meaning behind elements of African cuisines.

SELECTED BIBLIOGRAPHY

—

Acholonu, Catherine Obianuju. *The Igbo Roots of Olaudah Equiano: An Anthropological Research*. Owerri, Nigeria: Afa Press, 1989.

Alden, Peter. *National Audubon Society Field Guide to the Southeastern States*. New York: Knopf, 1999.

Alford, Terry. *Prince among Slaves*. New York: Harcourt Brace Jovanovich, 1977.

Allen, William T., and T. R. H. Thompson. *A Narrative of the Expedition Sent by His Majesty's Government to the River Niger in 1841*. London: Cass, 1968. Originally published in 1843.

Austin, Allan D. *African Muslims in Antebellum America: Transatlantic Stories and Spiritual Struggles*. New York: Routledge, 1997.

Bagby, George William. *The Old Virginia Gentleman, and Other Sketches*. Ed. Ellen M. Bagby. New York: C. Scribner's Sons, 1910. Originally published in 1877.

Bailey, Adrian. *The Cooking of the British Isles*. New York: Time-Life Books, 1969.

Balandier, Georges. *Daily Life in the Kingdom of the Kongo from the Sixteenth to the Eighteenth Century*. New York: Pantheon Books, 1968.

Ball, Charles. *Slavery in the United States: A Narrative of the Life and Adventures of Charles Ball, a Black Man, Who Lived Forty Years in Maryland, South Carolina and Georgia, as a Slave Under Various Masters, and was One Year in the Navy with Commodore Barney, During the Late War*. New York: John S. Taylor, 1837.

Ball, Edward. *Slaves in the Family*. New York: Farrar, Straus and Giroux, 1998.

Bancroft, Frederic. *Slave Trading in the Old South*. New York: Ungar, 1959.

Baptist, Edward E. *The Half Has Never Been Told: Slavery and the Making of American Capitalism*. New York: Basic Books, 2014.

Bascom, William. "Yoruba Cooking," *Africa* 21 (April 1951): 125–37.

Basden, G. T. *Among the Ibos of Nigeria*. London: Seeley, Service & Co., 1921.

Bassir, Olumbe. "Food Habits of the Mendes." In *Africana: The Magazine of the West African Society*, April 1949, 23–24.

Behrendt, Stephen D. "Ecology, Seasonality, and the Transatlantic Slave Trade." In *Soundings in Atlantic History: Latent Structures and Intellectual Currents, 1500–1830*. Ed. Bernard Bailyn and Patricia L. Denault. Cambridge, MA: Harvard University Press, 2009.

Bennett, Chris. *Southeast Foraging: 120 Wild and Flavorful Edibles from Angelica to Wild Plums*. Portland: Timber Press, 2015.

Berlin, Ira. *Many Thousands Gone: The First Two Centuries of Slavery in North America*. Cambridge: The Belknap Press of Harvard University Press, 1998.

Blassingame, John D. *The Slave Community*. New York: Oxford University Press, 1972.

Blockson, Charles L. and Ron Fry. *Black Genealogy*. Englewood Cliffs, NJ: Prentice-Hall, 1977.

Bober, Phyllis. *Art, Culture and Cuisine: Ancient and Medieval Gastronomy*. Chicago: University of Chicago Press, 1999.

Boone, Sylvia Ardyn. *Radiance from the Waters: Ideals of Feminine Beauty in Mende Art*. New Haven: Yale University Press, 1986.

Bosman, Willem. *A New and Accurate Description of the Coast of Guinea*. 1705. Reprint, London, 1967.

Brock, Sean. *Heritage*. New York: Artisan, 2014.

Brown, Ras Michael. "'Walk in the Feenda': West-Central Africans and the Forest in the South Carolina–Georgia Lowcountry." In *Central Africans and Cultural Transformations in the American Diaspora*. Ed. Linda M. Heywood. Cambridge: Cambridge University Press, 2002, 289–318.

Burroughs, Tony. *Black Roots: A Beginner's Guide to Tracing the African American Family Tree*. New York: Fireside Book, 2001.

Burwell, Letitia. *A Girl's Life in Virginia Before the War.* New York: F. A. Stokes, 1900.

Carney, Judith Ann. *Black Rice: The African Origins of Rice Cultivation in the Americas.* Cambridge, MA: Harvard University Press, 2001.

Carney, Judith Ann, and Richard Nicholas Rosomoff. *In the Shadow of Slavery: Africa's Botanical Legacy in the Atlantic World.* Berkeley: University of California Press, 2009.

Carr, Lois Green, Russell R. Menard, and Lorena S. Walsh. *Robert Cole's World: Agriculture and Society in Early Maryland.* Chapel Hill: University of North Carolina Press, 1991.

Carson, Jane. *Colonial Virginia Cookery.* Williamsburg: Colonial Williamsburg Foundation, 1985.

Chambers, Douglas B. "'He Gwine Sing He Country'": Africans, Afro-Virginians, and the Development of Slave Culture in Virginia, 1610–1810." 2 vols. Dissertation, University of Virginia, 1996.

———. *Murder at Montpelier: Igbo Africans in Virginia.* Jackson: University Press of Mississippi, 2005.

———. "Tracing Igbo into the African Diaspora," in *Identity in the Shadow of Slavery.* Ed. Paul E. Lovejoy. London: Continuum, 2000.

Charles, Dora. *A Real Southern Cook in Her Savannah Kitchen.* New York: Houghton Mifflin Harcourt, 2015.

Chase, Leah. *The Dooky Chase Cookbook.* Gretna, LA: Pelican Pub. Co., 1990.

Chew, Elizabeth V. "Carrying the Keys: Women and Housekeeping at Monticello." In *Dining at Monticello: In Good Taste and Abundance.* Ed. Damon Lee Fowler. Chapel Hill: University of North Carolina Press, 2005.

Covert, Mildred L., and Sylvia P. Gerson. *Kosher Cajun Cookbook.* Gretna, LA: Publican Pub. Co., 1987.

———. *Kosher Creole Cookbook.* Gretna, LA: Publican Pub. Co., 1982.

———. *Kosher Southern-Style Cookbook.* Gretna, LA: Publican Pub. Co., 1993.

Craughwell, Thomas J. *Thomas Jefferson's Crème Brûlée: How a Founding Father and His Slave James Hemings Introduced French Cuisine to America.* Philadelphia: Quirk Books, 2012.

Crews, Jennie Wilson. *Plantation Recollections.* Richmond: Dietz Publishing Company, 1945.

Crofts, Daniel, W. *Old Southampton: Politics and Society in a Virginia County, 1834–1869.* Charlottesville: University Press of Virginia, 1992.

Crofts, Daniel W., ed. *Cobb's Ordeal: The Diaries of a Virginia Farmer, 1842–1872.* Athens: University of Georgia Press, 1997.

Crow, Hugh. *Memoirs of the Late Captain Hugh Crow of Liverpool: Comprising a Narrative of his Life, Together with Descriptive Sketches of Africa, Particularly of Bonny, the Manners and Customs of the Inhabitants, the Production of the Soil, and the Trade of the Country, to Which Are Added Anecdotes and Observations of the Negro Character.* London: F. Cass, 1970. Originally published in 1830.

Crump, Nancy Carter. *Hearthside Cooking: Early American Southern Cuisine.* Chapel Hill: University of North Carolina Press, 2008.

Dalziel, J. M. *Useful Plants of West Tropical Africa.* London: Published under the Authority of the Secretary of State for the Colonies by the Crown Agents for the Colonies, 1937.

DeCorse, Christopher. *An Archaeology of Elmina: Africans and Archaeology on the Gold Coast, 1400–1900.* Washington: Smithsonian Institution Press, 2001.

Deetz, James. *In Small Things Forgotten: An Archaeology of Early American Life.* New York: Anchor Books, 1996.

Delmont, Matthew F. *Making Roots: A Nation Captivated.* Oakland, CA: University of California Press, 2016.

De Marees, Pieter. *Description and Historical Account of the Gold Kingdom of Guinea.* Trans., ed. Albert Van Dantzig and Adam Jones. Oxford: Oxford University Press, 1987.

Diouf, Sylviane A. *Dreams of Africa in Alabama: The Slave Ship* Clotilda *and the Story of the Last Africans Brought to America.* Oxford: Oxford University Press, 2007.

———. *Servants of Allah: African Muslims Enslaved in the Americas.* New York: New York University Press, 1998.

Douglass, Frederick. *Life and Times of Frederick Douglass.* Grand Rapids, MI: Candace Press, 1996.

Douglass, Frederick, and Benjamin Quarles, ed. *Narrative of the Life of Frederick Douglass: An American Slave*. Cambridge, MA: Belknap Press, 1960.

Doumbia, Adama, and Naomi Doumbia. *The Way of the Elders: West African Spirituality & Tradition*. Saint Paul, MN: Llewellyn Publications, 2004.

Eddy, Kristin. "African Roots Transplanted." *Washington Post*, July 4, 1990.

Edgar, Walter B. *South Carolina: A History*. Columbia: University of South Carolina Press, 1998.

Edge, John T. *Foodways*. Chapel Hill: University of North Carolina Press, 2007.

————. *The Potlikker Papers: A Food History of the Modern South, 1955–2015*. New York: Penguin Press, 2017.

Egerton, John. *Southern Food: At Home, on the Road, in History*. New York: Knopf, 1987.

Eichstedt, Jennifer L., and Stephen Small. *Representations of Slavery: Race and Ideology in Southern Plantation Museums*. Washington, DC: Smithsonian Institution Press, 2002.

Eltis, David, and David Richardson. *Atlas of the Transatlantic Slave Trade*. New Haven: Yale University Press, 2010.

Equiano, Olaudah. "The Early Travels of Olaudah Equiano." In *Africa Remembered: Narratives by West Africans from the Era of the Slave Trade*. Ed. Philip D. Curtin. Madison: University of Wisconsin Press, 1967.

Ethridge, Robbie Franklyn. *Creek Country: The Creek Indians and Their World*. Chapel Hill: University of North Carolina Press, 2003.

Fehribach, Paul. *The Big Jones Cookbook: Recipes for Savoring the Heritage of Regional Southern Cooking*. Chicago: University of Chicago Press, 2015.

Feibleman, Peter S. *American Cooking: Creole and Acadian*. New York: Time-Life Books, 1971.

Feltman, William. *The Journal of Lt. William Feltman, 1781–82*. New York: New York Times, 1969.

Ferguson, Leland. *Uncommon Ground: Archaeology and Early African America, 1650–1800*. Washington, DC: Smithsonian Institution Press, 1992.

428 Selected Bibliography

Ferris, Marcie Cohen. *Matzoh Ball Gumbo: Culinary Tales of the Jewish South*. Chapel Hill: University of North Carolina Press, 2005.

——. *The Edible South: The Power of Food and the Making of an American Region*. Chapel Hill: University of North Carolina Press, 2014.

Fett, Sharla M. *Working Cures: Healing, Health and Power on Southern Slave Plantations*. Chapel Hill: University of North Carolina Press, 2002.

Fields-Black, Edda L. *Deep Roots: Rice Farmers in West Africa and the African Diaspora*. Bloomington: Indiana University Press, 2008.

Fischer, David Hackett. *Albion's Seed: Four British Folkways in America*. New York: Oxford University Press, 1989.

Fischer, David Hackett, and James C. Kelly. *Bound Away: Virginia and the Westward Movement*. Charlottesville: University Press of Virginia, 2000.

Fowler, Damon Lee. *Classical Southern Cooking*. Layton, UT: Gibbs Smith, 2008.

Gamble, David. *The Wolof of Senegambia*. London: International African Institute, 1957.

Gates, Henry Louis Jr. *Finding Your Roots: The Official Companion to the PBS Series*. Chapel Hill: University of North Carolina Press, 2014.

——. *In Search of Our Roots: How 19 Extraordinary African Americans Reclaimed Their Past*. New York: Crown, 2009.

Genovese, Eugene D. *Roll, Jordan, Roll: The World the Slaves Made*. New York: Vintage Books, 1976.

Gomez, Michael A. *Exchanging Our Country Marks: The Transformation of African Identities in the Colonial and Antebellum South*. Chapel Hill: University of North Carolina Press, 1998.

Grant, Rosamund, and Josephine Bacon. *The Taste of Africa*. London: Southwater, 2006.

Gray, Lewis Cecil. *History of Agriculture in the Southern United States to 1860*. Clifton, NJ: Augustus M. Kelley, 1973. Originally published in 1933.

Greene, Wesley. *Vegetable Gardening the Colonial Williamsburg Way: 18th-Century Methods for Today's Organic Gardeners*. New York: Rodale, 2012.

Grimé, William Ed, ed. *Ethno-Botany of the Black Americans.* Algonac, MI: Reference Publications, 1979.

Grosvenor, Vertamae. *Vibration Cooking: Or, The Travel Notes of a Geechee Girl.* Athens: University of Georgia Press, 2011.

Haley, Alex. *Roots.* Garden City, NY: Doubleday, 1976.

Hall, Douglas, and Thomas Thistlewood. *In Miserable Slavery: Thomas Thistlewood in Jamaica, 1750–1786.* Kingston, Jamaica: University of the West Indies Press, 1999.

Hall, Gwendolyn Midlo. *Africans in Colonial Louisiana: The Development of Afro-Creole Culture in the Eighteenth Century.* Baton Rouge: Louisiana State University Press, 1992.

———. *Slavery and African Ethnicities in the Americas: Restoring the Links.* Chapel Hill: North Carolina University Press, 2005.

Harbury, Katharine E. *Colonial Virginia's Cooking Dynasty.* Columbia: University of South Carolina Press, 2004.

Hatch, Peter J. *"A Rich Spot of Earth": Thomas Jefferson's Revolutionary Garden at Monticello.* New Haven: Yale University Press, 2012.

Hatch, Peter J. "Thomas Jefferson's Favorite Vegetables." *Dining at Monticello: In Good Taste and Abundance.* Ed. Damon Lee Fowler. Chapel Hill: University of North Carolina Press, 2005.

Hazelton, Nika Standen. *The Cooking of Germany.* New York: Time-Life Books, 1969.

Heath, Barbara J. "Bounded Yards and Fluid Boundaries: Landscapes of Slavery at Poplar Forest." In *African Reflections on the American Landscape.* Washington, DC: National Park Service, 2002.

———. *Hidden Lives: The Archaeology of Slave Life at Thomas Jefferson's Poplar Forest.* Charlottesville: University Press of Virginia, 1999.

Hess, Karen. "Thomas Jefferson's Table: Evidence and Influences." In *Dining at Monticello: In Good Taste and Abundance.* Ed. Damon Lee Fowler. Chapel Hill: University of North Carolina Press, 2005.

Heywood, Linda M. "Portuguese into African: The Eighteenth-Century Central African Background to Atlantic Creole Cultures." In *Central Africans and Cultural Transformations in the American Diaspora.* Ed. Linda Heywood. Cambridge: Cambridge University Press, 2002.

Heywood, Linda M. and John K. Thornton. *Central Africans, Atlantic*

Creoles, and the Foundation of the Americas, 1585–1660. New York: Cambridge University Press, 2007.

Hilliard, Sam Bowers. *Atlas of Antebellum Southern Agriculture*. Baton Rouge: Louisiana State Press, 1984.

———. *Hog Meat and Hoecake: Food Supply in the Old South, 1840–1860*. Carbondale: Southern Illinois Press, 1972.

Holloway, Joseph E. *Africanisms in American Culture*. Bloomington: Indiana University Press, 2005.

———. "The Origins of African American Culture." In *Africanisms in American Culture*. Ed. Joseph E. Holloway. Bloomington: Indiana University Press, 1991.

Hudson, Charles. *The Southeastern Indians*. Knoxville: University of Tennessee, 1989.

Jefferson, Thomas. *Notes on the State of Virginia*.

Johnson, Walter. *Soul by Soul: Life inside the Antebellum Slave Market*. Cambridge: Harvard University Press, 2009.

Jones, Katharine M. *The Plantation South*. Indianapolis: Bobbs-Merrill, 1957.

Joyner, Charles W. *Down by the Riverside: A South Carolina Slave Community*. Urbana: University of Illinois Press, 1984.

———. "The World of Plantation Slaves." In *Before Freedom Came: African-American Life in the Antebellum South*. Ed. Edward D. C. Campbell Jr. and Kym S. Rice. Charlottesville: University Press of Virginia, 1991.

Katz-Hyman, Martha B., and Kym S. Rice. *The World of a Slave: Encyclopedia of Material Life of Slaves in the United States*. 2 vol. Santa Barbara, CA: ABC-CLIO, 2011.

Kelley, Sean M. *Voyage of the Slave Ship* Hare: *A Journey into Captivity from Sierra Leone to South Carolina*. Chapel Hill: University of North Carolina Press, 2016.

Kelso, William M. *Kingsmill Plantations, 1619–1800: Archaeology of Country Life in Colonial Virginia*. Cambridge, MA: Academic Press, 1984.

Knight, Frederick C. *Working the Diaspora: The Impact of African Labor on the Anglo-American World, 1650–1850*. New York: New York University Press, 2010.

La Fleur, James Daniel. *Fusion Foodways of Africa's Gold Coast in the Atlantic Era*. Leiden; Boston: Brill, 2012.

Leach, Melissa. *Rainforest Relations: Gender and Resource Use Among the Mende of Gola, Sierra Leone*. Washington, DC: Smithsonian Institution Press, 1994.

Lewis, Edna. *The Taste of Country Cooking*. New York: Alfred A. Knopf, 2003.

Linton, Ralph. *Tobacco and Its Use in Africa*. Chicago: Field Museum of Natural History, 1930.

Little, Kenneth Lindsay. *The Mende of Sierra Leone: A West African People in Transition*. London: Routledge & K. Paul, 1967.

Littlefield, Daniel C. *Rice and Slaves: Ethnicity and the Slave Trade in Colonial South Carolina*. Baton Rouge: Louisiana State University Press, 1981.

Lundy, Ronni. *Victuals: An Appalachian Journey, with Recipes*. New York: Clarkson Potter, 2016.

Marone, Omar. "Teranga among the Wolof People." In *1990 Festival of American Folklife*. Washington, DC: Smithsonian Institution/ National Park Service, 1990.

McCann, James C. *Stirring the Pot: A History of African Cuisine*. Athens: Ohio University Press, 2009.

McKee, Larry. "Food Supply and Plantation Social Order: An Archaeological Perspective." In *"I, Too, Am America": Archaeological Studies of Afro-American Life*. Ed. Theresa A. Singleton. Charlottesville: University Press of Virginia, 1999.

McLeod, Malcolm D. *The Asante*. London: British Museum Publications, 1981.

McWilliams, James E. *A Revolution in Eating: How the Quest for Food Shaped America*. New York: Columbia University Press, 2005.

Mellon, James, ed. *Bullwhip Days: The Slaves Remember*. New York: Weidenfeld & Nicolson, 1988.

Mendes, Helen. *The African Heritage Cookbook*. New York: Macmillan, 1971.

Miller, Adrian. *Soul Food: The Surprising Story of an American Cuisine, One Plate at a Time*. Chapel Hill: University of North Carolina Press, 2013.

Miller, Jim Wayne. "From Oats to Grits, Mutton to Pork: North British Foodways in Southern Appalachia." In *Cornbread Nation 3: Foods of the Mountain South*. Ed. Ronni Lundy. Chapel Hill: University of North Carolina Press, 2005.

Miller, Joseph Calder. *Way of Death: Merchant Capitalism and the Angolan Slave Trade, 1730–1830*. Madison: University of Wisconsin Press, 1988.

Mintz, Sidney W. *Sweetness and Power: The Place of Sugar in Modern History*. New York: Penguin, 1986.

Mobley, Joe A., ed. *The Way We Lived in North Carolina*. Chapel Hill: University of North Carolina Press, 2003.

Monteiro, Joachim John. *Angola and the River Congo*. New York: Macmillian, 1876.

Moore, Stacy Gibbons. "'Established and Well Cultivated': Afro-American Foodways in Early Virginia." *Virginia Calvacade* 39:2 (1989): 70–83.

Morales, R. Isabela. "Letters from a Planter's Daughter: Understanding Freedom and Independence in the Life of Susanna Townsend (1853–1869)." *University of Alabama McNair Journal* 12 (Spring 2012): 145–74.

Morgan, Philip D. *Slave Counterpoint: Black Culture in the Eighteenth-Century Chesapeake and Lowcountry*. Chapel Hill: University of North Carolina Press, 1998.

———. "Slave Life in Piedmont Virginia, 1720–1800." In *Colonial Chesapeake Society*. Ed. Lois Green Carr, Philip D. Morgan, and Jean B. Russo. Chapel Hill: University of North Carolina Press, 1988.

Morgan, Philip D., ed. *Don't Grieve After Me: The Black Experience in Virginia, 1619–1986*. Hampton, Va.: Hampton University, 1986.

Morrison, Toni. *Beloved: A Novel*. New York: Knopf, 1987.

Moss, Kay, and Kathryn Hoffman. *The Backcountry Housewife*. Gastonia, NC: Schiele Museum, 2001.

Mukherjee, Siddhartha. *The Gene: An Intimate History*. New York: Scribner, 2016.

Nelson, Alondra. *The Social Life of DNA: Race, Reparations, and Reconciliation after the Genome*. Boston: Beacon Press, 2016.

Njoku, Onwuka N. *Mbundu*. Heritage Library of African People series. New York: Rosen, 1997.

Northrup, David. "Igbo and Myth Igbo: Culture and Ethnicity in the Atlantic World, 1600–1850." In *The Slavery Reader*. Ed. Gad Heuman and James Walvin. New York: Routledge, 2003.

Northup, Solomon. *Twelve Years a Slave*. New York: Penguin, 2012. Originally published in 1853.

Okigbo, Bede Nwoye. "Plants and Food in Igbo Culture." Paper presented at the Ahiajoku Lecture Series, Owerri, Nigeria, 1980.

Olmsted, Frederick Law. *Journey in the Seaboard Slave States*. New York: Capricorn Books, 1959. Originally published in 1856.

Osseo-Asare, Fran. *Food Culture in Sub-Saharan Africa*. Westport, CT: Greenwood Press, 2005.

———. *The Ghana Cookbook*. Hippocrene Books Inc, 2015.

Outen, Lon D. *A History of Lynches Forks and Extended Areas on Big and Little Lynches Rivers, South Carolina*. Ann Arbor, MI: Sheridan Books, 2012.

Park, Mungo. *Travels in the Interior Districts of Africa*. New York: Arno Press, 1971.

Perdue, Charles L. *Pigsfoot Jelly & Persimmon Beer: Foodways from the Virginia Writers' Project*. Santa Fe, NM: Ancient City Press, 1992.

———. *Weevils in the Wheat: Interviews with Virginia Ex-Slaves*. Charlottesville: University Press of Virginia, 1992.

Phillips, Ulrich B. *Life and Labor in the Old South*. Boston: Little, Brown: 1941.

Piersen, William D. *From Africa to America: African American History from the Colonial Era to the Early Republic, 1526–1790*. New York: Twayne Publishers, 1996.

Pogue, Dennis. "Slave Lifeways at Mount Vernon: An Archaeological Perspective." In *Slavery at the Home of George Washington*. Mount Vernon: Mount Vernon Ladies' Association, 2001.

Puckett, Newbell Niles. *Folk Beliefs of the Southern Negro*. Chapel Hill: University of North Carolina Press, 1926.

Randolph, Mary. *The Virginia Housewife; or, Methodical Cook*. New York: Dover, 1993. First published in 1824.

———. *The Virginia House-wife: With Historical Notes and Commentaries by Karen Hess*. Columbia: University of South Carolina Press, 1984.

Randolph, Peter. *Sketches of Slave Life; or, Illustrations of the "Peculiar Institution."* Boston: Peter Randolph, 1855.

Rawick, George P. *The American Slave: A Composite Autobiography*, vol. 16, *Kansas, Kentucky, Maryland, Ohio, Virginia, and Tennessee Narratives*. Westport, CT: Greenwood Publishing, 1972.

Rediker, Marcus. *The Slave Ship: A Human History*. Penguin, 2008.

Robinson, Sallie Ann. *Gullah Home Cooking the Daufuskie Way: Smokin' Joe Butter Beans, Ol' Fuskie Fried Crab Rice, Sticky-Bush Blackberry Dumpling, and other Sea Island Favorites*. Chapel Hill: University of North Carolina Press, 2003.

Root, Waverly, and Richard de Rochement. *Eating in America: A History*. Hopewell, NJ: Ecco Press, 1995.

Rountree, Helen C. *Powhatan Indians of Virginia: Their Traditional Culture*. Norman: University of Oklahoma Press, 1989.

Sauceman, Fred. "Of Sorghum Syrup, Cushaws, Mountain Barbecue, Soup Beans, and Black Iron Skillets." In *Cornbread Nation 3: Foods of the Mountain South*. Ed. Ronni Lundy. Chapel Hill: University of North Carolina Press, 2005.

Sellers, James Benson. *Slavery in Alabama*. Tuscaloosa: University of Alabama Press, 1950.

Serafin, Justin A. "Like Clockwork: French Influence in Monticello's Kitchen." In *Dining at Monticello: In Good Taste and Abundance*. Ed. Damon Lee Fowler. Chapel Hill: University of North Carolina Press, 2005.

Shange, Ntozake. *If I Can Cook / You Know God Can*. Boston: Beacon Press, 1998.

Shields, David S. *Southern Provisions: The Creation & Revival of a Cuisine*. Chicago: University of Chicago Press, 2015.

Singleton, Theresa A. "The Archaeology of Slave Life." In *Before Freedom Came: African-American Life in the Antebellum South*. Ed. Edward D. C. Campbell Jr. with Kym S. Rice. Charlottesville: University Press of Virginia, 1991.

Smith, James L. *Autobiography of James L. Smith*. Norwich, CT: Press of the Bulletin, 1881.

Sobel, Mechal. *The World They Made Together: Black and White Values in Eighteenth-Century Virginia*. Princeton: Princeton University Press, 1987.

Sorenson, Leni. "Taking Care of Themselves: Food Production by the Enslaved Community at Monticello." *Food History News* 18 (2006): 1, 6.

Spalding, Henry D., ed. *Encyclopedia of Black Folklore and Humor*. Middle Village, NY: Jonathan David Publishers, 1990.

Swann-Wright, Dianne. "African Americans and Monticello's Food Culture." In *Dining at Monticello: In Good Taste and Abundance*. Ed. Damon Lee Fowler. Chapel Hill: University of North Carolina Press, 2005.

Taylor, John Martin. *Hoppin' John's Lowcountry Cooking*. New York: Bantam Books, 1992.

Taylor, Raymond L. *Plants of Colonial Days*. Mineola, NY: Dover, 1996. First published in 1996 by Dietz Press for Colonial Williamsburg.

Thiam, Pierre. *Senegal: Modern Senegalese Recipes from the Source to the Bowl*. New York: Lake Isle Press, 2015.

———. *Yolele! Recipes from the Heart of Senegal*. New York: Lake Isle Press, 2008.

Thompson, Mary V. "'They Appear to Live Comfortable Together': Private Lives of the Mount Vernon Slaves." In *Slavery at the Home of George Washington*. Mount Vernon: Mount Vernon Ladies Association, 2001.

Thompson, Robert Farris. *Face of the Gods: Art and Altars of Africa and the African Americas*. New York: Museum for African Art; Munich: Prestel, 1993.

———. *Flash of the Spirit: African & Afro-American Art & Philosophy*. New York: Random House, 1983.

Thorne, John, and Matt Lewis Thorne. *Serious Pig: An American Cook in Search of His Roots*. New York: North Point Press, Farrar, Straus and Giroux, 1996.

Thornton, John. *Africa and Africans in the Making of the Atlantic World 1400–1800*. Cambridge: Cambridge University Press, 1998.

———. "The African Experience of the '20. And Odd Negroes' Arriving in Virginia in 1619." In *The Slavery Reader*. Ed. Gad Heuman and James Walvin. New York: Routledge, 2003.

Time-Life Books. *Tribes of the Southern Woodlands*. Alexandria: Time-Life Books, 1994.

Tipton-Martin, Toni. *The Jemima Code: Two Centuries of African American Cookbooks*. Austin: University of Texas Press, 2015.

Townsend, Stephen A. *Everlasting Foundations: The Genealogy and History of the Bellamy, Hancock, Hughes, Mabry, Todd and Related Families*. Stephen A. Townsend, 2012.

Twitty, Michael. "Divine Cravings: Soul Food as Edible Scripture." Unpublished paper presented at "Uncovering Connections: Cultural Endurance between Africa, the Americas and the Caribbean," Medgar Evers College, City University of New York, March 15, 2003.

Uchendu, Victor Chikezie. *The Igbo of Southeast Nigeria*. New York: Holt, Rinehart and Winston, 1965.

Umeh, John Anenechukwu. *After God Is Dibia: Igbo Cosmology, Divination & Sacred Science in Nigeria*. London: Karnak House, 1997.

Usner, Daniel H. Jr. *Indians, Settlers & Slaves in a Frontier Exchange Economy: The Lower Mississippi Valley before 1783*. Chapel Hill: University of North Carolina Press, 1992.

van der Post, Laurens. *African Cooking*. New York: Time-Life Books, 1970.

Vlach, John Michael. *Back of the Big House: The Architecture of Plantation Slavery*. Chapel Hill: University of North Carolina Press, 1993.

———. *By the Work of Their Hands: Studies in Afro-American Folklife*. Charlottesville: University of Virginia Press, 1991.

Walker, Sheila S. "Everyday Africa in New Jersey: Wonderings and Wanderings in the African Diaspora." In *African Roots/American Cultures: Africa in the Creation of the Americas*. Ed. Sheila S. Walker. Lanham: Rowman & Littlefield Publishers, 2001.

Wallace, Ira. *The Timber Press Guide to Vegetable Gardening in the Southeast*. Portland, Oregon: Timber Press, 2013.

Wallach, Jennifer Jensen, ed. *Dethroning the Deceitful Pork Chop: Rethinking African American Foodways from Slavery to Obama*. Fayetteville: University of Arkansas Press, 2015.

Walsh, Lorena S. "The Chesapeake Slave Trade: Regional Patterns, African Origins, and Some Implications." *William and Mary Quarterly* 58, no. 1 (January 2001): 139–70.

———. *From Calabar to Carter's Grove: The History of a Virginia Slave Community.* Charlottesville: University Press of Virginia, 1997.

Walter, Eugene. *American Cooking: Southern Style.* New York: Time-Life Books, 1971.

Washington, Booker T. *Up from Slavery.* Oxford: Oxford University Press, 1995.

Watson, Benjamin. *Taylor's Guide to Heirloom Vegetables.* Boston: Houghton Mifflin, 1996.

Weatherford, Jack. *Indian Givers: How the Indians of the Americas Transformed the World.* New York: Crown Publishers, 1988.

Weaver, William Woys. *Heirloom Vegetable Gardening.* New York: Henry Holt and Company, 1997.

Wheaton, Thomas A. "Colonial African American Plantation Villages." In *Another's Country: Archaeological and Historical Perspectives on Cultural Interactions in the Southern Colonies.* Ed. J. W. Joseph and Martha Zierden. Tuscaloosa: University of Alabama Press, 2002.

Williams-Forson, Psyche A. *Building Houses Out of Chicken Legs: Black Women, Food, and Power.* Chapel Hill: University of North Carolina Press, 2006.

Wilson, Gaye. "A Declaration of Wants: Provisioning the Monticello Table." In *Dining at Monticello: In Good Taste and Abundance.* Ed. Damon Lee Fowler. Chapel Hill: University of North Carolina Press, 2005.

Wilson, Mary Tolford. "Peaceful Integration: The Owner's Adoption of His Slave's Food." *Journal of Negro History* 49, no. 2 (April 1964): 17–32.

Wilson-Fall, Wendy. *Memories of Madagascar and Slavery in the Black Atlantic.* Athens: Ohio University Press, 2015.

Wood, Peter H. *Black Majority: Negroes in Colonial South Carolina from 1670 through the Stono Rebellion.* New York: Knopf, 1974.

Yentsch, Anne Elizabeth. *A Chesapeake Family and Their Slaves: A Study in Historical Archaeology.* Cambridge: Cambridge University Press, 1994.

ACKNOWLEDGMENTS

—

There is nothing more difficult than saying thank you. Whenever we do, we cede a bit of the idea that we can, or did, do it all on our own. I'd like to thank my stalwart agent, the cheerful and focused Jason Yarn, for proving himself worthy time after time of having the task of bringing this very complex project to the fore. And I want to thank Bill Strachan, editor at large at HarperCollins, and the entire HarperCollins family, for taking on this massive book and giving it life. I assure you that you have not only my thanks but that of my ancestors, the enslaved and their descendants, for giving them just a bit more immortality and peace and justice.

Before this book was born, it was a crowdfunding project called the Southern Discomfort Tour and without it and over a hundred people generously giving their resources to help us—from our first big donor, culinary maven and cookbook author Nancie McDermott and family (best massaman curry ever), to our last big donor, Anna Links (who on May 5, 2012 sealed our fate)—this book would not have a basis. Kat Kinsman, Mat and Ted Lee, Bill Daley, Jane Aldrich, Therese Nelson, Donna Pierce, Nicole Moore, Toni Tipton-Martin, Michael Pollan, Helen Hollyman of Vice's *Munchies*, my sister "dem" Tonya Hopkins, Annie Hauck-Lawson, and the voice of the UpSouth, the one and only Nicole Taylor, Gretchen McKay (who wrote the first big piece about us in the *Pittsburgh Post-Gazette*) and the generous support of Lucey Bowen and Rabbi Ruth Adar—all luminaries and movers and shakers—ensured that all of the right people heard about this project and the word got out. Once it did, one of the finest genealogists I know, Toni Carrier of Lowcountry Africana, sprang into action, spending the next several years helping me firm up as much of my family tree as we could using all available documentation to date. Without Toni the ancestors' stories you read within would be anchorless, and for Toni's help I am grateful for several lifetimes. I acknowledge and defer respect to the lifelong work of my uncle Stephen Townsend for documenting both sides of my maternal lineage, and to the many folks doing genealogical work on my father's side, providing the core basis for the narrative of this work.

So many people from the Meit family, to Andrew Melzer and family, to friends like Susan Snyder Kamins Solomon, the fermentation evangelist Sandor Katz (who shared this project with Michael Pollan), Afro-vegan master chef Bryant Terry, Katrina Brown, Rose McAphee, Ira Wallace and Southern Exposure Seed Exchange, the Southern Foodways Alliance, Todd Richards, the D. Landreth Seed Company, Tricia Brooks, the incredible Andrew F. Smith, Monica Brooks, Richard Josey, Mr. C. Weierke and his family, including Darcy, Loren, and Rena and his uncle Dick of blessed memory, Harold Caldwell, Robert Watson, Marc Steiner, Kathe Brown, Ser Sheshsh Ab-Heter, Sam Black, Dr. Edda Fields Black, John W. Franklin, Peter Wood, Peter Hatch, Joseph McGill, Chelius Carter and family, Chef Matthew Raiford and Jovan Sage, Chef Benjamin Dennis, Peggy Cornett, Simon A. Thibault, Wesley Greene, Jerome Bias, Dontavius Williams, Marvin Alonzo-Greer, Emmanuel Dabney, Susan Floydson-Kanu, Wisteria Perry, the encyclopedic John Martin Taylor, Nathalie Dupree, George McDaniel, Bill Ferris, Marcie Cohen Ferris, David Shields, William Woys Weaver, Jennifer and Nathan Wender, Beth Roach, Adam Tenney, Andrew Kornylak, Velma Jacobs, Chef Michael Moore and family, Jeff Bannister and family, Chef Kevin Mitchell, Professor Regina N. Bradley, Chef Vincent Henderson, Spike Chef Leah Chase and family, Rachel McCormack and family, Lisa Feldstein, Kennard Bowen, Janet Stanley, Jago Cooper, Glenn Roberts, Adam Duckworth, Jackie Gordon, my Todd and Townsend kin, my cousin Marsha Williams, my uncle Albert Townsend and my aunt Virginia, Susan Park, David Woolridge and family, Jennifer Cumby his wife and her distant cousins Andi Cumbo Floyd and Andrew Kearns, Garrett Matthews and family, Chef Jennifer Booker, Lavada Nahon, Teresa Vega, Virginia and Preston Hinkle, the Keith family, My Mungo and Twitty kin, especially cousins Tracy and Skip, Richard Cameron and his husband Doron, Delroy Cornick Jr. and family, Michael Nocerino and family, my cousin Benita Ramsey, my hosts in North Carolina—Josh Parel and Michael Howard and Kerry Joel Beck and Zechariah Sanders who kept me hosted and entertained while I wrote this book, and hundreds of supporters and readers were key to not only making the initial tour happen but making sure that we were housed, fed, paid, and sustained. I am embarrassed that the full list of contributors, benefactors, and institutions that set us on our way and made the experience unforgettable cannot be presented here.

The Colonial Williamsburg Foundation is to be especially thanked for a growing and empowering relationship during the growth of this project. I am particularly grateful to be a Revolutionary in Residence and have the confidence of Mitchell Reese at the helm of the effort to tell the story of early African American foodways in colonial America. I want to thank Barbara Scherer of Historic Foodways for encouraging me and teaching me during this process and for her lovely bottle of Welsh ale. Magnolia Plantation in Charleston, South Carolina, thank you for starting me on my journey in the Low Country, and I thank Middleton Plantation in Charleston, South Carolina; Old Alabama Town in Montgomery, Alabama; Somerset Place in Creswell, North Carolina; Sotterley Plantation in Hollywood, Maryland; Hampton Plantation in Towson, Maryland; Chippokes Plantation State Park in Surry, Virginia; Stagville Plantation in New Durham, North Carolina; Melrose Plantation in Natchez, Mississippi; Evergreen Plantation in Edgard, Louisiana; and Whitney Plantation in Wallace, Louisiana. Atlanta History Center friends and staff including Joanna Arrieta Potter and my new friend, little RJ; Historic Phillipsburg Manor in Tarrytown, New York; Kingsley Plantation near Jacksonville, Florida; Thomas Jefferson's Monticello near Charlottesville, Virginia; Walnut Grove Plantation, near Roebuck, South Carolina; the Heinz History Center in Pittsburgh, Pennsylvania; the Hermitage in Nashville, Tennessee; Carnegie-Mellon; the Yale Center for Sustainable Agriculture; and the International Festival of Arts and Ideas held at Yale University; and Jas. Townsend and Sons are just a few of the institutions and programs that really helped to promote me and my work and empower this project. I want to thank African Ancestry and, in particular,

Gina Paige for her early and consistent support as well as Andrew Zimmerman, Dr. Henry Louis Gates Jr., and renowned modernist master chef Rene Redzepi, who I still can't believe had the faith in me to bring me on his stage at MAD in Copenhagen. TED and my incredible class of 2016 TED Fellows, *Saveur*, First We Feast, and *Southern Living*, among many, have been indispensable in amplifying this project.

It is important to acknowledge the people who have been in my personal life who have played a role throughout the long duration of this project. My former partner and fabulous visual artist Jacob Dillow not only extensively photo-documented the journey but helped me lead the online crowdfunding campaign, combed through archives with me for hours at a time, and drove every mile of that initial 2012 journey and beyond; no matter the future, I will carry to my end an undying gratitude to him. It is bittersweet to me that the journey of this book is the journey of changing relationships, stressors, strains, tragedies, including the death of my mother, and other issues in my family and personal life, but through it all nobody let me give up. Johnathan M. Lewis also brought this project to life through his photography and his early and sustained commitment, and I am proud to call him a lifelong friend and brother. Latonya Lawson Jones, a passionate genealogist in her own right, executed a beautiful family tree for this volume and has been a sustaining voice during the writing period. Phil Lueck went through this book with me, word for word and line by line, from across the country and demonstrated the kind of dedication, love, and friendship that will last a lifetime, but most of all he took me to the Pacific so I could get my mind in order. I must give gratitude to and express love for my partner, Taylor D. Keith, who has been on this journey with me as well, going to archives, traveling miles down the road, and being there for me when I was under stress getting ready for presentations.

Tonia Deetz Rock (another lay editor in chief) and Kelley Fanto Deetz thank you for the incredible support of your learned and generous family to polish my work but also to get my name out there. Elah Levenson, your work on this book to ensure the bibliography would be complete and that fact-checking was done among other important work is incredible and I am grateful. I am thankful for Barbara Forbes Lyon, master writing teacher R. S. Williams, Mordy Walfish, Grant Menzies, Danielle

Alexander, Julia Skinner, Ren Vogel-Hanley, Adante Hart, and many others who helped me edit chapters and organize chapters out of the good of their heart. My distant cousins Hasani Carter-Nze and Terence Dixon gave me their time and energy to break down and interpret my genetic tests results. Martha Katz-Hyman, material culturalist extraordinaire, thank you for looking over records with me and offering critical thoughts. Leni Sorensen, thank you for your mentoring. My play sister, Crystal Campbell, and my donut shop family, I thank you for cheering me on and keeping me motivated day after day.

I want to acknowledge my grandmother of blessed memory Hazel Clintonia Todd Townsend, and my aunts of blessed memory Sheila Townsend Williams and Anna Townsend, and my beautiful, creative, genius of a mom, Patricia Anita Townsend of blessed memory, the keepers of a culinary dynasty that was passed down to me. I also mourn my uncle of blessed memory Walter Townsend Jr. and so many other family members who did not make it to see this book come to pass in this life. Without their love and strength from beyond, I couldn't have done this, besides my mother always said she'd pray for me and that I'd make it. The Yoruba say when your mother prays for you, you are unstoppable. My grandfather Gonze Lee Twitty, a lifelong pioneer for the Southern Black Farmer and Cooperative Hall of Fame awardee and founding member of the Federation of Southern Cooperatives, I acknowledge the standard you set for us all and the pride you have in your descendants. Thank you to my daddy for teaching me about the old ways and giving me part of my life's path. This is for you.

Finally, to my people, the African American people, a diverse civilization long-suffering and proud, bittersweet and spicy, always overcoming, always striving, always getting stronger and better, this is my present for you, as we reach four hundred years in British North America. With this milestone, may we recommit to tell our stories, record them and pass them on so that when we have been a people for a millennium, the world will speak lovingly of the culinary genius that flows in our veins. Without us the Atlantic world, global culture, the American experiment and nation would not be possible. Without our ancestors, we would not be possible. Without G-d, neither would they. Thank you King of the World.

ABOUT THE AUTHOR

—

MICHAEL W. TWITTY is a culinary historian, living history interpreter, and Judaics teacher from the Washington, DC, area. He is the creator of *Afroculinaria*, the first blog devoted to African American historic foodways and their legacy.

He has been honored by the website First We Feast as one of the twenty greatest food bloggers of all time, and was named one of "Fifty People Who Are Changing the South" by *Southern Living* and one of the "Five Cheftavists to Watch" by TakePart.com. Twitty has appeared on NPR's *The Splendid Table* and *Morning Edition* and has written for the *Guardian*, *Ebony*, the *Local Palate*, the *Jewish Daily Forward*, and the *Washington Post*. He has given more than 250 talks, from the Smithsonian to Yale in the US to the Oxford Symposium on Food and Cookery at St. Catherine's College in England and the MAD Symposium in Denmark.

Michael is a Smith fellow with the Southern Foodways Alliance, a TED fellow and speaker, and the first Revolutionary in Residence at the Colonial Williamsburg Foundation. He is the first recipient of Taste Talks Culinary Pioneer Award and has received readers' choice and editors' choice awards from *Saveur* for best food and culture blog. *The Cooking Gene*, based on his 2012 Southern Discomfort Tour, is his first major book.